2000 of the Best Films of All Time – 2019 Edition

By Dr. Arthur H Tafero

;

Forward

Want to see a couple of dozen GREAT films that you have never heard of? Well, then this book is for you. This is the 11th Edition of *2000 of the Best Films of All Time*. I have published this list for Amazon.com for a decade. In that span of time, I have added over 200 films to the list; including new films and oversight gems from the past. Conversely, I have had to eliminate over 200 films from the original list; not an easy task, because several of them were very good films. But this list is not intended for just very good films; it is intended to be among the BEST films.

Of course, best is a relative term, and a hundred critics will have 100 different lists as to what they believe the best films to be. While I might concur with over half of a well-researched list, such as the NY Times top 1000 list, I certainly do not agree with all of them. And omissions from them, such as *Cinema Paradiso*, are glaring mistakes that I feel must be corrected. In addition, I had to add another 1000 films to the list.

We will include bonus sections on Best Picture, Best Actress, and Best Actor opinions over the history of the Academy and we will continue to publish our special Charlie Chan section as well. Enjoy all the features.

Arthur H Tafero

AskMrMovies.com

- If you vehemently disagree with any of my choices (or LOVE my choices) feel free to email me at arthur_tafero@yahoo.com

Best Picture of the Year – My Choice Year by Year with 20-20 Hindsight and Place Viewed

1927-28 Winner – Wings

My Choice: Wings (on TV in West Paterson 50s)

1928-29 Winner: The Broadway Melody

My Choice: The Patriot (but Winner OK) (on TV 50s West Paterson)

1929-30   Winner – All Quiet on the Western Front

My Choice: All Quiet on the Western Front (on TV 50s West Paterson)

1930-31 – Winner: Cimarron

My Choice – Front Page (much better film; much better script) (on TV 50s West Paterson)

1931-32 Winner – Grand Hotel

My Choice: Grand Hotel, but Shanghai Express a very close second (on TV 50s West Paterson)

1932-33 Winner- Cavalcade (they must have been joking)

My Choice: I Am A Fugitive From a Chain Gang (not even close) (on TV 50s West Paterson)

1934 – Winner – It Happened One Night

My Choice: It Happened One Night (on TV 50s West Paterson)

1935 – Winner - Mutiny on the Bounty

My Choice – Mutiny on the Bounty (on TV 50s West Paterson)

1936 – Winner – The Great Ziegfield

My Choice – Mr. Deeds Goes to Town (close) (on TV 50s West Paterson)

1937 – Winner – The Life of Emile Zola

My Choice – (tie) Lost Horizon and The Good Earth (both films HEAD and SHOULDERS above The Life of Emile Zola) (on TV 50s West Paterson and the Criterion Theater NYC)

1938 – Winner – You Can't Take It With You

My Choice – Grand Illusion (on TV 50s West Paterson)

1939 – Winner – Gone With the Wind

My Choice –(tie) – The Wizard of Oz and Goodbye, Mr. Chips; both films far better than GWTW (on TV 50s West Paterson)

1940 – Winner – Rebecca

My Choice – The Grapes of Wrath (close) (on TV 50s West Paterson)

1941 – Winner – How Green Was My Valley

My Choice – Citizen Kane (by a mile) (on TV 50s West Paterson)

1942 – Mrs. Miniver

My Choice – Mrs. Miniver (on TV 50s West Paterson)

1943 – Winner - Casablanca

My Choice – Casablanca (on TV 50s West Paterson and Criterion Theater NYC)

1944 – Winner - Going My Way

My Choice: Double Indemnity (not even close) (on TV 50s West Paterson)

1945 – Winner – The Lost Weekend

My Choice: The Lost Weekend (on TV 50s West Paterson, Criterion Theater NYC)

1946 – Winner – The Best Years of Our Lives

My Choice – The Best Years of Our Lives (on TV 50s West Paterson)

1947 – Winner – Gentleman's Agreement

My Choice – Gentleman's Agreement (on TV 50s West Paterson)

1948 – Winner - Hamlet

My Choice – Hamlet (on TV 50s West Paterson)

1949 – Winner – All the King's Men

My Choice – All the King's Men (on TV 50s West Paterson)

1950 – Winner – All About Eve

My Choice – tie: Sunset Boulevard (close) (Born Yesterday close) (on TV 50s West Paterson, Criterion Theatre NYC)

1951 – Winner – An American in Paris

My Choice – A Streetcar Named Desire (on TV 50s West Paterson, 42nd Street Theaters NYC)

1952 – Winner – The Greatest Show on Earth (joke right?)

My Choice – Anything else: High Noon best of lot for weak year (on TV 50s West Paterson)

1953 – Winner – From Here to Eternity

My Choice – From Here to Eternity (another weak year) (Totowa Drive-In, West Paterson)

1954 – Winner – On the Waterfront

My Choice – On the Waterfront (by a mile) (Totowa Drive-In, West Paterson)

1955 – Winner – Marty

My Choice – Marty (Totowa Drive-In, West Paterson)

1956 – Winner – Around the World in 80 Days (amusing, but average script)

My Choice – The Ten Commandments (not even close) (Totowa Drive-In, West Paterson, Loew's NYC)

1957 – Winner – The Bridge on the River Kwai

My Choice – The Bridge on the River Kwai (Totowa Drive-In, West Paterson)

1958 – Winner – Gigi

My Choice – Gigi (weak year) (Totowa Drive-In, West Paterson)

1959 – Winner – Ben-Hur

My Choice – Ben-Hur (not even close) (Loew's NYC with St Bons class)

1960 – Winner – The Apartment

My Choice – Elmer Gantry (close) (saw both at the Totowa Theater in Totowa) (adult only)

1961 – Winner – West Side Story

My Choice – West Side Story (Loews Journal Square, Jersey City)

1962 – Winner – Lawrence of Arabia

My Choice – Lawrence of Arabia (not even close) (The Stanley, Journal Square, Jersey City) (Loews NYC)

1963 – Winner – Tom Jones

My Choice – Tom Jones (weak year) (State Theater, Journal Square, Jersey City)

1964 – Winner – My Fair Lady

My Choice – Becket (close) Stanley Theatre, Journal Square, Jersey City

1965 – Winner – The Sound of Music

My Choice – The Sound of Music (weak year) Loews Journal Square, Jersey City

1966 – Winner – A Man For All Seasons (Stanley, Journal Square, Jersey City

My Choice – Who's Afraid of Virginia Woolf, State Theater, Journal Square, Jersey City

1967 – Winner – In the Heat of the Night

My Choice – The Graduate (by a mile) – Eastside Theaters Uptown, NYC

1968 – Winner – Oliver!

My Choice – The Lion in Winter – Military Base: Machinato, Okinawa

1969 – Winner – Midnight Cowboy – Upper East Side 60s, NYC Theater While On Leave

My Choice – Midnight Cowboy

1970 – Winner – Patton – State Theater, Journal Square, Jersey City

My Choice – Patton (close) (weak year)

1971 – Winner – The French Connection – State Theater, Journal Square, Jersey City

My Choice – The French Connection

1972 – Winner - The Godfather – Loews NYC

My Choice - The Godfather (by a mile)

1973 – Winner – The Sting (highly overrated)

My Choice – The Exorcist (by a mile) Eastside Theaters 60s NYC

1974 – Winner – The Godfather Part 2 (by a mile)

My Choice – Godfather Part 2 (by a mile) – Loews NYC

1975 – Winner - One Flew Over the Cuckoo's Nest – Eastside Theaters 70s NYC

My Choice – Jaws – (close) Wildwood Theater, New Jersey (didn't go in the water for a week)

1976 – Winner – Rocky (Loews Colosseum Theater, Washington Heights NYC

My Choice (tie) Rocky and Network (Eastside Theaters 60s NYC)

1977 – Winner – Annie Hall

My Choice – Star Wars (by a light year) Loews 44th Street NYC Premiere

1978 – Winner – The Deer Hunter

My Choice – The Deer Hunter (Midnight Express –close) – both at Eastside Theaters 70s NYC

1979 – Winner – Kramer vs Kramer

My Choice – Apocalypse Now (close) Ziegfield Theater 54th Street NYC

1980 – Winner – Ordinary People (ordinary movie)

My Choice – The Elephant Man – Eastside Theaters 70s NYC

1981 – Winner – Chariots of Fire

My Choice – Raiders of the Lost Ark – Loews Colleseum, Washington Heights, NYC

1982 – Winner – Gandhi – Ziegfield Theater 54th Street NYC

My Choice – Gandhi (close) (ET) – 33rd Street Cinema NYC

1983 – Winner – Terms of Endearment

My Choice – The Right Stuff (close) – 33rd Street Cinema, NYC

1984 – Winner – Amadeus

My Choice – Amadeus – Forest Hills Theater NYC

1985 – Winner – Out of Africa (Dreadful)

My Choice – Witness – Forest Hills Theater, Queens, NYC

1986 – Winner – Platoon (not even close)

My Choice – Platoon – Forest Hills Theater Queens, NYC

1987 – Winner – The Last Emperor – Forest Hills Theater Queens NYC

My Choice – The Last Emperor

1988 – Winner – Rain Man – Forest Hills Theater Queens, NYC

My Choice – Rain Man

1989 – Winner – Driving Miss Daisy

My Choice – Field of Dreams (by a mile) Forest Hills Cinema Queens, NYC

1990 – Winner – Dances With Wolves

My Choice – Goodfellas – by a mile Hollis Queens Cineplex NYC

1991 – Winner – Silence of the Lambs

My Choice – Silence of the Lambs – Hollis Queens Cineplex NYC

1992 – Winner – Unforgiven

My Choice – Unforgiven – Hollis Queens Cineplex NYC

1993 – Winner – Schindler's List

My Choice – Schindler's List – Hollis Queens Cineplex NYC

1994 – Winner - Forrest Gump

My Choice – Forrest Gump – Forest Hills Cinema, NYC

1995 – Winner – Braveheart

My Choice – Braveheart – Hollis Queens Cineplex NYC

1996 – Winner – The English Patient

My Choice – Fargo by a mile – Hollis Queens Cineplex NYC

1997 – Winner – Titanic – Levittown Cineplex, Long Island

My Choice – Good Will Hunting (close) – Whitestone Bridge Cineplex, Long Island

1998 – Winner – Shakespeare in Love – Levittown Cineplex, Long Island

My Choice – Saving Private Ryan (close) – Levittown Cineplex, Long Island

1999 – Winner – American Beauty – Levittown Cineplex, Long Island

My Choice – American Beauty

2000 – Winner – Gladiator – Levittown Cineplex, Long Island

My Choice – Gladiator

2001 – Winner – A Beautiful Mind – Hollis, Queens Cineplex NYC

My Choice – A Beautiful Mind (weak year)

2002 – Winner – Chicago

My Choice – The Pianist – Levittown Cineplex, Long Island

2003 – Winner – Lord of the Rings: Return of the King – Levittown Cineplex, Long Island

My Choice – Lord of the Rings

2004 – Winner – Million Dollar Baby – Levittown Cineplex, Long Island

My Choice – Ray – Forest Hills Cinema NYC

2005 – Winner – Crash – Jupiter Multiplex, Florida

My Choice – Good Night and Good Luck – Port Saint Lucie Multiplex, Florida

2006 – Winner – The Departed – Port Saint Lucie Multiplex, Florida

My Choice – Letters From Iwo Jima – Port Saint Lucie Multiplex, Florida

2007 – Winner – No Country for Old Men – Port Saint Lucie Multiplex, Florida (perfect setting)

My Choice – No Country for Old Men

2008 – Winner - Slumdog Millionaire – Kunming International Movie House, Kunming, China

My Choice – Slumdog Millionaire

2009 – Winner – The Hurt Locker - Xiamen Multiplex SM, Xiamen, China

My Choice – The Hurt Locker

2010 – Winner – The King's Speech – Kunming International Movie House, Kunming, China

My Choice – The Social Network (weak year) – Kunming International Movie House, Kunming, China

2011 – Winner – The Artist – Xiamen Multiplex SM, Xiamen, China

My Choice – War Horse – Beijing Multiplex, Beijing, China

2012 – Argo – Tianjin International Multiplex, Tianjin, China

My Choice – Life of Pi – Kunming International Movie House, Kunming, China

2013 – Winner – 12 Years a Slave – Wenzhou University Multiplex, Wenzhou, China

My Choice – Gravity – Guangdong Multiplex, Guangdong, China

2014 – Winner – Birdman – Hong Kong Multiplex, Hong Kong, China

My Choice – The Imitation Game – Kunming International Movie House, Kunming, China

2015 – Winner – Spotlight – Kunming International Movie House, Kunming, China

My Choice – The Martian – Fuzhou Multiplex, Fuzhou, China

2016 – Winner – Moonlight – Kunming International Movie House, Kunming, China

My Choice – Lion – Jimei University Multiplex, SM, Jimei, China

2017 – Winner – The Shape of Water – Jimei University Multiplex, SM, Jimei, China

My Choice – Three Billboards Outside Ebbing Missouri (close) – Kunming International Movie House, Kunming, China

Tafero Choices for Best Actress of the Year in 20-20 Hindsight

By Arthur H Tafero

The following are the winners of the Best Actress of the Year Award from the first year of the presentation in 1928 to the present. Sometimes I agreed with the selection and other times I found myself laughing at a particular choice. My choices, with the benefit of hindsight, are made directly underneath the winners from that year

1927/28 Winner – Janet Gaynor – Seventh Heaven

My Choice – Gloria Swanson – Sadie Thompson

1928/29 Winner – Mary Pickford - Coquette

My Choice – Mary Pickford

1929/30 Winner – Norma Shearer – The Divorcee

My Choice – Greta Garbo - Anna Christie- in a close one

1930/31 Winner – Marie Dressler – Min and Bill (hilarious)

My Choice – Marie Dressler

1931/32 Winner – Helen Hayes – The Sin of Madelon Claudet

My Choice – Marie Dressler – Emma – much better

1932/33 Winner – Katherine Hepburn – Morning Glory (weak year)

My Choice – Katherine Hepburn

1934 Winner – Claudette Colbert – It Happened One Night

My Choice – Bette Davis – Of Human Bondage – in a close one

1935 Winner – Bette Davis – Dangerous – Academy made up for previous year's goof and gave it for this mediocre film

My Choice – Bette Davis – a mediocre Bette Davis was still better than almost other actress at the top of their game

1936 Winner – Louise Rainer – The Great Ziegfeld

My Choice – Carole Lombard – My Man Godfrey – hilarious pick in a close one

1937 Winner – Louise Rainer – The Good Earth

My Choice - Louise Rainer – The Good Earth as she pulls off a Spencer Tracy. Case could be made for Janet Gaynor in *A Star is Born*

1938 Winner – Bette Davis - Jezebel

My Choice - Bette Davis – no contest

1939 Winner – Vivian Leigh – Gone With the Wind

My Choice: tie: Bette Davis – Dark Victory and Greer Garson for Goodbye, Mr. Chips in a great year for films. Case can be made for Leigh as well.

1940 Winner – Ginger Rogers – Kitty Foyle

My Choice – Joan Fontaine – Rebecca. A case could be made for Rogers, Davis or Hepburn. A very tough year for competition

1941 Winner – Joan Fontaine – Suspicion. Academy tries to make up for previous year's goof, but Fontaine would have been best, anyway with this great performance.

My Choice – Joan Fontaine

1942 Winner – Greer Garson – Mrs. Miniver

My Choice – tie: Greer Garson and Bette Davis for Now Voyager

1943 Winner – Jennifer Jones – worst pick for best actress in history of the Academy

My Choice – anyone else would have been fine. Ingrid Bergman best of the rest for Whom the Bell Tolls

1944 Winner – Ingrid Bergman – academy, as usual, makes up for last year's goof by selecting Bergman for this good film Gaslight instead of great performance in great film by Barbara Stanwyck in *Double Indemnity*

My Choice – Barbara Stanwyck – Double Indemnity

1945 Winner – Joan Crawford – Mildred Pierce

My Choice – Gene Tierney – Leave Her to Heaven in a close one

1946 Winner – Olivia DeHaviland in the average To Each His Own, robs the deserving winner, Celia Johnson, who was brilliant in Brief Encounter, a classic.

My Choice - Celia Johnson (not even close)

1947 Winner – Loretta Young – The Farmer's Daughter

My Choice – Loretta Young – (weak year)

1948 Winner – Jane Wyman in Johnny Belinda

My Choice – Olivia DeHaviland – Snake Pit – far more deserving

1949 Winner – Olivia DeHaviland; do you see a pattern here? – The Heiress

My Choice – Olivia DeHaviland (weak year)

1950 Winner – Judy Holliday in Born Yesterday

My Choice – three way tie among Holliday, Bette Davis for All About Eve, and Gloria Swanson for Sunset Boulevard (very tough year)

1951 Winner – Vivien Leigh – Streetcar Named Desire

My Choice: tie Leigh and Katherine Hepburn for African Queen

1952 Winner – Shirley Booth – Come Back Little Sheba – This was a joke, right?

My Choice – anyone else, but most likely Bette Davis – The Star

1953 Winner – Audrey Hepburn – Roman Holiday

My Choice – Audrey Hepburn

1954 Winner – Grace Kelly – The Country Girl robs Judy Garland

My Choice Judy Garland – A Star is Born (not even close)

1955 Winner – Anna Magnani – The Rose Tattoo

My Choice – Jennifer Jones – Love is a Many Splendored Thing (not even close)

1956 Winner – Ingrid Bergman - Anastasia

My Choice – Deborah Kerr – The King and I (far superior)

1957 Winner – Joanne Woodward – The Three Faces of Eve

My Choice – Joanne Woodward

1958 Winner – Susan Hayward - I Want to Live

My Choice – Susan Hayward – 2 in a row

1959 Winner – Simone Signoret – Room at the Top

My Choice – Audrey Hepburn – The Nun's Story

1960 Winner – Elizabeth Taylor – Butterfield 8

My Choice – Elizabeth Taylor

1961 Winner – Sophia Loren – Two Women (tough year)

My Choice – Sophia Loren (her best film ever); case could be made for Hepburn's Tiffany and Wood's Splendor – 2 in a row

1962 Winner – Anne Bancroft – The Miracle Worker

My Choice – Anne Bancroft – 3 in a row – Case could be made for Lee Remick

1963 Winner – Patricia Neal - Hud

My Choice – Natalie Wood – Love with the Proper Stranger in a close one

1964 Winner – Julie Andrews – Mary Poppins – This was a joke, right?

My Choice – Sophia Loren – Marriage, Italian Style, much funnier and better-acted

1965 Winner – Julie Chirstie - Darling

My Choice – Samantha Eggar – The Collector in a close one

1966 Winner – Elizabeth Taylor – Who's Afraid of Virginia Woolf? - well-deserved

My Choice – Elizabeth Taylor

1967 Winner – Katherine Hepburn –Guess Who's Coming to Dinner – Playing the wife of Spencer Tracy; what a stretch

My Choice – THREE more deserving: Anne Bancroft as the immortal Mrs. Robinson and my pick, as well as Faye Dunaway in Bonnie and Clyde, and even Audrey Hepburn in Wait Until Dark were better

1968 Winner – Katherine Hepburn – Lion in Winter and Barbara Streissand in Funny Girl

My Choice – Katherine Hepburn without Streissand

1969 Winner – Maggie Smith robs Jane Fonda for The Prime of Miss Brodie

My Choice – Jane Fonda in They Shoot Horses Don't They? – much better

1970 Winner - Glenda Jackson – Women in Love

My Choice – Sarah Miles – Ryan's Daughter in a close one

1971 Winner – Jane Fonda in *Klute* to make up for snub of Horses, but she would have won anyway

My Choice – Jane Fonda

1972 Winner – Liza Minnelli for Cabaret robs Diana Ross in Lady Sings the Blues

My Choice – Diana Ross

1973 Winner – Glenda Jackson – A Touch of Class

My Choice- Marsha Mason – Cinderella Liberty much better

1974 Winner – Ellen Burstyn – Alice Doesn't Live Here Anymore

My Choice – Ellen Burstyn

1975 Winner – Louise Fletcher – One Flew Over the Cuckoo's Nest

My Choice – Louise Fletcher – 2 in a row

1976 Winner – Faye Dunaway for Network and 2 previous snubs

My Choice – Faye Dunaway – 3 in a row

1977 Winner – Diane Keaton – Annie Hall – This was a joke, right?

My Choice –anyone else, but my pick was Marsha Mason in the Goodbye Girl

1978 Winner – Jane Fonda in Coming Home to make up for second snub

My Choice – Jill Clayburgh far better in An Unmarried Woman

1979 Winner – Sally Field – Norma Rae

My Choice – Bette Midler – The Rose but a case could be made for Field

1980 Winner – Sissy Spacek – Coal Miner's Daughter

My Choice – tie: Sissy Spacek and Goldie Hawn for Private Benjamin

1981 Winner – Katherine Hepburn – On Golden Pond

My Choice – Meryl Streep – The French Lieutenant's Woman – much better

1982 Winner – Meryl Streep – Sophie's Choice to make up for French snub, but she would have won anyway

My Choice – Meryl Streep

1983 Winner – Shirley MacLaine – Terms of Endearment

My Choice – Shirley MacLaine – 2 in a row

1984 Winner – Sally Field – Places in the Heart

My Choice – Jessica Lang – Country – in a close one

1985 Winner – Geraldine Page – The Trip to Bountiful

My Choice – Geraldine Page – The Trip to Bountiful

1986 Winner – Marlee Matlin – Children of a Lesser God

My Choice – Marlee Matlin – 2 in a row

1987 Winner – Cher - Moonstruck

My Choice – Cher – Moonstruck – 3 in a row

1988 Winner – Jody Foster – The Accused

My Choice – Jody Foster – 2 in a row – 4 in a row

1989 Winner – Jessica Tandy – Driving Miss Daisy

My Choice – Jessica Tandy -5 in a row

1990 Winner – Kathy Bates - Misery

My Choice – Kathy Bates – 6 in a row

1991 Winner – Jody Foster – Silence of the Lambs

My Choice – Jody Foster – 7 in a row

1992 Winner – Emma Thompson – Howard's End

My Choice – Emma Thompson – 8 in a row

1993 Winner – Holly Hunter – The Piano

My Choice – Holly Hunter – 9 in a row

1994 Winner – Jessica Lange – Blue Sky

My Choice – Jessica Lange (weak year) – 10 in a row

1995 Winner – Susan Sarandon – Dead Man Walking (Academy ends a decade of agreeing with my picks)

My Choice – Meryl Streep – Bridges of Madison County better – end of streak

1996 Winner – Frances McDormand - Fargo

My Choice – Frances McDormand by a mile

1997 Winner – Helen Hunt – As Good as it Gets

My Choice – Helen Hunt – 2 in a row

1998 Winner – Gwyneth Paltrow – Shakespeare in Love

My Choice – Gwyneth Paltrow – 3 in a row

1999 Winner – Hilary Swank – Boys Don't Cry

My Choice – Hilary Swank – 4 in a row

2000 Winner – Julia Roberts – Erin Brockovich

My Choice – Julia Roberts – 5 in a row

2001 Winner – Halle Berry – Monster's Ball

My Choice – Halle Berry – 6 in a row and 16 of the last 17

2002 Winner – Nicole Kidman – The Hours – this was a joke, right?

My Choice – Salma Hayek – Frieda – Far more deserving

2003 Winner – Charlize Theron - Monster

My Choice – Charlize Theron in a runaway

2004 Winner – Hillary Swank – Million Dollar Baby

My Choice – Hillary Swank – 2 in a row

2005 Winner – Reese Witherspoon – this was a joke, right?

My Choice – Keira Knightly - Pride and the Prejudice

2006 Winner – Helen Mirren – The Queen

My Choice – Meryl Streep – The Devil Wears Prada in a close one

2007 Winner – Marion Cotillard – Edith Piaf – This is right up there with the Begnini selection

My Choice – Cate Blanchett - Elizabeth by two miles

2008 Winner – Kate Winslet – The Reader

My Choice – tie: Kate Winslet and Meryl Streep for Doubt

2009 Winner – Sandra Bullock – The Blind Side

My Choice – Helen Mirren – The Last Station in a close one

2010 Winner – Natalie Portman – Black Swan

My Choice – Jennifer Lawrence – Winter's Bone in a close one

2011 Winner

My Choice

2012 Winner

My Choice

2013 Winner

My Choice

2014 Winner

My Choice

2015 Winner

My Choice

2016 Winner

My Choice

2017

My Choice

2018

My Choice

Best Actor of the Year in Hindsight

By Arthur H Tafero

1927/28 Winner: Emil Jannings – The Last Command

My Choice: Emil Jannings

1928/29 Winner: Warner Baxter – In Old Arizona

My Choice: Warner Baxter – two in a row

1929/30 Winner: George Arliss – Disraeli

My Choice: Ronald Colman – Bulldog Drummond

1930/31 Winner: Lionel Barrymore – A Free Soul

My Choice: Richard Dix – Cimarron

1931/32 Winner: tie; Wallace Beery – The Champ and Fredric March Dr. Jekyll and Mr. Hyde

My Choice: Just Wallace Beery

1932/33 Winner: Charles Laughton – The Private Life of Henry VIII

My Choice: Obviously Paul Muni for I am a Fugitive from a Chain Gang in the first really big blunder for the academy in this category

1934 Winner: Clark Gable – It Happened One Night

My Choice – Clark Gable

1935 Winner: Victor McLaglen – The Informer

My Choice- Victor McLaglen – two in a row.

1936 Winner: Paul Muni – The Story of Louis Pasteur

My Choice: Gary Cooper; Mr Deeds Goes to Town. Academy gave it to Muni for mistake for Chain Gang. This would start a long and inglorious tradition of the academy giving the best actor or actress award to the wrong actor or actress because they were trying to make up for a previous mistake. This resulted in almost no one every winning for the year they actually had the best performance because the academy was giving it to someone else who had been snubbed previously.

1937 Winner: Spencer Tracy – Captains Courageous

My Choice: Fredric March – A Star is Born in a close one

1938 Winner; Spencer Tracy – Boys Town

My Choice – Spencer Tracy

1939 – Winner; Robert Donat – Goodbye, Mr. Chips

My Choice – a very prejudiced yes for Robert Donat

1940 – Winner; James Stewart – The Philadelphia Story

My Choice; Henry Fonda – The Grapes of Wrath; not even close

1941 – Winner; Gary Cooper – Sergeant York

My Choice – Gary Cooper (this made up for Mr. Deeds)

1942 – Winner; James Cagney – Yankee Doodle Dandy (this made up for Angels With Dirty Faces)

My Choice – Ronald Colman – Random Harverst (to make up for not even being nominated for Lost Horizon, for which he deserved to win) (now I'm doing it; choosing winners to make up for past snubs)

1943 – Winner: Paul Lukas – Watch on the Rhine

My Choice – Humphrey Bogart – This snub was a joke, right?

1944 – Winner: Bing Crosby – Going My Way (if only he could act)

My Choice – Alexander Knox – Wilson (weak year for films)

1945 Winner: Ray Milland – The Lost Weekend

My Choice – Ray Milland (thank God Crosby didn't win again)

1946 Winner: Fredric March – The Best Years of Our Lives

My Choice – Frederic March (although a case could be made for Stewart in It's a Wonderful Life

1947 Winner – Ronald Colman – A Double Life (which was dreadful – to make up for Lost Horizon)

My Choice – John Garfield in Body and Soul in a close one over Gregory Peck for Gentleman's Agreement. A tie would have been fine.

1948 – Winner – Laurence Olivier – Hamlet

My Choice – Laurence Olivier – Hamlet

1949 – Winner; Broderick Crawford – All the King's Men

My Choice; Broderick Crawford. Two in a row.

1950 Winner; Jose Ferrer – Cyrano de Bergerac

My Choice: William Holden – Sunset Boulevard in a close one

1951 Winner; Humphrey Bogart – African Queen

My Choice: Tie between Bogart and Brando for Streetcar Named Desire

1952 Winner; Gary Cooper – High Noon

My Choice – Kirk Douglas – The Bad and the Beautiful in a close one

1953 – Winner; William Holden – Stalag 17

My Choice; Burt Lancaster - From Here to Eternity

1954 – Winner; Marlon Brando – On The Waterfront

My Choice; Marlon Brando

1955 – Winner: Ernest Borgnine – Marty

My Choice – Ernest Borgnine. Two in a row.

1956 – Winner; Yul Brenner

My Choice – Laurence Olivier for Richard III

1957 Winner – Alec Guinness – The Bridge on the River Kwai

My Choice – Alec Guinness

1958 Winner – David Niven – Separate Tables

My Choice – David Niven – Two in a row

1959 Winner – Charlton Heston – Ben-Hur (if only he could act)

My Choice – Jack Lemmon – Some Like it Hot

1960 Winner – Burt Lancaster – Elmer Gantry

My Choice – Burt Lancaster

1961 – Winner Maxmilian Schell – Judgment at Nuremburg

My Choice – Paul Newman – The Hustler (now they will have to make up for this snub)

1962 – Winner – Gregory Peck for a lifetime achievement award for the decent To Kill a Mockingbird, instead of Peter O'Toole, who was absolutely robbed blind for his brilliant performance.

My Choice – Peter O'Toole – Lawrence of Arabia

1963 – Winner – Sidney Poitier for Lilies of the Field

My Choice – Paul Newman – Hud (weak year for films)

1964 – Winner – Rex Harrison for My Fair Lady

My Choice – Peter O'Toole robbed again for Becket with an honorable mention to Peter Sellers, who was also better than Harrison.

1965 – Winner – Lee Marvin – Cat Ballou

My Choice – Rod Steiger for The Pawnbroker. Another theft.

1966 – Winner – Paul Scofield – A Man For All Seasons

My Choice – Richard Burton for Who's Afraid of Virginia Woolf in a close one.

1967 – Winner – Rod Steiger for In The Heat of the Night. Almost Laughable

My Choice – Dustin Hoffman for The Graduate – not even close

1968 – Winner – Cliff Robertson – Charly – richly deserved

My Choice –Cliff Robertson

1969 – Winner – John Wayne – True Grit – Give me a break. If you want to give him a lifetime achievement award, that's fine, but not at the expense of real actors like Dustin Hoffman and Jon Voight. Hoffman burned second time in three years.

My Choice - Dustin Hoffman – Midnight Cowboy

1970 – Winner – George C Scott - Patton

My Choice – George C Scott, though a case could be made for Jack Nicholson in Five Easy Pieces

1971 – Winner – Gene Hackman – The French Connection

My Choice – Gene Hackman, two in a row!

1972 – Winner – Marlon Brando – The Godfather

My Choice – Marlon Brando – three for three in the 70s

1973 – Winner – Jack Lemmon – Save the Tiger

My Choice – Al Pacino – Serpico – end of streak

1974 – Winner - Art Carney – Harry and Tonto – This was a joke, right? Another lifetime achievement award robs Pacino

My Choice – Al Pacino – Godfather Part 2, not even close and burned two years in a row

1975 – Winner – Jack Nicholson – One Flew Over the Cuckoo's Nest

My Choice – Al Pacino – Dog Day Afternoon – burned for a record three times in a row. Never to happen to any actor or actress again in our lifetimes.

1976 – Winner – Peter Finch - Network

My Choice – Peter Finch in a three way tie with DeNiro for Taxi Driver and Stallone for Rocky. Only three way tie ever for best actor

1977 – Winner - Richard Dreyfuss for Goodbye Girl

My Choice – Richard Dreyfuss for Goodbye Girl (weak year)

1978 – Winner – Jon Voight – Coming Home

My Choice – Robert DeNiro – The Deer Hunter, not even close

1979 – Winner – Dustin Hoffman –Kramer vs. Kramer (finally)

My Choice – Peter Sellers – Being There

1980 Winner – Robert DeNiro – Raging Bull

My Choice – Robert DeNiro – Raging Bull

1981 Winner – Henry Fonda – On Golden Pond – lifetime achievement award took it away from another lifetime achievement award that should have gone to Burt Lancaster.

My Choice- Burt Lancaster – Atlantic City and a case could be made for Warren Beatty in Reds

1982 Winner – Ben Kingsley - Gandhi

My Choice – Ben Kingsley – Gandhi, although a case could be made for Peter O'Toole in My Favorite Year who was used to getting jobbed by now.

1983 Winner – Robert Duvall – Tender Mercies – richly deserved

My Choice – Robert Duvall

1984 Winner – F Murray Abraham – Amadeus – right movie; wrong actor

My Choice – Tom Hulce - Amadeus

1985 Winner – William Hurt – Kiss of the Spiderwoman

My Choice – Harrison Ford - Witness

1986 Winner – Paul Newman – The Color of Money in another lifetime achievement award that robs James Woods for Salvador

My Choice - James Woods - Salvador

1987 Winner – Michael Douglas – Wall Street

My Choice – Michael Douglas

1988 Winner – Dustin Hoffman – Rain Man

My Choice – Dustin Hoffman

1989 Winner – Daniel Day Lewis – My Left Foot

My Choice – Kenneth Branaugh – Henry V – good Shakespeare is hard to find

1990 Winner – Jeremy Irons – Reversal of Fortune

My Choice – Kevin Costner – Dances With Wolves

1991 Winner – Anthony Hopkins – The Silence of the Lambs; absolutely no competition

My Choice – Anthony Hopkins – The Silence of the Lambs

1992 Winner – Al Pacino –Scent of a Woman – They give it to him for this crap and not for Serpico, Godfather 2 or Dog Day Afternoon. Is it me?

My Choice – Robert Downey Jr – Chaplin – not even close

1993 Winner – Tom Hanks - Philadelphia

My Choice – Liam Neeson robbed for Schindler's List

1994 Winner – Tom Hanks – Forrest Gump – Hanks pulls a Spencer Tracy with two in a row; much more deserving this time.

My Choice – Tom Hanks

1995 Winner – Nicholas Cage – Leaving Las Vegas

My Choice – Richard Dreyfuss – Mr. Holland's Opus

1996 Winner – Geoffrey Rush - Shine

My Choice – Geoffrey Rush - Shine

1997 Winner – Jack Nicholson – As Good As It Gets

My Choice – Tie: Matt Damon – Good Will Hunting and Robert Duval – The Apostle – BOTH MUCH BETTER

1998 Winner – Roberto Benigni – Life is Beautiful – Never to be seen again

My Choice – Tie: Edward Norton – American X and Tom Hanks – Saving Private Ryan MUCH better

1999 Winner – Kevin Spacey – American Beauty

My Choice – Kevin Spacey

2000 Winner – Russell Crowe - Gladiator

My Choice – Russell Crowe – Gladiator – two in a row

2001 Winner – Denzel Washington – Training Day – Run of the mill violent cop movie

My Choice – Will Smith - Ali

2002 Winner – Adrian Brody – The Pianist

My Choice – Adrian Brody

2003 Winner – Sean Penn – Mystic River

My Choice – Sean Penn – two in a row

2004 Winner – Jamie Foxx - Ray

My Choice – Jamie Fox – three in a row

2005 Winner – Philip Seymour Hoffman - Capote

My Choice – Philip Seymour Hoffman, but a case could be made for David Strathairn's Good Night and Good Luck. – four in a row

2006 Winner – Forest Whitaker - The Last King of Scotland

My Choice – Forest Whitaker – five in a row

2007 Winner – Daniel Day-Lewis – There Will Be Blood

My Choice – Daniel Day- Lewis – six in row!

2008 Winner – Sean Penn – Milk

My Choice – Sean Penn – Milk, although a case could be made for Frank Langella's chilling Nixon – seven in a row.

2009 Winner – Jeff Bridges – Crazy Heart

My Choice – Jeff Bridges (weak year). Eight in a row.

2010 Winner – Colin Firth – The King's Speech

My Choice – Colin Firth and an amazing nine in a row.

2000 of the Best Films of All Time

3 Idiots – India– 2009 -Directed by Rajkumar Hirani and starring R Madhaven as Farhan, an engineering student who is at school to please his father. Farhan would rather be working in the wild jungles as a naturalist. Also featured are Sharman Joshi as Raju, the first member of his poor working- class family to attend college and Rancho, who is a bit of a lover boy and gets involved with the daughter of one of the more repressive professors. This is not the 3 stooges go to an Indian college. The characters are much more complex than that. The story is a bit convoluted, but we forgive that, because it is outright hilarious. Recommended.

8½-Italy–1963-Directed by Federico Fellini and starring Marcello Mastroianni as Guido, a famous Italian film director. I think it is safe to say this might be considered Fellini's autobiography with lots of room for creative license. This film won the Academy Award for Best Foreign Film of the year. It also won for costume design. The film's title refers to the eight films that Fellini had directed, and the half stands for the one he did with another director. The story of the film concerns a director, Guido, who is having current creative problems. He can't seem to go forward on his latest science fiction film (probably a reference to The Tenth Victim, a film that in real life, Fellini had some trouble with) and is suffering from a bad marriage at the same time. This is not a must-see film, but it is one of the best films to come out of Italy; and is certainly worth the time to view. Recommended.

10–1979-Directed by Blake Edwards and starring Bo Derek as Jenny, who is a10, Dudley Moore as George, the discontented husband of Sam, who is played by Julie Andrews. This is a story of a man who fantasizes about having the perfect girlfriend, a 10, such as Bo Derek, instead of the plain-Jane looking girl he has now. He finds out that perfect physical beauty is no substitute for substantial inner beauty. This is a typical farce comedy by Edwards. Sam just isn't sexy enough for George(Moore). He catches a glimpse of a woman, Jenny(Derek) on her way to her wedding and he becomes obsessed at finding out more about her. Recommended.

10 Rillington Place - 1971- Directed by Richard Fleisher and starring Richard Attenborough (*Great Escape*), John Hurt (*Elephant Man*), and Judy Geeson (To Sir with Love), in the lead roles. This tense serial murder film captures your attention from start to finish. Good filmmaking.

12 Angry Men—1957-Directed by Sidney Lumet and starring a strong cast including Henry Fonda, Jack Klugman, Lee J Cobb, Jack Warden, E.G. Marshall, and Ed Begley. This film is an actor's vehicle and was really made for the stage, because there is very little movement outside of the jury room. Somehow, Lumet is able to hold our attention for the full hour and a half with deft direction and the help of an outstanding script written by Reginald Rose. A great cast of professional veteran actors also helps in the task.

12 Monkeys-1995- Directed by Terry Gilliam, who, although very entertaining, is also a bit out of control as a director, and starring Bruce Willis as James Cole, a convict out on a work-release program that puts him in the past to retrieve a sample of a virus that killed most of the human race. The film also stars Madeline Stowe as the prerequisite romantic interest. Brad Pitt has a nice performance as a mental patient (good casting) named Goines (reminded me of Jack Nicholson *(One Flew Over the Cukoo's Nest)*. Also featured is Christopher Plummer as the evil Dr.Goines, father of Pitt, the man responsible for the virus, and David Morse (*The Fugitive* TV series) as Dr.Peters, the assistant to Dr.Goines. Interesting.

39 Steps–England-1939-Directed by Alfred Hitchcock and starring Robert Donat as Richard Hannay, a Canadian, who is having a night on the town watching an illusionist. Also featured are Wylie Watson as

Mr.Memory, the illusionist, Lucie Manhheim, as a frightened member of the audience, Annabella Smith, who seeks the help of Richard, and Madeleine Carroll, who as Pamela, becomes the ultimate love interest of Richard.

Hitchcock is a master at using actors as props, rather than having some dramatic actor or actress become the centerpiece of his films. He repeated that formula dozens of times with great success. This is easily one of the most convoluted of all the Hitchcock films. There is raw suspense in spots, but the plot twists and complications challenge the laws of mathematics. Hitchcock was well-known to be the master of suspense, and this film is a great illustration of that belief. Still recommended, although highly unbelievable, because a mediocre Hitchcock movie is still better than the best of what a lot of other directors can do.

45 Years – 2015 – Directed by Andrew Haigh and starring Charlotte Rampling and Tom Courtenay in the lead roles. This little package of repressed anger, hidden agendas, and passive-aggressive behavior combined with crisp dialogue from good writing produces a first-rate domestic drama. Recommended.

55 Days at Peking-1963–Directed by Nicholas Ray and starring Charlton Heston as Marine Major Matt Lewis, an arch-typical American officer who defends the International Compound from the Boxers. The Boxers are not Chinese packagers; they are part of a Chinese revolt intended to slaughter all the Christians in China; some analysts would consider that a worthy cause. Also featured prominently in the film is the competent David Niven, who, naturally, plays a British consulate official who is handy with weapons and other ingenious methods of strategy and survival. Dated material because crowds are now rooting for the Chinese instead of the colonials. Still fun to watch.

'71 – 2015- Directed by Yann Demange and starring Jack O'Connell in the lead role as a British soldier left behind by his unit in Belfast. This film examines key issues of both sides of the conflict without being preachy, and at the same time holds you in suspense about the outcome of the young soldier's fate. Well done. Recommended

101 Dalmations – 1963 – Directed by Wolfgang Reitherman, Hamilton Luske, and Clyde Geronomi and starring lots of cute puppies in a fairly amusing Disney tale of good overcoming evil (great villain; Cruela De Vil). Recommended for kids and adults.

300 Spartans -1962–Directed by Rudolph Mate and starring Richard Egan, Ralph Richardson, BarryCoe and David Farrar. Diane Baker is also in the film as a prop for the romantic interest. The film was remade as a graphic novel cartoon in 2007 as *300*. Once again, the original is better than the comic-book reproduction that was done many years later. Real people are always far more interesting than comic-book figures. Whereas the later version is not fit for children of most ages, the one made in 1962 is fine, even for the kids. I can recommend this as a great popcorn movie and a good history lesson.

13:10 to Yuma-1957—Directed by Delmar Daves and starring Glenn Ford and Van Heflin. Ford plays Dan, a hired hand, who has to deliver Heflin, playing the killer outlaw, Wade, to Yuma to stand trial. Ford was considered by many critics to be one of the more underrated actors of his generation, although he starred in numerous hits like *The Blackboard Jungle* and *Superman*, as well as *Cimarron*. At least Ford always had plenty of work. Heflin, on the other hand, was not as fortunate as Ford. Although a highly competent actor, he had the misfortune to have a German-sounding name just before, during and after WW2. This did not help his popularity with casting producers or with the public. Recommended.

400 Blows (France)-1959-Directed by Francois Truffaut and starring Jean Pierre Leaud as Antione Doinel, a misunderstood teen. Some critics have christened this film the *Rebel Without a Cause of France* (actually,I have christened it that). In this case, there actually was a very good cause, because he was constantly being mistreated and emotionally whipped by both of his parents. He was not a spoiled little brat like James Dean, who was in *Rebel Without a Cause*; he had no car or comfortable home, and no girlfriend to console him.

Antione had nothing but himself to fend off the slings and arrows of outrageous fortune. It is quite easy to bear when you have all the comforts of home, and quite another when you have practically nothing but the shirt on your back. The film takes us from one difficult disappointment in youth to another, but Antoine keeps forging ahead in life because there really is no alternative, but to go forward. Some of us learn this at an early age, and some of us learn it when we are older. And some us never learn this lesson at all.

1000 Eyes of Dr. Mabuse – Germany - 1960 - Directed by Fritz Lang and starring Dawn Adams, Peter Van Eyck and Gert Frobe. Although not exactly household names, these competent actors, along with Wolfgang Priess as Dr. Mabuse, play out a well-written scenario created by the novel by Jan Fethke with an adaptation by Lang. Lang was famous for setting up the viewer with a terrific foreboding atmosphere. Something bad was going to happen, and Lang would make sure you knew that there was nothing you could do to prevent it. His films were second in suspense only to the great Hitchcock; and there was not that much great a gap between them.

1900 (Italy)-1977-Directed by Bernardo Bertolucci and starring Robert DeNiro as Alfredo Berlingheri, Gerard Depardieu as Olmo Dalco, Donald Sutherland, in a creative bit of casting as Attila Mellenchini, Sterling Hayden in another bit of odd casting, as Leo Dalcoand. Burt Lancaster is perfectly cast as Bernardo's grandfather. Sutherland and Hayden are about as believable as Italians as Arnold Schwarzenegger would be, but fortunately, they are not the leads. This film chronicles the friendship of two Italian boys who go on to become influential politicians later in life. One becomes a conservative landowner, who mistreats his workers under the guise of fascism, and the other becomes an active socialist that fights for the rights of workers. This is one of the better films to come out of Italy in the seventies, and is highly recommended.

2001: A Space Odyssey --1968 - Directed by Stanley Kubrick and written by Arthur C. Clarke, and starring Keir Dullea and Gary Lockwood, two lesser-known actors. This film is not about the actors, but about the story. As Hitchcock use to say, actors are merely props to be used in a film, and with 2001 Kubrick follows that philosophy to the hilt. Kubrick continued to use his lead actors mainly as props in many of his films after the success of this one. Previous to this film, Kubrick had success with Kirk Douglas as a powerful actor in *Paths of Glory*, shot in black and white for a relatively small amount of money. *2001* was shot in expensive color, with numerous special effects, and for an enormous budget.

Later, Kubrick would go on to successfully make *Full Metal Jacket* with the same formula that he made 2001 (using the actors as props to the story). The sequel, *2010* tried to give some closure to the mystery of the original, but only succeeded in making things even murkier. Some mysteries are best left unsolved or unexplained. This is still a must-see film, and is consistently included in almost every movie critic's top one hundred films.

2010: The Year We Make Contact-1984–Written and Directed by Peter Hyams and starring Roy Scheider as Heywood, John Lithgow as Walter, Helen Mirren as Tanya, and Keir Dullea as himself, or rather Dave Bowman, the only role he ever had that people remember. The story is interesting, except for the corny, outdated US-Russia confrontation scenario. Russia couldn't afford the gas for this trip, much less the car and a place to stay. The world is not really concerned about outer space these days; aliens don't pay the bills. But other than the weak Russia-US on the verge of war subplot, it has a decent storyline.

The style of the director differs sharply with that of Kubrick, who directed the original of this series. Kubrick used actors as props, but in this production, you can clearly see the personalities of the lead actors, especially Scheider and Lithgow, who take over the film and its direction. Oddly enough, although Hyams was not as accomplished as Kubrick as a director, he was still able to pull off a pretty goods science-fiction yarn that was entertaining. Recommended.

2012–2009-Directed by Roland Emmerich and starring John Cusack as Jackson Curtis, a struggling writer who drives a limo to make ends meet. This income comes in very handy when the end of the world is approaching. Good, fast drivers won't get stuck in the thousands of cars that would absolutely jam every road in ten minutes if this actually happened, right? Chiwetel Ejiofor (try saying that three times fast) plays Dr. Adrian Helmsley, an advisor to the President, and a great admirer of Jackson because of his driving ability (actually, supposedly because of his writing).

Oliver Platt is another of the president's advisors, and Danny Glover is the President. Woody Harrelson has a silly cameo role as some meaningless hermit for comedy relief. This attempt is much better than the average end-of-the-world sagas that are usually served up by the Hollywood factories. There are surprises and complications from the start. However; I find it very interesting that you can drive at high speeds while everyone else is stuck in traffic.

10,000BC-2008-Directed by Roland Emmerich and starring unknowns Steven Strait and Camilla Belle. (she can never name her daughter Clara). This film by Emmerich that predates 2012 by a year uses the same formula as the latter film; it makes the actors secondary to the story and plot and tends to use them more as props rather than developed characterizations. Some would say that characterizations are pretty difficult to come by in 10,000BC because people were in more of a survival mode rather than seeking some type of long-range goal. One had to provide food, shelter, and clothing, ala Maslow, before one could think about taking any steps toward self-actualization. So for a few hours, we can imagine ourselves, thanks to Emmerrich, in a world where you literally had to fight for everything in your existence. Recommended.

20,000 Leagues Under the Sea-1954–Directed by Richard Fleischer and starring Kirk Douglas, James Mason, Paul Lukas, and Peter Lorre. This was the first major film production by Disney Studios and naturally, it was a huge success. The movie made a bundle at the box office because of the great combination of special effects and the great writing of Jules Verne. It was a can't-miss proposition for producer Disney, who took care of this baby all by himself from beginning concept to finished production.

A

Abandon Ship (England)–1957-Appropriately directed by Richard Sale and starring Tyrone Power as the unfortunate Captain Alec Holmes, who has to make life or death decisions in a matter of minutes, Mai Zetterling as Julie, a nurse and his girlfriend (you can bet she was never considered to be tossed overboard), Lloyd Nolan in his best performance ever, as the self-sacrificing Frank Kelly, and Stephen Boyd of *Ben-Hur* fame as Will McKinley (not the fat American President). A fine supporting cast rounds out the survivors of a catastrophic sinking of a luxury liner when it hits a mine. Recommended.

The Accidental Tourist–1988-Directed by Lawrence Kasden and starring William Hurt as Macon Leary, a writer of travel guides and a man who drifts away from his wife, Kathleen Turner, as Sarah Leary, the wife that Macon cannot commit to, Geena Davis as Muriel, the younger woman that Macon runs away with, and Bill Pullman, as Julian, his publisher, whose primary concern is that Macon continue to crank out Paul Theroux imitations. Music by John Williams adds intensity to the film. Kasden does a wonderful job of both drawing out the characterizations of the actors and moving along the plot of the film at the same time. Kasden is at home with the comedic melodrama as his vehicle, and the crisp dialogue of Ann Tyler makes his job a lot easier.

Across the Bridge (England)–1957-Directed by Ken Annakin (no relation to the Star Wars character) and starring Rod Steiger as Carl Schaffner, an embezzler on the run, Noel Willman as the chief of police who hunts him down and Inspector Hadden, played by Bernard Lee. This is a low-budget, black and white film that has nothing to offer the viewer except suspense and a good story. It has no color or special effects; it has no big shootouts. I will take a good story that is well done in black and white over a pretty color film any day of the week. Some up and coming reviewers disagree with this premise. They do not give their readers enough credit to be able to appreciate a simple black and white film (or they are too ignorant to appreciate them themselves). I have shown numerous black and white films in my film classes that young college students seemed to enjoy; so it could be a mistake to underestimate them.

Ace In the Hole—1951-Directed by Billy Wilder and starring Kirk Douglas as an unscrupulous reporter, Chuck Tatum, Jan Sterling as the miserable wife of the trapped miner, Lorraine Minosa, who angles for as much money as she can make from the unfortunate incident, Robert Arthur as a photographer, who gets wise during the incident, and an underrated performance by Richard Benedict as Minosa, the trapped miner. Highly recommended.

Action in the North Atlantic—1943-Directed by Lloyd Bacon and starring Humphrey Bogart as Joe Rossi and Raymond Massey as Captain Steve Jarvis as Merchant Marines sailing across the dangerous waters of the North Atlantic during the early days of WW2.

Adam's Rib—1949-Directed by George Cukor and written by Ruth Gordon, which proves she was a better writer than she was an actress, and she wasn't that bad an actress. The film stars Spencer Tracy as Adam Bonner, the prosecuting attorney for a case involving a woman who shoots her cheating boyfriend. Also starring In the film is Katherine Hepburn as Amanda Bonner, who opts to become the defense attorney in this case because she believes her client is not guilty of attempted murder. The film also features the enormously talented Judy Holliday, as Doris, the woman accused of trying to murder her boyfriend. Tom Ewell, as the adulterous husband, Warren, fills out the featured cast. The casting of the film is about as perfect as one can cast a film. It is extremely rare in film to find the four leading players to be perfect fits for the roles they are playing, but this movie shows how it should be done. Recommended.

Adventures of Mark Twain—1944-Directed by Irving Rapper and starring Fredric March as Mark Smith, a competent actress plays Olivia, his wife. We follow Twain in his early years at the Hannibal Journal newspaper in Missouri as Samuel Clemens. He covers local stories, state fairs, and mostly events affecting the local population. He is not happy writing for the paper. Twain goes on the road and becomes a Mississippi River Boat pilot. Recommended.

Adventures of Robin Hood—1938-Directed by Michael Curtiz and starring Errol Flynn as Robin Hood, Basil Rathbone as the evil Sir Guy of Gisbourne, Olivia DeHaviland, as the fair Maid Marian, and Claude Rains as the corrupt PrinceJohn, brother of Richard the Lionhearted.

Adventure yarns don't get much better than this one. Great casting for everyone in the film, and great cinematography and music to boot. The story of Robin Hood according to Hollywood is so much better than the real one. I prefer this version to the later versions by Connery, Costner and Crowe because Connery is too serious, Costner merely makes fun of the character, and Crowe is miscast. The Connery version was pretty good, but he was too damn old to play the role. Robin Hood, by the way, never really existed; and if he did, he did not rob from the rich and give to the poor; he just kept the money after he robbed or killed anyone foolish enough to go through Sherwood Forest too late in the day. So not really the first recorded incident of socialism.

Adventures of Robinson Crusoe (Mexico)—1954-Directed by Luis Bunuel and starring Dan O'Herlihy as Crusoe. This is a story of a man marooned on a desert island, but he is not completely alone. This classic, written by Daniel Dafoe, has been featured numerous times on the big screen and television in many different countries. This particular version was filmed in Mexico to lower the costs of sets and production. Almost all of the shots are exteriors filmed on the island itself on Manzanillo and near Colima. O'Herlihy was nominated for an academy award for his portrayal in this film, partly due to the fine direction of Bunuel and partly due to his great performance. He had practically no chance of winning that year because he was up against Marlon Brando for *On the Waterfront*.

Adventures of Sherlock Holmes–1939-Directed by Alfred Werker and starring Basil Rathbone as Holmes and the bumbling Nigel Bruce as Doctor Watson. Arguably, this is the most famous pairing of Holmes and Watson in the first 110 years of film. They will be difficult to replace as the number one team. The chemistry between the two was genuine, and highly believable. The plots were usually secondary to the repartee between Holmes and Watson. Also, any supporting roles were usually submerged when Rathbone and Bruce were on the screen. For example, Moriarity, the infamous third wheel in the series is always a highly forgettable actor. Do you remember any of their names? Very few people can name even one of them, but almost everyone remembers Rathbone and Bruce. By the way, this is the film which initiated "Elementary, My Dear Watson". Recommended.

African Queen-1951–Directed by John Huston and starring Humphrey Bogart as Charlie and Katherine Hepburn as Rosie. This film was a rare independent studio effort that proved to be successful at the box office. Bogart won the Academy Award for this film, even though many critics thought it was not his best work. *The Treasure of Sierra Madre* is considered his best by most critics, while *Casablanca* was considered by others to be his best. Katherine Hepburn never feared tackling any role, and this was just another of her great screen triumphs. She was nominated but did not win the Oscar in 1951. That honor went to Vivien Leigh for Streetcar Named Desire and deservedly so. I include this film in my top thirty, so I believe it is a must-see film for younger film fans.

After Life (Japan)–1998--Directed by Hirokazu Koreeda and starring Arata, Oda Erika, and Terajima Susumu. This is a small Japanese film with a big question. What would you keep for the rest of eternity as your favorite moment in time? At first, I was a bit reticent to see this film, since it was about death, a rather depressing subject. This film, however, had the opposite effect. It has a soothing, almost hypnotic effect on the viewer. It provides us with a gratifying positive view of the the hereafter that is not judgmental or pressurized. The film allows us to consider that things after death may not be as black and white as we have imagined them to be.

Aftershock (China)–2010-Directed by Feng Xiaogang and starring Xu Fan, Zhang Jingchu, and Li Chen. This film is much more than just your ordinary disaster movie. Based on a true story, it has a secondary plot that eventually turns into the main plot of the film. The earthquake is devastating enough, and the catastrophic scenes are unforgettable, but the emotional devastation of the people involved in this case lasts for a lifetime.

Against All Flags–1952-Directed by George Sherman and starring Errol Flynn as the heroic Brian Hawke, who is posing as a deserter in order to infiltrate Pirate terrorists (pirates were actually the terrorists of that time period). Also appearing is Anthony Quinn as Roc, a real Pirate, Maureen O'Hara, as the Pirate's sex object, Spitfire, and Alice Kelley as Princess Patma, a captured princess that falls in love with Brian. Recommended despite the lack of believability.

The Agony and the Ecstasy–1965-Directed by Carol Reed and starring Charlton Heston as Michaelangelo and Rex Harrison as Pope Julius II. It is the story of the painting of the famous Sistene Chapel and the fits and starts that accompanied the great undertaking. The music is appropriate for the time and place and one will feel as if he or she is painting the chapel along with Michaelangelo. The film had great production values and the intensity is there from beginning to end. Recommended.

Aguirre, The Wrath of God (Germany)–1972-Directed by Werner Herzog and starring Klaus Kinski as Aguirre, a commander of the Spanish expeditionary forces in the New World. Kinski over the top, as usual, but still a very interesting film to watch. Recommended.

Air Force–1943- Directed by Howard Hawks and starring John Garfield as Sergeant Winocki, Aerial Gunner, in his first major role. One can see the emerging star quality within the character that Garfield plays. He was to make many more films with that quiet, angry personality that you could virtually see smoldering on the screen.

   Also starring with Garfield in this very successful film is Gig Young as Lt. Williams, the co-pilot of one of the first planes to come to Pearl Harbor after the bombing. The film also features John Ridgely as the pilot, and Harry Carey as Sergeant White, whose son is killed in the raid on Pearl Harbor. Carey is particularly effective in his role as a military father whose military son predeceases him. The resolve of the character comes through to the audience without any histrionics by Carey. The rest of the supporting cast does a first-rate job filling out their roles.

Airplane! – 1980–Directed by the trio of David Zucker, Jerry Zucker, and Jim Abrahams and starring all the wise guys in the film business who were tired of doing straight roles such as Leslie Neilson, Peter Graves, Robert Stack, and Lloyd Bridges. Of these four, Neilson and Bridges steal the movie, but there are enough scenes for everyone to have some fun.

Airport–1970-Directed by George Seaton and starring Burt Lancaster, Dean Martin, Jackie Bisset, George Kennedy, (it was mandatory to have George Kennedy in almost every disaster movie ever made), Helen Hayes, Maureen Stapleton, and everyone else in Hollywood who was not working in a major motion picture. This film has become known as the serious version of *Airplane!,* a highly successful lampoon of this film. It does have a certain amount of tension, and is watchable, but it is almost impossible to take seriously (surely, you can't be serious; don't call me Shirley!) after a viewing of *Airplane!* The performances of Lancaster and Kennedy, in particular, stand out in this film, despite the amusing similarities to the satirical roles depicted in the later *Airplane!* film. Lancaster and Kennedy are both highly professional actors who were totally convincing in any role they tackled. Try to see this one BEFORE *Airplane!.* Recommended.

Alexander Nevsky (Russia) – 1938-Directed by Serge Eisenstein and starring a cast of relatively unknown Russian actors. This tale of a Germanic invasion of the Russian motherland in the Middle Ages was obviously a metaphor for the Nazi invasion of Russia on the Eastern Front in modern times. Some chilling moments.

Ali-2001–Directed by Michael Mann and starring Will Smith as Ali. Jamie Foxx, Mario Van Peebles and Jon Voight are also featured in the film. Mann had a number of successes before this film, including the origin of *The Silence of the Lambs*, called *The Red Dragon*. He was also famous for directing the famous TV show, *Miami Vice*, which put him on the map of Hollywood directors for style and action. Will Smith was a good choice for the brash role of Ali because of his physical similarities and his acting ability. Some critics, though, thought he was wrong for the role because he did not have the complex type of personality that was inherent in Ali. One critic joked that the role would have been perfect for Denzel Washington emotionally, but would have had to have been filmed strictly from the neck up. The man still remains an enigmatic legend. Recommended.

Alien–1979-Directed by Ridley Scott and starring Bolaji Bodejo as the Alien. Yes ,folks, that was a human being inside an alien outfit. The best-kept secret of a monster in a movie since Karloff was in *Frankenstein* (his only credit was Karloff; not including his first name, Boris). Bolaji was a Nigerian discovered at a bar by a member of the casting crew. Sigourney Weaver was the recognizable lead star as Ripley, the warrant officer on the spaceship, Nostromo. It was one of her first leading roles. Also appearing in the film were John Hurt as Kane, the Executive Officer and host for the Alien, Tom Skerrit as Captain Dallas, Harry Dean Stanton as Brett, the engineer, Ian Holm as Ash, who is actually an android and Yaphet Kotto as Parker, the Chief Engineer. This moody, atmospheric film really captures that outer-space feeling sometimes missing in other science-fiction movies. You get a real sense of being far away from earth and any sense of security of protection by earth authorities.

Aliens-1986-Directed by James Cameron and starring Sigorney Weaver as Ripley, Lance Henrikson as the new android, Bishop, and Bill Paxton as a marine (bit of a stretch, there). Adding to the film is child actor, Carrie Hennas Newt, the only survivor of a space colony. The primary difference between the sequel and the original, which was also very good, is that this film has a great deal more action. However, it does not have as much atmospheric suspense as the original. We already know the Alien exists; so that surprise is taken away and replaced with other surprises. It follows the successful formula of *Frankenstein* and the sequel, *Bride of Frankenstein*, which many critics, including myself, thought was superior to the original. This film is not superior to the original, in my opinion, however. My son, Thomas disagreed with me vehemently on this one; one of the few times we did not agree or slightly disagree. The addition of Bishop, played by Henrikson, is a real boon to the sequel, as he was not in the original. He gives us the real feel of an android. In this case, the sequel is ALMOST as good as the original. Recommended.

All About Eve–1950–Directed by Joseph Mankiewitz and starring Bette Davis as Margo, a very successful and popular stage star, George Sanders as Addison, as the wonderfully acidic (and my role model) critic, Anne Baxter, in the greatest role of her career as Eve, and a solid supporting cast. This is a first-rate film that many critics love , including myself. Bette Davis is at the top of her game in this one and that means she is unbeatable. GeorgeSanders is also at his best and the two of them are extremely formidable, but Anne Baxter holds her own with both of them in her portrayal as the back-climbing Eve, a character so devilishly conceived, that once seen, will never be forgotten. In fact, the writer of the short story (her first), Mary Orr, is astounding with her incisiveness about the play industry. She captures every aspect of Hollywood's greed, deception, malice and insincerity in a matter of a few pages, while many had tried to write books about the subject, and had failed miserably. This film was nominated for an astounding 14 Academy Awards; a feat unmatched until *Titanic* (not really in the same class). This is a must-see film.

All My Sons–1948-Directed by Irving Reis and based on a play by the husband of Marilyn Monroe, ArthurMiller. It stars Edward G. Robinson as Joe Keller, an overly-ambitious man who is willing to sacrifice American lives in WW2 so his family can live well, and Burt Lancaster as Chris Keller, the eldest son of Joe, who is horrified to find out what his father has done. Howard Duff, who appeared with Lancaster previously in *BruteForce*, plays George Deever, and Harry Morgan, who always adds to any film, plays Frank Lubey.

All Quiet on the Western Front–1930-Directed by Lewis Milestone, and starring Louis Wolheim as one of the tragic German high school students who do on-the-job training on how to survive as soldiers in World War I. The film also stars Lew Ayres, John Wray, and Ben Alexander, with capable supporting players filling out the cast. This movie won Best Director and Best Picture of the year and both awards were well-deserved. It is one of the few American war films that depicts the tragedy of war from the side of the opponents. *The Young Lions* would attempt to duplicate this feat, but with far less success. Of course, more recently, we have the highly successful *Letters From Iwo Jima*, which is sympathetic to the Japanese soldier's plight.

The point of all these films is that young men who are soldiers are seldom very political; they are merely young men who are caught up in the machinery of wars. *All Quiet on the Western Front* is the classic anti-war film. It shows the horror and stupidity of war in numerous scenes without using a great deal of dialogue or preaching about it to the audience. That is the body and soul of good film-making .The scenes of whistles blowing and men going over the top to almost certain death at a rate of 50% or higher on each charge is heart-rending. The idiotic orders of officers who are safe behind the lines is also highlighted in the film. It is easy to give orders if you do not have to go over the top yourself. The beauty of the film is that both sides in the war are idiotic, as war is an idiotic endeavor. I highly recommend it to all movie buffs who want to see how a real war movie is made. Despite the age of the film, it is not in the least bit dated because everything that happens in this film still happens in every war we have. Highly Recommended.

All The King's Men–1949–Directed by Robert Rossen and starring Broderick Crawford in his Academy-Award winning performance as WillieStark (Governor Huey Long of Louisiana). Crawford gives a tour-de-force performance not only to win the award, but to gain eminence in acting circles for future roles for many years to come. Best remembered for his role on TV in *Highway Patrol*, we see that he far exceeded those performances with both this and his other film triumphs, such as *BornYesterday*. Crawford was usually cast as a heavy, but made his greatest impression when he stretched his considerable acting range to include comedy and a sense of clumsy romanticism. I highly recommend this film to all movie buffs as a top-notch biopic.

All The President's Men–1976-Directed by Alan J Pakula and starring Dustin Hoffman and the *Sundance Kid*, I mean Robert Redford, as the Washington Post reporters CarlBernstein and Bob Woodward, respectively. Of these two, it is my opinion that Hoffman is the stronger actor, and he pretty much dictates the flow of the action from the pair. Also prominent in this film in probably the most important role of his career is Jason Robards Jr., as the editor of the Washington Post, Ben Bradlee. This is a key role in the film because it gives guidance to the limits that these two reporters can go to in order to get their stories.

Almost Famous–2000-Directed by Cameron Crowe and starring Patrick Fugit as William, Cameron Crowe's alter-ego, Kate Hudson as Penny Lane, a groupie, Billy Crudup as the rock star, and the very talented Phillip Seymour Hoffman as a mentor of William. This is a tale of a young man seeking adventure as a reporter of contemporary music and the groups that play it. It also follows his experiences with the groupies that follow the musicians. Sometimes, what appears to be a glamorous lifestyle is not all that glamorous. This is a delightful little film that demonstrates how far passion for your work can take you. Recommended.

AloneAcrossthePacific(Japan)–1963–Directed by KonI Chikawa and starring Yujiro Ishihara in a tale about a Japanese man who attempts a Kon (norelationtothedirector)-Tiki-type trip to San Francisco from Japan. Recommended.

Along the Great Divide–1951-Directed by Raoul Walsh and starring Kirk Douglas, Virginia Mayo, John Agar, and Walter Brennan, who used to make a great living as a second banana in Hollywood Westerns. He was so good at it, he won the Academy Award for Best Supporting Actor three times which tied him with Jack Nicholson as the most honored actor in Hollywood film history. This was Douglas' first role in a Western; he was rejected for the Montgomery Cliff role in Red River. Why they would ever choose an effeminate actor like Cliff to play a rugged cowboy over Douglas was beyond me, but time eventually showed that they made the wrong choice. Douglas is very good in this film as the sheriff similar to the character of the sheriff in 3:10 to Yuma, who has to bring a suspect in for trial in another town. As usual, Mayo is just window dressing in this Western, as most women were for most Westerns, until someone like Barbara Stanwyck or MarleneDietrich came along and actually overwhelmed the male actors. Recommended with reservations.

AlteredStates-1980–Directed by Ken Russell, a director who had a problem avoiding excess, like I have avoiding pasta, and starring William Hurt in his first major film as Professor Edward Jessu,a Columbia?(it is filmed in the Columbia University area) University professor studying the effects of sensory deprivation (with a little bit of help from rare mushrooms). The original material of the film is what makes it so interesting, and the South American scenes are one of the best things in the movie, although the transformation scenes are kind of neat, also. There are a few holes in the plot, but we quickly forgive these because the on-screen candy is so sweet that we just want to see more and more. Russell has a way of mesmerizing the viewer with images and sometimes going to such great lengths to develop a scene, he sometimes loses the rhythm of the film itself. This is my favorite Russell film (I really don't care too much for his other work).

Amadeus–1984—Directed by Milos Foreman and starring Tom Hulce as the legendary Mozart, and F. Murray Abraham in his Academy-Award nominated role as Salieri, the jealous adversary of Mozart. Also prominent in the film is Elizabeth Berriage as Hulce's love interest and the wonderfully miscast Jeffrey

Jones as the delightful Emperor JosephII with his memorably funny line "The music has too many notes" which I have used in my classic film quote quiz. The film is told in flashback with Salieri as the wistful narrator. Foreman carries off the technique very well without getting bogged down in some of the usual flashback difficulties (too many cuts to the present, or staying in the past so long that we forget we are in flashback). This was one of the four films chosen by American professors to teach the Chinese about Western Culture at a major Chinese university. This film deserved every nomination it got and a few it didn't receive (like ignoring Hulce's stellar performance).

America, America–1963–Written, directed, and produced by Elia Kazan, and starring Stathis Giallelis (a low-budget actor, rarely to be seen again) as Stavros. Even though Kazan uses one of the greatest no-name casts of one-time actors in a big film, he is still able to pull off a good movie because he uses the Hitchcock formula of using actors merely as props to a good story, good dialogue, and good direction. Both Kazan and Hitchcock strongly felt that actors could be replaced much easier than a good script, and that good direction of any actors was a far better idea than poor direction of good actors. This film relies on a solid story and a series of events that show how some people who try to come here deserve being here more than a lot of the citizens that are already here.

America, Imagine the World Without Her – 2014 – This interesting documentary by Ginesh D'Souza is biased, but very inspiring at other levels. His clever premise of setting up the viewer when interviewing various miscreants creates great distaste for the interviewees. However, he quickly rebukes each of the generally accepted theories of these people with great research and content. This is when he should have quit while he was ahead, but, unfortunately, he began a diatribe against the left in the persona of Hilary Clinton, Obama and other liberals. The film loses its original energy and then falls into a rather boring rant against the left. Still, very good other than the political rant. My friend Red Eipert will love this film because as a Vietnam Vet like myself; we still love the US, despite its flaws.

American Beauty-1999- Directed by Sam Mendes and starring Kevin Spacey as Lester, a magazine writer having a midlife crisis. Also featured is Annette Benning as his money-hungry wife, Carolyn. The object of Lester's affection is Angela, a cheerleader played by Mena Suvari. She is a pretty hot number. Buddy Kane, played by Peter Gallagher, is taking good care of Lester's wife while he is out chasing his fantasy girl. Colonel Fitts (as in throwing a fit),is played by Chris Cooper and is another cardboard stereotype, although Cooper is a fine actor and gives the role his best shot. It appears as if Mendes had quite a load of stereotypes in the film, as opposed to the thorough character study that is Lester. He is the only character who we truly understand as a person. Spacey's tour-de-force performance is a must-see.

American Graffiti–1973-Directed by George Lucas and starring Richard Dreyfuss as Curt, a graduating high school senior, Ron Howard, as his lame friend Steve, Cindy Williams as a nice girl, Laurie, Candy Clark as a hot girl, Debbie, and Harrison Ford in a minor role that everyone has forgotten. Also appearing is Mackenzie Phillips (of the *Mamas and Papas*) as Carol, an annoying teen, and she does a great job. There is also a very interesting cameo by Wolfman Jack who plays himself in the film. Rarely do we get to see the voices of the people we have heard on the radio. The film fairly well captures the confusion and hopefulness of graduating seniors from high school. Some will go on to college, others will stay at home and become successes and failures, while others will leave their hometown to become successes and failures in other places. Such is life.

American Hustle–2013-Directed by David O. Russell and starring Christian Bale and others in a story about a scam from Camden, New Jersey (not very likely) and Atlantic City (very likely). Many hustle films are fun, and this one is no exception. Recommended.

An American Guerrilla in the Philippines–1950 – Directed by Fritz Lang and starring Tyronne Power as Ensign Palmer, a young, inexperienced Navy officer. Also appearing in the film isTom Ewell, as one of his Navy buddies. The story takes place at the beginning of World War2, right after the bombing of Pearl Harbor. The day after the bombing ,the Japanese began their invasion of the Philippines. The US troops were outnumbered and ill-equipped to fight the Japanese, but they were stubborn adversaries. This story gives a good illustration of the American will to fight.

American History X–1998–Directed by Tony Kaye and starring the electric Ed Norton as Derek, in the primary role with Ed Furlong cast as younger brother, Eric .Also featured in the film are Elliot Gould (who seems lost here) and Stacy Keach (who does a fine job as the scummy neo-nazi leader trying to take Norton's younger brother down the road to racial hatred). Recommended.

American Splendor–2003-Directed by Shari Springer Berman and Robert Pulcini and starring Paul Giamatti as Harvey Pekar, a guy that reminds me a great deal of my brother. Also in the film are Harvey Pekar himself, Hope Davis as Joyce, a woman with low self-esteem, and low expectations for male companionship, the real-life Joyce herself, James Urbaniak as Robert Crumb, the legendary underground comic writer, and various other slackers, who cannot connect in modern society at a professional or working-class level. For some reason, Hollywood loves slackers and slacker films. It glorifies slackers, so that they will spend money watching other slackers on the big screen and gain recognition for their slacker lifestyles.

   Occasionally, what makes these films popular is a slacker like Rocky, who learns how to become a winner. The truth of the matter is, though, that for every Rocky who turns it around, there are nine slackers who do not turn it around. It was good to see Giamatti follow up this film with the very chic *Sideways*, because the latter film helps to salvage his persona, which takes a severe hit in this one. Recommended.

Anatomy of a Murder–1959- directed by Otto Preminger and starring James Stewart as a small-town lawyer, Paul, Laura, the supposed rape victim, played by Lee Remick, husband of Laura and accused murderer, Manny, played by Ben Gazzara, and a big-city prosecutor named Dancer, played by George C. Scott. In addition to these major players, there are a number of good minor performances; including that of Eve Arden as a wise-cracking secretary. The cast is first-rate and the direction of Preminger, although at times heavy-handed, is still professional and detailed. Stewart is always believable as a lawyer, Remick is good casting here as well as Scott as a prosecutor. Scott could convince you he is just about anyone he wants to be. He is the heavyweight actor in this film, even though Stewart was better known. Scott would go on to win the Oscar for his performance in a future film (*Patton*). Recommended.

Andha Naal–India–1954–Directed by Veenai S. Balachander and starring Sivaji Ganesan, Pandari Bai, and Javar Seetharaman in a story about a murder with five suspects. This was one of the few Indian films not to have song and dance routines in the story, which would have been difficult, considering the plot. Interesting, from a historical perspective.

And Now For Something Completely Different (England)–1971-Directed by Ian McNaugton and starring the barely legally sane Graham Chapman, John Cleese, Terry Gilliam, Eric Idle, Terry Jones, and Michael Palin. The film is a collection of skits reproduced from the first two seasons of Monty Python's Flying Circus, an enormously popular and funny weekly show that broadcast primarily in England, but was rebroadcast on several occasions in the United States by Public Broadcasting Stations (PBS) throughout the country. The show was paid for by the donations of public viewers. It was one of the biggest fund-raisers for public television, because many people wanted to see more of Monty Python. The public couldn't get enough of them. Each show and movie seemed to outdo the previous one. The apex of the Flying Circus seemed to be the classic film, *Monty Python and the Holy Grail*, which some fans have seen over a dozen times. The film was so popular, that it was made into a very expensive play where people gladly paid over $100 a seat for good tickets to see just one more retelling of the movie.

Andromeda Strain–1969-Directed by Robert Wise, (the hills are alive with deadly bacteria) based on the best-selling novel of Michael Crichton and starring a number of B actors who are merely props for the real star of the film, which is the extra-terrestrial disease. This was a very unusual project for Wise, who was used to lighter fare such as *The Sound of Music* (not to mention much bigger budgets). But he was able to put together a nice tight little low-cost science-fiction thriller, which makes him one of the more versatile directors in the history of film.

How many directors have a hit musical and a hit film in science-fiction besides Wise? None that I can think of. The novel by Crichton provides the ample guideline for the tight script and engenders suspense from the opening scene through the entire film. It is a rare piece of science-fiction that can grab the reader or viewer immediately and hold them for two hours. The book was such a great page turner that it was on the best-seller list for months, and some contend the book was better than the film (which is the norm). This is a wonderfully creative science-fiction plot; based on science rather than monsters or aliens attacking the earth. I can highly recommend it.

And Then There Were None – 1945 - Directed by Rene Clair and starring Barry Fitzgerald, Walter Huston, and a long list of additional competent B actors. This is the original film version of the Agatha Christie novel of the same name. Sometimes, there is difficulty in translating a mystery novel to the big screen, but a story such as this one is a perfect vehicle for a film. Christie does a great job of honing all the characters, so that the director has a very easy job of keeping them in character. Very few screenwriters could match the detail that Christie brought to the screen.

Clair directs the ensemble with a deft touch and there is very little in the way of heavy-handedness that one sometimes sees in other detective vehicles. Of course we all know that the vast majority of the characters are doomed from the start and part of the fun is figuring out who will next to get their eternal reward. Another fun aspect is trying to figure out who is the power behind all the killings and what is the motive of the killer.

Angel Face – 1952 - Directed by the heavy-handed Otto Preminger and starring Robert Mitchum as Frank, an ambulance attendant and Jean Simmons as Diane, the psychopathic killer who looks like an angel. You could not find a hotter duo in the early fifties. Herbert Marshall, a thoroughly competent actor, is also featured. Although the film was good, it could have been sensational under the hand of a more subtle director, like Michael Curtiz, for example. Preminger bludgeons us with the beautiful girl, who is really Satan in disguise, right from the beginning of the film.

   A better director would have used a lot more nuance and a lot less hitting us over the head with blatant music and innuendo. Mitchum looks like one of the world's biggest chumps in this film. If his character had been handled by a more talented director, it could have been a much more sympathetic and tragic figure. As done by Preminger, Mitchum appears as if he almost deserves what happens to him, despite not having an evil bone in his body. On the other hand, I used to absolutely adore Jean Simmons, and I can understand, to a point, how Mitchum's character could forego all good judgment just to have a fling with her. Diane's character is so despicable, she makes Theron's character in *Monster* sympathetic in comparison. Recommended.

Angel on My Shoulder – 1946 –Directed by Archie Mayo and starring Paul Muni as Eddie Kagle, a gangster who has met an untimely end, Claude Rains, wonderfully cast as the Devil, who offers Eddie a chance for revenge on his best friend who killed him, Smiley, played by the relatively unknown actor, Hardie Albright, and Anne Baxter, the romantic interest in the film, as Barbara, the fiancée of Judge Parker, whom we never see in the film.

Angels With Dirty Faces - 1938 - Directed by Michael Curtiz and starring James Cagney as Rocky Sullivan, a lifetime gangster, Humphrey Bogart, oddly miscast as a crooked lawyer, Jim Frazier, and Pat O'Brien as Father Jerry Connolly, and best friend of Rocky. The Dead End Kids led by tough-guy Bim (Leo Gorcey) and the funny Crabface (Huntz Hall) pretty much steal the movie from the veteran stars. They were so popular in this film, that the studio had to make another film resurrecting Cagney and Bogart called *Dead End*. After this second film, the Dead End Kids became so popular, that they could practically carry a movie on their own. They then made a long series of films until each of the Dead End Kids was well into their thirties.

Animal Farm (England) – 1955 - Directed by John Halas and Joy Batchelor and starring Mauric Denham. This is the George Orwell tale of farm animals acting act how life would be under communist rule. The lesson we are supposed to learn from this is that both systems, capitalism and communism, are pretty much the same in their end results. Only a select few get to enjoy the benefits of the work of the many. Both systems promise greater freedom for the working man, eh animal, and but then both systems wind up exploiting the workers about the same.

   The political, industrial and military leaders take all the power for themselves, whether it be in the capitalist system or in the communist system. So there is really very little to distinguish one from the other. The animal metaphors work as a better illustration than humans, because humans rationalize a lot more and animals get to the heart of the matter much quicker than dumb humans. After all, pigs are pigs regardless of whatever political or economic system they might be in. It is interesting to see such complex elements like communism and capitalism get rightfully spit-fried by Orwell, who is a master of simplifying these principles for mass understanding.

Animal Kingdom – 2010 – Directed by David Mechod and starring a relatively unknown cast of B actors, but a riveting script and tight direction make this film a cut above the usual crime drama. The story of a younger brother in a crime family is fascinating from beginning to end.

Anna and the King of Siam – 1946 - Directed by David Lean and starring Linda Darnell and Rex Harrison as the King of Siam. The casting here was a bit askew, but that is quickly forgiven because of the great dialogue and the absence of musical tunes which tortures the musical version of this film in The King and I. I am not a big fan of Hollywood musicals. Although Rex Harrison did not go on to play the Western English version of this film (that was performed by Yul Brenner), he did go on to play Professor Higgins in the Broadway hit, **My Fair Lady**, opposite Julie Andrews, then he went to star in the film version opposite Audrey Hepburn. He won an Oscar for his efforts in that role. He was described by Noel Coward as the finest light comedy actor in the world (although Cary Grant would later challenge for that title). Not bad.

Annie Hall – 1977 - Directed by Woody Allen and starring Woody Allen and Diane Keaton as two offbeat Manhattan lovers. We follow Woody and his emotional frailties as well as the insecurities of Diane Keaton in her manly, but stylish clothes, which started a new fashion trend that Fall in New York and the rest of the country. Along the way, we are treated to a number of great scenes within New York City and a map for out- of- towners of where to go and what to do while in New York. My favorite scene is the one where the couple is waiting on line for a movie and Woody gets into an argument about the meaning of media in the eyes of Marshall McCluan, who taught at Columbia University. Some smart-ass on the line mentions that he went to Columbia and he knows all about what McCluan taught in his class. Woody goes on to pull McCluan from another part of the line, and McCluan chastises the student by telling him he knows nothing about his work. Woody speaks to the audience at this point and says don't you wish you could do this in real life? I am picking this film (against my better judgment) to win the Best Picture Oscar for 1977.

Annie Oakley - 1935 - Directed by George Stevens and starring Barbara Stanwyck and Preston Foster. This is perhaps the greatest role (Annie Oakley) ever performed by Stanwyck. She was to go on to play numerous Western heroines plus a successful long-running TV series, *Big Valley*. She was also considered to be one of the most popular film actress in Hollywood in the thirties with audiences, directors, film crews and ordinary people. The Brooklyn-born native was popular with just about everyone she met. I must admit while other boys my age were dreaming about mounting horses they saw in Westerns, I was dreaming about Stanwyck in *Annie Oakley*.

She deserved at least a nomination for this film, if not the award, itself. I have seen the performances of all the other films and actresses for that year, and hers is at least as good, if not better. Unfortunately, at that time, Westerns were considered an inferior genre, and were not considered serious films.

Preston Foster is more than adequate in his role, as Frank Butler, the Irish immigrant sharpshooter, but it is Stanwyck that steals the movie from beginning to end. Highly Recommended

Anthony Adverse – 1936- Directed by Mervyn LeRoy and starring Fredric March and Olivia DeHaviland in the leading roles. A fine supporting cast, including Donna Woods, Edmund Glenn, Claude Rains, and Akim Tamiroff round out the production. This is a story about an unwanted child, who is shifted around until he reaches adulthood. As an adult, Anthony, played by March, falls in love with Maria (just like in *West Side Story*), who is played by DeHaviland. There are numerous complications and the giving away of personal fortunes before the desired happy end result is accomplished. I wish I had a fortune I could just give away on a whim; but then I wouldn't have given it away, I guess. Recommended.

Ant Man - 2015- Directed by Peyton Reed and starring Paul Ruddand Michael Douglas in the lead roles of Antman and an aging scientist, respectively. The director is fine, the actors are fine, and the production values are very good, but the script had one serious problem. A cat burglar as the superhero? Please. His brain must have shrunk as well. If someone possessed technology like that, they could make a hundred times more from private industry and governments than what they could steal. I hate dumb logic. Other than that horrible mistake, an entertaining film.

Anzio – 1968 – Directed by Edward Dmytryk and starring Robert Mitchum, Peter Falk and Robert Ryan. Also featured is an early performance of Giancarlo Giannini (*SweptAway*). This WW 2 film highlights the stupidity of the upper American military command for digging in at Anzio rather than moving unopposed to Rome. Not all European Theater of War decisions by the Allies were brilliant .

Apache – 1954 -Directed by Robert Aldrich and starring Burt Lancaster as Massai, the renegade Apache warrior, and Jean Peters, his lovely blue-eyed squaw. How Jean Peters got cast in this film is beyond me, but she is pretty sexy, even if she looks nothing at all like an Apache woman. Burt Lancaster, on the other hand, is quite believable as a renegade because he was pretty much one in real life. Lancaster brought believability and passion to almost every role he ever played and this one is no exception. His physique matched that of a renegade, also. Of all the actors in Hollywood at the time, there was never an actor who did more of his own stunts than Lancaster, who started out in Hollywood as a trapeze artist and super-athlete. He didn't get the role of *Jim Thorpe* because he was a pretty boy. It is a bit ironic that Charles Bronson is in this film, because Bronson played Indians convincingly in a number of his films, and would, no doubt, have been perfect in this role. This is one of the earliest films out of Hollywood where people were rooting for the Indians over the evil white man. Recommended to see Burt in action.

Aparajito (India) – 1956 - Directed by Satyajit Ray and starring Penaki Sengupta as Apu as a boy, Smaran Ghosal as Apu as anadolescent, Karuna Banergee as his mom, and a brief appearance by Kanu Banergee as his father. This film is considered to be one of the greatest Indian films ever made. It is no coincidence that the director of the film is also considered the greatest Indian director in film history. Ray is to Indian cinema as Hitchcock is to English and American cinema. It used to be that Indian cinema was wildly popular in India, but not so popular outside of that country. That was until recently. The recent spectacular international success of *Slumdog Millionaire* has now put India on the international cinema map, and more great films from India will now be expected to emerge from that great cinema-loving nation. One can only hope that they can rise to the occasion and create more classics.

The Apartment – 1960 — Directed by Billy Wilder and starring Shirley Maclaine, Jack Lemmon, and Fred MacMurray. This film about working and loving in Manhattan is given a shot in the arm by the great work of the three lead actors. MacMurray makes a rare appearance as a sleazebag, instead of the usual good guy roles he was known for. He immediately returned to his good guy persona by enlisting for the popular TV series, *My Three Sons* following this and a few other films. He had, however, been very successful once before in playing a bad guy in *Double Indemnity*, a great film about murder and collecting insurance, many years earlier with Edward G Robinson and Barbara Stanwyck. He is a little less dark in this film, but effective, nevertheless. Lemmon does his usual professional job as the guy who picks up the pieces for Shirley MacLaine. Maclaine, by the way, is really very good in this film and it is one of the best roles of her career.

Apocalypse Now – 1979 – Directed by Francis Ford Coppola and starring Martin Sheen and a very fat Marlon Brando. Brando was so fat in this movie, all his scenes had to be shot in the shadows of his jungle cave, so viewers would not be able to see how enormous he was. Part of the plot of the movie was that he was a super-athlete that whipped himself through Ranger training at an advanced age. Well, that didn't quite jibe with the actual pictures we saw. But the film is not about Brando's big belly or his training success; it is about the Vietnam War, and the mass confusion from the generals down to the privates is wonderfully illustrated by one line in the film. When Sheen asks who's in charge to a battle-beleaguered front-line veteran, the soldier merely states "I thought you were". This pretty much sums up the entire Vietnam War; mass confusion. The helicopter scene combined with music from *The Ride of the Valkyries* is considered by many to be one of the greatest war scenes ever shot.

The more famous quote from this film is when Robert Duvall utters: "I love the smell of napalm in the morning!". The movie was nominated for numerous Academy Awards, but won only for best cinematography (which it richly deserved) and for best Sound. The film is on practically every best ten war movies of all time lists of the vast majority of critics. I have it placed at number 32 of best films of all time, but it will fall a few notches as great new films are added over the years. I picked *Kramer vs. Kramer* to win Best Picture for that year because I knew how the academy votes, but I thought this film should have won. The supporting cast included such well-known actors as Laurence Fishburne, Dennis Hopper, Harrison Ford, and Scott Glenn. The real star of the film, however, is the confusion of the war itself.

Apocalypto – 2006 - Directed by Mel Gibson and starring Rudy Youngblood and a fine supporting cast. Mel Gibson may do and say some dumb things once in a while, but he certainly knows how to both select a good script, and then direct it. The casting for the film is letter perfect. You feel as if you are part of Jaguar Paw's tribe and are rooting for him all through the film. The cinematography is outstanding, and of Academy-Award level production. As a matter of fact, all the production values were very high in this film. The music is vibrant and pulsating, and Gibson keeps the action at a fever pitch for most of the film. There is almost too much going on in each frame of each scene, so that the viewer is overwhelmed by the images. Gibson certainly knows how to make an action film, and provide a good story at the same time.

The lead actor, Youngblood, is highly sympathetic to the viewer, and the sequence of events that he suffers through are horrific, yet highly representative of that time period and place. It was a time and place that I certainly would not have enjoyed being in, and I doubt that few others who view the film would have had any desire to have lived through those events. The film makes one very thankful that we live in an ordered and civilized society, despite patches of world disorder and starvation. Because whatever difficulties we now face in the modern world pale in comparison to what Jaguar Paw and the Mayans had to face when the Spanish landed on their shores.

Apollo 13 – 1995 -Directed by Ron Howard and starring Tom Hanks as Jim Lovell, Kevin Bacon as Jack Swigert, and Bill Paxton as Fred Haise. There is also a great supporting cast, particularly Ed Harris as the flight director. This is a well-acted story depicting the fateful flight of Apollo 13 in 1970. A film about a problem flight, *Maroooned*, was made shortly before and ballyhooed by everyone before its release. After its release, I took my mother to the film, and she said it was the most boring movie she had ever seen, and I had to agree with her. It was a major disappointment for everyone and I thought for sure there would never be another film about the subject ever made after that turkey. But I was wrong. Universal Studios miraculously picked up the script, and said we can do a lot better than *Marooned* and they did. Good for them.

The Apostle – 1997 – Directed and written by Robert Duvall and starring Robert Duvall as a Christian who returns to the path of righteousness in Louisiana after leading committing a violent act as a preacher in Texas. The film is a tour-de-force for Duvall, and he most certainly deserved the Oscar that year for his performance. He is letter-perfect casting for this type of role. The role is a very complex one. The character played by Duvall is both a man of frightening potential violence and a river of compassion. There is almost no limit to the goodness of the man when he is control of his temper. His belief is so strong, and his character outside of his bad temper is so rock solid, that one cannot help but be influenced by his passionate words and sermons. Recommended.

Appointment in Berlin – 1943 - Directed by Henry Levin (one of his first films) and starring George Sanders and various forgotten actors. As is very common in films with George Sanders, the leading lady, Marguerite Chapman, is an afterthought to the massive wit and good lines provided by Sanders. He completely steals this film (like most films he was in) despite trying to be generous to his fellow actors. The man just could not help dominating the big screen. If a film called for a witty, urbane, middle-aged man with charm to spare, then Sanders was on the top of the A list. He could play villains or heroes with equal aplomb. In this typical B film, he fights the Nazis for England as a spy and has plenty of time to dally with Margo.

This is well before the Bond films, and are far more realistic because WW 2 actually happened, unlike most of the scenarios in Bond movies. That is why I prefer films like these to the entertaining, but not very realistic, Bond movies. Recommended.

The Apprenticeship of Duddy Kravitz (Canada) – 1974 - Directed by Ted Kotcheff and starring Richard Dreyfuss as Duddy Kravitz, a struggling young man trying to make his way in the world. Dreyfuss is greatly assisted by an accomplished supporting group of actors who bring humor and realism into all the scenes and roles. The director skillfully manipulates all of the actors along with Dreyfuss in order to get the very most out of a very low budget. We are not even aware that the film is made for much less than the average Hollywood production for the same type of story. The Canadian film industry has an excellent reputation for producing quality films for very moderate amounts of money. One of their few weaknesses is when they try to pass off Toronto as a setting for New York; that almost never works. Outside of that error, Canadians make some very well-made films and this is a prime example of one of them.

Armageddon – 1998 -Directed by Michael Bay and starring Bruce Willis, Ben Affleck, Billy Bob Thornton, and Steve Buscemi, who has the most famous quote in the film "embrace the horror". This is a sci-fi thriller with all the trimmings. It has great cinematography and music, a good script, good actors and great scope. It is one of the best science-fiction movies of all time because even though it goes over the top on occasion, it never loses focus of the effect of the catastrophe on human beings. The scenes of the redemption of the character played by Thornton are particularly touching. There are other complications from each of the characters, such as the mandatory love interest story with Affleck and a no-name actress. Willis is quite good in the film in his own semi-hysterical way. I really enjoyed all the wisecracks of Steve Buscemi, who is one of my favorite actors (*Fargo, The Big Lobowski* etc). The supporting cast does a wonderful job of working together as a team in the film and allowing each other to feed off of throwaway lines. The production values are first-rate and we get the feel of impending doom and great human drama.

Army of Shadows – 1969 – France – Directed by Jean-Pierre Melville and starring a cast of relatively unknown French actors who do a much more efficient job concerning the true essence of the French Resistance during World War Two than the four hour marathon, *The Sorrow and the Pity*. There is a tendency for eventual victors of a struggle to candy-coat the actual events during the struggle. A perfect case in point would be the Chinese struggle against the Japanese incursion of 1937 that lasted for eight years.

Nowadays, Chinese films glorify tremendous deeds of derring-do that portray the Chinese Resistance as brilliant, fearless and always triumphant, whereas the Japanese were stupid, cowardly, and always lost. Nothing could have been further from the truth, or the Japanese could not have possibly conquered two-thirds of China for eight years. The French Resistance falls into that same category. This film highlights some of the more probable realities. Recommended.

Arrival –2016 – Directed by Denis Villeneuve and starring Amy Adams, Jeremy Renner, Forest Whitaker, Michael Stuhlbarg, and Tsi Ma (wasn't there a drink called Zima?). This sci-fi plot is given the epic treatment and is quite intricate. The storyline of visitors from another planet is not new; but the approach to the subject in this film is fairly unique. Recommended.

Arrowsmith – 1931 – Directed by John Ford and starring Ronald Colman and Helen Hayes in the lead roles. Colman plays a new doctor who is far more concerned about his research than he is about the woman he supposedly loves. He never heard of Confucius' saying "moderation in all things". Intriguing.

Arthur – 1981 -Directed by Steve Gordon and starring Dudley Moore, Liza Minnelli and John Gielgud, who won a best-supporting actor award for his outrageous portrayal of a sarcastic butler. The best line in the movie comes from Gielgud who dryly suggests: "Shall I hold it for you, sir?". This said to Arthur while he is drunk and trying to urinate. Very funny stuff. Minnelli, who always seems to have a wrapper of plastic around her screen persona, is adequate in this film as Arthur's romantic interest.

But of course, it is Moore who steals the movie with his self-absorbed, immature, spoiled portrayal of a rich man who really contributes nothing at all to society. Gielgud richly deserved his award and it is considered my most critics that this was the crowning achievement performance of a highly distinguished career. The director, Gordon, does an outstanding job of pacing within the film, and the highly entertaining music is only one of the lush production values associated with the movie. The photography and sound are also quite impressive. All of these components add up to very entertaining movie with characters that we can root for. . Recommended.

As Good As It Gets – 1997 - Directed by James L Brooks and starring Jack Nicholson as a novelist (as if), Helen Hunt, as the believable love interest, and Greg Kinnear as a homosexual artist (not a big stretch for him). This overrated film won best actor and actress in a VERY lean year for films in 1997. Although I like all of these actors, and I liked the film as well, I cannot place it in Academy Award-level performances or films. Despite that, it is a very GOOD film; it is just not as good as it gets. Nicholson, who would probably get an Oscar for a remake of *Little Shop of Horrors* or one of his early biker movies with his wild popularity at this point in his career, is very good in the film. We even believe he could be a writer (if we shut our eyes tight enough), or at least a Hollywood writer (which requires a lot less belief). Hunt is always good in everything she does, and Kinnear is a very dependable second banana. Recommended.

Assembly 2007 (China) -Directed by Feng Xiaogang and starring Zhang Hanyu, Deng Chao, Yuan Wenkang, Tang Yan, Wang Baoqiang, Liao Fan, HuJun, Ren Quan, and Li Naiwen. This is a rational telling of the Chinese Civil War without the usual histronics (or at least limited use thereof) or overblown references to the actual facts. The story is based on actual events, which to put it mildly, are a bit unbelievable, but within the realm of possibility, so we must suspend our disbelief. Some of the feats described in the film would be considered very unlikely to have been accomplished by anyone except Superman, but the nice touch of whether one of the officers actually heard a retreat bugle, or merely imagined it during a fierce battle, still remains at the core of the story. Zhang, as Captain Gu, goes on a painful journey of discovery, which, at the ending that I will not reveal, allows Gu to finally fully understand what happened. Recommended.

The Asphalt Jungle – 1950 - Directed by John Huston and starring Sterling Hayden as a hardened lifetime crook, Dix, Louis Calhern as a delightful white-collar criminal, Emmerich, Jean Hagen as Doll, the sex interest in the film, the capable James Whitmore as Gus, a part time diner operator, who really enjoys crime much more, and Sam Jaffe as Doc, one of the most memorable characters in the film. This group is assembled, executes the crime, and then the double crosses and games begin. I recommend this film noir gem without reservation.

Atlantic City – 1981- Directed by Louis Malle and starring Burt Lancaster and Susan Sarandon. Malle is an experienced and talented director who has a fistful of French cinema triumphs and was imported by Hollywood to see how he would be able to handle a big-budget film. The experiment was highly successful, as Malle proved he could handle a big budget just as deftly as he handled all his small budget films in the past.

His directorial sytle is unrushed and polished, as he slowly, but surely, develops the personalities of his leading man and leading lady. The photography and music are first-rate, and add to the ambiance of the film. All of the production values point to the fact that the studio did not hold back on any assets that would add quality to the film. The studio was gambling that an aging actor like Lancaster, and an emerging actress such as Sarandon would have sufficient screen chemistry to pull off this risky venture. Luckily, the two were able to convince audiences with their ample acting ability that are an odd couple who had found love. I found this to be a very entertaining film and can recommend it. It was nominated for five Academy Awards, but did not win any that year.

At Play In The Fields Of The Lord – 1991 - Directed by Hector Babenco and starring Aidan Quinn, who is supposedly married to Kathy Bates and has a son, and understandably has not moved from his missionary position (who thought of that romantic match-up?), Kathy Bates, as a woman who goes crazy (unbelievable stretch, huh?), Darryl Hannah as Andy Heuben , the unlikely hot wife of Lithgow, Tom Beringer as Lewis Moon, a stranded pilot who takes drugs (another big stretch) , the talented John Lithgow, as the demonic missionary, Leslie Heuben, with a hot wife, (if anything, Hannah should have been Aidan's wife and Bates would have been perfect as Lithgow's wife) and Tom Waits, as Wolf, Lewis' co-pilot. All of these characters interact with the Indians in the background. This is a story of both missionary meddling and governmental indifference to native Indians. It is too bad a story to be good, and too good a story to be bad. So I will not pan it. But, as you can see, the casting is horrendous, but the story line is interesting. The acting is good, but the story line just drifts away. This film is a model of inconsistency.

Attack! – 1954-Directed by Robert Aldrich and starring Jack Palance, Eddie Albert, Lee Marvin, and Buddy Epsen. This film transcends most other war movies because it examines the abuse of power of officers over regular frontline troops. Jack Palance is a hard-fighting lieutenant respected by his men, Eddie Albert is a coward and lets other men do his fighting, and then does not back them up with reinforcements. Lee Marvin is also a manipulator, and uses his subordinates like pawns instead of flesh and blood men. Buddy Epsen makes a good contribution to the film also. Albert sends Palance on a suicide mission and Palance makes it out alive and comes back to kill Albert. I will not reveal the ending, but a certain amount of justice is metered out. This is a good war film and I recommend it.

Au revoir Les Enfants – 1987 –France- Directed by Louis Malle and starring Gaspard Manesse and a solid cast of B actors with an A script and director. This story about a boarding school in Nazi-occupied France is rife with suspense.

Avatar –2009 -Directed by James Cameron and starring a group of unknown actors, plus veteran actress Sigorney Weaver as a scientist, Dr. Grace. This film was nominated for many awards and should win three Oscars; best cinematography, visual effects and art direction. This would clearly indicate that the production values of this film were top-notch and they were. The film also used state of the art 3D effects in many of the theaters it played in and some of the effects were quite interesting. But,in the end, it is the story that must hold up for a few hours, and in that category, the film is a bit short on the dramatic side. It was a good try, and certainly worth seeing, but the story is just not engaging enough for most mature viewers. It is a clear cut tale of the good guys against the bad guys. Recommended.

B

The Babe – 1992 - Directed by Arthur Hiller and starring John Goodman, in the role of his lifetime, perfectly cast as Babe Ruth. The film traces the early years of George Herman Ruth before he became known as Babe Ruth. This film differs from the original attempt with William Bendix because it has excellent production values and a professional director who really knows what he is doing. Goodman gives us a tour-de-force as Ruth and is highly believable in the role. A very good supporting cast is put through the paces by Hiller, and complements Goodman's performance in every way. This is a story that needs to be told in a special way that both projects the humanity of Ruth and his legend as a ballplayer and public figure. It is fairly obvious from the film that there will never be another personality anywhere near as popular as Ruth was with the Yankees in the twenties and the thirties. Ruth was not merely a Yankee personality; he was a national personality. Highly recommended.

1942 - 2012 (China) - Directed by Feng Xiaogang and starring Zhang Guoli, Adrian Brody and Tim Robbins along with a superlative supporting cast of Chinese actors depicting the horrendous events of the Henan famine, and refugee movement of 1942 that was comparable to about half of the entire Holocaust in the number of lives lost and 30 million lives involved. Human suffering and loss of life in an unimaginable scale. Feng almost duplicates his success of *Aftershock*, but with a little less emotional TNT than his first film.

Back to Bataan –1945 - Directed by Edward Dmytryk and starring John Wayne and Anthony Quinn. This film helped to cement Quinn as a positive screen persona (any war movie where you were a loyal fighting American put you in that category immediately). You can see the talent Quinn possessed in every scene he was in, as he easily out-acted the wooden John Wayne. The expert direction of Edward Dmytryk is realistic, and his pacing is right on the money. One gets the feeling of revenge dripping through the entire film because of the earlier retreat, and events at Bataan. MacArthur had indeed promised "I Will Return" and was now fulfilling his promise.

Back to School – 1986 - Directed by Alan Metter and starring Rodney Dangerfield, Sally Kellerman, Burt Young and Robert Downey Jr. This is a fairly ridiculous comedy that I kept imagining how great it would have been with W.C. Fields, the older version of Rodney Dangerfield, in the lead role. But Dangerfield is great himself in this very silly movie. Robert Downey Jr. appropriately plays his son, and Sally Kellerman plays the romantic interest. Metter keeps the action and dialogue (which is quite funny) moving.

Back to the Future – 1985 - Directed by Robert Zemeckis and starring Michael J Fox as Marty, a time traveler who tries to back in time to correct some of the things his father might have made mistakes doing, and Christopher Lloyd as the scientist who creates the machine and the process that allows Marty to make the trip back in time. Time travel films are often very popular with audiences and most of the previous ones like *The Time Machine* and *Time After Time* usually are primarily serious films with occasional funny moments.

Back to the Future is just the opposite. It is a comedy with occasional serious moments. But both formulas will work well, if the right director and cast is behind them and this film works just fine primarily as a comedy with some serious moments. This film did so well at the box office that they had to make two more sequels. The first one is the best, however. This is a sci-fi comedy made with great skill. It is very difficult to unite those two genres successfully. Mel Brooks failed miserably when he tried to do it with *Spaceballs,* and he made the two highest ranking comedies in film history.

The Bad and the Beautiful – 1953 – Directed by Vicente Minnelli and starring Kirk Douglas, Lana Turner, Barry Sullivan, Gloria Grahame, Dick Powell and Walter Pidgeon. Douglas plays a ruthless director whose only goal is success of the film. He does not care about his actors or anyone else. Lana Turner is one his leading ladies along with Gloria Grahame, and they are both treated like props in a Hitchcock film. Sullivan, Powell and Pidgeon give wonderful performances of Hollywood actors and executives who have a love/hate relationship with Douglas' character. They cannot stand him personally, but they respect him professionally for his results.

This is a wonderful insider story about Hollywood that is a bit similar to *All About Eve*, but it has Douglas as the overly-ambitious newcomer instead of Eve. Like Eve, Douglas is a ruthless, heartless individual who cares only about his own personal success. And like Eve, Douglas tries to manipulate all the people around him in any way he can (personal or professional) in order to come to the final result that he desires.

Bad Company – 1972 - Directed by Robert Benton and starring Barry Brown and Jeff Bridges as two cowboys looking for trouble. The story begins with a young man dressed as a woman, Drew, who is trying to avoid the draft for the Civil War. His mother gives him $100 and tells him to head West. When Drew, played by Barry Brown, reaches St. Joseph's, Missouri, he is robbed by Jake Rumsey, a small-time thief in the town who is the head of a kid's gang. While recovering from a pistol-whipping administered by Jake, Drew meets him again in a minister's home and has a long fight that he loses with him. After the fight, Jake convinces Drew to join his little gang. There are a number of complications afterward with Drew generally taking the high moral ground in all of them except the ending, which I found to be a bit preposterous, but I will not reveal what that was. The film is entertaining and realistic up to the unlikely ending, which some viewers may disagree with me about. Recommended with reservations.

Badman's Territory – 1946 - Directed by Tim Whelan and starring Randolph Scott and Gabby Hayes. This is a story of a US marshal who goes hunting for his younger brother in No Man's Land. No Man's Land was the Oklahoma panhandle which was not under the legal jurisdiction of any state. Needless to say, this area of the old West was a major haven for all types of criminals seeking refuge from the law. Oddly enough, there was a certain amount of law and order in this area, and the rules were rather strictly enforced. No one asked anyone else about their identity or business. The primary law was to mind your own business. Scott follows these rules and is strictly concerned about finding his brother without riling the James and Dalton gangs, which are prominent in this area. I will not reveal the end of the film, but suffice it to say there is a great deal of gun play and license with historical fact. But who cares about historical fact; this is a fun movie, so watch and enjoy it. Recommended.

Ball of Fire – 1942 - Directed by Howard Hawks and starring Barbara Stanwyck and Gary Cooper as polar opposites who are attracted to one another. Stanwyck plays a stripper named Sugarpuss and Cooper plays a stodgy professor doing research on slang. There are a few elements of *Blue Angel* in this film, but only a few. Most of it is wonderfully original and the expert hand of Howard Hawks keeps everyone in character. Dana Andrews is great as Lilac, the mobster, who wants to marry Sugarpuss to keep her from testifying against him. His other option, of course, is to take her for a ride. Meanwhile, she is taking the professor for a ride of a lifetime. I really enjoyed this film, and can recommend it to everyone. It might also be a good vehicle for a play in the future.

Balzac and the Little Chinese Seamstress (China) – 2002 - Directed by Dai Sijie and starring Zhou Xun, Chen Kun and Liu Ye. This is a tale of the repression of the Cultural Revolution between 1971 and 1974. This is another gem to come out of Chinese cinema, and is greatly undervalued in the West. The director Sijie is masterful in developing the sensitive aspects of characters we can root for in a horrendous political situation that tries to strip them of all of their intellectual curiosity.

The Cultural Revolution is hardly known in the West. It was a lot more than mobs of robotic-like Chinese youths marching around the country with their red scarves and little red books. It was similar to the repressive communist states under Russian rule in the 1950s before the eventual breakdown of Russian communism in 1989. Fortunately, for the Chinese, it only lasted twelve years and not the eternal 72 years that occurred under the Russians. The Chinese were able to recover from the catastrophe after 1978. Russia is still feeling the effects of its seventy years of repression over twenty years after it ended.

Bananas – 1971 - Directed by Woody Allen and starring Woody Allen, Louise Lasser and with a guest cameo by Howard Cosell and his famous hairpiece. This is one of Woody's earlier, funnier films, as some might say, although I would disagree with that assignation. Woody plays Fielding Mellish (a name no one could possibly have), a blue collar worker trying to impress his goofy girlfriend, social activist, Nancy. Many of Allen's fans liked his earlier films more than his later more sophisticated comedies and dramas. I count myself among those who prefer his later films, because they have a great deal more substance than his earlier ones.

That being said, there is nothing wrong in making a mindless comedy that is very funny. Practically anything that makes people forget their troubles for two hours and makes them laugh is a laudable achievement. Allen was always able to do that with his earlier slapstick films. He should not be vilified for moving on to more mature material, which, by the way, won him many more professional accolades and prizes than his earlier "funny" films were able to garner. This film, though uneven in places and having pacing problems, at least has crisp, funny dialogue. It was one step up from Allen's previous "funny" films and one step closer to his sophisticated later films.

Bandit Queen – 1994 – India – Directed by Shekhar Kapur and starring Seema Biswas as the main character, a woman forced to become a bandit due to political prosecution in India. One could easily blow off this film as exploitation, but it is not that kind of film. This true bio is about a woman who went on to become a respected member of the Indian Parliament, Phoolan Devi. Fascinating.

Bang the Drum Slowly – 1973 - Directed by John D Hancock and starring Robert DeNiro and Michael Moriarity as two professional baseball players. Henry, played by Moriarity, is a talented pitcher, while Bruce, played by DeNiro, is a bumbling second-string catcher. This is not just your usual fluffy baseball story, it is a love story about two athletes going in different directions in life. One is going on to become a star, and one is quickly going to come to the end of his life.

Some critics felt the story line was corny and manipulative, but since the story is based on real-life incidents, how can a critic say anyone's life is corny? Yes, the premise is a bit depressing, but there is a lot to recommend the premise as well. It takes a lot of human compassion to live with someone who is dying every day they are still alive. And it takes even more compassion to treat them like any other human being, and not drip sympathy on them every day until their death. There are a number of very good lessons to be learned from this film. DiNiro can do anything, and he takes this challenging role and turns in a superlative effort.   Moriarity also turns in a very good performance, and is sometimes underrated as an actor. Many actors are intimidated when they are in scenes with DeNiro, but Moriarity comfortably holds his own in every scene.

The Bank Dick – 1940 - Directed (as if you could direct Fields) by Edward F Cline and starring W.C. Fields as a bank detective, Edgar Souse. The last name of the main character is obviously meant to refer to his excessive drinking habit. There are other actors in the film, but they are merely props for Fields, and no one (particularly Fields) takes any of them seriously. The plot, if you can call it that, is that Fields convinces the boyfriend of his daughter to embezzle money from the bank so the family can buy a nice house. We are supposed to believe that he and his future son-in-law get away with this ridiculous plan (as if neither of them would be prime suspects in real life). But we forgive the giant holes in the plot because the trip through the film is pretty funny and Fields is at the top of his game in this one. I can still recommend it as a great popcorn movie because as unbelievable as the story is, it is still funnier than the vast majority of modern comedies.

Barabbas – 1962 - Directed by Richard Fleischer and starring Anthony Quinn as the thief, Barrabas, who was supposed to be crucified for his crimes. The film was made in Italy by Italian producers, so the production values are mixed. Italian filmmakers are great at making small movies, but tend to get carried away a bit when they are commissioned to make blockbusters. Dino DiLaurentis was famous for his blockbuster flops like *The Bible* and other forgettable attempts. This film would have fallen in that category, except for the mighty effort of Quinn, who, as a top-notch actor, saved the film from the land of mediocrity. The movie is still a bit uneven, with scenes a bit dull, to scenes that are highly engaging. The cinematography ranges from inspiring to insipid at times. You could see the effort of the filmmaker to attempt to make a blockbuster, but you could also see it fall short in a number of scenes and in some production values.

Barbarian Invasions – 2003 – Directed by Denys Arcand and starring Remy Girard as the lovable, womanizing History professor we met in the earlier installment of this character in *The Decline of the American Empire*. Almost as good as the first installment, but not quite as fancy free due to the serious nature of the professor's illness. Arcand succeeds in easily overcoming that one problem (illness), and produces another gem of a comedy. First Canadian film to win Best Foreign Film Award from the Academy that year.

Barfly – 1987 - Directed by Barbet Schroeder and starring Mickey Rouke and Faye Dunaway. Rouke gives the best performance of his acting career in this relentlessly depressing film and Schroeder accurately captures the world of drunks, bums and alcoholics. Quite frankly, we are all glad to get out of the theater after this film and to know that we have absolutely nothing to do with this tortured world that Charles Bukowski writes about. The story is fascinating, but fairly disgusting in most aspects and falls under the category of sucks to be you and I'm glad its you and not me.

The Barretts of Wimpole Street – 1934 – Directed by Sidney Franklin with a powerhouse cast of Frederic March, Norma Shearer, and Charles Laughton. This tale of the poet Robert Browning romancing the daughter of a protesting father is actually fairly trite, as it happens several times in real life with others, but it is his technique that saves the film.

Bataan - 1943 - Directed by Tay Garnett and starring Robert Taylor, Robert Walker, Lloyd Nolan and Thomas Mitchell. The tone of the film is dark and grimmer than most film noir efforts. Garnett deftly captures the period depression that was apparent from the beginning to the end of the film. Inevitable defeat wears heavy on both the viewer and on the people living through the actual nightmare that happened to the soldiers trying to hold on to an indefensible island. The US unpreparedness for WW 2 is starkly portrayed in the film and we can see most of the soldiers dressed and outfitted with weapons that are more generally associated with WW1 rather than WW 2.

The incompetence of the US government and the US military is quite apparent, also. The soldiers must suffer for this incompetence by sacrificing their lives for their unprepared country and politicians. Taylor, a veteran of thirties Hollywood films, is able to translate the feeling of the Depression right into his role in this film. The Depression and the Battle for Bataan have a lot in common. Mitchell, another veteran of thirties films is quite comfortable in his role as a soldier on the losing side because he had made a number of films as an IRA fighter in Ireland. Nolan would go on to star in over another half dozen WW 2 films and dies in just about every one of them. His war characters are always sympathetic and the audience always roots for him.

The Battle of Algiers (France) – 1966 - Directed by Gillo Pontecorvo and starring a group of relatively unknown actors who play their roles with relish as urban guerrillas in a movement against the French colonial powers in Algiers. Algiers for the Algerians is the theme of the film. It shows how ordinary people in a European colony, regardless of what colony it is, are quickly politicized into taking action against the colonial power that is occupying their country. This film is countered by the peaceful resistance philosophy of Gandhi in India, which was also successful in removing a colonial power. However, it appears as if the Algerians did not have a Gandhi within their midst, and even if they did, it was possible the French were not as flexible as the English were in dealing with colonials. This film really captures what it feels like to be the underdog and then succeeding. This was the first foreign film I ever went to after graduating high school.

The Battleship Potemkin (Russia) (Silent) – 1926 - Directed by Sergei Eisenstein and starring a cast of unknowns. This film chronicles the Russian Revolution and all the reasons why the people of the country rose up against the Czar. From war adventures that the country could ill afford to mistreatment of the farmers and working class; this film has it all and the cinematography is legendary. Eisenstein captures every element for the reasons of the Great Russian Revolution. Common people were treated like dogs or worse.

There was no equal application of the law; the rich received privileges and the poor had the privilege to serve them. Farmers were stripped of their produce. Workers were exploited on a daily basis. The absolute worst elements of capitalism were being practiced without any thought or consideration for the common man. The story of the excesses of the Czar and those in authority under him are shown without pounding the viewer over the head with dramatic scenes, but with scenes that gradually show us the absolute necessity of the working classes and the farmers, as well as the military men being pressed to such outrages, that they had no other choice but to revolt. Highly Recommended.

Beau Geste – 1939 - Directed by William A. Wellman and starring Gary Cooper, Ray Milland, Robert Preston, Susan Hayward, Broderick Crawford (a little out of place here) and Brian Donlevy, who won an Academy Award for Best Support Actor for this film. Three orphaned brothers, Beau (Cooper), Digby (Preston) and John (Milland) all join the French Foreign Legion together because of a family disgrace for a missing jewel. They are trained by Sergeant Markoff, played to the hilt by Brian Donlevy. Cooper gives one of his best performance in this film, and Milland probably gives the second best performance of his entire career (other than his academy-award winning performance in *Lost Weekend*).

A Beautiful Mind – 2001 - Directed by Ron Howard and starring Russell Crowe as John Nash, a math whiz at Princeton, Paul Betany as Charles, his roommate, Jennifer Connolly as Alicia, love interest of John, and a nice creepy performance by Ed Harris, as William, the slimy US Department of Defense toady. Ron Howard shows us a very deft hand in directing the eventual breakdown of Nash, and his filmmaking is always very professional at every level. The production values of the film are very good, but there seems to something missing from the end result.

Becket -1964- Directed by Peter Glenville and written for the screen by Edward Anhalt, who did an outstanding job. The film stars the dynamic duo of Richard Burton and Peter O'Toole. One critic said he hadn't seen so much ham in one place since he had worked in a butcher shop in Union City. The vast majority of critics, however, felt that the dialogue was crisp and forceful and that both actors were at the top of their game. I would agree with that assessment. Although nominated for nine awards, it won only one for best screenplay (so richly deserved).

This film followed O'Toole's tour-de-force performance in *Lawrence of Arabia* and he was expected to win best actor for Becket to make up for his unfathomable snub for Lawrence. But fate was against him again as both he and Burton (who gave an equally fine performance) split their votes for best actor and Rex Harrison sneaked in for his work in *My Fair Lady*. It would be fair to say of all the major actors in the history of the Academy Awards, Peter O'Toole was the least fortunate. My low opinion of musicals is directly related to my experiences of 1964 when I picked *Becket* to win Best Picture and O'Toole to win best actor. I then learned afterwards to never underestimate the academy's love of musicals. This is a must see film for all movie buffs.

Before Night Falls – 2000 - Directed by Julian Schnabel and starring Javier Bardem (*No Country for Old Men*), Johnny Depp, and Sean Penn in a story about a Cuban poet and writer, Reinaldo Arenas, a literary version of Che Guevarra, who lived through the Cuban revolution with the Castro rebels. Interesting.

Being There – 1979 - Directed by Hal Ashby and starring Peter Sellers in one the best roles of his career as Chauncey, a mentally challenged individual with an IQ roughly equal to that of a borderline moron. He is ably assisted by a fine supporting cast including Shirley MacLaine as Eve, the wife of an aging politician and Chance's love interest, Melvyn Douglas as Ben, his benefactor and major economic adviser to the president, and Jack Warden as the President. Everyone in the cast gives a first-rate performance, and the dialogue is witty and diabolical. The film is wonderfully paced by the talented director, Ashby, and there is never a dull moment in the film. Sellers, of course, steals the show from everyone else with his understated, yet over the top, portrayal of Chauncey, the man that is so stupid, that in a place like Washington, DC, he is considered a genius. This tells us a lot more about Washington, DC than it does about the nature of low IQ. Recommended (sorry, Maryanne)

Believer – 2002 - Directed by Henry Bean and starring Ryan Gosling as an Orthodox Jew who becomes a Neo-Nazi. It traces the life of one, Daniel Balint, a troubled student at a New York Yeshiva. Daniel has an identity crisis. Is he destined to be another long-suffering Jew like the millions before him, or can he obtain the power that he sees inherent in the Jewish God who dominates the behavior of Jew? Daniel initially opts to go for the power over others which is fostered by the Neo-Nazi movement. Unstated in the film is the sexual attraction that Daniel may have had for his fellow Neo-Nazis as he has no normal female relationships at the Yeshiva or afterwards. Daniel is constantly torn between his past and his current activities with the skinheads. Eventually, he decides to commit suicide when he is outed as a skinhead. Things could have been worse. He might have continued his gene pool had he lived. Recommended with reservations as the ultimate self-hating Jew movie.

Ben-Hur – 1959 –A- Directed by William Wyler and starring Charlton Heston as Judah Ben-Hur, Stephen Boyd, in the greatest role of his career as Messala, a boyhood friend of Judah, and a cast of thousands (sic). This blockbuster film was the one that bested *Gone With the Wind* for winning the most Academy Awards (11) for one film. This feat was later equaled by *Titanic* and *Lord of the Rings*: The Return of the King, although most critics still believe it to be superior to both of those films. The musical score by Miklos Rozsa is magnificent. This is considered one of the top half dozen epics ever made and is a must-see film.

Best in Show – 2000 - Direction in credits by Christopher Guest, but actually co-written and directed by Eugene Levy, and starring Christopher Guest as Harlan, Eugene Levy as Gerry, Catherine O'Hara as Cookie, Fred Willard as Buck, and a superb supporting cast. Although it would have been easy to give this film a dog rating since it is about dogs and dog shows, it would not have been fair, because this is a very funny movie. Almost anything that Eugene Levy touches is funny (no, I don't mean body parts). As we go through an array of eclectic dogs and dog owners, we come to see how quite ridiculous the whole concept of dog shows really are. Why not have pet goldfish shows? Or pet gerbil shows? They would be popular with many of the same people, I am sure. The film is meant to be silly and, of course, does not take itself seriously as it is a mockumentary to show the silliness of these shows. It reminded me of Borat for some reason. Recommended.

The Best Man - 1964– Directed by Franklin J. Schaffner and starring Henry Fonda as William Russell and Cliff Robertson as Joe Cantwell. The film is wonderfully paced by the director, Schaffner and the production values are first-rate. The screenplay by Gore Vidal is based on a montage of political personalities of the past in US history, but certainly not John F Kennedy or Lyndon Johnson, the main political figures of the period, when the film was shot.

The Best Years of Our Lives – 1946 - Directed by William Wyler and starring Dana Andrews, Fredric March and amateur actor Harold Russell as a disabled veteran. The able women characters were played by Myrna Loy, Cathy O'Donnell and Teresa Wright. There is a strong case here for the women actually stealing some of the scenes from the men; that is how strong the female cast is here. The film won several awards including: Best Picture, director, actor, supporting actor, editing, screenplay, and original score. I might add it deserved a few awards for the female actors. Myrna Loy is the ultimate woman waiting for her man to come home and is as stable as a rock. Cathy O'Donnell and Teresa Wright, always a strong actress, play girlfriends trying to understand the moody men who have returned home from a horrendous war.

   The story follows the men of the armed forces after they have returned home; it does not dwell on the war itself. It dwells on the war after the war. That would be the one where a man tries to fit in again into a gentle society with rules rather than a harsh society with no rules like war. One would think at first that the soldiers with severe physical disabilities like Homer (he lost his hands), would have the most trouble readjusting to civilian life, but that would not always be the case. There were thousands of guys like the Dana Andrews character, who returned from the war without a scratch on them, yet had a miserable time readjusting to civilian life. Only veterans will know what I am talking about here. As long as there are wars, you will have thousands of men like these. This is a must see film and in the top 100 of almost every critic's list.

Beverly Hills Cop - 1984 – Directed by Martin Brest and starring Eddie Murphy as Axel Foley, in the role that spawned a number of sequels. As usual, the first in the series of films is best by far. We are introduced to Murphy's character and his associations with various questionable personalities as a Detroit police detective. Axel meets an old friend who is murdered for his role in an illegal bond scheme. Axel is denied access to the case because of his close personal relationship, so he takes a vacation in Beverly Hills to try and solve the crime on his own. The Beverly Hills police are on the verge of giving him a one-way ticket out of LA when Axel finally cracks the case. I can recommend this film as a good popcorn movie because I enjoy Eddie Murphy in just about any comedy venue he chooses; whether it is stand-up, doing Velvet Jones, or Mr. Robinson.

Beyond a Reasonable Doubt – 1956 - directed by the gifted Fritz Lang and starring Dana Andrews in one of his greatest roles as Tom Garrett, who agrees to a scheme by a newspaper publisher to pose as a murderer based on phony evidence. Why does he do this? Because the newspaper editor is his future father-in-law and his future wife, Susan Spencer, played by Joan Fontaine, goes along with the scheme, also. When the only two people who can prove that Tom is actually not a killer die themselves, then Garrett is left to literally hang out to dry. In imminent danger of being executed for a crime he did not commit, Tom must come up with some device to delay his gruesome fate. I will not reveal how the story is finished, but I will say it is a rather inventive, but believable plot. Recommended.

Beyond Rangoon – 1995 - Directed by John Boorman and starring Patricia Arquette (that's the Arquette sister who can act), as Laura Bowman, a grieving American tourist in Burma during 1988, where there is tremendous political unrest. Director Boorman is a master of atmosphere (see *Excalibur*) and has the knack of making us feel we are right in the middle of the jungle with Laura. Boorman is also good with lush settings and sensual photography. He surrounds a well-written script with great production values and the end result is a first-rate film. The music itself is worth the price of admission. It is inspiring. I love films that have a big twist in the middle and this is one of the best of them. The lush surroundings of the film only tend to heighten the experiences of the scenes we witness on the big screen. This is a film to be enjoyed in a theater, not on a computer or even on television.

Bicycle Thieves - Italy – 1948 - Directed by Vittorio De Sica and starring Lamberto Maggiorani as Antonio, the victim of a bicycle theft and Enzo Staiola as his son, Bruno. This is a very simple story, but is profound in its meaning. The theft of a bicycle shortly after WW 2 in Italy would be as devastating to someone as getting their horse stolen in the Old West or your car stolen in the US. Not only are the economic ramifications terrible (lose your job, minimize work chances), but the social fall of not having transportation usually marginalizes you as a person in others' eyes. This is basically the situation that Antonio, the father and Bruno, the son, find themselves. Voted best foreign film by the Academy Awards before they had the actual category. A must-see film.

Big – 1988 - Directed by the talented Penny Marshall and starring Tom Hanks as Josh, a young boy who makes a wish to become big and is a man the next day, Elizabeth Perkins, his much older girlfriend, Robert Loggia, as Mr. MacMillan, the owner of a NY toy company that Josh gets a job with, and John Heard, as Paul, a competitive adult who cannot stand the success of Josh. The story is loosely based on an Italian film, *Da Grande*, but the actual story comes from an old German fairy tale about a ball of string. A boy wants to be older and as he unravels the string he gets older and older. He doesn't get wise until he is an old man and then lives out the rest of his life knowing that whatever age you are, you should do the best you can with it.

The Big Chill – 1983 - Directed by Lawrence Kasdan and starring Tom Berenger, Glenn Close, Jeff Goldblum, William Hurt, Kevin Kline, Mary Kay Place, Meg Tilly and Jo Beth Williams. Kevin Costner was supposed to be featured in the film, but was left out in the final cut. This is pretty much a star-studded cast with great range. The story revolves around a reunion of friends in a country house setting in South Carolina.

The Big Clock – 1948 – Directed by John Farrow and starring Ray Milland as George Stroud, a harried editor of a crime magazine, Maureen O'Sullivan, miscast as his wife (she is strictly a period actress, just like Charlton Heston; once you put them in modern films, they lose their screen effectiveness), Charles Laughton in a secondary role as the short-sighted publisher who fires George for taking a vacation (in real life, that would never happen because the time you spend in finding a new, experienced editor would take longer than the vacation itself), Elsa Lanchester, and the dependable Harry Morgan. Film had enormous female attendance one Friday night when the marquee light failed for the letter L.

The Big Country – 1958 - Directed by William Wyler and starring Charton Heston, Gregory Peck, Jean Simmons, Chuck Conners, Charles Bickford and Carroll Baker. The film has a stirring soundtrack created by Jerome Moross. The tempo of the film varies from intense to humdrum, as Wyler is not as comfortable in the Western genre as he would later be in the Biblical epic genre (he made *Ben Hur* just a year afterwards). This film is a B movie, but with A movie production values.

Big Deal on Madonna Street (Italy) – 1958 - Directed by Mario Monicelli and starring Marcello Mastrianni and Victorio Gassman. There is also a good supporting cast to provide plenty of laughs about a gang that can't pull off a simple heist. The story begins with Cosimo getting jailed for trying to steal a car. He tells his friends he has a plan to make a big heist, but he is stuck in jail and they have to break him out in order to put the plan into effect. So these morons go for this story and spring Cosimo for the heist. The heist is a mess from beginning to end. The gang has to break into a private home currently occupied by a pretty woman before they can get into the safe of the pawn shop they are really after. Peppe begins to have an affair with the woman who lives next to the pawn shop and complications begin to occur. The heist is, of course, a predictable disaster. This film is a lot closer to real-life Italians in crime than the Godfather movies. Most criminals of all nationalities are mostly incompetent, that is why most of them get caught. The fun is in the trip, not the final destination for this film. Recommended.

Big Fish – 2003 - Directed by Tim Burton and starring Albert Finney as Edward Bloom, a master story-teller or big liar, depending on your sensibilities, Ewen McGregor as the young Edward, Jessica Lange as

Edward's long-suffering wife, Sandra, Alison Lohman as the young Sandra and Billy Crudup as William Bloom, Edward's son, who is estranged from his father, but comes around when he is dying for a reconciliation.

The Big Heat – 1953 - Directed by Fritz Lang who produced the gem, *M*, years earlier and starring Glenn Ford, Gloria Grahame and Lee Marvin in a classic film noir piece. Ford plays Bannion, a hardboiled detective and Grahame plays the moll, Debby, girlfriend to Lee Marvin's brutish (isn't he always brutish?) aptly named Vince Stone, the gangster who enjoys murdering people. The moll befriends Ford and eventually turns on Stone, who then throws acid on her face to disfigure her (nice guy eh?). Stone then threatens to kidnap Bannion's daughter. I will not reveal the ending, but everyone pretty much gets what they deserve.

The Big Lebowski - 1998 - Written and Directed by the dangerous comedy team of the Coen Brothers, Joel and Ethan, starring Jeff Bridges as Jeff or The Dude, John Goodman as the priceless Walter, who plots to keep all the ransom money (oh, there is a kidnapping in the film, by the way), Steve Buscemi, as Donny, who will always be remembered for his line in Armageddon "Embrace the Horror", Julianne Moore, a first-rate actress willing to be a second banana in this film as Maude, who makes the introductions for the kidnapping negotiations, Philip Seymour Hoffman, another first-rate actor as Brandt, who plays a low-key assistant, Ben Gazzara as the highly believable Jackie, a loan shark and pornographer, John Turturro as Jesus, a role he can play, easily, and Sam Elliott as the Stranger, who narrates the film (as if it needs narration).

The Big Red One – 1980 - Directed by Samuel Fuller and starring Lee Marvin, Mark Hamill, and Robert Carradine. This is a WW2 film written and directed by someone who was actually in the action with the First Infantry Division, which is what big red one stands for. Fuller saw plenty of action in the European theater and many of the scenes are ones that he actually lived through during the war. The film traces the advance of the First Infantry from the beaches of Normandy to the death camps in Germany and the freeing of the unfortunate inmates there.

The Big Sky – 1952 – Directed by Howard Hawks and starring and starring Kirk Douglas. There is a decent supporting cast of B actors including: Dewey Martin, Elizabeth Threatt, and Arthur Honeycutt. The plot is a bit different from most Westerns. It has an adventurer, Jim, who is joined by a buddy, Boone, played by Dewey Martin, and a cute squaw, played by Elizabeth Threatt. There is also a partner, Frenchy, played by Steven Geray. The group travels 2000 miles to trade with the Blackfoot tribe and runs into a number of problems, the least of which is a fight with some Crow Indians. The real threat, however, comes from the Missouri Trading Company, and a pack of traders headed by Streak, played by Jim Davis, who wants to kill off the competition. And you thought Wall Street was ruthless. Recommended with reservations about white people playing Indians.

The Big Sleep – 1946 – Directed by Howard Hawks and starring Humphrey Bogart as Philip Marlowe in an iconic role. Yes, I know all about the holes in the plot and about some of the logic not being exactly precise; and I don't give a damn. The film is fun to watch. Lauren Bacall is Vivian, and she has both an on and off-screen chemistry with Bogart that is fairly obvious. Elisha Cook Jr. provides a nice turn as a small-time crook. This is classic film-noir at its finest. The scenes with Cook in the seedy part of town are the most poignant in the film, and really capture the grit of noir. I can recommend this film wholeheartedly, despite a few holes; after all, it Bogey and Bacall.

Bill and Ted's Excellent Adventure – 1989 – Directed by Stephen Herek and starring Keanu Reeves, before he got smart and sophisticated in future films, and Alex Winter, as a geeky airhead. This is certainly a film that is destined to be lobbed off of the top 2000 in the near future. However; that time has not yet been reached. So enjoy the review and the film. This film was a forerunner to *Dumb and Dumber*, but with more panache. George Carlin is the only actual legitimate comedian in the film. Generally speaking, I don't like movies about successful stupid people (with the exception of *Being There*), because there are enough successful stupid people in real life, and too many talented people who go through life virtually unrecognized. That being said, the movie was flat out funny because the characters are endearing, despite their mental handicaps.

Billy Budd – England - 1962 - Directed by Peter Ustinov and starring Terrence Stamp as innocent Billy, the alter ego of a young Hermann Melville, Robert Ryan as the sadistic John Claggart, the Master at Arms, and Peter Ustinov as the weak-kneed Captain Vere of the vessel, *The Avenger*. This, unfortunately, is one of those films that is always depicted as a critical success, but a failure at the box office. It really is a shame, but in 1962, people were not rushing to the theaters to see the last work of Hermann Melville. Ustinov must have known as the producer, director and long-time film veteran of the screen, that this production had little chance of being a commercial success, but he went ahead with it, anyway. That will always be to his credit.

Biloxi Blues - 1988 – Directed by Mike Nichols, based on the book by Neil Simon, and starring Matthew Broderick as Simon's alter ego. This is a story of one GI's remembrances of basic training at the army post in Biloxi, Mississippi. The film tends to take a lighthearted view of the basic training process, and concentrates on the sexual coming-of-age process of the very young recruits. There are some very funny sequences with whorehouses and young soldiers, but it is certainly not material for young children, so be warned in advance that this is not a "family" film even though it has squeaky clean Matthew Broderick in it. Other than that, the film stands up on its own without any sensationalistic sex scenes or excessive violence because it is well-written, and does not need those crutches. I can highly recommend it to more mature audiences.

Birdman – 2014 - Directed by Alejandro Inarritu and starring Michael Keaton in an Academy Award worthy performance as Riggan Thomson, a former film superhero who is now betting everything he has on a new Broadway play. Emma Stone is also featured. The cinematography is outstanding. Recommended .

The Birdman of Alcatraz – 1962 - Directed by John Frankenheimer and starring Burt Lancaster as the Birdman and Karl Malden, the jailer, who eventually befriends the Birdman. The film is shot in black and white and this adds to the stark atmosphere of the prison on Alcatraz. The direction of Frankenheimer is well-paced and we are not left for wanting good dialogue on the screen. Lancaster, who won the best actor award the year before for his performance in *Elmer Gantry*, was still at the top of his game in this movie.

The Birds – 1963 –A- Directed by Alfred Hitchcock and starring Tippi Hedren and Rod Taylor. The supporting cast adds their talents to this film, as they did to just about every Hitchcock film ever made. Hitchcock was famous for accumulating good secondary talent in his films. He saw little need for A name actors and actresses to be in his films, because the star of the film was always Alfred himself, and his ability to use actors as props as a master storyteller. Make no mistake about it, Hitchcock was easily one of the greatest storytellers of all time on film. The movies he made were always about the story and almost never about the characters.

There were exceptions, of course with *Vertigo* and possibly *Notorious*, but almost all of his other films centered upon the story, rather than the people in the story. He always had a good guy who overcame obstacles. But in this film, the good guy is unable to overcome the obstacle of the birds. Although the plot is simple, don't underestimate the master of suspense, because the conclusion is terrifying. Recommended.

Bite the Bullet – 1975 – Directed by Richard Brooks and starring Gene Hackman as Sam, a contestant for a cross country horse race, James Coburn as Luke, a friend of Sam's who is competing against him, and Candice Bergen, as the unlikely love object, who is a bit of a whore (bad casting here). Also featured are Ben Johnson, a sick, old, cowhand taking his last shot, a punk kid hotshot, played perfectly by Jan-Michael Vincent, and another perfectly cast role for Dabney Coleman as the rich, unscrupulous Parker who wants to win at any cost. The cinematography of this film is magnificent, and it richly deserved its Academy Award for it. The editing also won an Oscar. Highly recommended as a great Western.

Black Angel – 1946 – Directed by Roy William Neill, this classic film noir entry stars Dan Duryea as an alcoholic pianist composer, who goes around solving murders (that happens all the time in the music business, you know), June Vincent (who?) as the wife of a falsely convicted (aren't they all?) murder prisoner, and Peter Lorre as a shifty night club owner (perfect casting here). There is also a preview of Broderick Crawford as a policeman (a role he would master later in the hit TV series *Highway Patrol*).

The plot borders on high camp, but we watch out of pure fascination because director Neill (of Sherlock Holmes fame) is so highly skilled in keeping the story going forward. I kept thinking this is really going to help Duryea with his next piano composition. Recommended with reservations if you are looking for reality to go along with your film noir.

The Blackboard Jungle – 1955 - Directed by Richard Brooks and starring Glenn Ford and Anne Francis as two endangered teachers in the inner city (oooooooh). The capable Louis Calhern, and a very young Sidney Poitier (who would go on to make his own classroom opera; *To Sir with Love*), also add to the casting. Calhern plays just about every Social Studies teacher I ever met when I taught in NYC high schools; one who was smug, crass, unconcerned about the students, and one who considered students lower life forms. This film is a fifties icon. Recommended.

Black Fury – 1935 – Directed by Michael Curtiz (*Casablanca*) and starring the talented Paul Muni as a Pennsylvania coal miner who is a witness of the harsh working conditions of the mine that is owned and operated by an indifferent prosperous management. Great stuff and not to be missed.

Black Narcissus - England – 1947 — Directed by Michael Powell and starring Deborah Kerr, Sabu, David Farrar, Flora Robson, and Jean Simmons in a minor role. This atmospheric drama is fraught with sexual tension, and focuses on the breathtaking views of the Himalayan valley and the isolation that is inherent in living there. Powell was legendary for creating atmosphere with his letter-perfect filming techniques, which have seldom been matched. You not only see the relative remoteness of the Himalayas, but Powell actually makes you feel lonely and detached during the film.

Powell also creates some of the best sexual tension ever captured on film. Nudity and sex scenes pale in comparison to the techniques used by Powell to stimulate the viewer's imagination, rather than hit him over the head with tasteless love scenes. Kerr is excellent, and shows a wide range of emotions. David Farrar, a B actor, rises to the occasion, and gives an exceptional performance. Jean Simmons shows off her exotic beauty, and gives us a wonderful promise of many great performances from her in the future. The camera is absolutely in love with her image. Sabu, however, cannot act his way out of a paper bag, and is always cartoonish in his efforts to give an even performance. One of the best small budget films ever made, with greater scenery than the vast majority of blockbusters.

Black Robe (Canada) – 1991 - Directed by Bruce Beresford and starring Aden Young, Sandrine Holt, Tantoo Cardinal, August Schellenberg, Gordon Tootoosis and Raoul Trujillo. This film escapes from the usual Hollywood formula movies, and has a nice, fresh feel to it. The unheralded cast is partially responsible for this. There are no A-list actors in this film; but they all give a very competent performance. The producers spent their money on production values, and the exhilarating atmosphere and scenery of the North country.

The Black Cannon Incident (China) – 1986 - Directed by Huang Jinxin and starring Gao Ming, Gerhard Olschewski, and LiuZifeng. Liu plays an engineer who is also a German interpreter for a mining company. He works well with a German national played by Olschewski. After he loses one of his chess pieces which happens to be a small black cannon, and sends a telegram to the hotel where he last stayed to see if they found it. The highly censored communications in China (and now the internet in China) misinterprets the telegram, and the authorities make Liu resign his post; thinking he has lost a real cannon. He is replaced by an incompetent bureaucrat, played by Yang Yazhou, and both the company and the Chinese authorities begin to lose a lot of money. I will not reveal the ending of the film, but it certainly illustrates restraints that businesses must work under if they expect to operate in China. A good black comedy. Recommended.

Black Hawk Down – 2001 - Directed by Ridley Scott, and starring Ewan McGregor and Josh Hartnett. This is a story about a military operation that goes terribly wrong. It concerns a raid on Mogadishu to nab a Somali warlord, Aidid. Sam Sheppard and Orlando Bloom are featured in the film which won two technical Oscars in the Academy Awards. The film highlights the frustrating role that unfortunate American troops have to play as the policemen of the world.

The editing and sound for this film are first-rate, and both won Academy Awards. The action sequences, as would be expected with the direction of Ridley Scott, are intense and very well done. The film, by design, is made to make you feel uncomfortable being in this place, and greatly relieved once you have left it. I am sure the soldiers in the battle felt exactly the same way as Ridley wanted to make the audience feel. I highly recommend it.

Black Stallion -1979 – Directed by Carroll Ballard and starring an Arabian horse named Cass Ole as the Black Stallion. The good human supporting cast includes Kelly Reno as Alec Ramsey, the boy who is shipwrecked with a black stallion (how lucky is that?), Mickey Rooney as Henry the horse trainer, Teri Garr as Alec's mother, and Hoyt Axton as his father. As you can see, this is not exactly a heavyweight cast, so how does this film get into my top 100? For one thing, the cinematography was easily the best of that year even though it wasn't even nominated. There is an extreme prejudice in Hollywood for any cinematography done in animal or children's movies. Only "serious" films seem to be eligible for the cinematography award. What a bunch of elitist baloney.

The best photography is the best photography, regardless of what movie it is in. The music is outstanding, and so is the editing (which was nominated, but lost to the "serious" films). This film brought back memories of *Fury*, a Saturday TV show I used to watch as a kid. Other shows featuring horses included The Long Ranger with Silver and Roy Rogers with Trigger. You would be hard-pressed to find too many kids in America who didn't want to own one of these horses when they were young. This kid got one.

Blade Runner –1982 - Directed by Ridley Scott and starring Harrison Ford as Rick Deckhard along with Rutger Hauer as Roy Batty, an out-of-control replicant. Also starring in the film are William Sanderson as Sebastian, and Daryl Hannah as Hauer's love interest (I didn't know that robots could have a love interest). Ridley Scott is noted for his directorial action sequences, and this film will not disappoint anyone looking for a good action sequence.

Harrison Ford plays this role much more seriously than his Indiana Jones characters. Rick is all business. But the actor who steals the film is Rutger Hauer. Roy is a computer that considers itself greater than human. It is Roy's contention that robots are more noble than men because they do not lie, cheat or steal, so they are morally superior. Robots are also smarter and stronger than man. But Rick shows that man has a few things that robots do not have. William Sanderson plays a very interesting role as a software developer who is more sympathetic to machines than to real people. The film raises a few philosophical questions about man and machines and the interrelationship between both. Highly recommended.

Blazing Saddles - 1974 – Directed by Mel Brooks and starring Clivon Little and Gene Wilder along with a wonderful supporting cast. This is one of Brooks' three best comedies. The other two are in the top hundred films of all time: *The Producers* and *Young Frankenstein*. This one is not quite as good as those other two, but it is certainly better than most films that pass for comedies.

Blind Shaft (China) - 2003 – Written and directed by Li Yang and starring Li Yixiang, Wang Shuangbao, and Wang Baoqiang. The story is about two street hustlers who con a migrant worker who is very young (only sixteen) into taking a job working in an illegal coal mine. After the worker gets paid, they murder him for his signing bonus and repeat the scam over and over. The film shows the horrendous conditions of China's illegal mining industry, which is enormous, because it gathers migrant workers from all over China who will eagerly risk their lives for a few hundred RMB a week (that is $30 a week US) in order to work 12 hour shifts in an unsafe and unhealthy environment. According to the director and producer of this film, they were threatened on several occasions by companies and government officials. I found the film to be entertaining, and it seems it could have been made about any number of countries with illegal mines, but this one was a good choice. Recommended.

Blue Angel – 1930- Germany - Directed by Josef Von Sternberg, one of the greatest German directors of all time, and starring Marlene Dietrich as Lola and Emil Jannings in a tour-de-force performance as the Professor, who comes to ruin because of his love for a tawdry burlesque queen. This is considered a classic of the silver screen. It is usually one of the first films a film student is shown to enlighten them on the process of how a great film is made and how great acting can be measured. Von Sternberg may be a little bit stiff for some tastes, but one thing he certainly knows how to do, is set up the audience for dramatic impact. He is also very good at slowly developing the two major characters in the film. German directors like Von Sternberg and Fritz Lang are often underrated because of old stereotypes held by filmgoers that early German directors were rigid, and had little emotional range. Nothing could have been further from the truth, as this film clearly shows. This film is not dated in the least, and holds up well in modern times. I highly recommend it.

Blue Collar – 1978 - Directed by Paul Schrader and starring the talented trio of Richard Prior as Zeke, Yaphet Kotto as Smoky, and Harvey Keitel as Jerry. Schrader is a director that knows how to use his actors well. He directs the action at a crisp pace, and in some scenes, he achieves electrifying results. Prior shows us that he is much more than just a stand-up comedian in this film; and one can see the great potential in Prior (never realized) for other great dramatic roles. What a pity he allowed his personal vices to shorten such a promising career. Harvey Keitel was another fine actor who more often than not booby-trapped his own career with substance abuse, and fits of anger with writers and directors. This often led directors and producers to skip him for consideration for roles he might otherwise have landed with ease. The fact he was never used by Scorcese again after *Mean Streets* has a lot of significance attached to it. Scorcese had been very loyal to all the other actors that were with him from the start except for Keitel. Other directors and producers took note of this.

Blue Dahlia - 1946 – Directed by George Marshall and starring Alan Ladd, Veronica Lake, and William Bendix. This was the third pairing of Ladd and Lake. This film noir piece tells of a Navy Lieutenant, Johnny, played by Ladd, who returns from action in the Pacific along with two friends, one of which is Buzz, played by Bendix, who has a serious recurring head wound, and George, played by *Leave It To Beaver* dad, Hugh Beaumont. Johnny finds his wife living and partying in her love shack. He thinks about killing her, but figures she is not worth it. Even Buzz goes a few rounds with Johnny's wife, not knowing who she is (how likely is that?). Meanwhile, Johnny somehow upgrades as he gets picked up by Joyce, a gangster's moll, played by Veronica Lake. Johnny's wife is found murdered, and he is the prime suspect. Recommended.

Blue Gardenia - 1953 – Directed by Fritz Lang and starring Anne Baxter, one of the queens of B movies, as Norah, a woman of questionable character, Richard Conte as Casey, a newspaperman, also of questionable character, Ann Southern, a highly capable supporting actress as Crystal, Raymond Burr in his usual sleezy urban role as Harry Prebble, and George Reeves, before he becomes Superman, in the role of police captain, Sam Haynes. This is film noir at it sleeziest. Everyone is a lowlife, or has major defects. Norah gets drunk and sleeps with Harry, who gets murdered. Casey covers the story and tries to help Norah rid herself of the murder charge using his superior investigative skills. Of course they both fall in "love" with each other. In some ways the film is depressing, and in others, it is very realistic. One feels like taking a shower after the credits begin to roll. Recommended with reservations about the image of everyone in the city as being of inferior character.

Blue Kite (China)- 1993 – Directed by Tian Zhuangzhuang and starring Tian Yi, Wenyao Zhang and Xiaoman Chen. This film was banned in China because it shows the ideological mistakes of the communist party over the years before the opening of China under Deng Xiaoping. The three big mistakes were the *Hundred Flowers Campaign* which encouraged criticism a then punished those who criticized, *The Great Leap Forward*, which was actually a great leap backward, although some progress was made in steel production, the overall economy was neglected, and finally the horrendous *Cultural Revolution*, which lasted for almost ten years and destroyed millions of valuable books and artifacts within China, not to mention millions of lives being disrupted or lost for no good reason. Mao was great for China in the beginning, but these three periods brought him down in stature. A really incisive film. Highly recommended.

The Blue Max – 1966 - Directed by John Guillerman and starring George Peppard as Bruno, James Mason as the General, and Ursula Andress as anyone she wants to be because she is there strictly to look at (if only she could act). There are a number of other Hollywood B actors doing their imitation of World War Two Nazis even though there weren't any nazis during the era of this film. One of the problems of the film is that the actors are trying to play German instead of trying to play people. A good war story is a good story, regardless of where the setting is.

Blues Brothers – 1980 - Directed by John Landis and starring John Belushi and Dan Aykroyd as the Blues Brothers, as Jake and Elwood, respectively. Landis is pretty good in creating fantasies for comedies. He is not capable of doing a serious film, but as far as doing physical comedy, he is more than capable of creating numerous situations for the actors to show their comedic skills. The film is stolen by Kathleen Freeman, who plays Sister Mary Stigmata, also known as The Penguin. Sister Stigmata is the head of a Catholic Orphanage who runs the institution with an iron fist, and threatens both physical and emotional mayhem on the two boys if they fail in their quest to pay off the school's debt. Of course the role is a stereotype of the worst kind that the Catholic nunnery had to offer. There were many nice, patient nuns who used to teach for the church and that still do so today.

That being said, there really were nuns like this. We had one just like her in West Paterson, New Jersey at Saint Bonaventure Grammar School in both the 4th and 7th grades. Her name was Sister Aloysius, and she was FAR worse than the nun portrayed in this film. She must have broken over 100 of her pointers (mostly over the head of Jeffrey Lovas) during our 200 days of school in the 7th grade. She used to go into tirades of cursing, and stamping up and down the class when we misbehaved. She was retired the year after our 7th grade finished. She made Sister Stigmata look like a saint in comparison. One of the weaknesses of the film is that we don't get to see enough of Sister Stigmata. She deserved double or triple the face time of the other actors. Recommended.

Blush (China) – 1994 - Directed by Li Shaohong and starring He Saifei, Wang Ji, and Wang Zhiwen. This film takes a more humorous view of government reform when two prostitutes are re-educated to become useful citizens in the People's Republic. This film actually makes the CCP look good from the public relations standpoint, because everyone knows that prostitutes are a repressed segment of any society, and at least the CCP was trying to do something about it within their country. It is the director's job to make this situation funny; not an easy task. Recommended.

Bob Roberts – 1992 - Written and Directed by the talented Tim Robbins and also starring Robbins, Gore Vidal, Brian Murray and Alan Rickman as some very nice sleaze. This film about the quagmire of politics is shot in similar fashion as Meathead used in his mocumentary of a rock band several years earlier. Meathead being Rob Reiner and the film being *This is Spinal Tap*. If you enjoyed that kind of film, you will most certainly enjoy this one. *Bob Roberts* touches all the bases on a home run about the sleaze factor in politics. I particularly liked the scenes with Alan Rickman, who is a wonderful over the top actor who should be used more in films. It is refreshing to see the main character as an emerging conservative, rather than another of the tired rising liberals usually portrayed in these kinds of films (*The Candidate*, *The Best Man*, etc). Political beliefs are not really all that important in the film; it is the backroom bargaining, and the manipulation of the media that make the film entertaining, as well as the great job done by Robbins. Highly recommended.

Body and Soul – 1947 - Directed by Robert Rossen and starring John Garfield as Charlie Davis, a boxer who can't escape the moral pit of the boxing underworld, Lili Palmer, and William Conrad as the heavy (sic) are also featured. This is one of the granddaddies of the boxing genre, and also some pretty good film noir. Garfield got nominated for an Oscar for this performance, and the technique of filming inside the ring by the master cinematographer, James Wong Howe, earned the film the Academy Award for best film editing. This technique was later copied by Martin Scorsese in *Raging Bull* with great success. Garfield is offered the classic deal of throwing a fight for a lot of money. If he doesn't, he could wind up with a lot less than empty pockets. I will not reveal the end of the film to you, but this is classic John Garfield (a highly gifted actor), and is a must-see film. Highly recommended.

Bodyguards and Assassins (China)- 2009 – Directed by Teddy Chan and an all-star cast including Zhang Honyu, Donnie Yen, Nicholas Tse, Tony Leung Ka-Fai, Leon Lei, Wang Xu Simon Yam, Hu Jun, Eric Tsang, Wang Po-chieh and Fan Bingbing. The film begins with the subject of the 1911 Revolution which changed China from a monarchy to anarchy, or a very loose version of democracy, depending on your point of view. Good guys in the film are the revolutionaries, and the bad guys are the assassins sent by the evil empress Cixi to kill them. It begins in 1905 with Sun Wen, played by Zhang Hanyu, coming to Hong Kong to help overthrow the decaying Qing Dynasty. He is aided by Chen Shaobai, the chief editor of the China Daily, Li Yutang, who is a financier for the revolution, Li Chongguang, the financier's son, Deng Sidi, a common rickshaw driver who sacrifices himself for the cause, and Fang Hong, a fictional woman who knows martial arts. It was highly unlikely this last character ever existed. Yang Quyun plays a university professor who is assassinated after the successful revolution. The film is chock full of violence and action, but i also has a very interesting historical perspective. I recommend it.

Bone Collector -1999- Directed by Philip Noyce and starring Denzel Washington and Angelina Jolie. Washinton plays Lincoln, a paralyzed forensics specialist, who teams up with Jolie's Amelia, who is an average patrol officer. (how come I don't have any patrol officers in my neighborhood who look like Jolie?). There are a series of murders by a clever killer who takes a piece of bone from each victim. Eventually, the talented pair begin to piece together the necessary clues that lead them to a book of short stories. The short stories reveal the names of victims, and they figure out the next victim in advance. They arrive in time to save one victim, but not the other. Eventually, they figure out that the murderer is going to come after Lincoln. I can recommend the film based on its intelligent storytelling. Recommended.

Bonnie and Clyde - 1967- Directed by Arthur Penn and starring Warren Beatty as Clyde Barrow and Faye Dunaway as Bonnie Parker, two notorious bank robbers from the 30s Depression era. One must understand the era before one can appreciate the movie. These people were not bank robbers or outlaws to the majority of the public at that time. They were folk heroes. They were people other people wish they could have had the guts to have been. There were millions who were out of work and wished they could have done the things that Bonnie and Clyde did, despite their anti-social behavior. It was a time of desperation and these were desperados.

Boogie Nights -1997 – Directed by Paul Thomas Anderson and starring Mark Wahlberg as Eddie, a high school dropout and male prostitute, Luis Guzman as Maurice, a night club owner, (Luis used to teach with me down at Henry Street Settlement on the lower East Side of New York), Burt Reynolds as Jack Horner, a porn director, Heather Graham as Rollergirl, porn star, and a great supporting cast including the talented William H Macy. There were about a dozen ways this film could have gone bad, or have been nothing but sensationalistic crap, but it avoided every one of them. The director takes the actors through their marks with great precision and confidence, and it shows in the film. Some of the characters are extremely likable, despite their sexually excessive personalities. This is not an easy trick to pull off in a film. Burt Reynolds is absolutely believable and outstanding in his role.

Boomerang - 1947 – Directed by Elia Kazan and starring Dana Andrews, Lee J. Cobb, and Jane (*Father Knows Best*) Wyatt. This is a film noir story about a drifter who is picked up and charged with a murder he didn't commit. A priest in Connecticut was shot dead and the police cannot immediately find the killer. Arthur Kennedy plays the drifter, John, charged with the murder. Andrews plays a State's attorney , Harvey, and Jane Wyatt plays his wife. She is good at playing wives. Lee J. Cobb dominates the movie with his persona as the police chief who has the political pressure to get a suspect under arrest as soon as possible to satisfy the public and the papers. Eventually, the suspect confesses from lack of sleep, but Harvey is not convinced he did it, and continues his investigation. I will not reveal the ending of the movie, but it is fairly sobering. Recommended.

Borat (Cultural Learnings of America Make Benefit Glorious Nation of Kazakhstan)- 2006 - Directed by Larry Charles and starring Sacha Baron Cohen as the manic Borat from Kazakhstan; easily the most famous anything to ever come out of Kazakhstan. This film is easily the best comedy so far in the 21st Century. If you can't laugh at this movie, there is something seriously wrong with you. For the first few minutes of the film, one is not sure if this is a real documentary or a mocumentary. We find out it is the latter in very quick time. The trick is, of course, that many people in the film are sucked into believing that Cohen is actually making a documentary instead of a searing satire.

We trace the beginnings of Borat in his native country of Kazakhstan, where he is now public enemy number one, and meet his so-called family of illegitimate and illiterate sisters and brothers. Borat is proud of the high rating of his sister as one the ranking prostitutes in the country. The introduction of his relatives and neighbors, and the third-world town that he lives in is hilarious. This film is so over the top with poor taste, one cannot even begin to address each of the pc taboos that Cohen tramples on; Anti-Semitism, racism, sexism and scatological humor are good starters. Not to mention bestiality, promiscuity, and anti-Americanism as chasers. Of course one must take all of these personality traits in stride because IT IS ONLY A MOVIE. It is not a real person, and these are not the actual sentiments of the author and actor It has elements similar to those found in South Park and if one likes that show, one will love this film. If one does not like South Park and finds it offensive, then they will find this film offensive as well.

I personally think it will be very difficult for Cohen to make another comedy as good as this one in the near future and maybe not for the rest of his career. He is a highly creative artist, and a master of lowbrow humor, as well as a talented physical comedian. That is a fairly lethal combination. Charles does a great job in directing Cohen and keeping him under control (and I use that word advisedly). By the way, Borat reminded me a great deal of a tennis teammate I had in college, Clay Costantino. As a movie, Borat is hilarious and I recommend it without reservation as it is now in my top 100 films of all time.

Bordertown – 1935 -Directed by Archie Mayo and starring heavyweights Paul Muni and Bette Davis, who seldom co-starred together in film. Muni plays a Hispanic man called Johnny, who wants to be a lawyer, but loses his first case and assaults the opposing lawyer for being smarter than he is. Not an auspicious beginning to a legal career.

Born on the Fourth of July - 1989 – Directed by Oliver Stone and starring Tom Cruise as Ron Kovic, a disabled Vietnam veteran. Cruise is unusually understated in this film, and is not his usual over the top persona. Stone keeps him well in line with the character portrayed in the movie. Great music as well. And Stone was quite familiar with the material since he was a Vietnam vet, himself. He was familiar with all of the contradictions of the war both at home and in Vietnam. At home, you had the liberals and hippies who were against anything that had to do with the military or national defense. It didn't make any difference if you honestly believed you should serve your country; you were considered a sucker.

The conservatives, on the other hand, were against liberals and hippies because of their life styles, haircuts, and sexual mores. Sometimes the two groups actually even thought about the politics behind each other's causes, and were opposed for those reasons. In Vietnam, troops were divided as well. Most were against the war, but some thought they were doing the right thing for the right reasons, and that was the real tragedy of the war. Kovic was one of those who believed he was doing the right thing. Recommended.

Born to Kill – 1947 - Directed by Robert (The Hills Are Alive with The Sound of Music) Wise and starring Lawrence Tierney, Claire Trevor and Walter Slezak, in a high-quality film noir special. Helen, played by Trevor, is recently divorced and on the prowl. She becomes attracted to a killer, Sam Wilde (not the Oscar kind of Wilde, but the wild kind of wild), who has no socially redeeming values. Helen dumps her rich boyfriend, (sound choice, but highly unlikely in real life) and rolls in the mud with Sam. Then the police get on Sam's trail and all the sleaze begins to unravel. I loved every second of this highly immoral film. Highly recommended.

Born Yesterday - 1950 – Directed by George Cukor and starring William Holden as Paul, honest professor, Broderick Crawford as a crook, Harry, Howard St. John as Jim Devery, a sleazy lawyer and Judy Holliday as Billie, the ditzy moll of Harry. Cukor was a master at directing melodramatic comedy and it shows here in spades. This is one of the top ten comedies of all time. The dialogue is absolutely first-rate and there is never a dull moment in the film. Holden gives one of his best performances ever, and Holliday literally does give the performance of her career. St. John is great as the sleazy lawyer and Crawford steals the movie as Harry.

Crawford would go on to great success as the star of the fifties hit Highway Patrol on TV. This was the vehicle that led to that TV role. The plot has Harry intending to marry Billie so she cannot testify against him (in real life, he would just ice her). Then he hires a tutor, Paul, a local college professor, to teach her some class (as if Harry has any himself). Naturally, Paul and Billie fall for each other and the triangle has some very funny moments. I can highly recommend this film as a premier comedy.

Bound For Glory – 1976 – Directed by Hal Ashby and starring David Carridine as Woody Guthrie (perfect casting) and a strong supporting cast. Ashby is generally considered a lightweight director, but he rose to the occasion for this film, and produced a beautiful period piece. He really captures the essence of the Depression, but does not dwell on the sad and hopeless issues that were prevelant during the period. Instead, the film gives us a feeling of pulling together to beat this thing, and that despite very tough times, the human spirit can rise to the occasion and overcome practically any adversity. David Carridine was another Hollywood personality that was considered to be lightweight by most professionals in the industry. He also rose to the occasion for this film, and gave an outstanding performance. It was probably his best in his career with the exception of the Kung Fu series that successfully ran on TV for a few years.

The Bounty – England - 1984 – Directed by Roger Donaldson and starring a rare combination of Anthony Hopkins and Mel Gibson. I certainly hope that you guessed which roles Hopkins (Bligh) and Gibson (Christian) played. This was the fifth rendering of this great story, all of which I have enjoyed immensely and highly recommend. I love any film about the South Seas. Hopkins, naturally, does a great job as cold-fish Bligh; and we already know how hot-blooded Gibson is in practically every role he takes. It is inevitable that this film was compared to earlier versions of the same story.

The first successful Mutiny on the Bounty, was highly popular at the time of its release in the thirties, with Clark Gable as Christian (he had to shave off his famous mustache for the role) and Charles Laughton in a wonderfully over the top performance as Bligh. That film is still considered to be the best of all these productions, because no one will ever match Laughton as Bligh. This film, however, is still very good in its own right, and superior to the last remake that was done with the moody Marlon Brando in the role as Christian (by that time in the sixties, Brando had gained enough weight to play Bligh, and might have been much better cast in that than the tepid Trevor Howard). The waste of Richard Harris at the time in a secondary role instead of the role of Christian doomed the film to mediocrity). The casting of Brando as Bligh and Harris as Christian might have been electric. In this version, the casting is letterperfect and no one can rouse himself into a greater state of passion than Mel Gibson. Oddly enough, one of my favorite actors of all time, Anthony Hopkins, seems to give too understated a performance for Bligh; making him far more sympathetic than the character portrayed by Laughton in the earlier version. Highly recommended.

Bourne Identity - 2002 – Directed by Doug Liman and starring Matt Damon as Bourne. If you change just a few letters in Damon's character's name, can you figure out what type of character Bourne will be? This is the Americanized version of James Bond written by Robert Ludlum. Bond and Fleming are infinitely more interesting than Bourne written by Robert Ludlum, but this isn't about writing, it is about filmmaking. And the Bourne series of films spawned from this original film easily equal and sometimes surpass the Bond films in quality.

Boyhood – 2014 – Directed by Richard Linklater and starring Ellar Coltrane as a young man getting ready to enter college who reflects back on his boyhood. An interesting premise that is seldom done in film. Interesting.

The Boy in the Striped Pajamas – 2014 – Directed by Mark Herman and starring Asa Butterfield as a privileged German boy, son of a Nazi death camp commander, David Thewlis as the Jewish boy prisoner, and Rupert Friend as the commander. This simple Story of the horror of WW death camps gets right to the core of the insanity of the Nazis. Must be seen to experience a great Holocaust film.

Boys Don't Cry - 1999 – Directed by Kimberly Peirce and starring Hilary Swank in her spectacular debut as Brandon Teena, a transsexual, and Chole Sevigny as his/her love interest, Lana. This is some pretty gritty stuff, and quite a debut for Swank. Sevigny is also very good in the film as well. The essence of the film was rather taboo stuff in the late nineties (and still is that matter). The sexual liaisons of transsexuals are not usually highlighted in Hollywood mainstream films, so the film had to be quite exceptional to make up for the loss of mass audience appeal that is built into the story, and guaranteed it would not make a fortune at the box office. And yet, the film did quite well at the box office, despite having to play in several houses and secondary theaters to obviously limited adult audiences. Peirce does a wonderful job in her first big film attempt at directing. She shows a special tenderness to both characters and does not let the film slip away into any sentimental quagmire. She is in full control from beginning to end. I can recommend the film without reservation.

The Boys From Brazil - 1978 – Directed by Franklin J Schaffner and starring Gregory Peck and James Mason as lovable Nazis relocated in Brazil, pursued by the erstwhile Laurance Olivier, a Nazi-hunter of great renown. The film is a great escapist yarn that has a thin thread of reality attached to actual events, but there seems to be a great deal of creative liberties taken with the historical realities. Schaffner does a good job of setting up the audience for the inevitable confrontations at the end of the film. The only element of the film that I found a bit distasteful was the casting of Steve Guttenburg in a serious role as Olivier's assistant who is sent to gather more data from Brazil. Guttenburg is incapable of playing straight roles. The best part of the movie, however, is when Steve Guttenberg is killed. I believe it was the only film in which he was ever killed, though I am sure many viewers would have preferred otherwise in a large number of his films. Recommended.

Boys in Company C - 1977 - Directed by Sidney J. Furie and starring Stan Shaw, Andrew Stevens, Craig Wasson, Santos Morales, and Michael Lembeck as young men caught up in the Vietnam debacle. This fine group of unknown actors was able to take a serious subject like Vietnam and turn it into a MASH-like version of a black comedy. This is no easy trick. This is the light version of Full Metal Jacket as it follows five marines from boot camp all the way into combat in Vietnam.

Boys in the Band - 1970 – Directed by William Friedkin and starring Leonard Frey as Harold, Kenneth Nelson as Micheal, Peter White as Alan, Cliff Gorman as Emory, Frederick Combs as Donald, Laurence Luckinbill as Hank, Keith Prentice as Larry, Robert LaTourneaux as Cowboy, and Reuben Greene as Bernard. This film was a landmark movie that highlighted the gay lifestyle. Everyone in the cast does an outstanding job with the terrific dialogue provided by the electric screenplay. Especially good in the film is Kenneth Nelson as Michael, who has a secret about his roommate from his college days. The actor who steals the film, however, is Leonard Frey, who is absolutely riveting on the screen from his first scene until his last. He delivers his lines with all the authenticity that one could possibly imagine. He really should have been nominated for an Oscar for this role, but unfortunately, the film was made during a less enlightened era. If it had been made around the same time as Brokeback Mountain, it would have proven superior to that film in most respects (except for the photography). The movie revolves around Harold's birthday and the boys who are invited to celebrate it. O of the hilarious parts of the film is the prize for winning a game invented by Harold; the prize being a male hooker named Cowboy (probably named after Midnight Cowboy). Cowboy is wonderfully portrayed by Robert LaTourneaux (now there's a stage name to rival the director in The Producers). This film is still clinging to its top 100 status, but is sliding down into the ratings as new films come along and push it downward.

Boy's Town - 1938 - Directed by Norman Tourag and starring Spencer Tracy as Father Flanagan and Mickey Rooney as Tommy. Tourag does a great job of keeping the action moving at a crisp pace. This was the style of most thirties moviemakers. There are no lulls in this low-budget film. It shows how you can make a great film without spending multimillions of dollars. Shot in stark black and white, it is truly a no-frills film from start to finish. Tracy, who was by far the most dominant actor in this film, is generous, and gives the glib performance of Rooney every chance to succeed. Rooney would become a much better actor in the latter part of his life; especially in roles like the trainer in *Requiem For a Heavyweight*. Rooney mentioned on several occasions that his favorite mentor in films was Tracy and that he learned more from him than any other actor in Hollywood. MGM was noted for their fine supporting casts in almost all their films, and this one was no exception. Every member of the cast contributes to the finished product, which is quite impressive. The film won an Oscar for Spencer Tracy for Best Actor and I would heartily recommend it for viewing; especially for younger audiences.

Brainstorm -1983 - Directed by Douglas Trumbull and starring Christopher Walken, Natalie Wood, Cliff Robertson and a riveting performance by Louise Fletcher, who deserved an Oscar nomination, but did not get one, for this great job.   An unheralded star of the film was director Douglas Trumbull, who in essence, sacrificed his career at MGM to make sure that the film reached theaters, and was not shelved for the insurance money due the film for the death of one of its famous stars, Natalie Wood, in the end of the film. There were many lurid rumors that surrounded her death. One was that she was having an affair with her co-star Christopher Walken. Another was that she was drunk, and tried to swim in deep water and drowned. It seems the truth of the matter might never be known for sure. Brainstorm is about the development of a new technology that people do not really know how to use correctly or safely. In that sense, the film was outstanding and ahead of its time. In essence, you are able to leave your own body and live out fantasies created by your own mind. You can even record the events of your fantasies. Unfortunately, there are some downside elements to the invention. Highly recommended.

The Bravados - 1958 –Directed by Henry King and starring Gregory Peck as Jim Douglas, a rancher, who pursues the four outlaws that killed his wife, Lee Van Cleef, Stephen Boyd, Henry Silva and Albert Salmi, get to play the bad guys. Joan Collins is, as always, the best actress from the neck down in film. King paces the film very well and there is never a lull. Peck, however, seems oddly cast as a vigilante type. He carries it off because he is such a fine actor with a very wide range, but I would think that someone like Charles Bronson or Steve McQueen may have been a better choice for this role. Both of those actors would appear in the same film just a few years after this one in *The Magnificent Seven*.

Braveheart - 1995 - Directed by Mel Gibson and starring Mel Gibson as Sir William Wall, a 13th Century Scottish knight who challenges the authority of England. A strong supporting cast includes Patrick McGoohan as an English Lord and Ian Bannen as Robert the Bruce, a Scottish Lord who befriends Wallace, only to turn on him at a key point in a major battle. McGoohan is predictably cold-hearted and Bannen is very good as Robert the Bruce. Gibson excels in these types of films, and is a master of action sequences. His direction is impeccable in both the lively action scenes, and the personal encounters between the major actors. Gibson has a fine instinct for observing the elements of emotion within actors, and brings out the best of them for their performances. His personal and political life may be a mess, but his films are pretty much on the money. He is, however, much better in the costume drama genre than he is in modern settings (except for a few of his cop films). In that respect, he a quite a bit like Charlton Heston of a former era. Heston could never master modern roles as well. I can recommend it as a very entertaining movie with the reservation that you will most likely not visit the butcher after a viewing.

Brazil – 1985 - Directed by Terry Gilliam and starring Jonathon Pryce as a worker overwhelmed by the bureaucracy. There are a host of guest stars in this production. The original title of this film was One Day in the New York City Board of Education, but was changed at the last minute. We see the individual, regardless of whom it might be, getting completely annihilated by the enormous machine that is bureaucracy.

Bread, Love and Dreams (Italy) - 1954 – Directed by Luigi Comencini starring Vittorio DeSica as Antonio and Gina Lolobrigida as Maria. The story follows the familiar pattern of post-WW2 Italy where the people are still struggling to regain some form of normalcy. It shows Antonio as a marshall of a small mountain town who wants to marry Maria, the local beauty. But Maria is not in love with Antonio; she loves his shy assistant, Pietro, played by Roberto Risso. Antonio finally gives up his pursuit of Maria and settles for a local midwife, Annarella, played by Marisa Merlini. I will not reveal the ending, but things get complicated in the small village when passions begin to get out of hand. I can recommend this film because of the nice performances of the lead actors.

Breaker Morant –Australia-1980 – Directed by Bruce Beresford and starring Edward Woodward as Breaker Morant, Bryan Brown as Peter Handcock and Lewis Fitz-Gerald as George Witton. This is a relatively unknown cast, except for Woodward, who went on to fame and fortune in a popular TV series, *The Equalizer*. The Australian supporting cast gives a lively performance and everyone is very believable in their military roles. The director Beresford does a wonderful job of unraveling the rationale for executing apparently blameless soldiers for doing what they thought best during a difficult guerilla assignment. Despite its low budget, the film has excellent production values and is never boring.

 Breaking Away -1979 - This film is directed by Peter Yates and stars a young Dennis Quaid as Mike, Dennis Christopher as Dave, Daniel Stern in his first film as Cyrll, Jackie Earle Haley as Moocher, and Barbara Barrie, who received an Oscar nomination for her role as Evelyn, Dave's mother. This is one of the few coming of age films that one can watch without having the need to leave the room for any extended period of time for a beer or two. The coming of age genre is particularly hard to master for most directors, but Yates carries it off well. Some of the few other good coming of age films that I can remember seeing that was as good as this one were *Stand By Me* and *American Graffiti*. I give the film my heartiest recommendation because it makes a social statement that you can overcome odds, on occasion and, in addition, the film was highly entertaining.

Bride of Frankenstein -1935 - Directed by James Whale and starring Boris Karloff as Frankenstein, Elsa Lanchester as his spanking new bride, and Colin Clive as Dr. Frankenstein, that's Frankensteeeen (as per the pronunciation according to Gene Wilder, who played the Colin Clive role as the good doctor in one of the greatest comedies ever made) and the usual good supporting cast that always delivered for Universal Studios. Many consider this Frankenstein entry superior to the original one because of the atmosphere and character development of the surroundings and the monster, respectively. A line in this film led to the title of a modern film treatment of the life of Whale called *Gods and Monsters*. "A toast to a new world of gods and monsters".

Karloff, an underrated actor, was always good in anything he did and Elsa Lanchester does a high-camp, hair-raising job as his artificial mate. Colin Clive gives a nice over the top performance as Dr. Frankenstein and this particular film seems to have had much better production values than the original made just a few years earlier. It was evident that Universal studios made a bundle on the original and plowed a substantial amount of money into the sequel to ensure its success. And they were right on the money, because this sequel is clearly better than the original. Recommended.

Bridge on the River Kwai - 1957 – Directed by David Lean and starring William Holden and Alec Guinness. This is the greatest WW 2 prison camp movie ever made according to the vast majority of film critics. Jack Hawkins and Sesue Hayakawa have great supporting roles in this film. Holden had played serious roles before in such films as Sunset Boulevard, but this role cemented his ability to play both dramatic and comedic roles equally as well. Alex Guinness, of course, is one of the sublime British actors of all time, and not capable of a bad performance. He would go on to win the Oscar for this portrayal. Hawkins would have future success in blockbuster films like *Ben Hur* and Lawrence of Arabia. David Lean would also go on to make additional successful blockbuster films such as *Lawrence of Arabia* and *Dr. Zhivago*.

Alec Guinness had a whole new second career with the original Star Wars trilogy as well as many other successful roles in between. He was also destined to be in Lawrence of Arabia. The supporting cast also does a very good job. The technical aspects of the film were letter perfect and the production values were first-rate. The film won numerous Academy Awards including: Best Picture, Best Director for Lean, Best Actor for Guinness, who , by the way, disliked Lean, but worked with him again on *Lawrence of Arabia*, Best Screenplay, Best Musical Score and Best Cinematography, which it richly deserved. The film is on several top fifty lists of most movie critics, on the top list of many critics, and is a must-see film.

Bridges of Madison County – 1995 – Directed by Clint Eastwood and starring Clint Eastwood and Meryl Streep as killer gunslingers who have a big showdown where one is certain to get shot down (only kidding). Eastwood made a love story? And it was successful? Wow! Meryl Streep won the Academy Award for best actress in this film. That is not really a big surprise; as she is the best actress of the 20th century. The big surprise is that Clint Eastwood was such a romantic, and could direct a romantic film with such insight and finesse. Eastwood has been successful in a wide range of films outside of the Western genre. His successes include modern cops as in Dirty Harry, a modern fight manager in *Million Dollar Baby* and a modern astronaut in *Space Cowboys*.

Brief Encounter – England-1946 – Directed by David Lean, who was more noted for making epics than fine little films like this one. This is a gem of a little movie made on a budget lower than most big, modern commercials. It stars Celia Johnson as Laura, a suburban housewife, and Alec played by Trevor Howard as a general practitioner, who has an interest in preventative medicine. The filming in stark black and white adds to the simplicity of the story. There are no bells and whistles in the production values. Everything in the film is focused on the two main actors. The dialogue is superb and highly introspective. Many critics considered this one of the most romantic films of the first half of the 20th century.

Broadcast News - 1987 – Directed by James L. Brooks and starring William Hurt as anchor Tom Grunick, the funny Albert Brooks as the bumbling Aaron Altman, who occasionally fills in for Grunick, Holly Hunter as Jane Craig, a talented producer, and a great supporting cast including Robert Prosky, John Cusack, and Joan Cusack. The movie shows the everyday workings of a major television station and its news team. The stock of anchors rise and fall along with the events they cover. There are many laughs on trip through the film, especially when Brooks is on the screen. He is a very funny man. The film was nominated for a number of Academy Awards, but was unable to garner any. I can heartily recommend this wonderfully acted film to everyone.

Broken Arrow -1950 – Directed by Delmar Daves and starring Jeff Chandler as Cochise a James Stewart as Tom Jeffords. Also featured as a love prop is Debra Paget. This is one of the first post WW 2 movies to portray the American Indian in a positive light. This is actually a triangle movie about the peace established by Jeffords with Cochise and the breakaway Apache leader, Geronimo, played by an authentic Indian, Jay Silverheels, (Tonto, of Lone Ranger fame). Geronimo is constantly bedeviling the white settlers and mail couriers, and Cochise must either support his new white blood brother or Geronimo. He decides to back Jeffords and then to prove that no good deed goes unpunished, is promptly punished by the white establishment for the death of Jefford's new indian wife, Morningstar, played by the alluring Debra Paget. I will not reveal the ending of the film, but it does justice to the film. The film is based on historical data with some license for filmmaking. Recommended.

Brooklyn – 2015 – Directed by John Crowley and starring a cast of unknown actors with a good script. The story of a young Irish woman who comes to Brooklyn and falls in love with a Brooklynite is entertaining. A soap-lover's special.

Brother Orchid -1949 - Directed by Lloyd Bacon and starring Edward G Robinson, Ann Southern, and Humphrey Bogart as the heavy. Robinson plays Little John Sarto, a crime boss on the run from Bogart's Jack Buck mobster character. Southern plays Flo, Little John's loyal girlfriend. Sarto becomes a monk who is hiding out in a monastery from his foes. The film deliciously captures the conversion of Sarto into becoming a "sucker" like all the other suckers in the monastery. The conversion is slow and believable, because of the fine acting job by Robinson and the great supporting cast. Eventually, Jack Buck finds him at the monastery and Sarto must confront him and his own changed perspectives. I will not reveal the ending, but it is interesting. This film has been copied numerous times by Hollywood, including the Whoopie Goldberg classic, *Sister Act*, and a few others. I can recommend this film highly.

Brute Force – 1947 – Directed by Jules Dassin and starring Burt Lancaster as Joe Collins, Hume Cronyn as the sadistic warden, and Charles Bickford as Tom, Joe's friend in prison. This is the best prison movie of all time according to many critics; including myself. The music by Miklos Rozsa at the beginning of the film will give you an idea of the intensity of the movie later on. The dialogue may be a bit dated, but no one will mistake the mood of the film; desperation. The brutality of Cronyn is wonderfully set against his usual casting as a nice, gentle man. The action in the last part of the film is explosive. The story begins in prison, where Joe Collins, a violent, lifetime criminal, plans an elaborate escape with the help of a few other prisoners. Some of the other prisoners are also desperate to escape, as we learn from their flashback sequences. This is a must-see film for film-noir fans and especially fans of prison movies.

Buccaneer – 1958 – Directed by Anthony Quinn, who took the place of his ill father-in-law, Cecil B DeMille. Quinn was a great actor, but his directing ability left a lot to be desired; and it showed in the film. The movie starred Yul Brenner as Jean Lefitte, the French pirate who aided Andrew Jackson against the British in the Battle of New Orleans. Jackson's role is played by Charlton Heston. Both actors tried their best, but both of them were badly miscast. Brenner, who, looks nothing like a Frenchman, did not really have the demeanor of a pirate, and Heston had no clue how to portray Jackson. Both men seemed lost in their roles. The only reason they were there in the first place is that they were both together in the original production of *The Ten Commandments*, made earlier by DeMille. DeMille incorrectly figured that if they were good i one film together, they would be good again in another.

Buck Privates - 1941 – Directed by Arthur Lubin shortly before WW2 and starring Bud Abbott and Lou Costello as well as a turn by the Andrews Sisters, a popular WW2 singing group. This is the film that put Abbott and Costello on the movie map. Let's see; Abbott and Costello plus the US Army as a prop. What could be more conducive to comedy? Oddly enough, the film was made before Pearl Harbor and the outbreak of the war. You can see just how badly the US soldiers were trained and equipped, just a few months before the war began. If one looks at the US army five years later and compares it to the soldiers that were being prepared in this film, it gives the appearance that is a movie about World War 1, and not World War 2. That aside, there are just so many convenient situations in a boot camp for Abbott and Costello to use as props, they probably couldn't fit them into one movie. The film proved to be hugely popular with American audiences. Recommended with reservations about the sappy love story.

Buddy Holly Story - 1978 – Directed by Steve Rash and starring Gary Busey as Budd and a strong supporting cast. The film is a biopic of the tragic figure of Buddy Holly, a rising superstar in rock and roll who died in a plane crash just as his career was taking off. The film traces Buddy's beginnings in Texas and a band called the Crickets. An error in early bookings gets them a gig at the Apollo and three white Texans have to entertain an all-black audience. After a shaky start, Buddy wins the crowd's approval and his legend begin. The band breaks up, and Holly goes solo. In Iowa, during a snowstorm, Holly makes the fateful decision to charter a plane along with the Big Bopper and Richie Valens and the flight never gets to Minnesota. This is a first rate biopic without over-glorifying the star. I recommend it heartily.

Bull Durham - 1988 – Directed and written by Ron Shelton, who played minor league baseball, and starring Kevin Costner as Crash Davis, Tim Robbins as Nuke Laloosh and Susan Sarandon as the slutty groupie, Annie E Savoy. The E in her middle name stands for easy. The movie unfolds at a leisurely pace, and we see Costner as a catcher rotting away in the minors, despite his decent skills. Nuke is a promising young pitcher that needs to be babied by both Costner and Annie, but eventually Annie wants a piece of Crash as well. Sarandon is very convincing as a baseball camp follower. Costner is one of the greatest physically gifted actors in the history of film, and has mastered dozens of difficult movie stunts. This role was a piece of cake for him. Robbins is always very engaging, but it was difficult for some in the audience to consider him the moron he portrays on the screen, because of his innate intelligence. I will not reveal the ending, but it does have a nice twist, and I can recommend the film to everyone.

Bullitt - 1968 – Directed by Peter Yates and starring Steve McQueen, Jackie Bisset and Robert Vaughn. The real star of this film is the car chase at the height of the movie. The story has politician Walter

Chalmers played by Robert Vaughn trying to eliminate organized crime in San Francisco (good luck with that idea). He eventually leans on Frank Bullitt played by Steve McQueen (who eventually leans on Jackie Bisset, but in a much friendlier way), who is given the simple job of eliminating organized crime in San Francisco. As you can see, the plot is preposterous, but that doesn't really matter; the car chase is so good, it makes up for the silly plot.

Steve McQueen was great casting for this film, and he did a lot of h own stunt driving in the film since he was a renowned racing car driver. However, for the really dangerous collision shots, doubles and stuntmen were used because McQueen was too valuable an asset to risk in those situations. The hills of San Francisco are great props for car chases. Robert Vaughn is perfect as the smug and overly-ambitious city politician. Jackie Bisset played somebody in the film, but I really can't remember who it was, because I was too busy drooling over her screen persona. I don't care if she can't act that well; she looked gr Sort of a female version of Ricardo Montelban. This film contains one of the top two or three chase scenes in the history of cinema, depending on whose opinions you believe. This film has very little socially redeeming value, but it sure is a lot of fun to watch. I recommend it without reservation.

Bulworth – 1998 - Directed by and starring Warren Beatty. The film uses John Jay Hooker, Tennessee politician, as its role model. Hooker is supposedly a friend of Beatty. Beatty plays California Senator, Jay Billington Bulworth, who is running for reelection and is supposedly b stalked by an assassin at the same time. An admirable supporting cast gives a little heft to the film including Halle Berry as Nina, Oliver Platt, who always plays a good bureaucrat, as Dennis Murphy, Paul Sorvino as Graham Jack Warden, as the crotchety old Eddie Davers, and Isaiah Washington as the crucial black community liaison for the black vote. By the way, if this is the way that Warren Beatty portrays his so-called friends on the screen, then I am very glad not to be one of his friends. Who wants their dirty wash done in public? Beatty does reinforce the fact that he is able to direct and act at the same time (a skill the vast majority of other actors cannot master) and produces a very nice finished product. Recommended with reservations.

Bus Stop – 1956 - Directed by Joshua Logan and starring Marylyn Monroe and Don Murray. This is a simple boy meets girl movie that pits a rough and tumble rodeo man, Beau, played by Don Murray against a local lizard lounge singer in a small time bar, played by Mary Monroe. Well, what guy wouldn't want to run away with and marry Marylyn Monroe? But Marylyn is high maintenance, and wants to take a shot at success in Hollywood. How ridiculous, who would want to see her in a movie? Anyway, Beau chases her down, and kidnaps her on a bus (how the hell do you do that, anyway?). After Beau comes to his senses, he lets Cherie go her own way, and then she decides to go Montana with him, anyway. Of course, after a few years of living on a rodeo cowboy's wages in various trailer parks, Cherie may reconsider her decision, but we don't see that in the movie. I can recommend it, even with the overbearing performance of Murray because Monroe is actually a fine actress, and deserves some recognition as such.

Butch Cassidy and the Sundance Kid – 1969 - Directed by George Roy Hill and starring Paul Newman, Robert Redford, and Katherine Ross. This is one of the most overrated Westerns of all time because of the box office appeal of its two top stars. The story is entertaining enough, but there must be at least 100 westerns that are better, and yet this film is always rated near the top of the Western heap. The film follows Butch and Sundance through various escapades, until things get too hot for them to operate in the US. They then try their luck in Mexico, and do pretty well for a while. Katherine Ross does well as a woman of easy virtue who services both cowboys. This was a very popular premise in 1969; dated now. Despite the small flaws, the film is very engaging, and the characters are amusing. I would recommend it, even though it is not a top 100 Western.

The Butler -2013 - Directed by Lee Daniels with an all-star cast headed by Forest Whitaker in the lead role as a butler in the White House from 1952 to 1986, covering the Eisenhower, Kennedy, Johnson, Nixon, Carter and Reagan administrations (you can throw in Ford, if you like). A feeling of powerlessness overtakes both the character and the viewer.

207

C

The Caine Mutiny -1954 – Directed by Edward Dmytryk and starring Humphrey Bogart, Fred MacMurray, Van Johnson, and Jose Ferrer. This very talented cast makes this film gripping from beginning to end. Bogart plays against type in this film, and does a great job as Captain Queeg. He is the captain of a US destroyer who is beginning to get battle fatigue. Van Johnson plays the honorable junior officer, Lieutenant Maryk, who tries to reason with Queeg. On the ship is the shallow, cynical, Fred MacMurray character, Lieutenant Keefer. Ferrer, as usual, gives a great performance as the defense lawyer for Maryk after the mutiny.

Calcutta -1947 – Directed by John Farrow and starring Alan Ladd as Neale Gordon, an American commercial pilot, Gail Russell as Virginia Moore, his romantic interest (these types of films almost always have a romantic interest), and William Bendix as the tough, but funny comic relief as Pedro (Pedro? Who in their right mind would ever consider William Bendix to be Mexican? That would be like casting McKenzie Phillips as Tina Turner), Blake, Neale's sidekick and comic relief (these films almost always have comic relief). The movie is shot in film-noir fashion and the Gordon character does not trust women, which is why he has survived so long according to his logic.

California – 1946 – Directed by John Farrow and starring Ray Milland (miscast), Barbara Stanwyck, and Anthony Quinn(miscast). Although two thirds of the leading cast was miscast, this Western is a cut above the usual B Western because of the quality director and production values. Highly entertaining.

California Suite – 1978 - Directed by Herbert Ross and starring Alan Alda, Jane Fonda, Maggie Smith, Michael Caine, Walter Matthau, Elaine May, Richard Pryor, and Bill Cosby. This is an updated comedic treatment of the Hollywood classic, *Grand Hotel*. The characters' names are quite forgettable, but the performances of the stars in the film are very good; especially that of Alan Alda, whose sardonic sense of humor never fails to entertain on the big screen. In addition to Alda, the performance of Maggie Smith earned her a real Oscar for Best Supporting Actress (a case of life imitating art) as a struggling actress nominated for an Oscar. I also enjoyed watching and listening to the banter between Elaine May and Walter Matthau, who can be more sour than lemonade without sugar. This was really an enjoyable comedy, and a great date movie. I recommend it without reservation.

Calvary – 2014 – Directed by John Michael McDonagh and starring Brendon Gleeson, a fine actor, with a solid supporting cast in a story about a priest in a small Irish town who gets a death threat from one of his parishioners in the confessional box. Rather unique plot.

Candidate – 1972 –A- Directed by Michael Ritchie and starring Robert Redford as Bill McKay, a Senatorial candidate who is a little wet behind the ears, Peter Boyle as Marvin, a political strategist for Mckay, and Melvyn Douglas as John McKay, the candidate's father and former governor of the state. This film hasn't dated itself much in the last forty years; it is still as relevant now as it was then. It shows the dirty infighting during the primaries, and the even worse mudslinging that goes on in the main election. The story shows McKay as a thoughtful liberal in the beginning, who through some luck, gets the nomination and a chance to get thoroughly trounced in the main election. So McKay starts to court the middle of the road and gains in the polls. A debate with his opponent makes it an even race. I will not reveal the end of the film, but there is a very famous line from it: "Marvin, what do we do now?" I can recommend this film wholeheartedly.

Cape Fear – 1962 - Directed by J. Lee Thompson and starring Gregory Peck as Sam Bowden, the lawyer, Polly Bergen, the B actress, as his wife, and Robert Mitchum, who steals the film as Max Cady, the recently released rapist who begins to stalk Bowden and his family. The film was remade in 1991 with Robert DeNiro in the Cady role, but most critics, including me, prefer the Mitchum version. The story begins with the release of Cady, who blames Bowden for his conviction. Initially, Cady makes only veiled threats on Bowden's family, which Bowden uses various methods to try and thwart. He asks the local sheriff to help; to no avail. I will not reveal the ending of the film, but I would have shot Cady down like a dog, and would have planted a gun on him. But this is Hollywood. So enjoy the fantasy, which I can recommend.

Capote –A-2005 – Directed by Bennett Miller and starring Phillip Seymour Hoffman in his Academy-Award-winning role as Truman Capote. Hoffman is assisted by an able supporting cast including Chris Cooper, among others. The film centers on Capote's incisive research on a murder case in Kansas that would eventually lead to his blockbuster book and film, *In Cold Blood*. The film is masterfully crafted by the director to show us Capote is gradually sucked into the frenzy surrounding the crime, and how he came to intimately know the defendants in the case. In truth, Capote probably knew more about the case than all of the law enforcement and judicial branches involved with the case put together, because he was actually there, and did a painstaking amount of first-hand research.

Capricorn One – 1978 - Written and directed by Peter Hyams and starring James Brolin and Sam Waterston as astronauts who participate in a grand hoax to convince the public that there has been a space mission that has safely landed on Mars. The justification for this hoax is that a faulty life-support system will kill the astronauts in space, but cancelling the mission would be extremely costly and result in the mission being cancelled. Elliot Gould, as Robert Caulfield and Hal Holbrook as Dr. James Kelloway, are also featured. There are a few minor women's roles in the film for Karen Black and Brenda Vaccaro, but they are primarily just props. One amateur actor makes a token appearance, but the action is carried by Brolin and Waterston.

Captain America – 2011 - Directed by Joe Johnson and produced by Ivan Reitman and starring Chris Evans as Captain America, Steve Rogers and Hugo Weaving as the EVIL NAZI GUY, Red Skull. There is an unconvincing woman who plays the romantic interest for Chris Evans, but since he is completely asexual, her role is completely wasted in the film. A bizarre collection of military stereotypes round out what is supposed to be a WW 2 era film (which it fails miserably at doing), and some other forgettable characters round out the cast. . The plot is convoluted, and the obvious set-up for the sequel(s) at the end is really amateurish in every conceivable way. It will make a ton of money, just like Vegas does by illustrating form over substance. Recommended to show how to make money with an inferior film.

Captain Blood – 1935 - Directed by Michael Curtiz and starring Errol Flynn as Doctor Peter Blood, Olivia De Haviland as Arabella Bishop and Basil Rathbone as Captain Lavasseur. These three will star together again in the future in the popular film, *Robin Hood*. Flynn is his usual physical, sexy self, and DeHaviland knows how to play the heroine to the hilt. Rathbone, however, steals most of the pictures he is in because of the strength of his evil characters. No one remembers Luke, but they do remember Darth Vader. A good bad guy is much better than a mediocre good guy. The English are fighting the French (don't they always?), and eventually Blood can get a pardon for himself and his men if he joins the fight against the French. Even though we can all guess how this ends, the film is a lot of fun to watch and moves quickly under the professional hand of Curtiz. I recommend it as a top-notch popcorn film.

Captain Horatio Hornblower -1951 – Directed by Raoul Walsh and starring Gregory Peck as the heroic Captain Horatio Hornblower, the worst-named hero in the history of film, Virginia Mayo, as the ravishing, red-headed (especially for these technicolor productions), Lady Barbara Wellesley, who understandably diverts the attention of our hero, Robert Beatty, a B actor, as Lieutenant William Bush (if only all the Bushes knew they were B actors), Stanley Baker, a British A actor, who does a nice turn as the bosun for Hornblower, and Christopher Lee, hilariously miscast as the SPANISH captain of the ship *Natividad*, who goes wildly over the top in a role that was clearly meant for someone who was not an Englishman. (If you believe Lee as a Spaniard, you might also believe John Wayne could be a Mongolian...wait, he was a Mongolian in *The Conqueror*). Despite the miscasting step, the film has plenty of action and is nicely managed by the highly competent Raoul Walsh.

Captain Newman, M.D. -1963 – Directed by David Miller and starring Gregory Peck, as Captain Newman, a shrink, Tony Curtis as Leibowitz, his assistant, who helps with various cases in rather unorthodox fashion, and is always able to scrounge up rare resources for Newman, Angie Dickinson as a sexy nurse (not much of a stretch there), Eddie Albert as a nut case officer (not much of a stretch there, either), Bobby Darin, as a troubled GI, Jim, who makes a great debut in this film as a decent actor, and Robert Duvall, who, as usual, can play any role convincingly and plays the depressed Captain Winston. The movie is dominated by the performances of Curtis and Darin and the strong supporting cast really contributes to the film as a whole. Not a great film, but entertaining. Recommended.

Captains Courageous - 1937 – Directed by Victor Fleming and starring Spencer Tracy and Freddy Bartholomew. Victor Fleming would be famous two years later for directing *Gone With the Wind* and would go from a basically a one studio shooting lot in *Captains Courageous* to an enormous production in *Gone With the Wind*. Spencer Tracy as Manuel, the fisherman's fisherman, guides little Freddy from childhood to adolescence in just a few weeks. Bartholomew plays his usual spoiled brat persona to the hilt.

Unfortunately, this would wear thin as he got older, and parts for him gradually disappeared. His other co-star, however, Mickey Rooney, would go on to have dozens of other successful films, and would costar with Tracy again in *Boys Town* as well as *Mad Mad Mad Mad World* many years later in the sixties. The film is really a tour-de-force for Tracy who overpowers the less talented Freddy in just about every scene, and as a result won the Best Actor award for 1937; no small feat in the late thirties. Many consider this and *Boys Town* to be the best films in Tracy's career. This film is on numerous top fifty lists and even more top 100 lists. It is a must see film.

Captive Heart – 1947 – Directed by Basil Dearden and starring Michael Redgrave and a solid supporting British cast in a film about a Czech officer assuming the identity of a dead British officer from a concentration camp, and also initiates a relationship with the dead officer's wife. Very good B war movie.

Carnal Knowledge – 1971 - Directed by Mike Nichols and starring Jack Nicholson, Arthur Garfunkel, and Ann Margaret. This film examines the importance of sex in relationships and how different people react differently to the sex act. The story begins with Nicholson, Garfunkel (who is badly miscast in this movie and is a pretty horrendous actor to boot) and Ann Margaret all going to college together (how come I didn't get to go to college with Ann Margaret?) Garfunkel clumsily has sex with with her (how could that ever happen in real life?) and Nicholson easily sweeps her away from his good friend (there is nothing like a good friend who takes your women).

As all of their lives progress, we see Garfunkel actually marrying her, and Nicholson having a string of unsatisfying sexual encounters with various women. Despite the heavy dose of philosophical baloney in the film, it is a lot of fun to watch Jack Nicholson in one of his earlier films. It is even more fun watching Arthur Garfunkel trying to act. Recommended.

Carpetbaggers - 1964 – Directed by Edward Dmytryk and starring George Peppard as Jonas Cord, a character very loosely based on Howard Hughes. Also featured in his last film, was Alan Ladd as Nevada Smith, a gunman who has evolved into an actor. This character was later portrayed by Steve McQueen in a prequel called *Nevada Smith*. The movie also stars Carol Baker as a character that is supposed to be Jean Harlow, who stars in the eventual Academy Award winning film, *Hell's Angels* of the 1920s. To be perfectly honest, this film is all over the place, and the characterizations are either of a cardboard nature or completely over the top.

That is with the exception of a fine, controlled performance by Alan Ladd shortly before his real-life death a few months after the film was concluded. The film was a great commercial success. The performances of the secondary actors in this film far exceed the performances of the A actors, Peppard and Baker, who, as time would eventually reveal to us, were actually B actors. Recommended only for the Ladd performance and the B actors.

Casablanca - 1942 – Directed by Michael Curtiz and starring Humphrey Bogart as Rick, a shady, but lovable character in Casablanca, who is often on the wrong side of the law, and Ingrid Bergman as Ilsa, a Czech freedom-fighter fending off the Nazis with her ethical husband. Great supporting turns by Claude Rains as Captain Louis and Paul Henreid as the ethical husband, Victor, whose wife has already had an affair with Rick in Paris ("We'll always have Paris"; a notoriously famous line that has been quoted millions of times since) also contribute to the film's atmosphere. Considered by many critics to be one of the finest films ever made, it appears in the top ten list of almost every critic. It is considered the greatest Bogart film ever made, and the best thing that Bergman ever did, although some would argue the point that her performance in *Gaslight* was superior.

The casting in this film was brilliant from the top to the bottom of the troupe. Everyone makes a contribution. Sidney Greenstreet, normally a top actor with a lot of impact in most of his films, almost gets lost in this one because of the fantastic cast. Bogart, of course, steals the film with his legendary performance of Rick Blaine, a shady American expat living in Casablanca who owns and runs a gambling house and bar that is filled with intrigue. Peter Lorre kicks things off with a mysterious letter. No one can ever ignore Lorre in his prime; he is hypnotic. When Ingrid arrives on the scene, we find that she and Rick were former lovers in Paris, but now she is with the Czech resistance along with her husband, Paul Henreid. It is classic film-making at its best ,and even the music in the film is iconic: *As Time Goes By.*

Casino - 1987 - Directed by Martin Scorsese and starring Robert DeNiro, Joe Pesci, and Sharon Stone. DeNiro plays Sam Ace Rothstein (sorry, not buying Bobby as Jewish), as the gambling boss of a mob-run casino (that's redundant, isn't it?). Joe Pesci, as Joe Santano, a potty-mouthed Italian mobster (buying this completely), who skims money for the mob, and keeps the Vegas mobsters in line. Also starring is Sharon Stone as Ace's wife. She was one of the first actresses in Hollywood history to get an Oscar nomination as a prop in an Italian gangster movie (maybe the only one?). There is also a nice turn by James Woods as Stone's ex-boyfriend. I will not reveal the ending of the film, but it is interesting. I recommend this as a great popcorn movie despite the 122 uses of the bad word Pesci loves to say.

Casino Jack - 2010 – Directed by Stephen Belber and starring Kevin Spacey, Barry Pepper, Kelly Preston, Jon Lovitz and Rachelle Lefevre. This is a pull all the stops look at the excesses of lobbyists in our nation's capital. This is primarily why the average citizen of the United States hates politicians in general, and Washington in particular. While this film is satanically funny, it does show how billions of our tax dollars are wasted and how we partially got into the mess we are in today with the global financial crisis. It's all about unbridled greed. Spacey and Pepper play two slick lobbyists who get things done on the Hill. You want a casino (hence, the title), you see them. You want to get re-elected, you see them. You want to raise money for any particular cause, you see them. These guys make Al Capone look like a nickel and dime punk thief. When I was a senior in high school, I wanted to be a lobbyist. Now I know why. A thoroughly enjoyable romp with a bravura performance worthy of an Oscar for Spacey. While I am at it, I am convinced that Lovitz deserves one also in a supporting role. Highly Recommended.

Cast Away -2000 – Directed by Robert Zemeckis and starring as Tom Hanks as Chuck Noland, a FexEx shipping supervisor whose plane crashes and strands him on an uninhabited island in the South Pacific. Also featured in the film in minor roles is Helen Hunt as his finacee, Kelly Frears, who lives in Memphis Tennessee and Wilson, a volleyball that takes the place of human companionship as one of the few inanimate objects that have ever had a significant role in a major motion picture. Recommended.

Cat Ballou - 1965 – Directed by Elliot Silverstein and starring Jane Fonda as Cat, Lee Marvin, in his Oscar-winning role as Kid Shelleen (I believe this portrayal is the oldest KID ever seen in film history; the Kid was at least 60 years old in this movie), the drunken gunfighter who can shoot better drunk than most men can shoot when they are sober. There was a great deal of controversy among critics over the decision to give this award to Marvin over the scintillating performance of Richard Burton in *Virginia Woolf*. Marvin also plays the gunfighter Tim Strawn, also known as Silver Nose (he got his nose shot off in a fight), who is stalking Cat's father, a rancher. Cat hires Shelleen to kill Strawn, but not before her father is killed. Cat turns on the town and becomes an outlaw in revenge. Recommended for the Marvin performance.

Catch Me If You Can - 2002 - Directed by Steven Spielberg and starring Leonardo DiCaprio as the world's youngest con-man, Frank Abagnale Jr., who posed as a pilot, a doctor and a prosecutor. He was also highly adept at writing rubber checks. He was good enough at the check scam to be enlisted by the FBI. This film is highly reminiscent of *The Imposter*, a film made half a century ago about a similar fellow, starring Tony Curtis (another screen pretty boy like DeCaprio). Also featured in this film is Tom Hanks as Carl Hanratty, an FBI bank fraud agent, in one of his first roles that is clearly that of a supporting actor instead of the lead. The cast is rounded out with veterans Christopher Walken, who plays Frank's dad, Frank Abagnale Sr. and Martin Sheen in a minor role.

Cavalcade -1933 -Directed by Frank Lloyd and starring Diana Wynyard as Jane Marryot, who lost to Katherine Hepburn that year for best actress, Clive Brook as her husband, Robert, and a number of other forgotten British actors and actresses who contribute to the authenticity of the film. This is British soap at its finest. Although I generally do not do soap, I make rare exceptions like *Gone with the Wind* and this film, if they are very well done. The Titanic scene is particularly touching. This film has dated horribly, as has England itself for the most part, so the film must be considered strictly in a historical context. It is fun to watch, and takes us through the lives of families we really begin to care about. It is the engagement of the film that makes it so successful. I can recommend it wholeheartedly.

Champion - 1949 - Directed by Mark Robson, and skillfully acted by Kirk Douglas as Midge Kelly, a successful, but tormented boxer, as well as Marilyn Maxwell as his girlfriend, Grace Diamond. Douglas was so good in this film that he received an Academy Award nomination. The film also received four other nominations and won for best editing. Douglas is very well cast here as a fighter, and there were a half-dozen different ways this film could have been mediocre or worse. First, the film avoided cliches, which by this time, were rife in boxing films. Stuff like "I gotta win this one for my kid,;he needs an operation" and similar junk. Secondly, the filming of the movie was first-rate (it also garnered a nomination). Even the most mundane movie can be interesting, if it is filmed well. And the supporting cast all did a fine job. This can sometimes ruin other films where the supporting cast is less than stellar.

Chan is Missing - 1982 - Directed by my old tennis buddy, Wayne Wang, and starring Wood Moy, Marc Hayashi, and Laureen Chew. This is one of the first movies ever made in the US with native Chinese as leading and secondary characters.

Charge of the Light Brigade -1936 - Directed by Michael Curtiz and starring Errol Flynn, Olivia DeHaviland, and David Niven. The story tells of Major Geoffrey Vickers, played by Flynn and his brother, Captain Perry Vickers, played by Patric Knowles going to India to keep the local Indian population in their place for the East India Company. I was rooting for the Indians in this one. Perry is a great brother in this movie; he tries to steal the fiancee of Geoffrey , Elsa (played by the indecisive Olivia DeHavlland). So I was also rooting for the younger brother to die in combat, and for Elsa to contract a venereal disease. As if some geek can take a girl away from Errol Flynn; this is really suspending disbelief. The other way around, I might believe. Despite an appalling excess in romanticism, the film is well-photographed and is very exciting with the music of Max Steiner, one of my favorite score creators. Recommended.

Chariots of Fire (England) -1981 - Directed by Hugh Hudson and starring Ben Cross as Harold Abrahams, a Jew running in the Olympics to fight anti-Semitism, and Eric Liddell, played by Ian Charleson, who is a missionary from Scotland. Both athletes are attending Cambridge, the other prestigious university in England (other than Oxford). They eventually compete and Eric beats Harold. Harold takes it to heart and gets a private coach (Ian Holm) to improve his running skills. Both athletes are selected to run for Great Britain in the 1924 Olympics in Paris. I can highly recommend this film.

Charly - 1968 -Directed by Ralph Nelson and starring Cliff Robinson as Charly, a mildy retarded man who temporarily becomes a genius and Claire Bloom as the doctor, Alice, who is there initially with him to better his condition in life, and then is also there at the end of his brief trip through intellectual stardom. The story is taken from a science fiction classic, *Flowers for Algernon*, written by Daniel Keys. Robertson won the Academy Award for Best Actor that year and deservedly so. His performance ranging from the shy and plodding, low- IQ Charly, to the supremely confident and intellectually incomparable Charly is truly a marvel to watch on the screen. The direction by Ralph Nelson is beautifully paced, and the characters are developed in a highly believable manner. Claire Bloom is wonderfully sensitive as the doctor, Alice, monitoring Charly's progress. This story is considered to be one of the top ten science-fiction stories of all time by almost every literary critic who has ever done a review. There is not an ounce of waste in either the short story or in the film. Highly Recommended.

CHARLIE CHAN.................. You have arrived at the Charley Chan section of this

book. Please remove your hat (unless you are wearing a white fedora), shoes, all metallic items on your person, and any concerns you might have about the economy. The Charlie Chan films are listed chronologically rather than alphabetically. I have also prefaced each film with the appendage Charlie Chan at the beginning of a title. This is to prevent films about Charlie Chan without his name in the title from appearing in other places in the book. As usual, the earlier films are usually the best in any series, and this is the case with Charlie Chan. Warner Oland was the best of all the Charlie Chans, and was its star from 1931 until his death in 1938. Sidney Toler, who did a competent job, but was a bit broader, and a bit less talented than Oland, made the most Chan films from 1938 to 1946. By that time, with the passing of World War 2, (there was only one Chan film in 42 and none in 43) and the ignorance of the general American public to distinguish one type of Asian (Chinese) from another (Japanese) (they all look alike), the popularity and box office of Chan films began to descend into the solid B category.

Roland Winters took over from Toler from 1947 to the end of the series in 1949. There were mild attempts at revivals, but another war (Korean) in Asia led Americans to disdain anything Asian by the end of 1950. The Films Charlie Chan and The House Without a Key - 1926 –B- (silent) - Directed by Spencer Bennet and starring Japanese actor George Kuwa as the Chinese detective Charlie Chan. This, of course, was wildly appreciated by all the Chinese audiences who saw the film. I am being sarcastic unless you haven't noticed. The Chinese audiences, particularly the ones in Shanghai, stayed away from this film in droves because its star was a Japanese. It is amazing that, despite this serious initial blunder, general audiences still went to this film in moderate numbers . This is the first Charlie Chan feature. The mystery revolves around the first book about Charlie Chan, *Seven Keys to Baldpate*, written by Earl Derr BIggers, the creator of the character. The setting of the film is in Hawaii, and the nephew of a murdered man comes to the island to try and solve his uncle's death. The film is interesting, but not compelling. Kuwa was an inadequate actor to portray Chan and a more experienced and stronger personality was needed to fill out the character. Recommended as a curiosity.

Charlie Chan and The Chinese Parrot -1927- (Silent) – Directed by Paul Leni and starring Kamiyama Sojin, another Japanese actor as Charlies Chan. The second film based on the second book of Charles Derr Biggers was a bit more interesting than the first book and film. The setting moves from Hawaii to California and Chan disguises himself as a houseboy in order to investigate the murder of both a man and a Chinese-speaking parrot. This film provided a bit more intrigue than *The House without a Key*, but it still lacked the grace and charm of later Charlie Chan films. Again, however, the Japanese actor, Sojin, goes through the paces of Chan, but one can easily see that his film presence wanes in comparison to his two major (not the Korean actor, E.L. Park, but the two after him) successors in the future. Recommended as a curiosity.

Charlie Chan Behind That Curtain - 1929-- (silent) – Directed by Paul Leni and appearing (only in the last ten minutes of the film) as Charlie Chan, is a Korean actor, E.L Park, who makes one of those famous tidying-up sequences that Charlie Chan films were noted for. Chan was famous for completely explaining heretofore obscure references in the film as important clues for solving the crime. Park delivers the goods as well as can be expected in a rather mediocre detective story. But Fox Studios, which acquired the rights to the series that year, was about to make profound changes that would turn the books of Biggers (this was his third) and the films of Charlie Chan into the stuff of legends. Recommended as an oddity.

Charlie Chan Carries On – 1931 - Directed by Paul Leni and starring the first talkie of the Charlie Chan legends, Warner Oland, as Charlie Chan. The setting is a cruise ship where a series of crimes takes place. Many of the suspicious passengers are prime suspects for the crimes, and Charlie must sift through the evidence to pinpoint the criminal. This is the first talking film of the Charlie Chan series and the Chan character is greatly modified by the the gentle, yet controlled acting of Oland. This was the fifth novel of Biggers and actually preceded his fourth novel on the screen, which came out a bit later. Unfortunately, the print of this film was lost and only a Spanish version remains. If anyone finds it, please give me a buzz at my email address and I will gladly pay you $50,000 for the print. This was the third novel of Biggers. Recommended as an oddity if you can find the Spanish version.

Charlie Chan and the Black Camel -1931 -Directed by Hamilton MacFadden and starring Warner Oland as Charlie Chan and none other than Bela Lugosi as a mysterious psychic, Tarnevarro . Not only do we get Lugosi, but we also get the debut of Robert Young (*Father Knows Best*) in a minor role. A Hollywood actress who just finished a film in Tahiti and who was resting in Hawaii is murdered. It is the second murder of an actor connected to the suspicious psychic, Tarnevarro. In this film, Charlie is part of the Honolulu police department and begins to solve the crime. There is no black camel in the film; it is a metaphor for murder as explained by Charlie. This was the fourth Biggers novel and the best -written Charlie Chan film up to this point in time in the series. It actually came out after his fifth novel was used for Charlie Chan Carries On. Recommended.

Charlie Chan's Chance - 1932 - Directed by John Blystone and starring Warner Oland as Charlie Chan. The plot of the film is a little different from the other films previous to this one in the series because the victim of the crime is Charlie, himself, and it is only by chance that Charlie escapes his murder. There is some confusion as to where the plot of the film came from. It is often attributed to Charlie Chan behind That Curtain. But if that were true, than this film would be a remake of the 1929 silent film of the same name as the Bigger's novel. It was more than likely it was a Hollywood rewrite of the book, so the producers at Fox could save money by not paying Biggers. Not as good as The Black Camel. Recommended with reservations.

Charlie Chan's Greatest Case – 1933 – Directed once again by Hamilton MacFadden, who had success with a previous Chan film, Charlie Chan and the Black Camel. The two MacFadden films are superior to any of the other Charlie Chan films up to this point in time in the series, The film once again teams up MacFadden with Warner Oland, who plays Charlie Chan. Fox once again saved money on the script by using material from Bigger's first novel, The House Without a Key, rather than opting for a completely new novel by Biggers. Although it took some material from the original film, this production is quite different. Recommended.

Charlie Chan's Courage -1934 - Directed by Eugene Forde and starring Warner Oland as Charlie Chan. Fox continues its strategy of remaking all of the earlier Chan films made during the silent era. This reduced the payments they had to make to Biggers (the author the book, The Chinese Parrot, which this film is based on) because Fox had already acquired the rights to the silent films. See the entry for Charlie Chan and the Chinese Parrot for the details of the film. Recommended with reservations.

Charlie Chan in London - 1934 - Eugene Ford takes his second turn at directing Warner Oland as Charlie Chan. By this time, Biggers had stopped writing novels and wrote strictly for Fox and the big screen. This story is about Charlie arriving in England and finding a young man about to hang for a crime he didn't commit. His family hires him to find the real killer who is hiding out in an expensive mansion with a lot of suspects (especially the butler). This was only the second film in the series that was available for later DVD publication aside from The Black Camel. All the other ones were tragically lost due to poor storage. Recommended.

Charlie Chan in Paris - 1935 - Directed by Louis Seiler and starring Warner Oland in the seventh Fox Charlie Chan production. This film is especially noted for the first extended appearance of Charlie Chan's Number One Son, played by Keye Luke. The addition of Luke added a great deal more humor to the film series and was very popular with audiences. This inclusion of Luke makes this film the best in the series up until point in time. Charlie investigates a phony bond scheme when the criminals try to kill him and others who stand in their way. A fairly interesting plot makes the film even more enjoyable. Highly recommended.

Charlie Chan in Egypt - 1935 - Directed by Edward Lowe and starring Warner Oland as Charlie Chan in the 8th Fox production of the series and the eleventh Charlie Chan film ever made. This plot has Charlie investigating the theft of some Egyptian artifacts and some murders surrounding the thefts. Rita Hayworth makes her major film debut as some nice scenery, but number one son has temporarily disappeared (or was he at school in Paris?). The usual suspects and wonderful atmosphere of Cairo (even though it is shot at the studio) makes for an interesting film. Recommended.

Charlie Chan in Shanghai -1935 -Directed by James Tinling and starrin Warner Oland as Charlie Chan. This was the ninth Fox production of the series and the 12th Charlie Chan film in all. The best part of this film, which is the first Charlie Chan film that takes place in China, is that it marks the return of Number One Son played by Keye Luke. Crowds loved the give and take between the modern son and the old-fashioned father and it was to become a keynote in every good Charlie Chan film. Charlie is now a spy for the US in China to uncover an opium smuggling ring (they should have gone to England where the real bosses of Chinese opium smuggling were for hundreds of years). This film, like most Charlie Chan pictures, has a neat little ending that wraps up all the loose ends very conveniently, and reminds us that we should have been looking for these clues earlier in the picture (even though some of them were not on film). Still entertaining. Recommended.

Charlie Chan's Secret - 1936 - Directed by Gordon Wiles (it appeared at this time as if no director wanted to make more than one or two of these films) and starring Warner Oland as Charlie Chan in the tenth Fox production of the series of 13. Although this one is missing Number One Son, it is still very entertaining because of the mass of suspects and their motives. It is a bit like a game of Clue. A man who was heir to a large fortune is murdered to maintain the status quo of the fortune, and Charlie must figure out which of the main five suspects is the murderer. Recommended.

Charlie Chan at the Circus - 1936 - Directed by Harry Lachman and starring Warner Oland as Charlie Chan and Keye Luke as Number One Son (who finally gets to have a substantial role for the first time). This is one of the silliest Charlie Chan films of the entire series. The gorilla is really a terrible actor and obviously not real. The plot is a bit goofy as well. There are a spat of murders at the circus and obviously someone is training the gorilla to kill the victims. I mean, really now, how many people would be capable of training a gorilla to kill various victims? This was the 11th (and the worst) of Fox Charlie Chan productions and 14 in all of the series. The only saving grace of this film is the humor between Charlie and Number One son. Barely recommended.

Charlie Chan at the Race Track - 1936 - Directed by H. Bruce Humberstone. The film stars Warner Oland as Charlie Chan in a big upgrade from the previous disaster made before this one about the gorilla at a circus. At least this story line is a bit clever (and they don't meet up with the Marx Brothers here or at the Opera, later). Number One Son gets a new name, Lee, but everyone still called him Number One Son. Again, the dialogue between Luke and Orland make the film move forward well in addition to the storyline. Recommended.

Charlie Chan at the Opera - 1936 - Directed by H Bruce Humberstone for his second turn at a Charlie Chan film and he makes a good one. It is considered by many critics, including myself, to be one of the best of the series. Fortunately, the Marx brothers were not at this performance. The addition of a master antagonist of the level of Boris Karloff (who was a fine actor in addition to being a monster) makes this a great Charlie Chan film. Warner Oland appears for the 13th time. Number one son or Lee Chan adds to the film as well, providing necessary light moments to offset the seriousness of the film. Highly recommended. Amazingly, even though Charlie and the Marx Brothers both went to the Opera and the race track at the same time, they never met.

Charlie Chan at the Olympics – 1937 - Directed by H Bruce Humberstone, who becomes the leading director of Charlie Chan films at this point in time with his third entry. Starring as Charlie Chan is Warner Oland in the 14th Fox edition of the film series and 17th overall Chan film. The Marx Brothers went to the opera and race track with Charlie, but not to the Olympics. This film also features Number One Son, Keye Luke, who was pushed down a bit in face time on the film, because the director considered him a mediocre actor. The movie centers on the 1936 Olympics and has a rather dreary plot, but the scenes of Charlie flying on the actual Hildenburg Blimp and some footage of the actual 1936 Olympics are very interesting. Recommended.

Charlie Chan on Broadway –- 1937 - Directed by Eugene Forde in his second effort on the series and starring Warner Oland as Charlie Chan for the 15th time and Keye Luke is elevated back to second banana as number one son after a one film demotion by the last director, Humberstone. Forde thought that the humor aspect of the film was as important as the plot (and he turned out to be right about that). The film begins on a cruise ship coming into New York. Of course there is a murder and there are five suspects on the ship (this is the usual number). Then the evidence is magically produced by both father and son and the series gets to live on. One of the weaker entries of the series, but still recommended with reservations for the cruise.

Charlie Chan at Monte Carlo - 1937 – Eugene Forde ties Humberstone as the two directors that give three tries at making Chan episodes. They are both evenly matched. Humberstone does a better job with the mystery aspect of the films and Forde does a better job of getting humorous characterizations from his actors. They both have strengths and weaknesses that complement each other. The role of Charlie Chan goes to Oland for the 16th and final time in the 19 film series and Keye Luke stays as second banana under the Forde regime. Sadly, this is the last appearance of Orland in the role as he would be replaced by Sidney Toler in the next episode. Recommended.

Charlie Chan in Honolulu - 1938 - Directed by H Bruce Humberstone for the fourth time (and takes away the lead from Forde again). The series comes full circle as it started in Honolulu in 1926 and 13 years later in the 17th Fox production and 20th film of the series, the plot returns to its roots. There is a complete cleaning of the house. A new director, a new Charlie Chan with Sidney Toler, and even a new featured son, Sen Yung as Jimmy Chan, or number two son, replacing the beloved Keye Luke, who was number one son. The plot is the usual murder and usual lineup of suspects, but under Humberstone, the material is always taken a bit more seriously than under Forde's direction. Both Toler and Sen do an ok job, but one already misses Oland and Luke. Recommended.

Charlie Chan in Reno - 1938 - Directed by Norman Foster (Humberstone takes a break after his fourth effort) and starring Sidney Toler in his second turn as Charlie Chan and Sen Yung in his second turn as number 2 son. This is the 18th Fox production of all 21 Chan films. The plot of the film is a bit interesting as it takes place in Reno, the Biggest Little City in the World. There is gambling, murder, a number of suspects and an amazing display of crime-solving by both Chan and his number 2 son (who is decidedly not as funny as Keye Luke) . In fact, number 2 is to number one son as Zeppo Marx is to Groucho Marx. Recommended despite the second best son.

Charlie Chan at Treasure Island - 1939 - Directed by Norman Foster for his second swing at the series and starring Sidney Toler in his third appearance. Returning for his third appearance as well is number 2 son, Victor (he added Victor as a first name to alleviate the difficulty Americans had from telling first and last names of native Chinese). Ceasar Romero, a noted actor, had a role in the film. The poster for this film is one of the coolest of all the posters in the series. This was the 22nd film of the entire Chan series, with Fox making its 19th entry. The plot of the film is rather exotic and convoluted, but at least it is not boring. One of the main characters may have chillingly been the model for the Zodiac killer that come to the fore many years afterward. Recommended.

Charlie Chan and the City of Darkness - 1939 – Directed by Herbert Leeds in his first effort in the series and starring Sidney Toler in his fourth appearance as Charlie Chan. Mercifully, number two son, Jimmy, has been cut from the series by this time, but the film suffers from a distinct lack of humor since Keye Luke is not featured as well. There is a bit more realism to this episode, however, as two decent actors, Leo G Carroll (Topper), and Lon Chaney Jr. (many horror films), are part of the supporting cast. The knucklehead police officer is once again played by Harold Huber (I've lost track of how many times he had played an incompetent police officer, but by now Huber actually outlasted both the Chan leads and the son second bananas in both years playing his role, although he did not make as many appearances. This was the 2oth Fox production of the 23 Chan films. An interesting entry and recommended.

Charlie Chan's Murder Cruise - 1940 - Directed by Eugene Forde in his fourth turn at directing Chan films and tying him with Humberstone for the top honor in that category. Sidney Toler plays Charlie Chan in his fifth version, and the series now stands at 21 for Fox and 24th overall. Victor Sen Yung unmercifully returns as Jimmy, number 2 son and Leo G Carroll (of Topper fame) takes his second turn in the series as a professor. The film is a rehash of the lost film, Charlie Chan Carries On made in 1931, and does its fans of the series a service by returning one of the lost episodes. That being said, this is one of the lesser entries. Recommended by habit.

Charlie Chan at the Wax Museum - 1940 - Directed by Lynn Shores in a first time effort and starring Sidney Toler in his sixth role in the series. Joining Toler once again is Victor Sen Yung as number 2 son (also known as Avis because he tries harder). This was the 25th Chan film and 22nd produced by Fox. The rest of the supporting cast are the dregs of Hollywood as Fox was noted for saving every nickel they could. The plot of a murderer hiding in a wax museum is pretty silly, but we watch it anyway because it is part of the series. One of the lesser episodes. Recommended again by habit.

Charlie Chan in Panama --1940 - Directed by Norman Foster, who makes his third appearance as a director in the series. Norman took the series seriously and downplayed (wisely), the banter between Charlie and number two son Victor Sen Yung (who had much less face time than in previous films). Victor was just not as funny as Keye Luke. The result was still a mediocre production as they were now grinding out four of these a year at Fox. This was the seventh turn by Toler in a 26 film odyssey. 23 of them were produced by Fox, one of the Silas Marners of film production. The rest of the B and C actors are of no note. Recommended by habit.

Chalrlie Chan and Murder Over New York - 1940 - Directed by Harry Lachman in his first try and starring Sidney Toler in his eighth try. The series at Fox now reached 24 and 27 for all Chan films. Victor Sen Yung removes his first name again and goes back to Sen Yung for reasons unknown. This made the fourth Chan film made in one year and one can see the watered down effects of constant production with limited production values. The supporting cast is of no note with the exception of a cameo by future Stooge – Shemp Howard. When one of the three Stooges is the highlight of your film, you are in a bit of trouble. Recommended by habit.

Charlie Chan in Dead Men Tell - 1941 - Harry Lachman returns to direct his second effort in the Chan series. Sidney Toler returns for the ninth time in the 28 film trip; 25 of them produced by cheapie Fox Studios. Sen Yung once again annoys us with Jimmy, number 2 son. George Reeves, the future Superman of film, has a small role in the film and is the only actor of any note. The story line is as trite as the previous half dozen since the first few efforts at promoting Toler. The series is now decaying into predictability for practically every line of dialogue in the film. Fortunately, Fox slowed down production of these films from four to two in 1941, but it was already a bit too late. And as soon as Pearl Harbor was to hit the US consciousness, anything vaguely associated with Asians would have a big marketing task ahead of itself, even though Charlie was Chinese. Americans at this time were pretty unsophisticated and considered Chinese the same as Japanese. Recommended by habit.

Charlie Chan in Rio - 1941 - Harry Lachman returns for his third turn at directing the series and Sidney Toler returns for the tenth time. Victor Sen Yung again assumes his English first name after the attack on Pearl Harbor and plays Jimmy, number two son. This is 29th film about Chan and 26th by the Fox Studios. The cast for this film returned Huber in the role of the clueless police chief and Victor Jory, who always played a good bad guy. An oddity in the film has a former director of the series, Hamilton MacFadden, playing a minor role in the film (a bit of comedown from director). This is, at least, one step up from the recent hack productions, and gives us some hope for the future productions. Recommended.

Charlie Chan and the Castle in the Desert – 1942- Directed by Harry Lachman who takes his fourth turn as the series director and ties both Humberstone and Forde in directing series episodes. Sidney Toler plays the role for the eleventh time and Fox produces it's 27th film in the series out of all 30 Chan films. Things were getting cheaper and cheaper in the production values and Toler eventually moved over to Monogram Studios for a better deal, beginning with his next film. This story is below average and the actors along with it, but recommended to see Toler.

Charlie Chan in the Secret Service - 1944 - Directed by Phil Rosen in his first crack at tackling the long-running series as Monogram Studios takes over production. Toler played Chan for the twelfth time and the series finally drops the tedious number two son, Victor Sen Yung. Toler had purchased the film rights from Fox, and now made the films for even less money than they were made before (more than 50% less) Number Three son is briefly seen in this film, but makes no impression. The rest of the cast tries their best, and it is a bit better than the previous few Chan efforts, but still lacks the sense of humor of the Oland films. This movie represented the 31st Chan film made by all three studios. Recommended as a slight upgrade from number two son films.

Charlie Chan and the Chinese Cat - 1944 - Directed by Phil Rosen in his second shot at the series, and starring Sidney Toler in his 13th appearance and the second of the series produced by Monogram Studios. It was also the 32nd Chan film produced. Mantan Moreland, a black comedian, played Charlie's driver in this one, and had some very funny lines, although critics are divided as to whether the character is racist or not. Anyway, see the film and judge for yourself. Recommended.

Charlie Chan in Black Magic -1944 -Directed by Phil Rosen in his third attempt at guiding the series and starring Sidney Toler in his 14th appearance as Charlie Chan. This was also the third Monogram production of the total 33 Chan films made. Mantan Moreland returns as the funny black driver. There are no other worthies in the cast, and the film is pretty silly as we know all the psychic stuff is as phony as a three dollar bill, but it is worth watching to see Toler in action. Recommended.

Charlie Chan and the Shanghai Cobra -1945 - Directed by Phil Karlston in his first try at directing the series and Sidney Toler makes his 15th appearance as Charlie Chan in the 34 films made about the detective. This is the fourth Monogram production of Chan and Toler is quickly approaching the record for most appearances of Charlie Chan held by Warner Oland (16). Mantan Moreland makes his third straight appearance as second banana and driver for Charlie (sort of a Rochester character that appeared in Jack Benny – now I never thought Rochester was very funny, and I could easily see how that character could be categorized as racist). The films at Monogram are beginning more and more to look like future television episodes (which some of them would eventually become). Recommended from habit.

Charlie Chan and the Red Dragon - 1945 - Directed by Phil Rosen for the fourth time who ties directors Humberstone, Forde, and Harry Lachman as directors with four credits within the series. Toler ties the number of appearances made by Oland with 16 as Monogram makes it fifth production of the series of films up to 35. Number Three son fails to impress, and a racist, dumb, Italian detective is added to the racist black driver, played by Mantan Moreland. The plot is insipid, as are the suspects and the action. These look more like TV shows. Recommended only for Toler's performance.

Charlie Chan and the Scarlet Clue - 1945 - Directed by Phil Rosen, who takes the lead with five mediocre efforts reminiscent of Ed Wood in the Chan Series. And Sidney Toler finally passes Oland as the Charlie Chan with the most screen appearances with 17 of the total 36 films made about the detective. Monogram makes its sixth TV episode...I mean feature film,; and Number Three Son adds to second banana, car driver Moreland (who appears in one of the posters with a wide-eyed Rochseter look). Moreland was known in these films as Birmingham and is now getting second billing. Story of nazi spy ring in radio production crew is incidental. Recommended only from habit.

Charlie Chan and the Jade Mask -1945 -Directed by Phil Rosen for the sixth time in the series and who was responsible for cranking out a Chan film every three months now for Monogram and starring Sidney Toler in the one of the longest running TV shows playing in the movie houses. Monogram and Rosen stuck to the Chan formula closer than Coca-Cola when it made its soda. Toler makes his 18th episode of the 37 films and Monogram makes its seventh. Edwin Luke, the younger brother in real life of Keye Luke, plays Number four son (at least the series kept that record straight). Edwin is certainly an upgrade over number two and number three sons, but he is not strong enough to save this dreadful story of an amorous cop and a mad scientist.

Charlie Chan and Dangerous Money – 1946 - Directed by Terry Morse in his first try at the TV series (actually called a movie, but seems more like a one hour TV show) starring Sidney Toler in his 19th appearance within the 38 Chan films. Monogram makes its eighth production of the series. Like a bad penny, Victor Sen Yung comes back as Jimmy, the annoying number two son. He had been gone since 1942 when last seen in *Castle in the Desert* (by the way, just how do you build a castle in the desert in 1942?). Another racist stereotype, (Willie Best), takes over from the last racist stereotype, Mantan Moreland, and there is not much else going on in this film.

Charlie Chan and the Dark Alibi - 1946 - Directed by Phil Karlsen in his second shot at the series and starring Sidney Toler in his 20th appearance as Charlie Chan. Of the 39 films in the series, Monogram had now produced nine of them. Dreary number two son once again mercifully disappears, and so does the new driver. Benson Fong plays number three son (who is almost as bad as number two son). Mantan Moreland returns as the racist driver character, Birmingham Brown, but is still an upgrade from the last driver, Willie Best as Chattanooga Brown. The rest of the cast and the story are lost at sea.

Charlie Chan and Shadows Over Chinatown - 1946 - Directed by Terry Morse in his second time around the block and starring Sidney Toler in his 21st appearance as Charlie Chan. Monogram makes it tenth production in the series of 40 Chan films. The bad penny, number two son, in the person of Victor Sen Yung, comes back to haunt us; this time in Chinatown in San Francisco. Mantan graces us again with his driver role, and nothing much else changes as we gratefully come to the end of the series in the next film.

Charlie Chan in the Trap - 1946 - Directed by Howard Bretherton and starring Sidney Toler as Charlie Chan in his 22nd and final appearance as the great detective in the 41 films made about him. Toler succumbed to cancer immediately after the eleventh production of Monogram Studios for this series. Number two son played by Victor Sen Yung, and Birmingham Brown played by Mantan Moreland are also featured. Recommend as a curiosity.

Charlie Chan and the Chinese Ring - 1947 - Directed by William Beaudine in his first effort in the series and produced by Monogram Studios as their 12th Chan production in the line of 42 films produced for the series. After the death of Sidney Toler, Roland Winters gives his best shot at imitating Charlie Chan, but does not fare very well. He is aided? by Victor Sen Yung playing one of the sons (not number one or two), and Philip Ahn (who would go on to become the Master in the TV *Kung Fu* series years later). Recommended to see Ahn.

Charlie Chan in the Docks of New Orleans - 1948 - Directed by Derwood Abrahams (not exactly a household name for directors) and produced for the 13th time by Monogram Studios (where you can still hear the screams of the buffaloes from the nickels they squeezed). This was the 43rd Chan film ever produced. Roland Winters goes through the paces for the second time as Chan. The usual suspects are in the film (the actors like Victor and Mantan, not the characters). It is so very near the end of the series that one can sense it.

Charlie Chan and the Shanghai Chest- 1948 -William Beaudine comes back for a second helping of Chinese folklore as director of this turkey. Roland Winters swings for a third time and misses wildly as Charlie Chan. The usual gang of idiots are there to "help" Charlie, and the plot rolls merrily along with no rhyme or reason. When one holds these TV shows up the early Oland Chan films, one can easily see the difference in quality and effect. These later films were sagging badly from cliches and hackneyed phrases. There was little or no original material at Monogram Studios by the time they produced the 14th entry of the total of 44 Chan films produced.

Charlie Chan and the Golden Eye - 1948 - Directed by William Beaudine who makes his third film of the series; all of which look and sound exactly the same. Roland Winters keeps on rolling along with his fourth portrayal of Charlie Chan and the 15th by Monogram Studios, with the 45 films made about Chan. That meant that a full one-third of the Charlie Chan films were the height of mediocrity, which is what Mogogram Studios strove for. Audiences were staying home in droves by this time and watching television that was far more creative than the junk that Monogram was producing.

Charlie Chan and the Feathered Serpent - 1948 - Directed by William Beaudine, who makes a mad dash for immortality as the director with the most Chan films under his belt, but will fall tragically short as this was only his fourth try and the next would have been his fifth (but he stopped here, mercifully) and final Ed Wood impersonation; falling one short of the immortal Phil Rosen, one of the greatest hack directors of all time. More important than Roland Winters making his fifth appearance in the 16 films produced by Monogram and of the 46 made about Chan, was the triumphant return of Keye Luke as number one son, which makes this film the best of all the Monogram attempts. However, not even Keye Luke could save this TV series episode masquerading as a real movie. The end would come in the next production. Recommended for Luke.

Charlie Chan and the Sky Dragon - 1949 —Directed by Lesley Selander, an unknown (and for good reason) talent. Also known as *Murder in the Sky* (and by some others privately as Thank God It's Over), this was the final film of the 47 movies about the Chan character. He would go on to more fame on TV with J. Carroll Naish doing a good job, but would never again flourish on the big screen as he did in the Golden Age of film during the Warner Oland period. The series had a twenty year run equal to that of Cy Young pitching in baseball. Roland Winters tried once again to portray the main character, but fell short. Keye Luke could not save it, either. It was over. It was a great run, and the character will live forever. Recommended. All good things must come to an end and *Sky Dragon* was the last of the real Charlie Chan films.

The Chase - 1946 - Directed by Arthur Ripley, who gained notieriey as the listed director for the 1958 film, *Thunder Road*, but in reality, was merely a technical advisor for Robert Mitchum, who wrote, produced and actually directed most of *Thunder Road* . Mitchum even co-wrote the music for Thunder Road; it was completely his baby. Ripley was a strictly a tepid technician whose few films never achieved very much recognition. *The Chase* was about as good as it ever got for him. It is a film-noir piece, naturally shot in black and white, and based on a screenplay by the very able Philip Yordan. So at least you know the dialogue will be believable and interesting.

The film is also based on a novel by Cornell Woolrich, called *The Black Path of Fear,* which contained two SEO words in the title, so Cornell was ahead of his time. The film stars Robert Cummings, a veteran of Hitchcock's film noir pieces, as Chuck Scott, a driver for a notorious gangster, Steve Cochran as the vicious hood, Eddie Roman, Peter Lorre as Roman's right-hand man, Gino, and, of course, the essential romantic interest, Lorna Roman, the unfortunate wife of the sadistic Eddie, played by Michele Morgan. Although this is obviously a B movie, it has some surprising elements that are unexpected. This is one of those hidden little gems you seldom hear about, so instead of renting something predictable, try this one on for size; you won't be disappointed.

Chato's Land – 1971 – Directed by Michael Winner and starring Charles Bronson and Jack Palance in the lead roles. This story about an Indian's struggle to both survive and maintain his dignity was a step in the right direction for Hollywood PC for Indian films.

Chief Crazy Horse- 1955 – Directed by George Sherman and starring Victor Mature (usually a sword and sandal or film noir actor) as Chief Crazy Horse. Suzan Ball and John Lund are also featured in the film as secondary characters. The film was produced by Universal Studios, which specialized in the horror genre, so the poster reflects the philosophy of the studio; it is meant to scare people rather than to explore the motives of the protagonist. The story is almost a complete work of fiction except for the actual battle of the Little Big Horn (and many historical aspects of the battle are not followed too closely as well. But this is the movies, and literary license allows the writers and director to take many liberties with the truth for effect. I can recommend it with...reservations.

Children of Huang Shi -2008 – Directed by Roger Spottiswoode and starring a B cast in a film about a British journalist who stays among a group of Chinese orphans during the Japanese incursion into China. Some good scenes.

China Syndrome- 1979 – Directed by James Bridges and employing an all-star cast that included Jack Lemmon as Jack Godell, a nuclear technician who fears the worst, Jane Fonda as Kimberly Wells, a nosy news reporter who is hunting for a sensational story, Michael Douglas in an early career supporting role as Kimberly's cameraman, who captures a nuclear accident in the plant on film, and a solid supporting cast including WIlford Brimley as Ted Spindler, another nuclear technician. This film is scarier than most horror movies because it is all too real.

As a matter of fact, less than two weeks after this film opened in theaters, there was a major nuclear accident in Three Mile Island in Pennsylvania, which the film mentions by name as a state the size of which would be affected by a nuclear mishap. The message is there that nuclear energy is not safe and that we desperately need far less dangerous energy resources to fuel our needs. Highly recommended.

Chinatown – 1974 – Directed by Roman Polanski and starring Jack Nicholson as Jake, a private investigator, Faye Dunaway as Evelyn Mulwray, the daughter of Hollis Mulwray and an unfortunate victim of incest, Darrell Zwerling as the corrupt Water and Power commissioner, Hollis Murwray, and John Huston as the mysterious Noah Cross, who knows where all the skeletons of the sleazy people in this situation are located. Polanski, only occasionally, slips into his sordid view of humanity and the perverse. Generally, he keeps the action moving forward without too many sordid scenes, such as the one where Jake gets his nose slit.

Faye Dunaway is great in this film and really makes the whole thing work. Her chemistry with Nicholson is sizzling, and it is the chemistry between these two fine actors that makes the film a classic. There doesn't seem to be much going on with the Chinese who are living in Chinatown, but then again, the story is not about them, despite the title. Recommended.

Chongqin Blues (China) - 2010 - Directed by Wang Xiaoshuai and starring Wang Xueqi as the father, Lin Quanhai, Fan Bingbing as the doctor, Zhu Qing, Qin Hao as a friend of the family, Xiao Hao, Zi Yi as Lin Bo, the son, and Li Feier as Xiao Wen, the girlfriend. This is a relatively rare Chinese film that is not shot in Hong Kong, Shanghai or Beijing. The three big cities in China account for well over 90% of the commercially released films in the country. This film also demonstrates that you can make a decent small film on a limited budget in China in other than the three big well-known cities.

The story begins with Lin as a sea captain who returns after a lengthy stay away from home. He is told that his son, who was only 25, was gunned down by the police. In modern China, it is very rare for anyone to be shot by the police, unless they are involved in a violent crime that is actually in progress. Incidents of citizens being shot by the police for any reason are sparse. Eventually, he finds out that his son was actually a criminal and the father feels guilt over the fact that he was not home enough in the early years of the young man to better guide his life choices. Despite his guilt and the knowledge that his son was actually a criminal, the father continues to investigate what happened on his own. There are a few surprises in the end which I will not reveal, but they are fairly believable. This is extremely sophisticated stuff for any movie audience from any country, but all the more amazing that the film was made in a smaller city within China.

A Chump at Oxford – 1940 - Directed by Alfred Goulding and starring Stan Laurel and Oliver Hardy in a full-length comedy. This is one of the best Laurel and Hardy features ever made, even though it is only sixty minutes long. There was never any comedy team on the planet as funny as Stan and Ollie. This film highlights their various talents in both slapstick and satire. I loved when they got lost in the maze garden. It is one of the funniest bits they ever did on film. Watch for Peter Cushing, of horror movie fame, as a university snob I can recommend this film much more than most comedies.

The Cider House Rules - 1999 – Directed by Lasse Hallstrom and starring Michael Caine, Tobey (*Spiderman*) Maguire, and Charlize (*Monster*) Theron. This is one of those offbeat films that you occasionally see produced in Hollywood. Hallstrom does a great job of developing the characters at a leisurely pace so that they are more than just shallow cardboard props. Each scene helps to reveal a bit more about each of the character's good and bad traits. Caine gives a beautifully layered performance of an imperfect man who means well. Maguire as Homer, on the other hand, despite a good attempt, cannot seem to escape his Spiderman persona. He tries the understated approach, but succeeds in only being dull. Theron does a nice job, but her part is really a secondary character, as the story is primarily about Wilbur and Homer and the orphans of the Cider House. I can recommend the film to all.

Cimarron – 1960 – Directed by Anthony Mann and starring Glenn Ford and Maria Schell (miscast) in the lead roles of big Western action film; especially the race to claim land at the beginning of the film. Unfortunately, the movie cannot maintain any momentum from the exciting beginning.

The Cincinnati Kid - 1965 - Directed by Norman Jewison, more commonly known for lighthearted fare, and featuring an all-star cast including Steve McQueen, Edward G Robinson, Ann Margaret, Tuesday Weld, Joan Blondell and Karl Malden. The story revolves around a highstakes poker game (before the days of Texas Holdem) between the Kid, played by McQueen and Howard, the reigning champ, who is played by Robinson. The dealers for the game are very important in the plot. Karl Malden is Shooter, a dealer with a great reputation for being honest and Joan Blondell is Ladyfingers, a wise-cracking dealer also noted for her honesty. Part of the story line is one (or possibly even both) of the dealers fixing hands. The odds on the climatic last hand were360 BILLION to one. Recommended.

A Christmas Carol (England) - 1951 - Directed by Brian Desmond Hurst and starring Alastair Sim as Scrooge. This is the best of the myriad of Christmas Carol films and it is because of the perfect casting of Alastair Sim who IS Scrooge. Anyone else who plays this part for the rest of time can only be compared to Sim and possibly be the second best ever. The film is wonderfully shot in atmospheric black and white which adds immeasurably to the authenticity of the setting and the story. The superb supporting cast gives Sim all he needs in the area of character development and we are drawn into the film almost from the very first shot. Of course, the movie is even better to be seen during the Christmas holidays as it imbues a spirit of thankfulness that is often seen missing by large numbers of both adults and children during that potentially wondrous season. There really are more important things in life than money (although, admittedly, one is hard-pressed to dismiss the importance of money). This is a must see film and is on practically every top 100 films of all time for just about every movie critic, except for our pal at the New York Times with his 1000 best movie list. He left this one completely off in his book! So much for the New York Times knowing all that much about film. Highly recommended.

A Christmas Story -1983 - Directed by Bob Clark, who also wrote the screenplay, this film is considered the best Christmas movie ever made by the majority of movie critics. It is also on numerous top 100 lists of best films of all time. The movie stars Peter Billingsley as Ralphie, a role with greater audience recognition than all of his other roles in his career combined. The outstanding supporting cast includes an inspired Darrin McGavin in the greatest role of his career as the old man, Melinda Dillon in the greatest role of her career as Ralphie's mom, and a host of child actors who carry off the cruelty of the children's world with great finesse. They are all aided, of course, by the great writing and characterizations of Jean Shepherd, the master of story-telling in America in the 20th century. Shepherd contributes his rascally voice to the alter-ego of Ralphie in the voiceover.

This is as close to a perfect film as one can be made, as far as I'm concerned. There isn't a wasted or overly long scene in the entire film. You actually hated the film to end. Unfortunately, Shepherd seemed to have been more comfortable in the radio world than in the TV or movie world. What a tremendous loss for the TV and movie world. By the way, our pal at the New York Times with his lame 1000 best movie list left this one off as well as Alastair Sim's *A Christmas Carol*. You will never convince me or the vast majority of Americans that some obscure French or Swedish soap opera with Shakespearian trappings and highly symbolic mumbojumbo is superior to either of these Christmas productions. Which would you rather watch? One of these two films or a dreadfully depressing Bergman film?

The story takes place in a wintry Mid-Western working-class neighborhood and highlights the Christmas season. We see the normally placid town light up at night with colorful Christmas lights and decorations, punctuated by the town's big toy store that has a magnificent toy display in the window. Raphie presses his nose against the window and sets his sights on a Red Ryder BB rifle. That becomes the obsessive object of his desire. Unfortunately, every adult he talks to about it says "You'll shoot your eye out, kid" and tries to talk him out of it, but he is relentless in his pursuit. There are bullies and a terrific sequence of double-dog dare you to stick your tongue on the frozen iron pole. There are just too many great scenes to mention. Highly recommended and a double razz to the New York Times top 1000 list for not including it.

Cinderella Man - 2005 - Directed by Ron Howard and starring Russell Crowe as Jimmy Braddock and Renee Zellweger as Mae (who is so poor, she doesn't even have a last name). This is an inspiring true-life biopic of Jimmy Braddock, a real-life Rocky that is far more impressive that the fictional one created by Hollywood and Sylvester Stallone. The fact that the miracles occur dead set in the middle of the Great Depression, only amplify the drama of the situation.

Cinema Paradiso- Italy - 1988 - Directed by Giuseppe Tornatore and starring Jacques Perrin as Tornatore's alter ego Salvatore as an adult and Philippe Noiret as his childhood mentor projectionist at an Italian movie house. Salvadore Cascio steals the film as Salvadore, the child, (Tornatore) forced to be an adult because his father has been killed in WW 2. The complex story of this film is told so simply that you don't even realize that the director is weaving coming of age, comedy, romance, the love of film, the love of family and good friends and the love of a small hometown all in one motion.

The music is spectacular, but that should be no surprise since it was done by Ennio Morricone, the great Italian composer responsible for the Clint Eastwood spaghetti western music as well as countless other great sound tracks, especially *The Untouchables*. It is an unforgettable film with great minor roles. Isa Danieli, as the adolescent object of Salvatore's love, is as inviting as the Mediterranean location of the film itself. The scenes with the Italian priest played by Leopoldo Trieste, who is also the film censor are priceless, as well as the kissing montage scene. The photography is rich and memorable, and each scene is measured and shot to perfection by the director. It is hard to believe that a movie could be made with each scene so perfectly directed.

The scene where the projector breaks and what appears to be the invention of the modern-day drive-in is created is inspirational. There is not a dull spot in the film. It was obviously a labor of love for the director. The story covers the youth of Salvadore as the assistant to local movie projectionist. Salvadore collects all the kisses in the films that are censored and cut by the local parish priest, who is absolutely hilarious. Listed as the greatest foreign film of all time by a few critics (including me). Not on the NY Times list of Best 1000 films because they are sometimes oblivious to great foreign films.

Citadel -1938 - Directed by King Vidor and starring Robert Donat, as the idealistic Scottish doctor, Andrew Manson, who treats poor tuberculosis patients, Rosalind Russell, who, though a fine actress, seems to be miscast in this role because of the location of the action (she is NOT British, Scottish or even vaguely European), Ralph Richardson and Rex Harrison, in one of his earliest roles. Robert Donat is a first-tier actor who won an academy award for *Goodbye Mr. Chips*. He carries out his role with ease. Rosalind Russell, although a credible actress, is just not on the same level as Donat, and, unfortunately, it shows up in the exchange of dialogue. The film needed a stronger actress in this lead role to make it a better film. With someone like Davis or Hepburn in the role of good doctor's wife, the movie might have been a classic or at least far more memorable. But when the doctor has all the good lines and deliveries, it becomes a one-person film. A good film and recommended.

Citizen Kane - 1941- Directed by Orson Welles, who also stars in the movie. This film is consistently in the top ten list of best films of all time and is listed as number one on several critics' lists. Orson Welles plays Charles Foster Kane, whose character is a thinly veiled copy of newspaper magnate William Randolph Hearst. Hearst was infuriated by this intrusion into his privacy and plagued the release of this and all other films associated with Orson Welles. Despite these obstacles, Citizen Kane opened to successful reviews and good box office receipts.

A strong supporting cast helped the production as well as an absorbing plot. Welles uses several unique shooting angles to evoke various reactions from the audience. The music and cinematography are impressive as Welles spared no effort to make each scene a piece of art. Joseph Cotton adds a great effort among the talented supporting cast. He is Kane's best friend and does not hold back from criticizing him. The black and white photography is absolutely essential to the emotional compositions of each scene formulated by Welles, and he has an obvious mastery of the black and white filming technique. We see Kane as a young boy with his sled (hint), taken away from his home and brought up by a rich uncle (Everet Sloane). He becomes a principled newspaper owner and begins a campaign to become a major politician. Highly recommended, even it is not the best movie of all time.

The City of God (Brazil) - 2002 - directed by Fernando Meirelles and Katia Lund and starring Alexandre Rodrigues as Firecracker, an adult, who tries to avoid life among the street gangs of Rio and concentrate on photography, Luis Otavio, as Firecracker as a child growing up on the mean streets of Rio, Leandro Firmino as Little Joe, as an adult, a psychotic, violent street gang member, Douglas Silva as Little Joe as a child, growing up in the same mean streets as Firecracker, Phellipe Haagensen as Benny as an adult, a gang member who wants to go straight, Michel de Souza as Benny as a child, also growing up in the same mean streets, Matheus Nachtergaele as Carrot, another gang member, Su Jorge as Knockout Ted, the lady-killer of the gang, Alice Braga, a girlfriend of Benny, who used to be a girlfriend of Firecracker, Luiz Carlos Ribiero as an honest cop, Mauricio Maques as a corrupt cop, and Thiago Matins as a child leader of a child gang called The Runts.

The Class (France) – 2008 - Directed by Laurent Cantet and starring Francois Begaudeau as a French teacher and Department Chair, Carl Nanor as a transfer student, Esmeralda Ouertani as a class representative, Frank Keita as Souleymane, a student who needs to be disciplined, Rachel Regulier as Khoumba, a student who doesn't like to read, and Vincent Robert as Herve, the teacher in charge of sports.

Clockers - 1995 - Directed by Spike Lee and starring Harvey Keitel as a detective looking to solve a drug problem in a Brooklyn neighborhood, (might have been better cast as a drug dealer), John Tuturro as another cop on the case (but more convincing than Keitel), and a supporting cast of unknowns playing various hoodies, punks, drug dealers, and just plain neighborhood folks who try and survive day to day in extremely difficult circumstances. When there are daily drug deals going on in your immediate neighborhood, it is hard to have a normal, peaceful existence. Lee is very good at this kind of human drama, and he captures the frustrations of both the police and the decent citizens of the neighborhood. Recommended

Close Encounters of the Third Kind - 1977 - Directed by Steven Spielberg and starring Richard Dreyfuss as Roy. a hopeless electrician, Francois Truffaut as a serious scientist, Melinda Dillon as the ditzy new friend of Dreyfuss with her son Barry, Teri Garr as the mashed potato-making, suffering wife of Dreyfuss, and many strange looking, but friendly, aliens. This film was a huge success when it opened and, although nominated for a host of awards, won nothing but Best Cinematography because this film picked a tough year to get nominated; it was up against *Star Wars* and *Annie Hall*, both smash hits, as well.

Most of the tech awards went to *Star Wars* (understandably) and most the acting awards went to Annie Hall (smaller movies seem to do better than blockbusters when it comes to acting awards most of the time). Despite the lack of awards, the film was a gigantic box office hit and later came out with two additional editions of the original film. Spielberg, needless to say, is one of the craftiest directors in the business. He seldom makes a dull film, and this is one of his best. He knows how to use his actors as props and is not really concerned about character development. In that way, he is quite similar to Alfred Hitchcock, who also thought of actors as mere props who were secondary to the story. And make no mistake, Spielberg makes this story the star of the film and not the actors. This is a must see film and one of the best sci-fi films of all time.

Coal Miner's Daughter - 1980 - Directed by Michael Apted and starring Sissy Spacek and Tommy Lee Jones. Spacek plays Loretta Lynn, the famous country and western singer and won the Academy Award for Best Actress for that year. Tommy Lee Jones plays her husband, and has a far less sympathetic role. The film is aptly directed by Michael Apted, who keeps the development of Lynn's life in a fairly nice order, while putting the supporting cast through the appropriate paces in a seamless fashion. The musical numbers are handled very well, and we get the impression that Sissy Spacek can really sing well (even though all of her songs are dubbed). The technical production values of the film are far above average in relation to most Hollywood films. The music is first-rate, and is matched by exceptional performances from almost everyone in the cast. Jones is willing to play second banana and does not try to steal any scenes from Spacek.

The supporting cast does a wonderful job of filling in all the various characters associated with the music business and the Grand Ole Opry. I don't particularly care for country and western music, but I found this film to be captivating. It is not, as some critic from the New York Times mentioned, Carrie with an Annie Oakley cowboy dress. The same guy said that Johnny Cash looked more like a mortician than a singer with all his black clothing. What a snob. This is an inspiring story regardless of how you may feel about country and western music, and Spacek richly deserved her award. I can recommend this film to everyone without reservation.

Coherence – 2014 - Directed by James Ward Byrkit and starring a cast of unhearalded and inexperienced actors that handle the interesting script with dexterity. The plot of a comet that causes dinner party participants to experience odd occurances seems a bit like a *Twilight Zone* episode (and could have been one).

The Colditz Story (England)– 1957 ~ Directed by Ivan Foxwell and starring John Mills, Eric Portman, Frederick Valk, Ian Carmichael and Brian Forbes as Allied POWS in a supposedly escape-proof castle. This is a bit better than your average POW film, because Portman and Mills are fine actors, and one is never aware it is a film instead of an actual event. The supporting cast is also very competent, and the English have a way of creating atmosphere for POW films that is a bit more realistic than the usual Hollywood set. It probably comes from a lot of first-hand knowledge. The planning and execution of the escape makes for very interesting viewing.

The Collector – 1965 – Directed by William Wyler and starring Terrance Stamp, as a shy, retiring bank clerk, Frederick, who collects butterflies and young women, and Samantha Eggar, a twenty-year old college student who is the object of Frederick's desire. Both Stamp and Eggar give electrifying performances in this film, which will grab your attention from beginning to end. The tension produced by the film is primarily due to the substantial directing skills of William Wyler, who usually did not direct films from this genre. He was noted for Westerns, such as *The Big Country,* and blockbusters like *Ben-Hur.*

The movie goes off the deep end almost from the very beginning, and keeps you glued to your seat. It is probably one of the greatest Hollywood films ever made about obsessive love, and Frederick's character is mesmerizing. Wyler does a great job of keeping the viewer glued to the screen, because one never knows what is going to happen next. It is extremely refreshing to watch a story that is not a candy-cutting formula that Hollywood used to crank out on a consistent basis. A good story with well-developed characters always has more suspense than slasher films with nameless and emotionless villains.

The story begins with Frederick winning a substantial amount of money in the lottery and he goes about spending it on some very unusual hobbies. The viewer is repulsed and yet, fascinated, by his actions. When he kidnaps Miranda, we are repulsed, but when he makes every attempt possible to make up for what he has done, we begin to feel sorry for him a bit. We must trust in our original instincts. Recommended as a great study in abnormal psychology.

Colossus, the Forbin Project -1972- Directed by Joseph Sargent (my uncle), and starring Eric Braeden, Susan Clark and Gordon Pinsent as the prime and relatively unknown actors of a great screenplay written by James Brooks. This sci-fi tale of the future grabs you right from the beginning and holds your attention to the very end. This is a common trait of many Sargent movies as evidenced by such hits as the Taking of Pelham, One, Two, Three (which was so good they remade it many years later). This is not nepotism speaking here (I haven't seen my Uncle Joe since he moved to Hollywood from New Jersey down the Jersey Shore.)

The plot is straightforward and frightening; peace has gripped the world, but so has complete control of all human behavior. Computers monitor everything and the only way for humans to regain their relative freedoms is to free themselves from the computers. Sound familiar? Tell me more than a billion humans are not slaves to their cell phones and computers today. A tale far ahead of its time, and well done at that. Highly recommended.

The Color of Money - 1986 - Directed by Martin Scorcese and starring Paul Newman as Fast Eddie Felson and Tom Cruise as his young protégé, Vincent. Cruise and Newman don't seem to mix as well on the screen as did Cruise and another older actor, Dustin Hoffman, when that duo did *Rain Man*. Cruise tries to repeat his success in that film with a veteran actor with his efforts in this one, but The Color of Money doesn't quite stack up dramatically against *Rain Man*. That being said, the film is fine in its own right. This film also does not have the grit and atmosphere of *The Hustler*, which was appropriately filmed in black and white, and had a much edgier feel than this modern technicolor cool movie.

There is something about black and white photography that enhances places like pool halls, and there is something about color cinematography that somehow softens the desperation that is reeking in almost every one of them in the country. I can recommend this as a decent sequel and popcorn movie that is entertaining.

Comedian – 2002 - A documentary directed by Christian Charles that examines the life of an established comedian (Jerry Seinfeld) and a newcomer trying to break through the recognition barrier (Orny Adams). Some very incisive moments that show us how really difficult doing stand-up comedy can be. Recommended.

Command Decision – 1948 – Directed by Sam Wood and starring Clark Gable, Walter Pidgeon, Van Johnson and Brian Donlevy. The supporting cast included Charles Bickford, John Hodiak and Edward Arnold. Gable, Donlevy, Bickford and Pidgeon are all officers in charge of strategy and implementation of the Allied air strike forces and Johnson, Hodiak and others are the pilots who have to carry out both their sound, and not so sound ideas.

You can say what you like, but the job of the pilots was a lot more dangerous, and a lot more difficult than managing a game of stratego from behind a desk somewhere in a comfortable office. But someone had to take these cushy jobs, and we follow the gnashing of teeth, rationalizations, hemming and hawing of all four of the leading officers. To be fair, there was a great burden of responsibility on the shoulders of those who ordered thousands of others to great peril, but I would still rather be behind a comfortable desk, instead of having flak shot at me by desperate German defenders.

Commandos Strike At Dawn – 1942 - Directed by John Farrow (father of Mia Farrow) and starring Paul Muni as the leader of the commandos, Lillian Gish, his romantic interest (even thought she was getting a bit long in the tooth at this point in her career), Sir Cedric Hardwicke as the officer in charge of strategy, and Robert Coote as one of the commandos. The film is a bit dated, but that is quickly compensated for by the intensity and immediacy of the time period. Just about any war film made in 1942 always had great war atmosphere because it was going on during the filming. And that sense of immediacy was not the only thing one senses in films from this period. Things looked pretty bleak at this specific time in the war and you could sense the desperation in the film which only added to the production values. Muni is always intense, and though he seems a bit ill at ease in military situations, he still carries it off well. and he not to the extent where they interfere with the enjoyment of the story.

Compulsion - 1959 - Directed by Richard Fleischer (in a film that was tailor-made for Hitchcock), and starring Bradford Dillman as Artie Strauss and Dean Stockwell, who always does a professional job, as

Judd Steiner, Artie's co-conspirator. Also appearing in the film is Orson Welles and E. G. Marshall as opposing attorneys. You really couldn't do any better for the casting of the entire production. The heavyweight actors here are the attorneys, and it shows about halfway through the film.

The director does what he can to rein in Welles, but that was a difficult job. Hitchcock would have been a much better choice for direction of this film, but there were complications, and he did not get the assignment. The movie does suffer a bit from rather frugal production values, but not to the extent where they interfere with the enjoyment of the story. The film is a disturbing, callous look at the perversions of class privilege. It examines how two, rich, spoiled, young men, with a bit too much time on their hands, take advantage of their class position to commit an apparently senseless murder of someone they really don't care about. I thought the film was well-done. Recommended.

Conan, The Barbarian - 1982 - Directed by John Milius and starring Arnold Schwartzenegger as Conan, James Earl Jones as Thulsa Doom (great name), hot Sandahl Bergman as Valaria, and Gerry Lopez as Subotai , an archer. Akiro, played by Mako, is also effective as a wizard. The film is ably directed by Milius at a crisp pace and the audience is never given time to go fetch a bag of popcorn. The cinematography and music are first-rate as are the production values, which keep pace with the story line. The music sound track is considered one of best ever produced, and is still popular to this day.

Although it is fairly obvious that Arnold cannot act very well in this, one of his first films, he is still quite watchable, and the action more than makes up for the unbelievable delivery of some lines. And did I mention that Sandahl Bergman is completely SMOKIN HOT as Valaria and the romantic interest for Conan? I cannot understand why Sandahl Bergman never became a Hollywood sex symbol because she sure had a great start as the female centerpiece of this sword and Sandahl classic. Arnold is almost laughable as an actor, but his physical presence made up for some things he was lacking such as English and a range of emotions. James Earl Jones is the only legitimate actor in this film, but it really doesn't matter because the eye candy is so filling. I highly recommend this film in an uncut version.

Confessions of a Dangerous Mind – 2003- Directed by George Clooney and starring Sam Rockwell as Chuck Barris, a game show host who allegedly was also a spy, Micheal Cera as the very young Chuck Barris, Drew Barrymore as Penny Pacino, a teenage friend of Barris, who later becomes his girlfriend, George Clooney as Jim Byrd, a CIA agent who recruits Barris as an assassin, Julia Roberts as Patricia Watson, a seductive CIA agent, Rutger Hauer as Keeler, a German-American spy who becomes friends with Barris, Jerry Weintraub as Larry Goldberg, the President of the American Broadcasting Company (ABC), and two amusing cameo appearances by Brad Pitt and Matt Damon as contestants on the *Dating Game* TV show. The rest of the supporting cast is highly competent in delivering their contributions to the production.

Confessions of an Opium Eater - 1962 -Directed by Albert Zugsmith and starring Vincent Price as the alter ego of author Thomas DeQuincey, a confirmed opium addict. DeQuincey was a master of the horror genre and the equal of Poe. Price, though a bit hammy, is ably supported in the cast by Richard Loo of *Barney Miller* fame and Philip Ahn, the Master from the *Kung Fu* TV series. Fun to watch.

Contact – 1997 – Directed by Robert Zemeckis and starring Jody Foster, Matthew McConaughey, and Tom Skerritt in the lead roles for a sci-fi flick that falls well short of its lofty goals. Aliens are sending us radio messages to build a machine. I want to thank one of my readers for giving me more insight into this film. It was not as good as I had wanted it to be. The actors are fine, the idea is good, but the weak director (he was a comedy guy), and execution of the scenes, guarantee a mediocre result.

The Conversation - 1974 – Directed by Francis Ford Coppola and starring Gene Hackman, John Cazale, Allen Garfield and Cindy Williams. With half the cast highly experienced comedians, this film could have easily gone wrong without the script and direction of Coppola. The director uses his sure-handed touches to make sure that the gravity of the film is kept at a high pitch and that the actors stay in character. Cazale, of course, is an old Coppola hand from the Godfather trilogy and knows exactly what the director wanted in each scene. Garfield is miscast, as is Williams. But the high-powered Hackman is easily able to overcome these small setbacks in every scene he is in. Hackman is the consummate Hollywood actor. He is able to be anyone, anytime and make you believe it 100%. He Is a male version of Meryl Streep. His range is amazing and his delivery is always on the money.

Cool Hand Luke –1967 -Directed by Stewart Rosenberg and starring Paul Newman, George Kennedy and Strother Martin. Newman plays Luke, a lovable loser who supposedly inspires the convicts that he associates with. If prison were as much fun as it is depicted in this film, then more people would go there voluntarily. However, despite that fallacy, the film is highly entertaining and both Kennedy and Martin give sound performances. Everyone still remembers Martin's famous line "What we have here is a failure to communicate" which has become part of the American lexicon. The film does show some of the excesses of the prison system on the negative side, but we are overwhelmed with the spirit of the inmates during the egg-eating contest and in other scenes. Despite the overly-comedic aspect of the film, and the fact that it does not stack up well against real chain gang films like *I am a Fugitive From a Chain Gang* with Paul Muni, I still give it a modified recommendation just because it is fun.

The Counterfeiters (Germany) - 2007 - Directed by Stephan Ruzowitsky and starring a cast of B actors riding a great script and storyline to a suspenseful conclusion. Director Ruzowitsky does a masterful job. The story about the Nazis using POWs to counterfeit the British Pound is true. The film has a definite feel of authenticity to it; sometimes difficult for modern films about World War 2 to obtain. Recommended.

The Count of Monte Cristo - 1934 - Directed by Rowland V. Lee and starring Robert Donat, Elissa Landi and Louis Calhern. This film later spawned many imitations. The timeless story by Alexandre Dumas tells about the loyal Edmond Dantes who is entrusted with a secret letter from Napolean to be delivered to mysterious man in Marsailles. Both Dantes and the letter are intercepted and Dantes is imprisoned for eight years. Dantes flees the prison in a daring escape at sea posing as a corpse. He finds a treasure bequeathed to him by a fellow prisoner on a deserted island called Monte Cristo. He now has a fortune behind him to wreak his revenge on those who falsely imprisoned him. A great popcorn movie.

Country Teachers (China) - 1994 - Directed by He Qun and starring Li Baotian, Ju Xue, Xiu Zongdi, and Wang Xueqi. In the mold of Not One Less, this film deals with a dedicated country teacher in the outlying areas of China. As everyone in China knows, Chinese teachers in the countryside really don't want to be there most of the time. They are usually the lowest academically rated students in their classes; the better ones all opting to teach in or near a major city. What happens, as is shown in this film, is that despite the agenda of wanting to teach in a better place, country teachers are often affected by the students they are currently with. They become empathetic with the needs and concerns of these country students, and soon put their own desires on the back burner. This film is very incisive when it comes to showing this phenomena. I can recommend it highly.

Creature From the Black Lagoon - 1954 - Directed by Jack Arnold and starring a cast of B actors headed by Richard Carlson. This film is one of the icons of 1950s horror, and was made on a very low budget. It shows what you can do with a simple script and an interesting monster. Worth seeing and still one of the champions of the B films. Obviously the model for *The Shape of Water* over a half century later.

Crime of Passion - 1957 - Directed by Gerd Oswald and starring Barbara Stanwyck and Jan Sterling as a smoking hot duo in a classic film noir. The chemistry between Stanwyck and Sterling is palatable, and the dialogue is crisp. A real gem in the rough.

Crimes and Misdemeanors - 1989 - Written and Directed by Woody Allen and staring Allen and a highly talented cast including: Martin Landau, as a cold-blooded murderer (but with just cause), Claire Bloom, Mia Farrow, Anjelica Huston, Jerry Orbach and Sam Waterson. Allen is at the top of his game here in both writing and movie-making. There are plenty of funny lines, but it is also a serious film. The film is mesmerizing from start to finish and I can recommend it heartily.

The Crimson Pirate -1952 - Directed by Harold Hecht and starring Burt Lancaster and some woman with red hair. This was one of my favorite films that I enjoyed watching over and over again on Million Dollar Movie. Lancaster hams it up big time and uses all his circus know-how for thrilling somersaults and trapeze-type entrances and departures. Flynn and Fairbanks had nothing on Burt. Lancaster was born to play a pirate. Highly recommended.

Crisscross - 1949 -Directed by Robert Siodmak, who had previously made the hit film noir classic The Killers with Burt Lancaster, who also stars in this film with Yvonne DeCarlo and Dan Duryea. Although this film is not up to the level of *The Killers*, it is not too bad in its own right. The story centers on a daylight heist of a armed truck and all the double-crossing that goes on afterwards. The plot, except for the romantic interest of Yvonne DeCalro, is quite believable and well-staged by the director. Lancaster was unhappy about the romantic storyline with DeCarlo as a subplot, and I agreed with him 100%. It was totally unnecessary, and detracted from the suspense of the main plot, which was the heist, the double-cross and the revenge. Despite the small romantic glitch (there always had to be a girl in the movie in the old days), the film passes muster, and I recommend it without reservation.

Crocodile Dundee (Australia) - 1986 - Directed by Peter Faiman and starring Paul Hogan as Dundee, and Linda Kozlowski as his well-matched love interest, Sue Charlton. This is the ultimate fish out of water film. The movie was a sensation in the US and number one at the box office in the world for 1986. First, Sue comes to Australia to view Dundee in action with the crocs and the local natives, and then she becomes romantically involved with him, which is perfectly understandable, considering the wuss she was going out with at the time. Dundee is invited to New York, where he undergoes a series of fish out of the water adventures, the most famous of which is the unforgettable mugging scene where one of the punks brandishes a switchblade and advises the couple that he has a knife; Dundee pulls out his enormous Bowie knife and utters the famous line " Now that's a knife" and slashes the punk's jacket. I will not reveal the end of the film, but the pleasure of this movie is in the trip, not the destination.Recommended.

Crossfire – 1947 – Directed by Edward Dmytryk and starring Robert Mitchum, Robert Young , Robert Ryan and Gloria Grahame. I understand there was a great deal of confusion whenever anyone on the set yelled out "Bob!" This was the second film from this year to deal with the subject of anti-Semitism; the first being *Gentleman's Agreement* starring Gregory Peck. Both Ryan and Grahame were nominated for best supporting roles, and this film became the first B movie to be nominated for Best Picture (although some of the A films in the past that were nominated could easily qualify as B films in my opinion).

   The film is more of a message movie than it is a taut film noir drama of crime and punishment. Despite being a bit preachy, the acting in the film is so strong (particularly that of Ryan) that it transcends it's B movie plot and rises to the top of dramatic performances from that year as evidenced by its Oscar nominations. I recommend it, even though it is a bit dated.

Cross of Iron - 1977 - Directed by the sensitive hand of Sam Peckinpaugh and starring James Coburn, Maximilian Schell, James Mason and a relatively hot Senta Berger. This is a tale of the war from the German point of view, and Schell is ok at playing a Nazi, but James Mason was born for these kinds of roles, as evidenced in previous hits of his like the *Desert Fox* and *Desert Rats*. Mason was just about the most believable Nazi ever on the screen. He was coldblooded and wore the roles like the leather gloves he always wore. Worth seeing for Mason alone.

Crouching Tiger, Hidden Dragon (China) - 2000 – Directed by Ang Lee and starring Chow Yun-Fat, Michelle Yeoh, Zhang Ziyi, and Chang Chen. This film won Best Film of the year at the Academy Awards for 2000. It also became the highest grossing foreign film in American history. Ang Lee shows us the great promise he had as a director by making each scene a thing of beauty, and completely gets our attention. Lee is also a master of pacing, and is able to keep the action flowing as steadily as a mountain stream. The technical production values of the film are first-rate and deserved all the awards they won at the Academy Awards.

   Zhang Ziyi catapulted to international fame as a result of this film, and became the natural successor to Gong Li as the leading young Chinese actress. American audiences were wowed by both the story and the special effects of the film. This movie began a parade of Chinese historical and mythical costume dramas that were eagerly consumed by the American public that was tired of the same old Hollywood fare that appeared on the screen, year in and year out. There had never been anything like this done before in either Hollywood or Hong Kong. I can recommend this film, which spawned dozens of copycat films, but could not capture the essence of the original.

Croupier (England) – 1999 – Directed by Mike Hodges and starring Clive Owen in one of his ground-breaking performances that helped launch his successful career. Owen gives a tour- de-force performance that grabs the audience from beginning to end and does not let go. He appeared to be born for this role and does a masterful job. The casino sequences are very realistic and well done. Highly recommended.

Crumb -1995 – Directed by Terry Zwigoff (no relation to Gary Dalgoff) and starring several Crumbs from the family. This talented cartoonist was a big hit in the 60s, but then faded into obscurity after a decade or so. Interesting to see his development. and this film highlights that with great accuracy.

The Crying Game – (England) - 1992 – Directed by Neil Jordan, who also wrote the story and starring Stephan Rea as Fergus, an IRA regular, Forest Whitaker as Jody an IRA prisoner, and the lovely Jae Davidson as Jil, Jody's girlfriend, who now becomes Fergus' girlfriend after he promises to protect her. This is a very engaging film at two different levels. The director is able to involve us in *The Troubles* at its most basic elements, and yet is able to develop a secondary romance plot without any difficulty. This is not a simple task for any director to do. Some would say the romance plot supersedes the drama within the IRA, and this may be true, but both plots are carefully and skillfully constructed so that they intertwine and create greater tension. I can heartily recommend this film for its nice, tight ending. (no bun intended).

Cry, the Beloved Country - 1952 - Directed by Zoltan Korda and starring Canada Lee as Stephen Kumalo, Charles Carson as James Jarvis, and Sidney Poitier as Reverand Msimangu. This film is based on the novel of the same name by Alan Paton, and was remade as a major production in 1995. The older version, however, holds up very well and does not have the hindsight that is available for the 1995 film. Kumalo is a black Anglican priest from a rural town who is searching for his son in Johannesburg and finds that both his son and the son of a neighbor, James Jarvis, have met with several difficulties. I prefer the older version. It has a much greater sense of reality than the 1995 version and does not have the pat answers that the later film has because in 1952, there were no pat answers. I highly recommend this film.

Curse of the Golden Flower (China) = 2006 – Directed by Zhang Yimou and starring Chow Yun-Fat as Emperor Ping (his name means cold in Chinese), Gong Li as Empress Phoenix, Jay Chou as Prince Jai, Liu Ye as Crown Prince Wan and Qin Jugjie as Prince Yu. The emperor is the controlling father of Prince Jai. There are various soapy affairs between all the leading actors and actresses, but these are quite secondary in the plot and in the enjoyment of the film. The real star of the film is the spectacualar special effects, none of which were spared for this film, because of the success of previous Chinese epics in the US. The battle scenes are spectacular and the costume design is cutting edge. Unfortunately, the technical aspects of the film dominate, and the performances are secondary. This is why the film was pretty much ignored by the Academy Awards in the Best Foreign Film category; it wasn't even nominated. But it did get nominated for Costume Design. Despite its flaws, I can recommend this film with slight reservations.

Cyrano deBergerac-1950 – Directed by Michael Gordon and starring Jose Ferrer in his Academy-Award winning role as Cyrano. Blank verse poetry translated by Brian Hooker from the original work, was used as the primary dialogue in the film. Mala Powers as Roxanne and William Prince as Christian, are also prominent in the production. Gordon could have failed with this vehicle in a half dozen different ways, but managed to avoid the various pitfalls and produced a highly entertaining film.

Producing a classic literary film for mass audiences, particularly in blank verse, and then expecting it to make a lot of money at the box office is a very big risk, indeed. But because of the tremendous strength of the story, which is universal in nature, the film succeeds at every level. Many of us have been in such a situation on a more basic level. Millions of people have had good friends fix them up with dates, and sometimes you actually fall for the person you set the date up with. The movie is fueled by a superlative performance by Ferrer, who richly deserved the Academy Award which he won. Mala Powers is properly seductive in her role and appears, at first, to be well out of the range of dating consideration for someone who looked as ridiculous as Cyrano. But as we quickly learn from the film, once cannot judge people by appearances alone. Cyrano is a dynamo of human emotion and intelligence and that intelligence comes blazing through his elegant and romantic speeches. How could Roxanne deny such a powerful emotional thrust? Recommended.

D

The Damned (Italy) - 1969 - Directed by Luchino Visconti and starring Dirk Bogarde, Ingrid Thulin, Helmut Griem, Helmut Berger and Charlotte Rampling, who is perfectly cast in this film. This film is a fascinating look at the excesses and surrealistic lives of high Nazi officials during the Nazi era in Germany before and during WW2. The film follows the Essenbecks (a very thinly disguised substitution for the powerful Krupp family) on their gradual rise and importance within the Nazi party. The family's patriarch is murdered on the night of the Reichstag Fire. This immediately sets the audience up to be sympathetic to the Krupps. The miseries continue for the Krupps as fanatical Nazis take over every aspect of the company and rid the family of anyone who even remotely opposes them. The film is very incisive on how even a powerful moral native German company is unable to withstand the assault of Nazi fanaticism. I can recommend this film very highly as a good historical reference to the inability of the German industrial complex to withstand unreasonable political demands before and during WW2.

Damn Yankees - 1958 - Directed by George Abbott and starring Tab Hunter, in one of his few palatable films as Joe Hardy, the young Senator phenom who threatens the Yankees, Gwen Virdon, as the devil's temptress, Lola, and Ray Walston as the lovable devil, Applegate. The story has a middle-aged Washington Senator's fan moaning about how the Senators are already out of the pennant race in May. The fan would sell his soul to the devil to beat the Yankees. The devil makes a deal with him and changes him into a young phenom who carries Washington into first place. I will not reveal the ending of the film, but it is quite satisfying in its own way. As a rabid Yankee fan, I enjoyed this film immensely because it shows even if you sell your soul to the devil, the Yankees will still win the pennant. Highly recommended.

Dances With Wolves- 1990 -Directed by Kevin Costner, who also stars in the film along with Mary McDonnell as Stands With Fist, a blue-eyed Indian woman, Graham Greene as Kicking Bird, Rodney Grant as Wind in His Hair, and various real Indians as real Indians. Costner does even a better job of directing the film than he does acting in it, although he does a splendid job in that area as well. His character Dunbar is a victim of war burnout; it really doesn't matter what war we are talking about, all burnout victims of war have universal symptoms. Too much time at the front lines, too much time away from home, too much battle fatigue, and a gradual degrading of the senses until one feels almost nothing of the world. Costner captures all of these emotions and more in his portrayal, which not overtly stated in the film, and is truly an anti-war movie. This film won best picture and a number of other Oscars. Great story. I recommend it.

Danton - 1983 - Directed by Andrzej Wajda and starring Gerard Depardieu as Danton and Anne Alvaro as Eleonore . The story revolves around the French Revolution and the *Reign of Terror*. It supposedly draws a parallel to the revolution in Poland against the Soviet Union, but I couldn't make the connection. Danton is a leading figure in the French Revolution. After creating the fall of the monarchy, he set about the *Reign of Terror*, beheading all those related to the monarchy, serving the monarchy or anyone who benefitted from the monarchy. Basically, he was on witch hunt for anyone who was not a revolutionary, which was probably more than 90% of the population. In the end, he turned out to be more corrupt than many of the people he had executed, and appropriately was beheaded himself in 1794. This was an object lesson in absolute power corrupting absolutely, and I enjoyed the trip through the film, although I still can't figure out how it was supposed to be connected to the Polish uprising against the Soviet Union. Recommended.

Dao Ma Zai (The Horse Thief) (China) – 1986 – Directed by Tian Zhuangzhuang (can you possibly get a better name than that?) and starring Daiba, Iiji Dan, Drashi, and Gaoba. The cinematography for this film is outrageous. How they could have made so many great shots on such a low budget boggles my mind. The simple story revolves around a Tibetan horse thief name Norbu, who after his crime is discovered, is cast out of the tribe to wander on his own with his wife and child. Norbu vows never to steal again, but because of the harsh poverty he has suffered, he if forced to steal again. I will not reveal the end of the film, but I truly admired the way the director was able to convey so much with so little dialogue. It was precisely the object lesson I try and teach my film students; more visuals and less dialogue. I can see why Scorsese put it on the top of his list for the 80s. Visually, there are few films to match it. I highly recommend the film.

Dark Command – 1940 - Directed by Raoul Walsh and starring John Wayne as Bob Seton, a union supporter who opposes Cantrell, Walter Pidgeon as Cantrell, the renegade raider, and Claire Trevor as the object of desire of both men. The plot is interesting and shows Cantrell as a peaceful teacher in a small Kansas town married to Claire Trevor's character, Mary McCloud. Cantrell is actually neither a Confederate nor a Union man, just an opportunist. He captures a load of Confederate uniforms in a raid, and decides to try and pass for a Confederate officer. Mary's younger naïve brother, Flecth, played convincingly by Roy Rogers, joins Cantrell believing he is a real Confederate officer. Eventually, Roy, Wayne and Claire all escape to town to warn them of an impending raid by Cantrell and we have a lively finale. Of course the outcome of the Hollywood version is quite different from the realities of the real raid where the entire town is massacred by Cantrell. Recommend with historical reservations.

Dark Days – 2000 – Directed by Marc Singer (documentary) – This is a stark vision of masses of people living underground in Manhattan because they are homeless and underserved by the American social services. Some unforgettable scenes.

Dark Journey – 1937 – Directed by Victor Saville and starring Conrad Veidt and Vivien Leigh (just before her role in GWTW). This ageless story of women falling in love with the wrong man never gets tired. A non-aligned Swede falls for a German during the war. Will she choose the man or the war? Interesting.

Dark Matter - 2008 - Directed by Chen Shi-Zheng and starring Liu Ye as a young, talented PHD candidate who is being shafted by his PHD committee because he has a theory that doesn't jibe with the majority. Aidan Quinn plays the evil Department Chair and Meryl Streep plays an unsuccessful ombudsman on Liu's behalf. The film has a shattering climax. I have seen cases like this in real life at Columbia. Recommended.

Dark Mirror – 1946 – Directed by the crafty Robert Siodmak and starring Olivia DeHaviland, Lew Ayres and Thomas Mitchell (always the trusty old Irishman) in the lead roles. This great piece of film noir has DeHaviland (who plays schizophrenic effortlessly), as a tantalizingly psychotic set of twins who must be correctly separated; one is a psychopath and the other is "almost normal" (whatever that means). Watch Ayres use all his tricks to do it. Recommended. Ayres, by the way, was banned from the film industry during WW2 because of his Conscientious Objector status.

Dark Victory – 1939 - directed by Edmund Goulding and starring Bette Davis as Judith, a devil-may-care Long Island socialite who smokes, drinks and lives hard, George Brent, as Freddy Steele, the doctor who falls in love with her, and stays with her to the end, and a horribly miscast stable hand named Humphrey Bogart, who loves Judith from afar. There is absolutely zero romantic attraction between Davis and Bogart, and it shows on the screen from the first second they are together. They had appeared quite successfully in a previous film together, *The Petrified Forest*, which was a big hit, but Davis' romantic interest was obviously Leslie Howard, and not Bogart.

An odd thing about both these great actors was that they had to be paired with the right man or woman, or they were absolutely wretched in any romantic scenes. Davis was more comfortable with British actors such as Claude Rains and, in particular, George Sanders, who co-starred with her over a half a dozen times, with a perfectly matching cool personality. Bogart, on the other hand, really only looked believable with the opposite sex a few times; with Lauren Bacall and with Ingrid Bergman. Somehow, he made us believe that he and Katherine Hepburn were in love in *African Queen*. But outside of those three actresses, can you really name another film he was a memorable romantic lead in? I can recommend the film despite its soapy appearance, because Davis is such a great actress.

Das Boot (Germany) -1981 - Directed by the talented Wolfgang Petersen and starring an unknown cast following a great script, a great sound track and a great director. How could you go wrong viewing the film? About the rise and fall of the German Submarine Corps and one sub in particular. Recommended.

Das Experiment (Germany) - 2001 - Directed by Oliver Hirshbiegel and starring an unknown cast that does a terrific job. The true story here is the real star. Shocking and sobering story about using prisoners for experiments in Germany. You would have thought that the Germans would have learned their lesson from WW2.

David Copperfield- 1935 -Directed by George Cukor and starring Freddie Bartholomew, Basil Rathbone, Edna May Oliver, Elizabeth Allan, Lionel Barrymore, W.C. Fields, Maureen O'Hara, and Lewis Stone (Judge Hardy). This is the classic Charles Dickens novel come to the screen. A few episodes in David's life are left out, but without much damage to the screenplay. We follow David and his unfortunate encounters with his stepfather, who eventually sends him to a boarding school in Salem. His mother dies, and he is recalled from the boarding school to work in his stepfather's factory. There, he is in misery until he runs away to Dover.

He grows to manhood and marries Dora, but she dies soon after the marriage. He remarries with a woman, Agnes, who has secretly loved him and they live happily ever after. Dickens has a way of making his good guys come to a good end and the bad guys come to a bad end, which fit very nicely with the needs of Hollywood film producers. I can recommend this film highly.

The DaVinci Code - 2006 - Directed by Ron Howard, which may be one of the few cases in Hollywood history where a director is miscast, although he was extremely talented for many of his other films, and starring Tom Hanks (another miscasting problem), as Robert Langdon, a Harvard University symbologist (sorry, I didn't buy Hanks as a PHD from Harvard), Audrey Tautou as Sophie, a cryptographer from France (her I bought), Sir Ian McKellen as Sir Leigh Teabing (perfect casting), Alfred Molina as Bishop Manual, Jean Reno as Captain Bezu Fache, and Paul Bettany as the Opus Dei monk, Silas, who almost steals the movie from everyone else with his eclectic performance. Nice fast-paced entertainment.

Davy Crockett, King of the Wild Frontier -1955 – Directed by Norman Foster and starring Fess Parker as Davy. I can guarantee you that this film is not among the top 700, 1000, or even 2000 films ever made, all of which I have written books on. However, it will always be in my top 700, 1000 and 2000 film lists because it is both an icon of my childhood and an icon of the Disney studios. You could take the last 100 Disney productions combined, and it would not come close to the impact that this film had on the youth of America in the 1950s. Buddy Ebsen as Georgie Russell, also does a great job as Davy's sidekick in this film. Ebsen was not the world's best supporting actor, either, but he brings us a sympathetic Georgie with a good sense of humor. It's all there in glorious technicolor; the fringe clothing that set a style for men and women, in the 1960s (and Jon Voight in *Midnight Cowboy*), the coon-skin cap, and the Bowie knife which took up almost half the screen when it was unsheathed. Crocodile Dundee was NOT the first guy in film to wield a bowie knife; that honor would go to Davy Crockett (or more accurately, Jim Bowie, who was in charge of the Alamo). The music, of course, is unforgettable. Anyone who has not heard of the Ballad of Davy Crockett has to be very young, indeed. Disney Studios has a great knack of keeping these types of songs current through repeated airings of the film on the Disney Channel. By the way, if you did not have a coon-skin cap in the 1950s as a boy, you were a social outcast. Highly recommended for children of all ages.

Dawn Patrol - 1938 - Actioner directed by Edmund Goulding and starring Errol Flynn, David Niven and Donald Crisp. The supporting cast includes Basil Rathbone for good measure. About the early days of air combat. Some harrowing moments and recommended.

Dawson City: Frozen Time – 2017 – Directed by Bill Morrison and starring the Gold Rush members of the old Dawson City boomtown. A million to one shot at being recovered; original prints from the actual events that took place in the town. Amazing.

The Day After Tomorrow – 2004 - Directed by Roland Emmerich and starring Dennis Quaid as Jack Hall, a climate expert, Jake Gyllenhaal as his son, Sam, Ian Holm as Terry Rapson, a climate expert from Scotland, and Emmy Rossum as Laura, a friend of Sam. The story is rather simple; that global warming is bad and that it will cause great storms to take place as well as other cataclysmic changes. Everyone from the North Is trapped in their houses and everyone wants to go South at the same time. I used to do this when I lived in New York and went to Florida for three months every year. It is a better-than-average science-fiction yarn.

Day For Night –France - 1973 – Directed by Francois Truffaut and starring Jackie Bisset and Jean-Pierre Leaud. This is the classic movie-within-a-movie film. The movie is the most important star in the film. Filming the movie, acting in the movie, directing the movie, editing the movie and solving various problems that come up in the movie is what this film is really about. It is a visual love letter to film-making. The meaningless love affairs, fights, friendships and all other human emotional events that take place pale in comparison to the actual completion of the film itself.

Although we follow the ups and downs of the characters that engage us, we are constantly aware that the most important thing in the world is getting this film in the can. This film was on my top 100 list for many years until finally getting pushed over the 100 mark by upcoming films, but it is still a great film. I recommend it highly.

Day of the Falcon (Black Gold) – 2013- Directed by Jean-Jacques Annaud and starring Mark Strong and Antonio Bandaras (the best role he has ever done) and a solid supporting Arab cast. This film is a fitting sequel to *Lawrence of Arabia*. It humanizes Arabs and Muslims, and illustrates the problems of tribal unity in the Mideast (similar to *Lawrence of Arabia*). The only drawback to the film was the use of two Westerners in lead roles, but that was probably due to the lack of talent among Arab actors currently in the market. The last great Arab actor that anyone could name was Omar Sharif; there hasn't been anyone to replace him. Great action sequences, tragic story line, good script, and a solid director make this an A film in my opinion. See for yourself.

Day of the Jackal – 1973 - Directed by Fred Zinneman and and starring a low-cost cast including Edward Fox and Michael Lonsdale. This film is not about the stars or their personas, it is about the compelling story of an assassination plot of Charles DeGaulle, the WW 2 leader of France and afterwards. The film traces the unrest caused by DeGaulle giving independence to Algeria, and the militant underground organization, the OAS, that decides that DeGaulle must be eliminated.

Days of Glory – 2006 - (France) - Directed by Rachid Bouchareb and starring Roschoy Zem, Samy Naceri, Jamel Debbouze, and Sami Boujila as four friends who fight all their lives against some type of enemy. When they are young, they fight against poverty and discrimination. In the military, they fight the enemy and still face discrimination. When they resume their lives, they make adjustments to an unfair society; especially the character played by Debbouze. Fascinating to watch and highly recommended.

Day of the Triffids (England) -1963 -Directed by Steve Sekely and starring Howard Keel (who does not sing in this). The real stars of the film are the triffids, intelligent plants that try to take over the world. Very cool sci-fi from John Wyndham (who originally had SIX family names before settling on John Wyndham). I almost expected Howard Keel to break out into song about the Triffids, but fortunately, he held back his desires.

Day the Earth Stood Still - 1951 - Directed by Robert Wise, who had planned to have Gort sing "Santa Claus is Coming to Town" as a metaphor for Klaatu. The film, which is the ultimate classic fifties science-fiction movie, stars Michael Rennie as Klaatu, Frank Conroy as Harley, the President's secretary (Truman was busy with the Korean War, so he couldn't come to see Klaatu), Patricia Neal as Helen Benson, whose husband was killed in WW 2 and her son, Bobby, played by Billy Gray. Every kid in the audience imagined him or herself being the kid that meets the alien.

The story begins with an alien ship landing in Washington, DC. First a robot emerges from the ship and, naturally, the overaggressive American troops fire upon it. They get what they deserve when the robot disintegrates them in one second. Now the US and the rest of the world realize that the visitors mean business, and begin to take a bit more of a reasonable stance. Klaatu comes out of the ship and give an impassioned speech about peace and a united world. The American audience listens intently then figures they can shoot him easier than the steely robot. After shooting Klaatu, the robot first disintegrates half the soldiers in the area, and then gently picks up the prone Klaatu and brings him into the ship, which has a very convenient life-restoring machine aboard (where you can you buy one of those? I'm getting old and I think I need one). This is a must see film and is included on almost every critic's top 100 list.

Days of Wine and Roses - 1963 - Directed by Blake Edwards and starring Jack Lemmon in an Academy Award nominated performance (that was very good, but no way nearly as good as Peter O'Toole for *Lawrence of Arabia* from that same year), Lee Remick, Charles Bickford and Jack Klugman. Joe Clay (Lemmon) meets and falls in love with Kirsten, a secretary. The two gradually descend into full-blown alcoholism. The film is reminiscent of *Lost Weekend* with Ray Milland, which also won an Academy Award for best actor. It seems the academy likes roles for alcoholics. *Weekend* was a superior film, and this one is not bad, but it is more reminiscent of something like Barfly, which was also relentlessly depressing.

Blake Edwards was far better known for doing a number of good comedies (especially the *Pink Panther* series), and he does not seem at ease in doing a 100% straight dramatic film, but he does the best he can and pulls it off. Bickford and Klugman (from *The Odd Couple* TV show) are fine supporting actors who never miss a beat, or a chance to steal a scene.

Dead End – 1937 – Directed by William Wyler and starring Humphrey Bogart, the Dead End Kids in their debut, Sylvia Sydney, Joel McCrea, Claire Trevor, and Wendy Barrie. This is one those cautionary tales that Hollywood was fond of making about the youth of America during the Depression. Crime Does Not Pay. Bogart, of course, is the poster boy for the bad guy in the neighborhood who is a hero to the kids who are poor. McCrea, as an honest working stiff, tries to steer the kids into the right direction, but is unsuccessful because they idolize Bogart. The real star of the film is the Dead End Kids, who completely take over the movie and begin a series of endless sequels (such as the Dead End Kids Meet_____(fill in name of monster here). The series of the Dead End Kids lasted longer than most acting careers, going well into the fifties when they became middle-aged adults. I can recommend this film because in this first film, the Dead End Kids are kept in line as actors and have to be serious in their roles. In all their later films, they are all much lighter in their approach to the subject matter.

Deadline at Dawn - 1946 - Directed by Harold Clurman and starring Susan Hayward in an early effort with Paul Lukas (good actor) and Bill Williams (not so good actor). Williams wakes up after an all-nighter with a hooker with a load of cash in his pocket (how come when I woke up in the same situation, I was broke?) Did he kill to get it? Would most guys really care? He looks for the owner of the money (yeah, that'll happen in real life) and finds more than he bargained for. Interesting, despite lightweight Williams.

Dead of Night (England) – 1946 - This film is a compendium of efforts from a number of directors guiding mostly unknown actors (with the exception of Michael Redgrave), in their efforts to enact fairly interesting short stores of horror. It has the distinct flavor of *Twilight Zone*, which copied one of the stories in this film (the one that give Kramer nightmares on *Seinfeld*). That would be the story of the living dummy. There are other interesting stories in the anthology including a premonition story of a bus crash, a ghost story with a sense of humor, a ghost story about a children's party, and all topped off with the concluding creepy dummy story.

Since this is the origin of the dummy story (I had thought it was in the *Twilight Zone* and used again for *Magic*), that was enough for me to check out the whole film. I can think of worse ways to spend a Friday night. Recommended.

Dead Poets Society – 1989 - Directed by Peter Weir, who is not usually noted for his comical touch, but with Robin Williams in your movie, you really don't have to do a lot of work in the humor area. The film stars Robin Williams as John Keating, an inspired English teacher, and Ethan Hawke, as the most notable student in a group under the guidance of Keating. Keating takes his students on a coming of age trip through the magic of poetry. Although Eastern poetry, such as *Tao Te Ching* and *Zhuangzi* is not mentioned, the film does a fine job giving Western poetry its proper place in society.

In my opinion, I believe this to be Robin William's best work, and he has had a number of successes. Williams was confident, erudite and empathetic without being cocky or sentimental. He gives the audience a great example of what a really good teacher can do in a classroom. The only teacher films I remember seeing that surpasses this one were *Goodbye, Mr. Chips* (Donat version) and possibly, Mr. Holland's Opus. That is pretty rarified country, and I can highly recommend this film to all without reservation.

Dead Reckoning - 1947 - Directed by John Cromwell and starring Humphrey Bogart and smoking hot Lizabeth Scott (I'm sure Bacall was thrilled). Marvin Miller of *The Millionaire* TV show is also featured in this film noir piece. There are more twists in this murder mystery than on a Chubby Checker album. Lots of fun.

Death of a Salesman - **1951** - Directed by Laszlo Bebedek and starring Fredric March as Willy, Mildred Dunnock as Mrs. Loman, Kevin McCarthy as Biff and Cameron Mitchell as Happy Loman. The film was based on the well-known play by Marilyn Monroe's husband (Arthur Miller). There have been many plays that have succeeded in film, but this one is a tough nut to crack, because audiences in the early fifties were filled with the American dream, and the notion of failure at all turns was not appealing to the masses.

   March, is of course, a first-rate actor, and he gave it his best shot, as did Dustin Hoffman in a later version. Both great actors wound up on the mat for the ten count when both films failed miserably at the box office. It may be professionally challenging to play Willy Loman, but, the poor producer who is trying to make money on a film can find a hundred better scripts than this if he wants to a have a good shot at having a hit. I can recommend the film for March's and McCarthy's performance, but the problem is that you are aware these are performances.

Death of a Scoundrel – England - 1956 - Directed and written by Charles Martin and starring George Sanders as the scoundrel, Sabourin, Zsa Zsa Gabor as pretty much herself, Yvonne DeCarlo as Miss Kelly, a shady lady, and Nancy Gates as a pretty secretary that Sanders considers a chippie shot. There were few, if any actors in the forties and fifties who could play the debonair raffish gentleman better than Sanders. His timing and delivery were ironclad.

   He was always a great A actor that had to settle for the best B actor roles for the majority of his career. In one way, he was a lot like Walter Brennan, who won numerous Best Supporting Actor awards because he was generally a better actor than the lead actors in many of his second banana films. Saunders fits that bill to a tee. He was the lead actor in this small film, but the vast majority of Hollywood roles he mustered generally found him to be a supporting actor who was more talented than most of his co-stars.

   Bette Davis recognized this right away, and made over a half-dozen films with Saunders over two decades. She was one of the few strong actresses who were strong enough on screen to do battle with Saunders, and they had great chemistry together as evidenced in *All About Eve*. Sanders was the ultimate lady's man in this film. He loves and betrays all of them and most deservedly needs to be killed by any one of them. Eventually, he is done in by one of them. I loved every second of this little, unpretentious movie. Even Zsa Zsa Gabor, that dahling who couldn't act her way out of a paper bag, was believable in this film (probably because she was playing herself, mostly). Sanders was just so outrageous that he was almost too good a bad guy to be true. He plays Gabor and the other ladies like violins, and laughs all the way to the bank. His audacious behavior is positively inspiring. This obscure film is rarely seen in DVD form and is occasionally aired on AMC. Tape it, if you can't get ahold of a DVD. This is a must see film for me, but for others, it might be considered just your average fare from England.

Not on anyone's top 100 list, except mine (that I know of). This is the kind of movie that should develop into a cult film.

Deathtrap – 1982 - Directed by Sidney Lumet and starring Michael Caine and Christopher Reeve. Dyan Cannon and various real-life film critics also have cameo performances. The clever film is about a playwright, Sidney Bruhl, played by Caine, who has had a bad string of Broadway productions (one in a row is a bad string of Broadway productions). Sidney is desperately seeking a hit (aren't we all) and is willing to do anything to achieve his ends; including murder. Enjoy it. Recommended.

Death Wish – 1974 - Directed by Michael Winner and starring Charles Bronson and Vincent Gardenia. This little film made a big splash with audiences all over America in 1974 because people were getting sick of the concept of Law and Order without the Order part being properly enforced throughout the country. Some critics thought this film was immoral because it portrayed vigilantism, and excessive punishment to criminals. The other 99% of the population could not have disagreed more with these critics; they loved it when Bronson laid into the criminal punks. This series lasted over twenty years with numerous copycat films, in addition to additional sequels for this financially successful series.

Bronson and Gardenia were perfect casting choices. Bronson as a reserved, understated businessman, who had no other desire than to go about his business, and Gardenia, as a hard-boiled, NYC detective who had seen it all as far as crime and punishment were concerned. The chemistry between the two is undeniable. Despite its violent concepts, the visceral gratification of seeing lowlifes get blasted away on the screen finally led to a real-life Kersey name Getz, who shot a number of black thieves on a subway in New York years later. Getz was eventually exonerated despite outcries from the black community. But the *Death Wish* series did not fixate on the black population. It was across the board racially. I recommend the film despite the overt violence because it correctly portrays the emotions of that time and place in New York.

Deconstructing Harry - 1997 - Written, directed and starring Woody Allen and a very strong supporting all-star cast. Unfortunately, the story is rather mundane and predictable, even with the dozens of dysfunctional characters in the film. Some say this was almost autobiographical, but it had the feel of been there and done that if you have seen all the other Allen films. Still recommended, because an average Allen film is superior to most others.

Deer Hunter – 1978-Directed by Micheal Cimino, who would go on to make the most expensive one-day movie in the history of Hollywood (*Heaven's Gate*, which also had a wedding scene that lasted longer than most marriages) and starring Meryl Streep, Robert DeNiro, Christopher Walken, John Savage, John Cazale and George Dzundza. This film is oddly broken down into two parts; a leisurely (to say the least) wedding scene, and some super-intense POW and Saigon gambling scenes. Naturally, I preferred the super-intense scenes.

This is Walken's best film ever. The film seemed to lose a little bit of steam at the end, but as a whole, it was still a very dynamic production. With a cast like this, it was virtually impossible to make a bad film. It really captured the ugly side of the Vietnam experience (is there any other side?) and it shows the effects of any war on any veteran who has been in one and survived, as evidenced by DeNiro's character,

Michael. The powerhouse cast also includes Meryl Streep, who gives a great performance as well. Unfortunately, solid B actors like John Savage, John Cazale, and George Dzundza get buried by the high-powered cast lead actors, but contribute as well to the overall production. The production values of the film are superior, particularly the Vietnam sequences. This film won Best Picture and Best Director of the year in the Oscar race for that year, and I would have highly recommended it if it hadn't won anything.

Deewaar – India - 1975- Directed by Yash Chopra and starring Amitabh Bachchan and Shashi Kapoor as rebels with a cause. This film established both of these stars as icons of Indian cinema. It also highlighted the political turmoil of India in the 70s. A must-see film.

Defending Your Life - 1991 - Written, directed and starring Albert Brooks with B actress, Meryl Streep (just being sarcastic here). Great to have the best actress on the planet as your co-star. Comedy about being judged on your life's deeds hits the spot. Highly recommended (I loved the candy on the pillow scene).

Deliverance – 1972 - Directed by John Boorman and starring Jon Voight, Burt Reynolds, Ned Beatty and Ronny Cox. The film is based on a novel by James Dickey, who combined with Boorman for the screenplay. Boorman has a genius for creating atmosphere, as evidenced by his success in his film *Excalibur*, when he perfectly reproduced the period of King Arthur with all the moody elements of the British countryside. He accomplishes the same feat for rural Georgia. Jon Voight, who was always solid in every film he made, is the lead character. Burt Reynolds, though playing his stereotype macho role, still turns in a decent acting performance. Ronny Cox is killed off early, so he doesn't get to do much. Ned Beatty, however, shows great range.. The film was nominated for three Academy Awards and is a must see movie.

Demetrius and the Gladiators - 1954 – Directed by Delmer Daves and starring Victor Mature, Ernest Borgnine, Susan Hayward, Micheal Rennie and a wildly out-of-control, over-the-top performance by Jay Robinson as the depraved emperor, Caligula. I also liked the scene of Micheangelo's David in the arena, which, as any eighth grade student will tell you, was created many centuries after these events supposedly occurred. But we do not go to movies for history lessons, or to see restrained acting. Victor Mature gives his usual sword and sandal performance as a beefcake movie hero, who enjoys baring his chest and killing inferior gladiators. Susan Hayward tries hard to overcome the lame script, but it is a hopeless fight for her, Micheal Rennie is completely wasted as a very good actor in a film that has no intention of using good actors.

    Daves does a very mediocre job as the director, and has practically no control of his actors. Robinson and Mature take turns hamming it up, and some of the scenes are downright embarrassing, but fascinating to watch. The toy lion scene is also very funny to watch. Demetrius wrestles with a supposed lion that is being photographed off camera, but on camera someone throws him a very large stuffed animal that resembles Pookie from the *Soupy Sales Show*. It is probably the funniest scene ever done in a serious movie. Demetrius goes on to "wrestle" the savage stuffed animal to the ground before killing him. If you don't laugh at this scene, there is something wrong with you. This film is a total no-brainer.

You just sit back, enjoy the scenery and action, and eat your popcorn; what could be better? Highly recommended at any level you like.

Deng Xiaoping: A Legend (2005) - (Documentary) – This made-for-TV documentary of China's greatest leader (yes, greatest leader; Mao was not that great) shows how Deng inherited the mess left behind by Mao Zedong after the Cultural Revolution and opened up China economically to reach heights that Mao never dreamed of. Recommended.

Dersu Uzala – 1975 - Mongolia - Directed by Akira Kurosawa and starring Maxim Munzuk as Dersu Uzala, a native guide to the wilds of Siberia, and Yuri Solomin as the Russian, Captain Arseniev, head of an expedition exploring the region. This exotic film looks at a subject rarely seen in American cinema; namely life in Siberia, which for the average American, conjures up visions of an icy wasteland. But this film shows us that far from being an icy wasteland, Siberia is a gorgeous, breathtaking, spectacle of nature that has some of the greatest forests and wildlife on the planet.

It also shows the depth of the character of the natives who live there as shown by the actions of Dersu. As an aging guide, Dersu is at first derided by his companions, but they quickly learn to respect and admire him in a very short time. I can highly recommend this film as great cinema; it won the Best Foreign Film Oscar for 1975, which was richly deserved.

Desert Fox – 1951 - Directed by Henry Hathaway and starring James Mason, Sir Cedric Hardwicke and Leo G. Carroll (*Topper*). This biopic of Rommel is not always accurate, but it is very interesting to watch. Rommel is defeated at El Alamein in 1942, and returns to Germany to recuperate from injuries received in the Afrika Korps. Rommel is put in charge of the defense at Normandy, but does not receive the men he requests to repulse the Allies attack because Hitler thinks it is only a false move. Rommel is approached by General Strollin, played by Hardwicke, as they go for a walk, or I guess in this case, a stroll. Strollin suggests they do away with the beloved Fuhrer before Germany goes completely down the tubes. Rommel is hesitant, so the plan to assassinate Hitler goes on without him. It fails and the repercussions are felt immediately all over Germany as numerous conspirators are jailed or executed. By this time, it is too late to save Germany, Rommel, or the Fuhrer from final destruction. Recommended as Mason gives a masterful performance.

Desert Rats – 1953 - Directed by Robert Wise and starring James Mason and Richard Burton. The 1951 version of *Desert Fox* was so successful at the box office that they had to make a thinly disguised sequel to it. This film resurrects Mason as Rommel from the 1951 film and adds Burton as Light Colonel MacRoberts, the English officer in charge of the Australian Volunteers (the English never really trusted any of their possessions to be in full charge of any large number of troops). There is no truth to the rumor that the title of this film was going to be The Hills Are Alive with a Bunch of Nazis. The spunky group of Australians holds out for over eight months in Torbruk under heavy pressure from the Afrika Korps and Rommel. The film covers a key battle at Torbruk, which would be the subject of a later film made in the sixties when poor box office was attributed to little interest in WW2 battles during the Vietnam War. This film shows the turning of the tide in the battle for control of the continent of Africa and is recommended.

Desperadoes -1943 - directed by Charles Vidor and starring Randolph Scott and Glenn Ford. This is a simple classic Western in which Sheriff Upton, played by Scott, maintains law and order in a small Utau town.

Desperate – 1947 - Directed by Michael Kraike and starring B actors, Steve Brodie and Audrey Long. This gritty little film show a simple story of an independent trucker named Steve Randall (this made it easier for him to remember his lines), who is hired for a job to haul freight (so far the story is plausible). When Steve picks up the freight, he finds out it is stolen goods. This would have been a good time to back out of the deal, but Steve goes ahead with the delivery, which does not bode too well when a cop is killed during the transaction. This is what happens when you make bad choices.

Desperate Hours —1954- Directed by William Wyler and starring Humphrey Bogart and Frederic March. This is a film about an escaped convict who holds innocent people hostage in a respected community. Bogart, predictably, is the escaped con, and Frederic March is the upstanding citizen in his household along with his faithful wife, lovely daughter, and adorable son. Bogart and two sleazy companions take over the house and make veiled threats to the family on several occasions.

This film is a reprise of Bogart's earlier great success, *Petrified Forest*, when he played Duke Mantee. This con, however, is not quite as sympathetic as Duke Mantee was. He is a bit less empathetic than the Mantee character, and does not really have the audience rooting for his getaway as Mantee did. The film is still effective as two pros like Bogart and March go through their roles effectively. After all, is there such a thing as a bad Bogart film? Recommended.

Desperately Seeking Susan – 1985 - Directed by Susan Seidelman and starring Rosanna Arquette and Madonna in an effective female buddy movie. It is about an unfulfilled surburban housewife from Fort Lee, New Jersey, who has a desire to take a walk on the wild side. Madonna, on the other hand, is pretty much just playing Madonna, but uses the name Susan. Actually, the movie could have just as easily been called Desperately Seeking Madonna, but the producers felt if they changed the name to Susan, that people might have thought the director was really cool instead of being a cold fish. Regardless of the name of the film, it is very entertaining to see a Jersey housewife make the transition from geek to cool. And Madonna is predictably very comfortable in front of the camera, which makes her character all that much more believable. This is a very entertaining film and I recommend it.

Destry Rides Again – 1939 - Directed by George Marshall and starring Marlene Dietrich as a bar room singer (there's a real stretch), and James Stewart as a tenderfoot lawyer who settles in a wild Western town. This fish out of water film is very funny from beginning to end. It has a great deal of energy and a wonderful script that is enthusiastically acted out by a sterling cast that includes Brian Donlevy as a bad guy saloon owner. Dietrich plays Frenchy (she doesn't look French), who is the moll of Kent, the unsavory saloon owner played by Donlevy. The town drunk is appointed sheriff, and sends for the son of a famous lawman, Tom Destry. Destry Jr. is a crack shot with a 45, but refuses to wear a gun. He eventually solves the town's problems with his brain, but still has to battle it out with Kent. Recommended.

Detective Story – 1951 - Directed by William Wyler, a master at making good B movies, and starring Kirk Douglas, Eleanor Parker, and co-starring one of my favorite undercard actors, William Bendix. This is film noir at its best. Lee Grant makes her debut in this film as a shoplifter. Douglas plays Detective McLeod, who has to wade hip-deep into the human cesspool that is the NY crime scene. He has to do this on a daily basis. Just about everyone in this film is a bit seedy. Mcleod, his wife, his bosses, his partner, his coworkers and, of course, all the petty slimeball lawbreakers. There is no real hero in the film to root for. So on that point, the film is pretty unsatisfying. But it does seem to mirror real life a lot better than most cop movies, because the cops are not perfect people in this one. So because of the reality of the film, I recommend it conditionally.

Detour —1946-Directed by Edgar G. Ulmer and starring Tom Neal, Ann Savage, and Claudia Drake in one of the best B movies ever made. Neal plays Al, a likable piano player hiking his way across the country to be with his girlfriend in California. The fact that Neal has no employable skills, and cannot even afford a ticket to the coast on a bus would indicate that he was not a very good catch, and that's why his girlfriend left him to go to California in the first place. Things only get worse.

Devdas - 1955 - Directed by Bimal Roy and starring Dilip Kumar (there are no White Castles in this film) and Suchitra Sen in the lead roles as star-crossed lovers. This classic highlights the Indian Caste system. A must-see film and a soap-lover's dream.

The Devil and Daniel Webster – 1941 - Also released with the title, *All That Money Can Buy*. Directed by William Dieterle and starring Walter Huston as the Devil, Edward Arnold in a rare sympathetic role as Daniel Webster, and James Craig, as the guy, Jabez Stone, who wants to get off easy after enjoying all the fruits of the devil. Director Dieterle was a master of atmosphere, as shown in his previous successes with the horror genre. Although this is not a horror movie in any sense of the word, it is a bit scary in spots, and the atmosphere created by Dieterle in many scenes of the film lends a very scary feeling to the viewer, even if one does not believe in the devil.

Arnold does a masterful job as the lawyer defending our poor victim, Jabaz. Arnold was noted for playing a variety of bad guys throughout his substantial career in Hollywood. This was a chance for him to be with the angels for a change. Walter Huston is positively delightful as the Devil. I never saw an actor have so much fun playing the Devil. This movie is not on the NY Times top 1000 list, and some may agree with that assessment, but not me. This film is on my top 100, but does not appear on too many other critics' top 100 list, but I can heartily recommend it.

Devils on the Doorstep (China) – 2000 — Directed by Jiang Wen and starring Jiang Wen as Ma Dasan, a local Chinese peasant, Kagawa Teruyuki, as a Japanese Sergeant, Yuan Ding, as a Chinese interpreter working for the Japanese, and Kenya Sawada, who has a grand old time as a cruel Japanese Captain. This is not the usual anti-Japanese films that China is famous for making. This one actually tries to get inside the head of the invaders and shows their human weaknesses. However, it does fall short of making the invading Japanese into any kind of sympathetic figure. They are still ruthless, cruel, and unfeeling toward their conquered opponents. Recommended as a much more accurate assessment of China's resistance to Japan than current Chinese propaganda TV or films.

Devil's Doorway – 1950 – Directed by Anthony Mann and starring Robert Taylor. Once again, Taylor is fortunate enough to have a solid director for a mundane Western plot. The whole film could have easily gone to Hell without Mann.

The Devil Thumbs a Ride - 1947 - Directed by Felix E Feist and starring the hard-boiled Lawrence Tierney as a killer, and poster boy for not picking up hitchhikers. Although the story bogs down, it is still fascinating to watch. Recommended with reservations.

The Devil Wears Prada – 2006 -- Directed by David Frankel and starring Meryl Streep as the intimidating Miranda Priestly, fashion magazine editor, and Anne Hathaway as Andy Sachs, as the recent college grad working as Priestly's assistant. In key supporting roles are Emily Blunt as the abrasive Emily, and the talented Stanley Tucci as the art director, Nigel. The film is a good-natured roasting of a Vogue editor. and dear friend of mine, Anna Wintour, who thought Streep did a wonderful job. This is actually a very interesting coming of age film that Hollywood rarely does.

With the exceptions of *The Graduate* and *My Favorite Year*, and possibly, the more recent *Me and Orson Welles,* there are scant films that do the coming of age of recent grads from college well. In all of those former films, the recent grad was a male. This is only one of the few recent grad roles that I can ever remember a woman as having a significant role in a film. This film received numerous Oscar considerations and is highly recommended.

Diabolique – 1955 – France - Directed by Henri-Georges Clouzot (the director, not the funny inspector) and starring Simone Signoret as the other woman, Vera Clouzot as the wronged wife, and Paul Meurisse as the cruel philandering husband in a story of the eternal triangle. But this triangle is more like the Bemuda Triangle, because of a mysterious disappearance. The two women agree to do away with the heinous Delassalle, the owner of a boarding school. But after the murder is committed, the body, for one reason or another seems to have disappeared. I will not reveal the ending of this really interesting thriller, but I can guarantee you that it will give you a bit of a surprise. Originally, this film was headed for production by Alfred Hitchcock, but was spirited away by Clouzot. Hitchcock had to then be satisfied with his second choice for a script; something called Psycho. This film is highly recommended.

Dial M for Murder – 1954 - Directed by Alfred Hitchcock and starring Ray Milland, Grace Kelly and Robert Cummings, an old Hitchcock prop. This is one of Hitchcock's better films in my opinion. The plot is fairly chilling. A man (Milland) carefully plans to kill his wife and have an ironclad alibi as she is supposed to be killed on cue by his phone call to her. Highly recommended.

Die Hard – 1988 - Directed by John McTiernan and starring Bruce Willis as Bruce Willis and a wonderful over the top performance by Alan Rickman as the evil Hans Gruber. This is your usual terrorists- take - over -a -building –in- a -major –city movie. Actually, it is a pretty preposterous plot, but we forgive it, because we like to see Bruce bedevil Hans throughout the film. The action sequences are well done and this movie spawned a number of sequels and copycats including the creatively titled Die Hard 2, Die Hard With a Vengeance, and Live Free or Die Hard, which suspiciously sounds like it was stolen from a state motto in New England. There was also a porn film named *I Want to Die Hard*, but it petered out at the box office. Anyway, this is a great popcorn movie and I recommend it.

Diner – 1982 - Directed by Barry Levinson and starring the lightweight actor, Steve Guttenburg, Daniel Stern, the excessive Mickey Rourke, Kevin Bacon, Paul Reiser and Ellen Barkin. A group of male high school friends that get back together for a short period of time when one of them gets married. This movie is the Candice Bergen film, The Group with men instead of women. Recommended.

Dinner at Eight – 1933 –A- Directed by George Cukor and starring Marie Dressler, John Barrymore, Wallace Beery, Jean Harlow, Lionel Barrymore, Lee Tracy, Edmund Lowe and Billie Burke. This MGM extravaganza pulled out all the stops with this all-star cast. The dialogue is crackling, and the innuendo is not all that reserved, because this is a pre-code film. The actresses dominate this film (with the exception of Wallace Beery), because they seem to have all the best written lines in the film. They certainly have the funniest lines.

This film drips with elegance and style that is so prominent during the era of art deco. Jean Harlow is ephemeral. And Marie Dressler steals the film with her one-liners. I can recommend the film as a study in human greed, arrogance, and self-pity.

The Dirty Dozen – 1967 - Directed by Robert Aldrich and starring Lee Marvin, Telly Salavas, Jim Brown, Charles Bronson and Ernest Borgnine. Marvin, as Major Reisman, dominates the film in both action and dialogue, but the plot is rather unique and had never been done before on film (it has been copied many times since). Marvin excels in macho roles and this is one of his best. Telly Salavas, plays a real sleazebag with great enthusiasm. He had much better success on the small screen as a detective. Jim Brown, who fortunately played fullback for the Browns much better than he could act, is not required to spend too much time on the screen emoting, so his role is believable. Charles Bronson always adds a great deal of authenticity to this, and most other roles he played when doing the male bonding thing. Most notably, he was famous for his role in *The Magnificent Seven* and had later success with a series of vigilante films beginning with *Death Wish*. Another TV actor, Clint Walker, gave it his best shot in this film, but was unable to make the transition to the big screen as a major actor. A very good actor, John Casavettes, plays his role of a psycho to the hilt, and cashed in on this mainstream Hollywood film. He was usually known for independent studio productions and low-cost experimental films. Trini Lopez is miscast as the token Hispanic psycho. He was a singer and obviously not an actor.

Dirty Harry – 1971- Directed by Don Siegel and starring Clint Eastwood as Dirty Harry, who has, of course, now become an American icon. This film was followed by no less than four successful sequels, all wisely named without reference to the name of Dirty Harry (like a mindless Dirty Harry II and Dirty Harry III. *Magnum Force*, *The Enforcer*, *Sudden Impact* and *The Dead Pool* all subsequently made large profits and had a huge audience following. Eastwood tired of the series after *The Dead Pool* and went on to do much more significant (at least critically speaking) films.

Dirty Rotten Scoundrels – 1988- Directed by Frank Oz and starring Steve Martin and Michael Caine as two hustlers of the overly rich. With talent like that, you would think that you would have a no-miss comedy, but the film suffers from poor pacing. Sometimes it is hilarious; other times it just ambles along. Still worth seeing.

Disraeli - 1929 - Directed by Alfred E Green and starring George Arliss as Disraeli, the brilliant Foreign Minister of England that secured the Suez Canal for England. Arliss deservedly won the Academy Award for this performance. Highly recommended.

The Divorcee – 1930 – Directed by Robert Leonard and starring Norma Shearer in the sensational lead role (for this time period, at least). This story about a divorced woman and her adventures was quite the eye-opener for 1930; now it is tame. Interesting.

Divorce Italian-Style – Italy – 1962 - Directed by Pietro Germi and is most often erroneously attributed to DeSica or Fellini. The film stars Marcello Mastroianni and a group of B actors. This black comedy packed the art houses in the 60s. Marcello became an icon of Italian cinema during this decade. Recommended.

Divergent – 2014 - Directed by Neil Burger (no jokes, please) and starring Kate Winslett and Ashley Judd among the more notable actors armed with an intelligent script that almost makes it to the A list. This story about a streamlined society in the near future is full of potential for accuracy. Good direction, too.

DOA – 1950 — Directed by Rudolph Mate and starring Edmund O'Brien in a classic film noir tale of man who has been poisoned, and will die in a matter of hours. This sets up a natural state of suspense right from the beginning of the film as the viewer knows there is a limited time for Frank Bigelow, played by O'Brien, to solve his own murder. It is easily one of the most creative sequences for a beginning of a film in cinemaict history, and ranks up there with Citizen Kane as far as creativity and innovation in film design.

Do Bigha Zamin – 1953 – Directed by Bimal Roy and starring Balraj Sahni and Nirupa Roy as the main characters. This simple story of a family that moves to Calcutta to get relief from a greedy landlord is heartfelt and authentic, two qualities seldom found in older or newer films. Recommended.

Dr. Ehrlich's Magic Bullet - 1940 - Directed by William Dieterle and starring Edward G Robinson. This is a biopic of Dr. Ehrlich, the creator of salvansan, the chemical cure for syphilis. The director, an expert on eerie settings, does the same for this film. The film is very intriguing and intense, and I recommend it.

Dr. Jekyll and Mr. Hyde – 1941 - Directed by Victor Fleming and starring Spencer Tracy as schizo-boy, Ingrid Bergman and Lana Turner as two of the hottest female leads ever cast at the same time in film history, and a professional supporting cast. Fleming, of course, directed *Gone with the Wind* and *The Wizard of Oz* (roughly equal in difficulty for a director), so this film was almost like a vacation for both him and Tracy. Tracy is wonderfully over the top in this film, and it is extremely amusing to see him ham it up a little bit from his normally reserved and controlled persona, which he used for almost all his other films. I think with two women like Bergman and Turner chasing you, you wouldn't need any drugs to go crazy; that would be enough, but we follow the somewhat tragic tale to its inevitable conclusion, anyway.

Dr. Strangelove – 1964 - Directed by Stanley Kubrick and starring Peter Sellers as Dr. Strangelove and a superlative supporting cast. George C. Scott, Slim Pickins, Sterling Hayden, Keenan Wynn, and Tracy

Reed are the co-stars in this all-male cast. You have to have an amazingly big ego to think you can make the subject of nuclear war funny, but Peter Sellers pulls it off. He was both a consummate actor and comedian. George C Scott, who was at odds with Kubrick during the entire production, was tricked by the director into acting over the top in several scenes. This later infuriated Scott, who did not seem to appreciate the humor in his own character.

Pickins is hilarious as the country air warrior who 100% gung ho, Sterling Hayden seemed to be enjoying himself with his conservation of his precious bodily fluids, and Keenan Wynn chips in with a good scene or two. This film is about an accidental incident that initiates a chain of events between the US and Russia (modeled after the book *Red Alert* by Peter George). Also, the model of the film was a similar story called *Fail Safe*, which had a good amount of critical success at the time. I would classify this as a must-see film if you would like to better understand the Cold War of the 60s, and have a barrel of laughs while learning about it.

Doctor Zhivago – 1965 - Directed by David Lean and starring Julie Chirstie, Omar Sharif, Rod Steiger, Alec Guinness, Geraldine Chaplin, and Tom Courtenay. This tale of the history of Communist Russia from the revolution until the mid-1960s centers around the tragic romance of Christie and Sharif. They are happy together for only a very short time until events overtake their personal lives, and they are both lost in the avalanche of the socialist order. The cinematography for this film was outstanding and the music, created by Maurie Jarre was memorable. At times the film is spellbinding, and at other times, it sags a bit, but generally speaking, it will hold your attention for over three hours.

Dodge City - 1939 - Directed by Michael Curtiz (of *Casablanca* fame) and starring Errol Flynn and Olivia DeHaviland, previously co-stars in the highly successful Robin Hood. Ann Sheridan is also thrown into the mix. If there is one thing Curtiz was good at, it was pacing. Plenty of action.

Dodsworth – 1936 - Directed by William Wyler and starring Walter Huston and Ruth Chatterton. Paul Lukas, Mary Astor and David Niven also appear. This is a film about a spoiled woman, a rich man and playing the dumping game. Good for soap-lovers.

Donnie Brasco – 1997 - Directed by Mike Newell and starring al Pacino and Johnny Depp. Depp plays Donnie Brasco, an FBI undercover agent who infiltrates the mob. The complication is that Brasco befriends Lefty, a high-ranking member of the mob, played by Pacino. The film is intense from beginning to end.

Don't Look Back – 1981 (TV) - Directed by Richard A Colla and starring Lou Gossett Jr. as Paige. Satchel Page could not pitch in the major leagues in his prime because he was black. So he made a comeback when he was an old man and was successful, anyway. An inspiring true story.

The Doors: When You're Strange – 2009 – Directed by Tom DeCillo and narrated by Johnny Depp. Very nice documentary on The Doors, and great insight to their lead singer, Jim Morrison. More than just a glossy, fawning documentary. Very incisive.

Double Indemnity – 1944 –A- Directed by Billy Wilder and starring Fred MacMurray as Walter, an insurance salesman (perfect casting), Barbara Stanwyck as Phyllis, a temptress (more perfect casting) and Edward G. Robinson as Barton, a dedicated insurance adjuster, (even more perfect casting). Robinson had often been typecast as a tough gangster in most of his previous films, but his true-life demeanor was much closer to this type of role. Wilder, the director, is much more famous for his comedies such as *Some Like It Hot*, but is extremely comfortable in this genre as well, as evidenced by his fine work in *Sunset Boulevard* later in his career.

There are not a lot of directors who can perform equally as well in both drama and comedy. One that comes to mind is Steven Spielberg and another is Ron Howard. MacMurray was an actor who fit Wilder's profile precisely. MacMurray was also equally proficient in both drama and comedy, as evidenced by his performances in films such as *The Caine Mutiny* and *The Apartment*. Stanwyck, of course, was a consummate actress who did anything well. She is positively chilling in this role. Highly recommended.

Doubt – 2008 - Directed by John Patrick Shanley, who also wrote the Pulitzer-Prize winning play of the same name. The film stars super-actors Meryl Streep as Sister Aloysius, the strict principal of a parochial school, (who chillingly reminded me of my own Sister Aloysius, who was ten times worse than Streep's character), Philip Seymour Hoffman as Father Flynn, the suspected child molester, and a lessor actress, Amy Adams, as Sister James (I am sure she was just thrilled to be in this company). Also featured in a key role is Viola Davis as Mrs. Miller, the mother of the altar boy, Donald, who has been experimenting with wine.

One can see immediately that Shanley is not only an excellent writer, but a wonderful director as well. You seldom find a writer who can direct as well as they write. Streep is, as always, brilliant as Sister Aloysius. You are happy you are no longer in the parochial school system while you are watching the film. Hoffman is an accomplished actor who can tackle any role with relish, and he attacks this one with great vigor (how Kennedyish). His range of characters in other films shows that he can play just about any type in the business. Viola Davis keeps her own with the heavyweights, but Amy Adams gets kind of lost in the tall trees. Sister James could have been played by anyone. Highly recommended and deserving of more than just nominations from the Academy Awards.

Down to the Sea in Ships - 1949 - Directed by Henry Hathaway and starring Richard Widmark and Lionel Barrymore. A young Dean Stockwell is also featured. This is a whale of a soap and you will need your Quaker Oats for the throbbing conclusion. Nicely done.

Dracula – 1931 - Directed by Tod Browning and starring Bela Lugosi as the Master of the Night. This is considered to be the classic Dracula of all time in cinema. Lugosi made his name as an actor based on this film, and there are literally hundreds of imitations ever since its inception. Frightfully good fun.

Dragnet – 1954 - Directed and starring Dr. Deadpan himself, Jack Webb as Sergeant Joe Friday. Delivered in breathtaking, monotone dialogue by Jack Webb and a bunch of B actors. Just the facts mam. You either love or hate this guy. I like him. Transitioned easily to TV.

Dream House – 2011 ---Directed by Jim Sheridan and starring a solid cast of Daniel Craig (007), Naomi Watts, and Rachel Weisz in a finely layered screenplay about a man who may or may not have killed his family in the recent past. Nice script and good direction. Might have been better in black and white. Highly reminiscent of *The Stepfather*.

Dressed to Kill - 1980 – Directed and written by Brian DePalma, and also considered to be one of his masterpieces. The film starred Michael Caine, Angie Dickinson and Nancy Allen. This is one of the rare films that allow the women to chew up most of the lines and scenery, yet women's groups did not like the film, and labeled it misogynist. The viewer must ultimately decide for themselves. Michael Caine plays against type here, and begins a new career as a potential creep in this and future films. Of course Michael can really turn on the charm when he wants to, and he does just that in this film. Angie Dickinson, who was among the sexiest female actors of this decade, gives a very credible performance as a woman who decides to take a walk on the wild side and comes to regret it. Nancy Allen sleepwalks through a not-too challenging role as a high-priced Prostitute. Entertaining.

The Dresser – 1983 - Directed by Peter Yates and starring Albert Finney and Tom Courtenay. Two powerhouse actors use a brilliant script to create an unforgettable film experience about an actor and his dresser. Highly recommended.

Drishyam (India) – 2015 - Directed by Nishikant Kamath and starring AJ Devjn, Tabu (love that name), Shriya Saran, and Rajat Kapoor in the lead roles. This entry as India's best film of the year is about the struggles of a middle class Indian family and the bumps in the road they endure.

Driving Miss Daisy - 1989 - Directed by Bruce Beresford and starring Morgan Freeman, Jessica Tandy and Dan Aykroyd. Popular social commentary film done with comedy rather than with preaching. A white woman with pre-conceived notions about blacks has a black driver. Racism that is entertaining and enlightening; not an easy trick.

Dr. No -1965- Directed by Terence Young and starring Sean Connery as 007. Ursula Andress adds her own particular talents to the scenery. This Ian Fleming book is the one that started it all. "Bond, James, Bond" became an icon quote from this film. Beefcake and cheesecake deluxe.

Drums Along the Mohawk - 1939 - Directed by John Ford and starring Henry Fonda and Claudette Colbert. Ford knew how to make actioners and this was a rousing one. John Carradine is also featured.

The Duellists - 1978 - Directed by Ridley Scott (his first feature film) and starring Keith Carradine and Harvey Keitel. I agree 100% with Leonard Maltin that the film is staggeringly beautiful. One of the top-ten best-filmed movies of all time; up there with Kubrick, Powell and Wong. However, there is no protagonist. It is good entertainment.

Dumbo – 1941 - Produced by Walt Disney Studios and introducing Dumbo, the flying elephant. Made just prior to WW2 and helped the country forget about the war for a few hours. One of Disney's early classics.

Dunkirk – 1958 - (England) -- Directed by Leslie Norman and starring John Mills and Richard Attenborough. This tale of a decisive battle early in WW 2 is told from the British view and is also featured in *Mrs. Miniver*. A good rouser.

Dunkirk – 2017 – Directed by Christopher Nolan and using a cast of mostly unknown actors, the film puts all of its money into the cinematography and special effects of the great migration from the French Coast back to the safety of England. The best scene I ever saw about Dunkirk was in *Mrs. Miniver* (without special effects). See that film after this one for more depth about Dunkirk.

442

E

Each Dawn I Die - 1939 - Directed by William Keighley and starring Jimmy Cagney and George Raft, two friends from the old neighborhood in New York. This is one of your better gangster in prison films. Cagney went on to a great career, while Raft seemed to be popular for only a short period of time.

The Eagle Has Landed – 1976 -Directed by John Sturges and starring Michael Caine, Donald Sutherland, and Robert Duvall. The film revolves around a plot to land Nazi paratroopers in England and assassinate Churchill. This is not exactly breaking news. There were at least a half dozen attempts by the Nazis on Churchill's life; all which failed miserably for one simple reason; British spies were much better at their jobs than were German spies.

Earth (Russia) – 1930 - Directed by Alexander Dovzhenko and starring a group of unknown Russian actors. This film highlights the schizophrenic nature of the Russian farmer in the Ukraine in the early years of communism under Stalin. Some welcomed collectivism and atheism, and others clung to the old ways. Interesting to see.

East of Eden - 1955 - Directed by the talented Elia Kazan and also known as Rebel Without a Clue by responsible parents, and starring James Dean as Cal, Julie Harris as Catie, his love interest, Raymond Massey as daddy, Burl Ives as a relatively slow-moving sheriff, and Jo Van Fleet as the not too happy hooker, Catherine, who is the secret mother of Cal.   This film is the epitome of good soap. I really loathe agreeing with a New York Times critic, but in this case, I will make an exception. Bosley Crowther, a prominent critic there, was right on the money when he tagged Dean's performance as a copy of a young Brando, but without the nuances.

"This performance was quite similar to the one in *Rebel Without a Cause;* full of self-pitying histrionics." If anything, Dean will always be remembered as the whiniest actor in film history. Both of these characters had plenty of life's advantages including their own cars and plenty of money to waste on extra-curricular activities outside of school. If anything, Dean was the poster child for high-school dropouts, and not exactly the best role model. The lame excuse that all adults were liars and cruel, and that no one understood teenagers was a lot of Hollywood baloney that was used to sell the film to spoiled teenagers, of which there were legions in the fifties.

Dean's characters had more advantages than 99.9% of the world's other teenagers and yet he still whined away at the world. Grow up. Unfortunately, Dean did not get the chance, as he died tragically in an accident at a very young age. As I mentioned in a previous review, there are a number of better coming of age films, in particular, *The 400 Blows* by Francois Truffaut, which accurately shows young people in the difficulty of adult transition, rather than this Hollywood pap that was slopped on the plate in the fifties.

Easy Rider – 1969 - Directed and starring Dennis Hopper as Billy aka Billy the Kid, as a drug-dealer living out his fantasy, Peter Fonda as Wyatt aka Captain America, who shares Billy's fantasy scenario, and Jack Nicholson, who steals the movie as George Hanson, an alcoholic ACLU lawyer, and is the most likeable character in the film. This a movie about two drug dealers going cross-country on their motorcycles and trying to reconcile their fantasies to the harsh realities of real life. Needless to say, they have great difficulties with issues like earning a respectable living, creating meaningful and long-lasting relationships, and establishing roots in a community That is why this film is so overrated. Hollywood likes to give the impression that the vast majority of people living out there have meaningless lives, and that we are supposed to fall in love with the romantic images of the free and easy, lawless life up on the screen. Baloney. Great performance by Jack Nicholson.

Eat Drink Man Woman – China - 1994 - Directed by Ang Lee and starring Kuei- Mei Yang, Chien-Lien Lu, Yu-Wen Wang as three daughters and Sihung Lung as the chef father of the three daughters. The story is about the various relationships of the three daughters and how it affects the family dynamic. Interesting.

Edge of Darkness - 1943 - Directed by Lewis Milestone and starring Errol Flynn, Ann Sheridan and Walter Huston. This is a WW2 tale of a Norwegian fishing village resisting Nazi domination. Some say it is a propaganda film, and others say it was a true story. Really doesn't matter if the story is engaging. See it and judge for yourself.

Edison, the Man – 1940 - Directed by Clarence Brown and Starring Spencer Tracy as Edison. This less-than-honest depiction of Edison may be candy-coated and have little to do with reality, but as a young man growing up, I was inspired by the film because of the intensity of Tracy's performance and the portrayal of the tenacity of Edison. I learned persistence from this film, as I am sure did millions of others who had viewed the movie. Of course, the film does not discuss the dark side of Edison, such as his bullying tactics with the budding motion picture industry and other bullying episodes.

Edwin Boyd, Citizen Gangster - 2011 - Canada - Directed by Nathan Morlando and starring Scott Speedman in a great performance as Edwin Boyd, a real-life gangster on which the film is based. Kevin Durand also turns in a wonderful performance. Great direction as well. A gritty, realistic film. Recommended.

Ed Wood – 1994 - Directed and produced by Tim Burton and starring Johnny Depp in a manic performance as Ed Wood, the C movie producer-director, Martin Landau in his Academy Award-winning performance as Bela Lugosi, the famous Dracula actor, and a superb supporting cast including Sarah Jessica Parker as Dolores, Ed's former girlfriend who is embarrassed by his transvestite behavior, Patricia Arquette as Kathy, Ed's eventual lifetime mate, Jeffrey Jones (who is absolutely hilarious), as the

Amazing Criswell, a character which inspired an entire film under a pseudonym a few years later starring John Malkovich, Lisa Marie Smith as Vampira, and Bill Murray, in one of the best and funniest roles of his career, as Bunny Breckinridge, an openly gay man who occasionally appears in Ed's fiascos.

His portrayal as The Ruler in *Plan 9 From Outer Space* is absolutely one of the funniest things he has ever done on the big screen. Of course, this comedy was not intentional at the time of the original filming of these C movies, but the end result is a centerpiece production for a comedy program like Science-Fiction Theater 3000. I have to be perfectly honest. After *The Producers* and *Young Frankenstein*, I would rank this in the top ten funniest comedies I have ever seen. Blind optimism is the byword for this movie. Highly recommended for everyone.

The Egyptian - 1954 - Directed by Michael Curtiz and starring Jean Simmons, Victor Mature, Gene Tierney, Michael Wilding, Peter Ustinov and Edmund Purdom as the Egyptian physician who has an event-filled life. This film was the precursor to The Ten Commandments, which would come out in the next few years. It is an attractive mix of human drama, pure fiction, and a degree of half-truths which keeps the viewer's interest. Not the model for Steve Martin.

Eight Men Out – 1988 - Directed by John Sayles and starring John Cusack as Buck Weaver, one of the wobbly White Sox conspirators of the thrown 1919 World Series, Bill Irwin as a key conspirator,as Eddie Collins, a major star for the White Sox, Michael Rooker as the prime mover among the ballplayers to throw the games, Chick Gandil, David Strathairn as the key pitcher needed to tilt the games as Eddie Cicotte, Clifton James as the miserable owner of the White Sox, Charles Comiskey who virtually forces the players to seek money on the side, Charlie Sheen as Happy Felsch and, of course, the most tragic figure of the thrown World Series, Shoeless Joe Jackson, one of the most talented players in the game, played by D.B. Sweeney.

Also featured is John Anderson as the righteous Judge Kenesaw Mountain Landis, who sends a message to all the players in the game with life-long suspensions. Sayles does a great job with this loving portrait of an event that has become an icon in American folklore. Sayles, who usually makes film in modern venues, had no problem at all capturing the flavor of the period. His subtle touches in other films such as *Brother From Another Planet* are readily apparent in this film as well. Everything from the newsboys to the crowds waiting for play by play relays in the streets of Chicago gives the film a sense of reality of the times. Because of the severe sentences of the players involved, and the tragedy of Shoeless Joe Jackson, there has never been another baseball game fixed in almost 100 years.

El Cid – 1961 - Directed by Anthony Mann and starring Charlton Heston as El Cid, the great defender of Spain during the Islamic invasion of the Middle Ages and the superhot Sophia Loren as his (and half the male population in the world) love interest. The film score by Miklos Rozsa was one of the most stirring scores ever created, but yet lost the Academy Award to *Moon River* because of the immense popularity of the title song, which was understandable. There is a great deal of spectacle in this film, as well as stirring music and spectacular photography. The choreography of the battle scenes is outstanding, and the movie can stand up to any epic ever produced. It is one of Marty Scorcese's favorite films, and one of mine, as well. Anthony Mann is a consummate film director and knows how to precisely mount every scene in the movie.

   Even the love scenes, with the questionable skills of Charlton Heston in that area, were successful, because of Mann's ability to frame the scene so well. Of course, Sophia Loren could play a love scene all by herself during the height of her career, and she visually carries Heston in all the scenes they have together. Loren is also a better actor than Heston, but she is generous with her lines and allows him to put across that constant macho image he liked to project. When Heston was doing his manly fighting scenes, however, there were few actors who could match him, and there were numerous chances in this film to show his physical prowess. The supporting cast, in general, is very good, especially his Islamic allies. Highly recommended.

Election – 1999 - Directed by Alexander Payne and starring Reese Witherspoon as Tracy, an oversexed, hyperactive, politically savvy student, and Matthew Broderick as Mr. McAllister, her hapless teacher/advisor, who becomes obsessed with the idea of having someone else defeat her in the student election for student president. There was great distress in one neighborhood when the movie marquee had an incorrect letter in the title.

Elegy – 2008 - Directed by Isabel Coixet and starring Ben Kingsley as David Kepesh, a professor and critic who has difficulty with the concept of commitment, Dennis Hopper as George O'Hearn, who supposedly won a Pulitzer Prize for something or other, and now is an expert on human relationships, and advocates a wife for day to day humdrum existence and a lover on the side for exciting sex; how novel. Other cast members include Penelope Cruz, as Consuela, a woman who is too stupid to realize that she cannot change a creature of habit like David into a committed man, and Patricia Clarkson as Caroline, another female sucker who has fallen fall this line of bull for twenty years and now is amazingly disillusioned. Can someone tell me why these women are so arrogant that they think they can change a worm into a snake? The women in this film deserve all the mistreatment that they receive from guys like David and George.

The Elephant Man – 1980 —Appropriately directed by David Lynch, the king of the bizarre, but admirably under control during this effort, and starring John Hurt as the unfortunate Joseph Merrick, a man with severely deformed features, but a beautiful personality and brain, Anthony Hopkins giving one of his peerless performances as Dr. Frederick Treves, a sympathetic surgeon, a delightfully inhumane Mr. Bytes, played with relish by Fredie Jones, who treats Joseph like a dumb animal in his freak show, the constantly professional Wendy Hiller, who plays a highly professional matron, and the impeccable John Gielgud, who plays the priggish Mr. Gomm, the governor of the hospital who really does not want Joseph there for assistance. This is a first-rate cast with a first-rate script, and that can only result in an Academy Award winning, first-rate film. Somehow, the corny and hysterical *Ordinary People* (which did have great music, though) beat this film out for Best Picture (probably because it was American and *Elephant Man* was perceived as British, and therefore Foreign).

   Robert Redford getting the nod over David Lynch as best director was even more laughable. Redford was a good, competent director, but his *Ordinary People* was no match for *The Elephant Man* in my book, but what do I know? I had picked this film for best movie, and it broke my string of correct Best Movie of the year picks at 20. I now have another streak currently at 30. Hopkins was exceptional in this film, and it guaranteed his top-notch A actor status for the rest of his career. Highly recommended.

Elevator to the Gallows- France - 1958-Directed by the astute Louis Malle and starring Jeanne Moreau and Maurice Ronet in the featured roles. This piece of French film noir about two small-time hoods is highlighted with a great jazz score from Miles Davis. Recommended.

Elmer Gantry – 1960 - Directed by Richard Brooks and based on the famous Sinclair Lewis novel, starring Burt Lancaster as Gantry, in an Oscar-winning performance, as well as Jean Simmons as Sister Falconer, a crusading evangelist. Other key roles in the film belong to Arthur Kennedy, as the reporter who follows the crusade, and Shirley Jones, who won a Best Supporting Actress Academy Award, as the prostitute who betrays Gantry. The film's energy is exacerbated by the thrilling musical score provided by Andre Previn, and the photography is first-rate. This film occasionally makes it into the top ten of all time for some critics. Lancaster gave the performance of his career, and he made a quite a number of good films in addition to this one. The direction of Brooks is impeccable, and his pacing is extraordinary. The film is not dull for one moment. The characters of Lewis' novel virtually come alive on the big screen, and we feel we are in the middle of the entire proceedings. The chemistry between Lancaster and Simmons is sizzling, and Arthur Kennedy gives what I believe to be, the best performance of his career (with the possible exception of the original *Invasion of the Body-Snatchers*). The supporting cast is superb in every aspect. This is a must-see film.

El Norte – 1983 - Directed by Gregory Nava and starring Zaide Silvia Gutierrez and David Villapando as two refugees from Guatemala who embark on a very long and dangerous trip to arrive in the United States. This film is one of the very few that captures the real desperation of refugees trying to enter the United States. Their desperation is palatable. And their trip is filled with pitfalls.

Elysium –2013 - Directed by Neill Blomkamp and starring Matt Damon and Jodie Foster (who have no chemistry whatsoever) is a flawed story similar to *In Time*, but nowhere nearly as well-made or directed. Watchable only for Damon.

Embrace of the Serpent – 2016 – Colombia – Directed by Ciro Guerraand starring a cast of unknown Colombian actors in a story about a turn of the century explorer who seeks a miraculous plant that can cure a terrible disease. What is different about this film is that the explorer returns to the location many years later to see how Western intrusion has changed the area and the natives. Fascinating.

 The Emerald Forest (England) – 1985 - Directed by the talented John Boorman, and starring a low-key cast including Powers Booth as Bill Markham, Meg Foster as his prop wife (fill in any name you like), an exceptional performance by William Rodriguez as Tommy, the abducted seven year old son of the Markhams, and Charley Boorman, son of the director, as Tomme, who is Tommy at a later age with his new family in the rain forest.

All of the performances are first-rate, and highly believable. But the real star of the movie is the script written by Rospo Pallenberg, which from the first few scenes of the film grips you, and does not let you go for an hour and a half. The film was nominated for numerous awards, but the one it most richly deserved, Best Screenplay, went to *Out of Africa*, a major crowd-pleasing soap, that swept all the major awards that year. Quite frankly, *Out of Africa* is boring compared to this film, and its screenplay is great soap, but it is not in the same category philosophically as *The Emerald Forest*. Pacing is one of the long suits of Boorman's directing talents, and it shows here in this film. He keeps the viewer on the edge of their seats from beginning to end. Booth easily gives the best performance of his career in this film, as do all of the other actors and actresses that are in it. Highly recommended.

The Emperor and the Assassin (China) - 1999 - Directed by Chen Kaige, a premier Chinese director, and starring Gong Li, Zhang Fengyi, Li Xuejian and Zhou Xun in the principal roles. This is the historically accurate story of the attempted assassination of the Emperor of the Qin, as described by Sima Qian, the Grand Historian of China. Fun to watch.

Empire of the Sun – 1987 - Directed by Steven Spielberg and starring John Malkovich, Miranda Richardson, and Christian Bale in his major film debut. Bale plays a boy stuck in the turmoil of China during WW2. He becomes a very young POW, and makes the best of it with the aid of John Malkovich. The highlight of the film is the bombing raid on the POW camp, and is nicely done with that Spielberg feel for WW2 aircraft. Recommended.

Empire Strikes Back- 1980 - Directed by George Lucas and starring the usual suspects of the Star War Trilogy, Mark Hammil as Luke, Harrison Ford as Han Solo , Carrie Fisher as Princess Leia, Chewbaca, R2D2, and 3CPO. Alec Guinness as Obiwan was killed off in the first episode, but his spirit lived on in the force, so they had to pay him again for this episode. In this episode, the Evil Empire (the Star Wars version, and not the New York Yankees) is building a new Death Star. The Rebel Alliance is still alive and well.

    The best part of the film is the confrontation between Luke and his father, Darth Vader (what a cool dad). Lukas continues his mastery of the genre with tight direction that is just as enticing as the first Star Wars film. Some critics have commented that this film is actually superior to the first one. I thought the second entry was just a tad better, as well. The weakest actor in this troupe is obviously Mark Hammil. He is pretty much a one-dimensional actor, and has no other film credits worth discussing. However, he is saved by the presence of the highly competent Harrison Ford and Alec Guinness. The Darth Vader character actually steals this film from everyone else and is the centerpiece of the film. Recommended as a great sequel.

Encore – 1952 – Directed by Harold French and Pat Jackson and starring mostly B actors no one has ever heard of. It is the stories of Somerset Maugham that are the stars of this film. If you are a fan (and I am), then this film will be a real treat for you.

Enemy at the Gates – 2001 –A- Directed by Jean-Jacques Annaud and starring Jude Law as a Russian super sniper, Vasily Zaytsev. Also starring are Ed Harris as Erwin Konig, his German counterpart, Rachel Weisz, the love interest of Vasily, Joseph Fiennes as Danilov, a Russian commissar, and a wonderful portrayal of Nikita Khrushchev by Bob Hoskins, who almost steals the film from Law. Also featured are Ron Pearlman as Koulikov, a Russian propagandist, and a nice bit by Mihail Matveyev as Vasily's grandfather, who teaches Vasily how to hunt as a young boy. Highly recommended. Another community had a problem with this title in the marqee; but the problem was eliminated.

The Enforcer - 1951 - Directed by Raoul Walsh, but credited to some bureaucratic government worker, this purely fictional film starred Humphrey Bogart as a fighting DA who did more than plea bargain. Fighting DAs that outwit Murder Inc. What a great fantasy. Fun to watch.

The English Patient – 1996 - Written and directed by Anthony Minghella and starring Ralph Fiennes as Count Laszlo de Almasy, a Hungarian geographer, and Kristin Scott Thomas as Katherine Clifton, his smoking-hot companion in the desert, who is married, but unhappy. The film also features great performances from Juliete Benoche, a nurse who looks after the Count after his disfiguring accident, and Willem Dafoe as David Carvaggio, a Canadian intelligence officer who has a vendetta to settle with the Count. Also in the film is Colin Firth, winner for the 2011 Oscar for best actor, in a small role as Geoffrey Clifton, who is the cockuld husband of Katherine.

The Entertainer – 1960 - Directed by Tony Richardson and starring Laurence Olivier in the role of an aging actor who loses himself in the arms of numerous ambitious young actresses. Oh, the horror. Interesting to see a self-pitying Olivier.

Enter the Dragon – China- 1973 - Directed by Robert Clouse and starring an icon of martial arts, Bruce Lee. Lee died under mysterious circumstances six days before the release of the film. Elements of the Hong Kong martial arts film community were said to be responsible according to Lee's son, who was also killed in an "accident". Some say this is fiction and others swear it is true.

ET – 1982 - Directed by Steven Spielberg and starring a cast of relative unknowns who later made no significant films with the exception of Drew Barrymore (and that might be debatable also). The real star of the film is the alien or extra-terrestrial, ET. He is a cute, adorable type of alien, not like the ones encountered in most alien films like *War of the Worlds* or *Aliens*, but more like a child version of friendly aliens like the ones we see in *Close Encounters of the Third Kind*....hmmm, who directed that? I guess Spielberg feels that all the aliens out there are nice; I guess we will see some day. Regardless of Spielberg's philosophy, his directorial skills in this genre are seldom matched, and he does a masterful job with this one as he slowly develops his alien character.

ET is almost too innocent and naïve to be true, but since it is the movies, we suspend disbelief. Spielberg's universe seems to be filled with altruistic aliens who want only the best for the human race. This philosophy clashes harshly with Lucas' vision of the universe in *Star Wars* where humans have to fight tooth and nail against a variety of bad guys from various galaxies. In political terms, you would probably define Lucas as a conservative and Spielberg as a liberal when it comes to film interpretations of the universe. Personally, I prefer an interpretation similar to that of *Star Trek* and the Borg. The Borg, for some reason, seem to be a much more logical extension of what aliens may turn out to be. My Chinese friend said the Borg reminded him of his in-laws. This is a must see film for children of all ages and is listed in the top 100 films of all time on practically every critic's list.

Europa, Europa- (Germany) (1991) - Directed by Agnieszka Holland and starring Marco Hofschneider as Solomon Perel as a young Jewish boy who evades extermination by posing as an elite German Aryan youth. Fascinating to watch. Sometimes confused with Van Trier's *Europa* of a later date.

Europa Report -2013- Directed by Sebastian Codero and starring a B cast with an interesting script about the exploration of Europa, the mysterious moon of Jupiter that is as smooth as a ping-pong ball with ice. Interesting and reminiscent of a short story written several years earlier in Marvel comics.

Evening Bell (China) - 1988 - Directed by Wu Ziniu and starring Tao Zeru and Chong Peipei in the principal roles. A very insightful film about the PLA (People's Liberation Army) and the events immediately following the end of WW2; a subject seldom covered in film. There was very little difference between the war and after the war for these soldiers. Recommended.

Every Day's A Holiday - 1937 – Directed by Edward Sutherland and starring and co-written by Mae West as Peaches, and a parade of men in a supporting cast who cannot possibly keep up with her. Sutherland does his level best to keep West under control, but like all other directors who had West as their leading lady, he met with dismal failure. Mae West dominates every scene she is in and, I am sure, completely ignored any requests by the director. She had the gift of turning B movies into A comedies. That is a very rare gift, indeed. The fact that she co-wrote the script indicates that she was well-aware of the fact that scripts for these B comedies were mediocre, at best.

   She used her considerable talent to liven them up whenever possible.   Mae West was known for broad characterizations and lean plots. She was the female version of WC Fields, but a lot better-looking. This was her final film for Paramount before moving on to her greatest triumph at Universal Studios in *She Done Him Wrong*, which I will review at a later part of the book. Mae West was the absolute queen of the double meaning and was able to be seductive, comedic and dramatic all at the same time. This is a rare attribute for any actor or actress, but she performed these complex emotions with ease. I unconditionally recommend this film to anyone who wants to see a real American icon of the thirties and forties.

Excalibur – 1981 - Directed and co-written by John Boorman, a master behind the camera, and starring Nigel Terry as Arthur, Nicholas Clay as Lancelot, a young and sexy Helen Mirren as Morgana, a young Liam Neeson as Sir Gawain, and Nicol Williamson as Merlin the Magician. Critics were sharply divided on this film. Some believed it to be visually lush and beautifully photographed (I am among those critics) and others, such as Roger Ebert, who is almost always on the money on the vast majority of films he reviewed, thought it was a mess (which I also happen to agree with).

   So I will say that the film has both of these attributes. It is far too well photographed to be bad, and far too messy in the story line to be considered a great film. But regardless of how you feel about the story line, the film is fascinating to watch and very easy on the eyes.   Terry is good as Arthur, Mirren is smoking hot as Morgana, and Liam Neeson shows the promise of a budding career as Sir Gawain. Nicol Williamson is very good as Merlin, by the way. Still recommended because a messy Boorman film is still better that the majority of tidy films by other directors.

Executive Suite - 1954 - Directed by the incomparable John Houseman (second only to Orson Welles for film creativity) and starring a heavyweight cast of Hollywood's best in 1954 including William Holden, Barbara Stanwyck, Fredric March, Walter Pidgeon, Louis Calhern and Dean Jagger. The female roles, unfortunately, hold little weight. This is arguably the best film of 1954 except for On The Waterfront . Corporate hijinx and drama abound.

Ex-machina – 2015 -Directed and written by the talented Alex Garland and starring Domhnall Gleason as the wide-eyed whiz kid, and Nathan Bateman as the Bill Gates-type recluse CEO who seeks top talent to keep his company on top. Nothing like intelligent sci-fi instead of mindless superhero crap. Leave the comic book heroes for the kids and sit back and enjoy some adult entertainment for a change in sci-fi. Recommended.

The Exorcist – 1973 - Directed by William Friedkin and starring Ellen Burstyn as Chris MacNeil, the mother of Regan, who is possessed by the devil (aren't we all?) and Linda Blair in her smash debut as Regan, the child tormented by the devil. The film also features a strong performance from Max von Sydow as Father Lankester Merrin, the older priest who is also a knowledgeable archaeologist, and Father Damien Karras, played very well by Jason Miller in a nicely understated performance, as the younger priest and psychiatrist, who convinces the Church to allow an exorcism in this case.

It was, and still is, the policy of the Catholic Church to keep these exorcisms to a minimum. Both Ellen Burstyn and Linda Blair were seriously injured during the filming of this picture. Back harnesses, primarily created for Blair, were also used for shock scenes on Burstyn for effect. Friedkin, who sometimes had trouble reining in his excesses (don't we all?), seems to be in control in this film with many expertly measured scenes.

Of course, Friedkin inevitably goes overboard as he almost always does, with a scene or two; such as the pea-spewing and gory stairs scenes. Despite those, the vast majority of the other scenes are quite gripping. The shot of Father Merrin arriving at the residence in the middle of the night under a very eerie light was an effect created by actually shooting in the early morning and then using a filter to darken the already dim light. The effect was quite creepy. The film won Best Sound and Adapted Screenplay Academy Awards, but lost out to *The Sting* for Best Picture that year. Recommended

Exterminating Angel – 1962 — France-Directed by Luis Bunueland starring a solid B cast of French actors who tell us a tale about a group of upper-class people who find themselves imprisoned in a room and begin to degrade themselves.

F

Face in the Crowd – 1957 — Directed by Elia Kazan of *On The Waterfront* fame, and starring an electric Andy Griffith as a rising singing star, Patricia Neal as a business agent, and Walter Matthau in a nice turn as a TV coordinator. This film shows the early days of television, and how a new star could rise from nowhere to be an overnight sensation across the country. The story begins with Griffith in jail getting bailed out by Neal when she hears a version of his song on the radio. She gets the idea to put him on TV so people can see his vitality along with hearing his music. The combination is dynamite, and the public cannot get enough of him. This is a top 100 film listed by many movie critics.

Fahrenheit 9/11 – 2004 - Directed by Michael Moore. This documentary is very well done and captures the anger, frustration, and hysteria surrounding the events and subsequent days after the attack of 9/11. It is also very incisive about the association of Saudi Arabia with the Bush family and Saudi Arabia's role in the event.

Fail Safe – 1964 - Directed by Sidney Lumet and starring Henry Fonda as the American President, Dan O'Herlihy, as General Black, Walter Matthau as Professor Groeteschele and in a very funny miscasting fiasco, Larry Hagman of Dallas fame as a translator! There was a very close relationship to this film and Dr. Strangelove, which is a parody of this film. Sometimes viewers get the two films mixed up. There really is a possibility that Dr. Strangelove might have actually been closer to the truth as well. Recommended, despite the grim atmosphere of the film.

Fair Game -2010--Directed by Doug Liman and starring Naomi Watts and Sean Penn in the lead roles. Watts plays a CIA agent whose cover gets blown by her husband, who writes a critical op-ed in a newspaper that offends the Bush Administration. Based on a true story. Judge for yourself.

Fallen Angel – 1946 – Directed by (of all people) Otto Preminger, not noted for doing cool film noir, but this is exactly what this film is. Starring Dana Andrews as a deliciously slick hustler, Alice Faye, the nice girl, and Linda Darnell, the Fallen Angel, who is a hot waitress at a local grease joint. Ok, here comes the cliché; they just don't make movies like this anymore.

Falling Down – 1993 - Directed by Joel Shumacher and starring Michael Douglas as William Foster, a common man who is bedeviled by numerous elements in his current life including, poverty, the economy and commercialism. Also featured is Robert Duvall as an aging and sympathetic Los Angeles police sergeant who has approached his retirement day. A fine supporting cast adds realism to the movie.

The Family Game- Japan – 1983 - Directed by Yoshimitsu Morita and starring a cast of unknown Japanese (except in Japan) actors. The film examines the new post-war Japanese family ethic, as opposed to the old Japanese family traditions in place before WW2. Interesting from a historical perspective.

Fantasia – 1940 - Produced by Walt Disney Productions and starring The Philadelphia Orchestra under the direction of Leopold Stokowski. Music critic Deems Taylor introduced each classical piece, instead of using a simple screen prompt, which would have pretty much served the same purpose. The use of a human giving prompts on the screen is much too serious for children and, particularly, young children, whom were the primary audience for these films.

In retrospect, it would have been better to use Mickey Mouse or Donald Duck to introduce the pieces. Mickey has worn tuxes before. This was a very labor-intensive project at the time because there was no computer animation or other time-saving special-effects devices. All the animation was drawn by hand, and the action had to mirror the classical music pieces that accompanied the visuals; not an easy task. In addition, it was also a difficult job from the musical side for Stokowski, who had to conduct according to the needs of the visuals. Both departments did a wonderful job.

The Disney artists, of course, are the real stars of the film, because without their patience and talents, none of the early Disney classics would have materialized. The production could have used more Mickey Mouse and was completely devoid of other Disney characters, including Donald Duck. In hindsight, this might have not been the best approach to promote the line of Disney characters, and young audiences would have certainly preferred Donald Duck or Mickey to many of the unknown cartoon characters that were featured in these pieces.   Highly recommended.

Farewell, My Concubine- China– 1993 — Directed by Chen Kaige and starring Gong Li. This film is considered one of the best ever made in China. It is about a woman forced to be a third wife (also known as concubine) to a rich Chinese businessman. Since Gong Li is smoking hot; it is a no-brainer for the businessman to quickly make her number one wife in the bedroom, but, unfortunately, number one wife has all the money and power and disposes poor Gong Li. Great soap.

Fast Runner (Canadian) - 2002 - Directed by Zacharias Kanuk and starring an unknown cast acting out an Eskimo legend about a man who overcomes extremely difficult obstacles within nature near the Arctic Circle to provide for his family during the first millennium. Quite frankly, I don't see much difference between living there in that millennium or this one, but the film is fascinating to watch, as are most frozen waste films.

Fat City – 1972 - Directed by John Huston and starring Stacy Keach and Jeff Bridges. Huston captures the gritty underbelly of small-time fighters in secondary cities. Keach is exceptional. Good viewing.

Fatal Attraction – 1987 - Directed by Adrian Lyne and starring Michael Douglas and Glen Close. This film about an affair gone to extremes scared off millions of men who had been cheating on their girlfriends and wives in 1987. Harrowing.

Father –2000 –(China) –Directed by Wang Shuo and starring Feng Xiaogang and Hu Xiaopei as a father and son who have relationship issues that are difficult to resolve. One of the best father and son relationship films ever made. I related to this film from a personal standpoint. Recommended.

Fear – 1946 - Directed by Alfred Zeisler and starring a cast of B actors working a very interesting story line. A poor medical student kills his dishonest professor, but is guilt-ridden about his crime. A lower-case version of *Crime and Punishment*.

Fear and Desire –1953 – Directed by Stanley Kubrick (his first major effort) and starring a B cast of actors depicting an event during a war where a plane crashes behind enemy lines and the crew must get back to their own lines. A fairly mundane plot, but a superior director rescues the script.

Fear Strikes Out- 1957 - Directed by Robert Mulligan and starring Anthony Perkins and veteran actor Karl Malden as real-life baseball player Jimmy Piersall and his father, respectively. The film examines the pressures of making it to the major leagues and staying there for a career. The pressure can be suffocating as evidenced by the film. Malden very good here. Recommended.

Fellini Satyricon - Italy- 1970 - Directed by Federico Fellini and starring a cast of Italian unknowns except for Capucine, who gained a bit of fame in the US. The film traces the experiences of various Roman citizens throughout history. Intriguing.

Ferris Bueller's Day Off - 1986 - Directed by John Hughes and starring Matthew Broderick in his signature role. Your usual the-kids-are-smarter-than-the-adults fantasy glazed to a fine finish. Strictly for teens and slackers, but fun.

A Few Good Men - 1992 - Directed by Rob Reiner, who is great with comedy, but is not too good at drama, and starring Jack Nicholson and Tom Cruise, who try to rescue Reiner, but cannot cut through the cumbersome script. Rob, "You can't handle the truth"; or maybe he can. Interesting just to see Nicholson try to overcome obstacles.

Field of Dreams – 1989 - Written and directed by Phil Alden Robinson and starring Kevin Costner. Also contributing to the success of the film are Ray Liotta, as Shoeless Joe Jackson, James Earl Jones as a university professor, and the final appearance of Burt Lancaster as a player who opted to become a doctor and gave up baseball. Amy Madigan plays the wife of Ray Kinsella (Costner).

   The film is considered the top sports movie of all time in cinema history by the majority of current critics. Kevin Costner was made to play this lead, and even though the film did not win any Academy Awards (it was nominated for three). It was still hugely popular with the public, who ate up the nostalgia that the film is saturated with. Robinson did a masterful job of creating the myth behind the film, and kept the momentum gained earlier in the movie going throughout the entire production.

   A few critics scoffed at the film, saying it was overly-sentimental, but they were drowned out by the vast majority of critics who loved the film, along with the millions who enjoyed watching it for the first time. It is the kind of movie that makes one forget their troubles, and there are damned few of those films that go for the distance over the years. Even the main character of the film is facing financial difficulties, and the resolution of them is quite satisfying. Even though this is obviously a fantasy, it is made with such loving care for the material, that the vast majority of audiences flocked to the film and gave it rave reviews. This is a top 100 film and a must see movie.

Fifty Shades of Grey – 2015 –Directed by Sam Taylor-Johnson and starring Jamie Dornan as Christian Grey, a billionaire, who is interviewed by a susceptible college girl reporter. One can guess where this is going, but the trip is far more important than the destination. Recommended.

The Fighting 69th - 1940 - Directed by William Keighley and starring Jimmy Cagney, Pat O'Brien, and George Brent as three New Yorkers from the 69th Regiment who are fighting in WW1. Despite the cliches and bromides, the film still delivers in the clutch.

The Fighting Sullivans – 1942 –A- Directed by Llyod Bacon and starring Selena Royle as Alleta, the real-life mother who loses FIVE sons at one time in a Pacific Theater battle, Thomas Mitchell as Thomas Sullivan, the father who must bear the unbearable, and Anne Baxter as Katherine Mary, the wife of Albert Leo Sullivan. Also prominent in the film are John Campbell as Francis Henry Sullivan, James Cardwell as George Thomas Sullivan, John Alvin as Madison Abel Sullivan, and George Offerman Jr. as Joseph Eugene Sullivan.

This was an event that changed Armed Forces policy for brothers serving in the same place at the same time during any war. It was called the Sullivan clause in Army Regulations. The change came too late for this family. We can't even begin to imagine the horror of this event for the Sullivan family. If you welled up a bit over the homage to this event shown in *Saving Private Ryan* (the scene where the mother is told of all the brothers' deaths), then you will really choke up on this one which is even more horrifying than the one portrayed in *Saving Private Ryan*. Bacon does a great job of not over-sentimentalizing the event of the deaths, and we see the Sullivans portrayed with all of their foibles. Obviously, this film was made at the beginning of the war, and served as one of the best recruiting propaganda films of all time during WW2. There wasn't a red-blooded American out there in the audience who did not want to get even for the Sullivans. Highly Recommended.

Finding Neverland -2004 – Directed by Marc Forster and starring Johnny Depp and Kate Winslet. Julie Christie (Dr. Zhivago) is also featured. The story of Barrie's inspirational family that leads to Peter Pan's creation never grows old.

Fire in the Sky 1993 - Directed by Robert Lieberman and starring D.B. Sweeney, James Garner (miscast), and Henry Thomas (good casting) in a story about alien abduction. And why would aliens want to abduct a forest firefighter? Too many holes in the lame, illogical script, but watchable.

Fire Over England (England) – 1937 - Directed by William K Howard and starring Vivien Leigh and Laurence Olivier. Also featured is Raymond Massey. This is the story of Elizabetho of England employing a pirate (Sir Francis Drake) to repel the Spanish Armada at sea. A bit of a rouser, eh, what?

First Men in the Moon (England) - 1964 - Directed by Nathan Juran and shot in Lunacolor (I'm guessing this process was never used again). The film used B actors because the real money went for special effects by the talented Ray Harryhausen. The story by HG Wells is only vaguely followed as the events in the film go way off the deep end. Fun to watch, though.

First to Fight – 1967– Directed by Christian Nyby, starring Gene Hackman and a solid B cast of actors in a story about a marine sergeant training raw recruits stateside during the birth of his first child. Not too bad.

Fist in His Pocket - 1968 - Italy - Directed by Marco Bellocchio and starring Lou Castel as a young man with a dysfunctional family he tries to help as much as he can. The entire cast is composed of unknown Italian B actors, but they do a pretty good job with the decent script and great music provided by the best in the business, Ennio Morricone.

Fistful of Dollars – 1964 –A- Directed by Sergio Leone and starring Clint Eastwood as the Man With No Name. This film was a ground-breaking production in more than one way. It initiated literally hundreds of copies of films with graphic violence.   There had been graphic violence in films before, but the sustained level of violence of this film exceeded all others before it. In Leone's world, people were either black or white, good or bad, with very few grey areas. It also marked the first film of a gunslinger killing three men at the same time in a fast draw; something that would only be possible if one or two of the men were almost completely incompetent with weapons.

   Another ground-breaking effect of this film was a highly successful Western made in Italy. Arrogant studio heads in Hollywood thought they knew everything, and predicted that no decent Western could be made outside of the US. They were dead wrong, and the age of the spaghetti Western began. The mundane story line is punctuated sharply by outstanding music by the legendary Ennio Morricone, one of the best film-scorers of all time, who later made the unforgettable *Cinema Paradiso* score. Recommended with reservations for violence.

 Five Easy Pieces – 1970 - Directed by Bob Rafelson and starring Jack Nicholson as Ralph Dupea, a classical pianist who works as an oil rigger and Karen Black as Rayette, his airhead waitress girlfriend, who is pregnant. This is primarily a story of a man who is unable to love in the spiritual sense. He is quite good at the physical part, though. It is also a film famous for one scene in a local luncheonette that some people can recite word for word; a rarity for the vast majority of films out there. When Ralph cannot get a simple order of toast from an obstinate waitress, he orders a bacon, lettuce and tomato sandwich with mayo. He tells the waitress to hold the bacon, hold the lettuce, (special orders DO upset us), hold the tomato and hold the mayo, so the result will be toast. The waitress fails to comply, and then he tells her what she can do with the sandwich. It is a classic piece of cinema and reflects the inflexibility of people, attitudes and mores of the time. Recommended.

Five Graves to Cairo – 1946- Directed by Billy Wilder and starring Franchot Tone, Anne Baxter and Erich von Stroheim. This is a WW 2 tale of fighting in the deserts of Africa, and there is also an element of mystery and romance not usually found in most other WW stories about African desert fighting. Worth viewing.

Five Star Final – 1931 – Directed by Mervyn Leroy and starring Edward G Robinson in the role as a ruthless editor, who is out to sell papers at any cost; facts be damned. The precursor to "fake news"? Fascinating, and has the feel that it is not very dated as well.

Flags of Our Fathers – 2006 - Directed, Produced and partially scored by the multi-talented and energetic Clint Eastwood. The film stars a group of relatively unknown actors including Adam Beach as the unfortunate Ira Hayes, one of the men who raised the flag on Iwo Jima. A previous film about Hayes had been made in 1961 as *The Outsider*. While that film was fairly well done, this one is superior from a number of standpoints. It has better production values, the acting is better, and the reasons for Ira Hayes erratic behavior are made clearer in the modern version. Recommended.

Flame and the Arrow - 1950 - Directed by Jacques Tourneur and starring a very athletic Burt Lancaster and a sexy Virginia Mayo (who became a prominent actress because of her brilliant red hair). Burt overcomes enormous odds with ridiculous ease, because he has had training as a trapeze artist. Irresistible.

Flame Over India (England) - 1959 - Directed by J Lee Thompson and starring Lauren Bacall (miscast here) with Kenneth More and Herbert Low (perfectly cast). This is a story about an attempt of British colonials to impose their will on a Muslim section of India (most likely Pakistan or thereabouts). They rescue a young Indian prince who has questionable qualifications to rule the Muslim population. We are supposed to hate the Muslims, and root for the British (Bacall can't do British), but we wind up rooting for the Muslims (just like we root for the Indians in Western in the modern era).

Flamingo Kid – 1984 -A- Directed by Garry Marshall, who was very good with comedy films and starring Matt Dillon and Richard Crenna. The story revolves around a poor, but handsome young man who takes a job at a summer resort on Long Island. A pleasant comedy with good soap elements.

Flashdance – 1983 - Directed by Adrian Lyne, who formally had done mostly television commercials and made a blockbuster with his first big chance. He exceeded this film with an even bigger hit, *Fatal Attraction* in 1987, but never really made another big box office film other than these two films. It appears as if one should never underestimate a producer and director of commercials. The film stars Jennifer Beals as Alex Owens, a young woman who is a welder by day and works as a dancer at a sleazy strip club at night.

Her dream is be accepted at the prestigious Pittsburgh Conservatory of Dance located in Downtown Pittsburgh, right between the bowling alley and tattoo parlor (actually it was a total fantasy; no such place existed in real life). She is aided and abetted by her boyfriend, Michael Nouri, as Nick Hurley, an actor of questionable ability who was never seen again in any major film, and various other unknowns. There is a nice turn from Lilia Skala, as Hanna Long, who as a retired Ballerina and dance teacher, encourages Alex to follow her dream. The real star of the film is the sound track, which is dynamic, and is sung by Irena Cara, who also did *Fame*. Music and quick-sequence photography are the primary mainstays of this film. Recommended.

Flight of the Navigator –1986 - Directed by Randall Kleiser and starring Joey Cramer and Paul Reubens. This light-hearted Disney offering of sci-fi fits the bill for audiences of all ages. A boy spends eight years in space and ages just a few minutes. Very interesting.

Flim-Flam Man – 1967 - Directed by Irvin Kershner and starring George C. Scott as Mordecai C. Jones, Sue Lyon plays the girlfriend of Curley, Harry Morgan, plays the hilariously funny sheriff, who cannot keep up with the antics of Mordecai, and Michael Sarazin plays Curley, an Army deserter during the Vietnam Era, who is on the run with Mordecai.

There is an absolutely first-rate supporting cast including Slim Pickins and Jarvis Bates as pigeons (suckers), and a wonderful turn by Strother Martin as a store owner who gets pickled by Curley and Mordecai in a punchboard scam. This is not an epic; it is just a simple little movie that was, for me, vastly entertaining, despite the soapy romance baloney with Lyon and Sarazin, which the director wisely kept to a minimum. Scott easily steals this film, and he is at the height of his skills as an actor, even in a small film like this one. Wasn't it Gloria Swanson that said there are no small roles, only small actors? It's a bit like watching Sgt. Bilko in action during his prime. Highly recommended.

The Fly –B- 1958 - Directed by James Clavell before he became a Shogunistic expert and starring a core of B actors led by an understated (only kidding) Vincent Price in the heavy role. I love the tag line " don't see it alone" It's not really that scary, but it did sell a few more tickets.

Flying Deuces – 1939 - Directed by the relatively unknown Edward Sutherland, who had an ongoing battle with Stan Laurel during the entire filming of the movie. The stars, Oliver Hardy and Stan Laurel play themselves (they always played themselves even when they had other names). Laurel and Hardy were arguably the greatest comedy team of all time to ever be on film. Some critics preferred Abbott and Costello, but the vast majority preferred Laurel and Hardy. Their shorts from the Hal Roach studios are still very funny and some are considered classics. Recommended, despite the silly storyline.

Flying Leathernecks – 1951 - Directed by Nicholas Ray and starring John Wayne and Robert Ryan as competing pilots with Janis Carter as the female prize.   Personally, I didnt think Janis was worth all the effort, but it is fun to watch the big dogs fight it out.

Flying Tigers – 1942 –A- Directed by David Miller and starring John Wayne in his first war movie as Jim Gordon, the leader of The Flying Tigers, the mercenary branch of the Chinese Air Force (which had very few of its own trained pilots) fighting against the Japanese invasion of 1937 in China. The group would be included in general hostilities after December 7, 1941.   These pilots were paid by the number of Japanese planes they shot down, which was a considerable number because they were better trained than the Japanese. Consequently, some of these pilots made quite a bit of money, if they survived. The film also stars John Carroll as Woody, a hotshot pilot who has trouble with the team concept, and Paul Kelly as Hap Smith, a pilot with failing eyesight. Recommended.

Follow Me Quietly - 1949 - Directed by Richard Fleischer and Anthony Mann, and starring B actors William Lundigan and Dorothy Patrick among others.   This is a vigilante film based on a serial killer who wants to eliminate people he feels are not worthy to live. An interesting premise rarely done in film. A bit bizarre, but interesting.

For A Few Dollars More – 1965 - Directed by Sergio Leone, and a sequel to the immensely successful Fistful of Dollars made a year earlier. It again stars Clint Eastwood as the Man with No Name, and also a very effective Gion Maria Volonte, as El Indio, who almost steals the film away from Eastwood. Also amusingly miscast as an American outlaw, is Klaus Kinski, who acts more with his eyes than his words. Lee Van Cleef, who would go to make another installment of this series in the *Good, the Bad and the Ugly*, is great as Colonel Douglas Mortimer, also known as The Man in Black. The music, as usual for these films, is wonderfully composed by Ennio Morricone and this is, in my opinion, his finest Western movie score. Recommended

Force of Arms – 1951 – Directed by Michael Curtiz and starring William Holden in this tale of war and romance hit the spot for many US viewers as Holden marries a WAC lieutenant and they become separated during the war (like the other millions of WW 2vets).

Force of Evil – 1948 - Directed by Abraham Polonsky and starring John Garfield and a new actress named Beatrice Pearson, who was supposed to be a femme fatale, but just turned out to be a dud. Garfield makes the film worthwhile, however. Garfield plays a lawyer (hard to buy that one), but being tough with the mob is right up his alley.

Foreign Correspondent– 1940 - Directed by Alfred Hitchcock and starring Joel McCrea as a reporter with the rather mundane name of Johnny Jones who is assigned by his editor in New York, played by Harry Davenport, to check out the latest goings on of Hitler and his gang in Germany. Herbert Marshall also stars as Stephen Fisher, a liberal leader of the Universal Peace Party in the Netherlands that is trying to solve WW 2 and Hitler through peaceful means (good luck with that idea). Also featured in the thriller is my favorite English actor, George Sanders, who just happens to be another reporter, and Lorraine Day is Carol Fisher, the daughter of the noble peacenik, Stephen, as the usual Hitchcock romantic prop for the hero, Johnny. Recommended.

Forrest Gump-1995- Directed by Robert Zemeckis, who, as a director, was noted for his light touch. Starring in the film is Tom Hanks as Forrest, a borderline retarded man from Alabama, Robin Wright as the woman who he loves, who goes off on her own adventures, and Gary Sinise as Dan, a Vietnam veteran wounded in the war, who is befriended by Forrest. The story takes place in Alabama, where a mentally-challenged child is born to a poor Alabama woman, whose husband has abandoned her. Despite his IQ, he gets a scholarship to Alabama for football, because of his great speed in running. The logic here is that if Bush can get into Yale, then Forrest can get a scholarship to Alabama. Recommended for fantasy lovers.

For Whom the Bell Tolls - 1943 - Directed by Sam Wood and starring Gary Cooper and Ingrid Bergman in the film version of the Hemingway novel. It is a story based on the memoirs and some fictionalization of Hemingway in the Spanish Civil War. Cooper was not known as a romantic, although Bergman was, so they were mismatched. The action was minimal, but the film was a success, and is worth seeing from a historical perspective.

Forbidden Games – 1952 - Directed by Rene Clement and starring Georges Poujouly and Brigitte Fossey in one of the best neo-realistic films ever made in France or anywhere else. It is right up there with The *Bicycle Thieves*. However, unlike the *Bicycle Thieves*, this film has no resolution, but makes a great statement about the effect of war on children. It is a two -hanky film made with great emotion and little soap.

Forbidden Planet - 1956 - Directed by Fred McLeod Wilcox and starring Leslie Nielson in a straight role, Anne Francis before she appeared on What's My Line, and Walter Pidgeon. The real star of the film is the special effects and Robby the Robot. Although the effects are tame by modern standards, they were pretty good for the fifties. Great fantasy.

Foreign Affair – 1948 - Directed by Billy Wilder, so you know the film will have a light touch , but can be serious at any moment, and starring Marlene Dietrich, Jean Arthur and John Lund. This story is not as funny as the title and poster would indicate. It is more of a melodrama, and a story of survival by Erika, Dietrich's character. Either way, the film is entertaining.

Fort Apache – 1948 –- Directed by John Ford and starring John Wayne as Captain Kirby York, a Civil War veteran now serving in the West. Also starring in the film is Henry Fonda as the Lieutenant Colonel Owen Thursday, a demoted Civil War general, who takes command of Fort Apache from Captain York. There is also an ample and talented supporting cast that includes Shirley Temple (all grown up), as Philadelphia, Fonda's daughter, John Agar as Second Lieutenant Michael Shannon O'Rourke, the son of Sergeant Major Michael O'Rourke (Ward Bond), who is a boozing, hard-fighting man.

Fort Bliss 2014 - Directed by Claudia Myers and starring Michelle Monaghan and additional B actors in an interesting premise; a returning medic from Afghanistan tries to readjust to life in the US and her young son. Interesting.

Forty Guns - 1952- Directed by Michael Curtiz and starring Barbara Stanwyck and Barry Sullivan. This Western has the most famous unedited line in Western history that slipped through the censors; it is not on Wikipedia or IMDB or any other movie review site that I know of, but here it is; Barry Sullivan is sitting at a table with Babara Stanwyck and she asks him if she can see his gun. The next line is when Sullivan says to her: "You better not touch it, it might go off in your face". Censors must have been asleep. Recommended with reservations.

The Founder (2017) - Directed by John Lee Hancock and starring Michael Keaton as Ray Kroc, an Elmer Gantry-like struggling salesman in the Midwest who goes on to create a burger empire. The movie somehow promises more than it can deliver, a lot like McDonald hamburgers, but still worth watching for the performance of Keaton.

The Fountain – 2006 -Directed by Darren Aronofsky and starring Hugh Jackman and Rachel Weisz in the lead roles of an interesting misfire of a sci-fi film concerning a scientist who will go to any lengths to try and save his wife dying from cancer. Might be betterto stop wasting billions of dollars on National Defense and use some of that money for research in real life. The film falls short in the script, which has more holes in it than Swiss cheese. Good try, though.

Four Faces West – 1948 – Decent B Western directed by Alfred E……Green (not Newman) and starring the dependable Joel McCrea, Frances Dee and Charles Bickford in his usual crusty character portrayal as Pat Garrett (the guy who got Billy the Kid). Watch for a streamlined version of William Conrad (under250pounds here). Fun to watch.

Four Feathers – 1939 - Directed by Zoltan Korda and starring John Clements, Ralph Richardson, June Duprez, and C. Aubrey Smith as childhood friends. The boys all serve in the Sudan during the war in the Middle East near the turn of the century. The significance of the feathers is they are connected to acts of heroism to redeem one's self if one has failed in his duties or courage in a previous situation. Henry Faversham, played by John Clemets, resigns his post just before his fellow soldiers are shipped out for duty. They all give him a feather. He must carry the feathers (in this case three from fellow soldiers and one from his fiancée) until he can perform an act of heroism to redeem himself. The film is action-packed, and the exotic location only adds to the atmosphere of the adventure. One by one, Harry saves each of his friends and to return their feathers. This film was made three times and is timeless as an adventure yarn. It is must-see fare.

The Foxcatcher – 2014 – Directed by Bennett Miller and starring Steve Carell, Channing Tatum, and Mark Ruffalo in the major roles. I love Steve Carell in just about everything he has ever done. He is so ingrained in my mind as a comedian, it was difficult for me to make the transition to his handling of this dramatic role, which he did effortlessly. There have been few comedians who could handle both drama and comedy as easily. The story of the infamous Dupont murder is morbid, but fascinating. Recommended.

Framed - 1947 - Directed by Richard Wallace and starring Glenn Ford and Barry Sullivan. Also starring is Janis Carter as a very bad girl in a classic film noir presentation that hits the mark. Janis frames Glenn for the killing of her boyfriend because she stole his money. Bad Janis.

Frankenstein – 1931 – Directed by James Whale and starring Boris Karloff as Frankenstein. Colin Clive, Mae Clark and John Boles are also in the film, but you hardly notice them because your eyes are continuously glued to Frankenstein. Poor Boris Karloff was typecast for the rest of his life because of this role, which, though it made him quite a bit of money, severely limited his role selection for the balance of his career. The film has a wonderful mood created by the director. One feels off-balance right from the start of the film. The cinematography is first-rate and worthy of an Oscar. This is a must-see film and in the top 100 of numerous film critics.

French Connection - 1971- Directed by William Friedkin and starring Gene Hackman as Popeye Doyle and Roy Schider as Buddy Russo, two cops trying to crack a difficult heroin case involving shipments from France to the United States. Also instrumental in the casting is Fernando Rey, playing the clever and stealthy French drug dealer, Alian Charnier. Charnier is the mastermind behind the entire drug operation between France and the United States and he is extremely difficult to corner. He always manages to stay away from potential drug busts by being cautious. Highly recommended, especially for the chase scene, considered one of the best in the history of cinema.

Frequency -2000 - Directed by Gregory Hoblit and starring Dennis Quaid and a solid B supporting cast in a nice storyline and script about a man who travels in time by radio to contact his father when his father was young. Extremely interesting, but falls just a bit short of expectations.

Freud -1962– Directedby John Huston and starring Montgomery Clift as Freud. Clift gives it the old college try, but the subject matter is just too complicated for the average movie fan to get excited about. Still interesting for the more intelligent viewer.

From Here to Eternity - 1953 – Directed by Otto Preminger and starring Burt Lancaster, Deborah Kerr, Montgomery Clift (predecessor to Leonardo DiCaprio as a sissy tough guy), Frank Sinatra, Ernest Borgnine, and Donna Reed. This film shows life in Hawaii before, during and after the attack on Pearl Harbor. It shows how quickly life can change. I recommend it conditionally because Lancaster carries most of the load in this film.

From Russia With Love -1964- The second installment of the James Bond series is directed by Terence Young, who also directed the first one. It also stars Sean Connery for the second time on a script developed from an Ian Fleming novel for the second time as well. More gimmicks than the first one, but about the same effect which is above average fare.

From the Earth to the Moon - 1958 – Directed by Byron Haskin and starring Joseph Cotton and Debra Paget. I'm trying to restrain myself from saying this film was a real blast...oh, I failed. Seriously though, with one of my favorite actors, George Sanders in a primary role, how can you go wrong? HG Wells was a genius, and this film highlights that.

The Front – 1976- Directed by Martin Ritt and starring Woody Allen and Zero Mostel. This is a rare film with Woody Allen where he is not the director. It is also a rare film in the sense that Allen is not used merely to gather laughs, but is in a much more serious role than he is accustomed to in almost every one of his countless films. This film might have had some problems with believability if the events portrayed had not actually happened. The frightening events of the McCarthy Era are brought to bear, and the viewer learns how life in the entertainment field was much different than it is today. Artists were routinely blacklisted because of their political activities, and therefore unemployable. In order to make ends meet for their families, they resorted to ruses such as ghostwriting, and using other people to make their artistic submissions for them. Highly recommended for historical value.

Frontier Marshall - 1939– Directed by Allan Dwan and starring Randolph Scott as Wyatt Earp. Cesar Romero plays Doc Holiday in a bit of creative casting, and John Carradine plays Ben Carter. There is a decent supporting cast that gives the film a feeling of the Old West. There would be many sequels in the future, including the Burt Lancaster version, and the Kevin Costner version, but this one is just fine. Recommended.

Frost/Nixon – 2008 - Directed by Ron Howard and starring Michael Sheen as David Frost and Frank Langella as Richard Nixon. This is a film about the Frost-Nixon Interviews that took place in 1977. The whole nation was interested in what Nixon would have to say about the whole Watergate affair, his eventual impeachment, and resignation as a result of it. This film is must-see cinema and in my opinion, Frank Langella deserved an Oscar for this movie. Highly Recommended.

Frozen River - 2008 - Directed and written by Courtney Hunt and starring Melissa Leo and Misty Upham as two down-on-their luck women who are forced to desperate measures to make ends meet in a border-crossing scheme between Canada and the US. Film is highly reminiscent of Thelma and Louise and hits the mark.

The Fugitive – 1947 - Directed by John Ford and starring Henry Fonda and Dolores Del Rio. This film noir special is very dark, and one gets claustrophobic from the photography. But that is by design. It reminded me of the cinematography in *The Informer*, which Ford made nearly a decade earlier. Good in spots.

The Fugitive – 1993 - Directed by Andrew Davis and starring Harrison Ford as Richard Kimble, the Fugitive from the extremely popular 60s drama series of the same name and Tommy Lee Jones as Samuel Gerard, the relentless pursuer of Kimble. There are some minor changes in the roles, such as having Gerard as a US Marshall, instead of a local detective from Indiana, but these changes are cosmetic in nature, as the film completely retains the suspense of the original series.

The killer of Richard Kimble's wife is a former police officer and not a one-armed drifter (which makes his detection more difficult). There is also a pharmaceutical company executive involved as the primary conspirator in this version. He had wanted his defective drug to be approved by Kimble. It must have impressed a lot of people because Tommy Lee Jones won the Best Supporting Actor Oscar that year. Recommended.

Full Metal Jacket – 1987 —Another great film directed by Stanley Kubrick (didn't he ever get tired of making great films?) starring Matthew Modine as Joker, Vincent D'Onofrio as Gomer Pyle and R. Lee Ermey as the legendary Sergeant Hartman, who completely steals the film, and wins an Academy Award to boot, in his first major role in a movie. Kubrick builds on the suspense and horror that he adds in some of his other films, such as *2001* and *The Shining*.

In this film, the suspense is built around the D'Oonfrio character, Pyle, Joker, and the Sergeant, played by Ermey. The closeness of boot camp is somewhat shaded by the abject failure of Pyle to blend in with the group. The dialogue is unbelievably good in the first half of the film, thanks to the delivery of Ermey, who makes every line he utters almost immortal.

This film is a classic because of the electric performance of R. Lee Ermey, who many critics believe gave the greatest performance in the history of cinema for a first-time actor. Every second he is on the screen, he completely dominates the lens. This is a must-see film that is shot to perfection (especially in the first half). Of course, this is no surprise with Kubrick at the helm, who won the Academy Award for Best Director for this film.

The Full Monty – 1997 - Directed by Peter Cattaneo and starring a group of unknown actors with the exception of Tom Wilkinson. Working class guys get a gig stripping for big bucks (good work if you can get it). Very funny.

The Furies - 1950 - Directed by Anthony Mann and one of the strangest casts ever put together. Barbara Stanwyck is fine in the lead role of Vance, a ruthless woman who runs a ranch and a prototype role for her later career on TV in *The Big Valley*. The rest of the cast is a mess, however. There is also no protagonist to root for in the film. What is Edith Anderson doing in this clunker? Walter Huston as a heavy is ok, but Wendell Corey as a ruthless rancher? Please. Wally Cox was more ruthless than Wendell Corey. Gilbert Roland is believable, but the plot isn't. Still entertaining to watch Stanwyck in her prime.

Fury – 1936 - Directed by Fritz Lang, who was among the cream of the crop of directors and starring Spencer Tracy as a wrongfully accused man who is accosted by mob violence. Sylvia Sydney is his ticket out of trouble, and she does a good job in the film. Walter Brennan is wasted, however, in his small role. Tracy is also a bit miscast, as he generally does not play vengeance roles in his other films. A better choice might have been Bogart, Cagney, Flynn, or any number of other male actors with a greater visceral potential for violence. Still very engrossing.

558

G

Gallipoli – 1981 - Directed by Peter Weir and starring Mel Gibson and a host of B actors. The film examines Australia's role in WW 1, and its domination by the British officers who used Australians more harshly than British troops. Historically interesting.

Games – 1967- Directed by Curtis Harrington and starring James Caan as Paul, a carefree, wealthy, Upper Eastside, spoiled brat who doesn't need to work for a living, and Katherine Ross as Jennifer, the female version of Paul. Outperforming both of these fine actors is Simone Signoret as Lisa, an older woman from France who sells Avon or some similar cosmetics line door to door. The real star of the film, however, is the writer, Gene R. Kearney. The story absolutely overwhelms all of the actors. The pace of the film is brisk, and there are no wasted or tedious scenes. It is over before you know it. I can recommend this film wholeheartedly, and I remember marveling at the story when I first saw it.

Gandhi – 1982- Written and directed by Richard Attenborough and starring Ben Kingsley as Gandhi. This film swept the academy awards for that year in almost every category. Attenborough does a highly professional job of recounting each of the important elements of the events in Gandhi's life. His pacing of a very long film is such that you do not even notice the length of the movie even with an intermission. Each of the scenes is carefully planned and executed. The music and cinematography are first-rate. The supporting cast is letter-perfect. The film depicts the life of Mahatma Gandhi from the time he was a lawyer in South Africa until shortly after the Indian independence movement. This film is a must see and is on the top 100 list of just about every movie critic in the US.

Gangster - 1947 - Directed by Gordon Wiles and starring Barry Sullivan in a nice psychological film noir piece about crime in the city, and the shady characters it attracts (not to mention shady ladies). Good stuff. Might have been written by the banned Dalton Trumbo.

Garden of Evil – 1954– Directed by Henry Hathaway, a dependable commodity, and starring a varied cast including Gary Cooper, Susan Hayward, Richard Widmark, Rita Moreno (*West Side Story*) and some good B actors, who help raise this oater into solid B territory. Watchable.

Garden of the Finzi-Continis – Italy - 1971 - Directed with impeccable taste by Vittorio De Sica, who generally does a stark portrayal of the lower classes very well. In this instance, he covers the upper crust of Italian society during the rise and fall of fascism. The B actors do a fine job under his master hand.

Garm Hawa (India) – 1973 – Directed by MS Sathayu and starring Balraj Sahni in the lead role of a Muslim businessman and his wife who must relocate to Pakistan from Northern India after the Indian Partition following the assassination of Gandhi. Film tackles complex issues with grace and insight. Recommended.

Gaslight – 1944 - Directed by George Cukor, who was skilled at portraying the upper levels of society, and starring Charles Boyer, Ingrid Bergman and Joseph Cotton in the principal roles. This is one of those "is my spouse crazy and trying to kill me, or do they just show their love in funny ways" films that were popular in the Golden Age of film. Angela Lansbury is also featured, and she is neither fat nor old in this one (pretty hot, actually).

Geisha (Japan) – 1953 - Directed by Kenji Mizoguchi and starring Michiyo Korgure and Ayako Wakao as an experienced Geisha and a novice Geisha respectively. The film highlights postwar Japanese men not being as civilized as the women now serving them in the Geisha houses. Fascinating to watch.

The General – 1926 - (Silent)- Directed by Clyde Bruckman with Buster Keaton as Johnny, the engineer, who was also the primary star of the silent classic. This film is supposedly in Roger Ebert's top ten films of all time, and for the life of me, I cannot fathom why. The film was a box-office disaster when it came out in 1926, and that was undeserved. It is a very solid comedy, and a fairly exciting film. But forgive me if I do not put it in the same category as silent classics such as *Potemkin*, which was far more exciting or *Modern Times*, which I thought was far funnier. I guess I like my films to be primarily one or the other and do not prefer films of mixed genres; but to each his own. Also featured in the film is Marion Mack as the love interest, Annabelle.

The General – 1998 - Directed by John Boorman and starring Jon Voight and a number of B Irish actors who, under the master direction of Boorman, perform admirably. This is a tale of a master Irish thief and his exploits. Interesting.

Gentleman's Agreement – 1947 - Directed by Elia Kazan and starring Gregory Peck as Phil Green, a widowed journalist posing as a Jew, Anne Revere as Mrs. Green, who must suffer the difficulties of her grandchildren being labeled Jewish, John Garfield as Dave Goldman, a Jewish WW veteran who is the role model for Green's undercover story. Also prominent is Dean Stockwell as Tommy, the young son of Phil, who has to learn what it is like to be Jewish.

Gentleman Jim – 1942 - Directed by Raoul Walsh and starring Errol Flynn and Alexis Smith in the principal roles. Jack Carson is badly miscast in a supporting role, and is uncomfortable in period films. This is the story of former heavyweight champion of the world, Jim Corbett, and how he was able to defeat the great John L Sullivan.

George Stevens: A Filmmakers Journey -1985– Directed by George Stevens Jr. and performed by an all-star cast, this documentary takes us through the various productions of George Stevens along his career in Hollywood. Interesting.

The Getaway - 1972 - Directed by Sam Peckinpah and starring Steve McQueen with a very hot Ali McGraw (who was able to shake her nice-girl image from *Love Story*). This is a story about a con who promises to rob a bank in order to get paroled. I am serious. Sally Struthers also appears weighing under 200 pounds. Eventually, in the near future, this film will not make the cut any longer for the top 2000.

Get Shorty - 1995 - Directed by Barry Sonnenfeld and starring John Travolta in black, rather than white clothes, Gene Hackman, as the only serious actor in the film, Rene Russo as a hot number, and Danny DeVito as comic relief. This is a nice, quirky comedy that clicks to a certain degree and is fun to watch.

GETT: The Trial of Viviane Amsalem - 2015 - Directed by Shlomi Elkabetz and Ronit Elkabetz and starring both the directors in the lead roles; an unusual occurrence in the vast majority of films. Having two directors that are also starring in lead roles could have been a mess; but this turned out to be a brilliant idea. Will grab you from start to finish. Recommended

Ghost Writer - 2010– Skillfully directed by Roman Polanski, who also co-wrote the screenplay along with Robert Harris, the novelist who wrote *The Ghost*, on which the film is based. The film stars Ewan McGregor as a ghost writer with no name, who accepts a job to write the memoirs of a former British Prime Minister named Adam Lang, played by Pierce Brosnan. Also featured are Olivia Williams as Lang's wife, Kim Cattrall as Lang's assistant and concubine, Eli Wallach as a mysterious old man, Tom Wilkinson as Professor Paul Emmett, who turns out to be a CIA agent, and Robert Pugh as Rycart, who had assisted the previous ghost writer in assembling data for the memoirs.

Gladiator- 2000 - Directed by Ridley Scott and starring Russell Crowe as Maximus and Jaoquin Phoenix as Commodus in the principal roles. The talented supporting cast is led by Oliver Reed, Richard Harris and Derek Jacobi. Scott does a masterful job with every single action scene (and there are plenty of them). The music and cinematography are absolutely stunning.

This film ranks up there with any gladiator movie ever made, and a good case can be made that it is the greatest gladiator movie ever with the exception of the classic *Spartacus*. It is head and shoulders above the rest of the sword and sandal genre. The film did win Best Picture and Best Actor for Crowe, and it richly deserved every award it won in every other category. It is a must-see film, and is listed on practically every top 100 best films of all time lists of most critics.

The Glass Key - 1948 Directed by Stuart Heisler and starring Brian Donlevy, a smoking hot Veronica Lake, and Alan Ladd, with William Bendix providing some comic relief. This is classic film noir in the finest tradition, and is not to be missed. Written by Dashielle Hammett.

Gleason - 2002 - Made for TV movie good enough for the top 2000 because of the great subject matter. This film has the distinction of being only one of two TV movies on the list. The other film from TV was *Don't Look Back*, a biography of Satchel Paige.

Glengarry Glen Ross – 1992 - Written and directed by David Mamet and starring one of the greatest lineups of actors in film history, including Al Pacino, Kevin Spacey, Jack Lemmon, Ed Harris, Jonathon Pryce and a demonic Alec Baldwin. Pacino's character is a great closer and sales pitch man, who seems to be the most organized and confident of all the salesmen, Spacey plays his character with his usual genius for turning into whatever it takes for you to believe what he is saying. Lemmon is the whiny, insecure former machine, who is now breaking down with the new world order taking over, Ed Harris is comparatively quiet, and is overwhelmed by the greater talent that surrounds him (that goes for both the film and the plot in the movie), Jonathon Pryce plays his role to a tee and is completely convincing. Alec Baldwin gives the performance of his life in this film, and he pretty much had to, considering whom he was surrounded by. I never forgot the line he uttered in the film, and use it in my classes for Strategic Management; " First Place is a car, Second Place is a set of steak knives and third place is you're fired."

David Mamet is one of the greatest writers of our time, and in my opinion, this film and its script is even better than *House of Games*, which up to this point had been Mamet's masterpiece. If you want to see writing, acting and directing at its very best, then this is the film you have been waiting for. This is a must-see film that lost money at the box office, but will be remembered more than the profits of a thousand other films.

Glory! – 1989- Directed by Edward Zwick and starring Matthew Broderick, as Captain Robert Gould Shaw, a reticent, sensitive, but fearless Northern Civil War leader and Denzel Washington as Trip, one of the African-American volunteers of the 54th regiment from Massachusetts. Also featured in key roles were Cary Elwes and Morgan Freeman.

Godfather – 1972 - Directed by Francis Ford Coppola and written by Mario Puzo, this is the first film of the trilogy of *Godfather* movies, but does not appear as highly rated as *Godfather 2*, primarily because Robert DeNiro is not in the first *Godfather* film. However, *Godfather 1* does have the benefit of a lot more screen time with Marlon Brando, which almost makes up for the absence of DeNiro. Robert Duvall, and particularly James Caan, give excellent performances in this gangster classic. Talia Shire and Diane Keaton also give strong performances, as the sister and wife of Al Pacino's Micheal Corleone character.

Coppola is letter-perfect in his direction of every single scene in the movie. He would repeat his perfection again in the sequel, but fall a bit short in the third installment. The cast is so talented, and the script is so apt, that the movie was guaranteed to be a success even before it was seen by the public.

The cinematography of this film is outstanding, and it is a must-see for every serious film buff. This movie is consistently in the top 100 films of all time.

Godfather Two – 1974 - Directed by Francis Ford Coppola and written by Mario Puzo, this is considered not only to be the best of the trilogy of Godfather films, but appears quite often on the top ten list of greatest films of all time for numerous critics, including myself. This tale of the Corleone family is both a flashback and a sequel to the original film. The major difference between the two films, however, is the explosion on the screen of Robert DeNiro, who won an Academy Award for his portrayal of Vito Corleone as a young man.

This film is only one of two that both Pacino and DeNiro are co-stars. The two of them would be enough to carry any film, but they had a tremendous supporting cast as well, combined with striking cinematography, and a haunting sound track that has become a classic piece.   You seldom get this kind of combination in many films. Robert Duvall and John Cazale stand out in supporting roles as do Talia Shire and Diane Keaton.   Lee Strasburg is excellent in his Havana scene as Hyman Roth. The early flashback story shows the young Godfather coming to New York, and the isolation of Ellis Island. Highly recommended.

Godfather III –1976- Directed by Francis Ford Coppola and starring his daughter, Sophia, Al Pacino, and the usual gang of suspects that are in most of the *Godfather* trilogy. This episode is considered to be the weakest of the three films, but that is like saying Mickey Mantle was not as good as Ruth or Gehrig. Mantle was still pretty good. This film is still head and shoulders over almost all other films made for that year and the performances are still first rate. The story about the Vatican is fascinating, and the cinematography is still outstanding, as well as the editing.

There really is not much of a fall-off here. I thought Sophia Coppola did a fine job in her role, and the subsequent criticism she received by various reviewers was, in my opinion, was far too harsh. If she didn't have any talent, then how was she able to win an Academy Award years later for *Lost in Translation*? Petty people are always jealous of others with more talent.

God Particle-2017–Directed by Julius Onah and starring a diverse cast including the successor to Gong Li, Zhang Ziyi, and a number of rather unknown actors in a very interesting concept for a story in science-fiction. One that does not include monsters or aliens, but nature; which can be FAR more terrifying. Recommended.

Gods and Monsters – 1998 - Written and directed by Bill Condon and starring Ian McKellen, Brandan Fraser, and Lynn Redgrave (*Georgy Girl*!). The film examines the late life of James Whale, the talented director of such classics as *Frankenstein* and *The Bride of Frankenstein* from which the title of the film is derived. Interesting.

Godzilla – Japan - 1956 Directed by Ishiro Honda and starring a number of unknown B Japanese actors. The real star of the film is Godzilla, of course. Godzilla is a result of nuclear weapons, and many psychologists have suggested the monster represents the nuclear nightmare for the Japanese. This film has spawned at least two dozen sequels. Recommended for historical interest.

Goldfinger – 1964 - Directed by Guy Hamilton and starring Sean Connery as 007, Super Spy, Honor Blackman as Pussy Galore, Shirley Eaton as Jill Masterson, and Gert Frobe, who lacked the suggestive names of the female co-stars, as Goldfinger. This film, as all Bond films, was based on the writings of Ian Fleming. The Bond Series was generally produced by veterans Albert Broccoli and Harry Saltzman, who specialized in the spy genre, and did another series of spy films with Michael Caine, such as The *Ipcress File* and others. The first two Bond films, *Dr. No* and *From Russia With Love,* had made enormous profits, and those profits were successfully reinvested into the production values of *Goldfinger*, which made more money than either of the other two.   Other than suspending disbelief, the film is quite entertaining, and I can recommend it without reservation.

Golden Voyage of Sinbad - 1973 - Directed by Gordon Hessler and starring John Phillip Law and a host of B actors who perform admirably. Music by the talented Miklos Rozsa adds to the production values. The special effects by Ray Harryhausen are the real stars of the film. Fun for all ages.

Gold Rush - 1925 (Silent) - Written, Directed, Produced and starring Charlie Chaplin as the tramp trying to make a go of it during the Gold Rush. Charlie even wrote the music and did everything for the film except shovel the snow (and he might have done that as well). A classic in every sense, anda must-see film.

Gone With the Wind – 1939 — Directed by Victor Fleming and starring Vivian Leigh and Clark Gable, plus a cast of thousands as they would say in the old days. Is there anyone out there who hasn't seen this movie, or read the book by Margaret Mitchell? Despite what some might say, this film is the zenith of soap. It is the Queen of soap. No other film or TV show in history can touch it for soap. Soap operas use this film as the benchmark. It is very high quality soap, however.

Leigh steals the film away from Gable quite easily, and is the dominant personality in the film. In case you are new to film, and haven't read the novel, I will quickly condense the thousand page tome. A Southern Belle, Scarlett, has over a half dozen boyfriends and struggles to keep her father's estate throughout the Civil War as she marries primarily out of convenience and necessity, rather than for love. She loves her best friend's husband, Ashley, played by Leslie Howard, who is married to Melanie, played by Olivia DeHaviland, but marries Rhett Butler, played by Gable.

There are additional husbands and boyfriends in the plot, but they are as meaningless as the Civil War, which just happens to be a major inconvenience for Scarlett, who is one of the greatest studies of self-absorbed personalities in screen history. The music for this film is legendary, and the cinematography is first-rate. This movie had more publicity than World War Two, and it continues as a favorite among the ladies in the audience as the greatest soap ever made. It is still a must- see film. It won numerous Academy Awards (more than any other film until *Ben-Hur*). Only poor Clark Gable was shut out in the 1939 awards.

 Goodbye, Columbus –1969- Directed by Larry Peerce and starring Richard Benjamin as Neil Klugman, (the name of the character which appears to be taken from Jack Klugman, who is also featured), a Jewish library clerk from Rutgers University, Ali MacGraw as Brenda Patimkin, a Jewish-American Princess from the Midwest, and prestigious Radcliffe College, who falls in love with Neil, Jack Klugman as

Ben Patimkin, Brenda's class-conscious father, and Nan Martin as Mrs. Patimkin, Brenda's severely class-conscious mother.

Goodbye, Mr. Chips– 1939- Directed by Sam Wood and starring Robert Donat as Mr. Chips and Greer Garson, in a rare supporting role, as his loving wife. Wood does a wonderful job creating the atmosphere of a boys' school in England, and the film progresses at a crisp pace without a lull. Donat won the Academy Award for this performance in 1939 over a highly favored Clark Gable from *Gone With the Wind*; an enormous upset.

   The award was well-deserved. Garson was also very good in this film, but the real stars were the magnificent supporting actors, who add authenticity and sincerity to each scene. There was not a bad performance in the lot. The dialogue in this film is outstanding, and Donat's award was well-deserved. This is a must see film and is consistently in the top hundred films of all time listed by the majority of film critics. It is one of my favorites, since I am a professor as well.

The Good Earth – 1937 - Directed by Sidney Franklin and starring Louise Rainer and Paul Muni. This is the best movie ever made about China in Hollywood history. The difficulties about making films about China were immense because of the language problems, and having Caucasians playing Chinese was a controversial subject, but at the time there were just not enough professional actors and actresses in China at the level of Muni and Rainer who could play the principal roles, so the ends justified the means in this situation.

   We will never see this type of film ever again, as China has caught up in the acting talent area as well as the technical area of film-making. For what it is, however, is still one of the ten best films ever made according to numerous critics. The photography by Karl Freund was magnificent, and won an Academy Award. The desperation of the family in the city was palatable, and the direction of the action was impeccable.

   The dialogue was crisp and intense, as well as the characterizations of a Chinese farmer's family. Muni, as always, gives a measured and professional performance, but it is Rainer who steals the film with her portrayal as O-Lan, the embattled wife of Wang Lung. Her range of acting is among the greatest in all of Hollywood history, as attested by her two Academy Awards. Her performance in this film is easily among the greatest ten performances by an actress in the annals of film. The solid supporting cast makes this a movie for one to enjoy just as easily in the 21st century as it was enjoyed a century earlier. A true classic.

Goodfellas – 1990 - Directed by Martin Scorsese and starring Robert DeNiro , Ray Liotta and Joe Pesci, who won the Academy Award for best supporting actor for this film. Scorcese is at his best when he is doing Italian hoods. He just knows them so well from the old New York neighborhood he came from. Robert DeNiro is another talent who has a special feel for Italian hoods. He knows them from his neighborhood as well in the Chelsea district. Joe Pesci is a piece of work. He uses the F word about a hundred times in about half of his films, and this time it won him an Oscar. Go figure. Pesci is an irresistible character, who always seems to be out of control, regardless of what movie he is in. This film is his best performance ever.

Good Morning, Vietnam - 1987 - Directed by Barry Levinson and starring Robin Williams as Adrian Cronauer, a Vietnam-era disc-jockey, who is constantly irritating his superior officers, Forest Whitiker as Private Edward Garlick, the eventual replacement of Adrian, a very funny Bruno Kirby (who was outstanding in *Godfather 2*) as Lieutenant Hauk, a corny, polka-playing, would-be replacement for Adrian, Nobel Willingham as General Taylor, who likes Adrian's show, and helps to protect him, Chintara Sukapatana as a Vietnamese girl, Trinh, that Adrian falls for, and Tung Tranh Tran as Tuan, the double-agent brother of Trinh.

The casting of an Indian woman as a Vietnamese infuriated many native Vietnamese citizens, who felt it was a slight against their female actors. They contended that there were plenty of Vietnamese actresses to choose from, just as when Tung Tranh Tran was chosen for his role. Recommended, despite a trite subplot, because of the great performance of Williams.

Good Night and Good Luck– 2006 - Directed by George Clooney and starring David Strahairn as the revered television journalist, Edward R. Murrow, who not only withstood a vicious attack from the political maniac, Joseph McCarthy, but was able to eventually be the catalyst behind McCarthy's inevitable fall. McCarthy is played by himself through old footage. This might have been a flaw in the production as face to face confrontations are far more dramatic than fighting an unseen enemy on film.

Maybe they couldn't find an actor ugly enough to play McCarthy. Also prominent in the cast is George Clooney as Fred Friendly, the CBS news boss, and loyal supporter of Murrow under all conditions. Frank Langella plays Paley, the head of CBS, with his usual convincing ability. Robert Downey Jr. is featured as a reporter, and may have been out of his element here. But that was only a mild miscasting mistake. A second problem for the film was not having someone play McCarthy, himself. If an actor can play Hitler, then they should have been able to find one who could have played McCarthy. Highly recommended for all.

The Good Shepherd - 2006 - Directed by Robert DeNiro and starring an all-star cast including Robert DeNiro, Matt Damon, Angela Jolie, William Hurt, Alec Baldwin, Joe Pesci, Timothy Hutton, Billy Crudup and John Tutturo. There was enough talent in this spy thriller to make three good films, but for some reason, too many good cooks seemed to have spoiled the broth. Still worth watching, however, because of a good story line.

The Good, The Bad and the Ugly – 1968 - Directed by Sergio Leone with great music by Ennio Moricone and starring Clint Eastwood, Lee Van Cleef, and Eli Wallach as the good, bad and the ugly, respectively. The film was the third spaghetti Western of a trilogy completed by Leone and starring Eastwood. *A Fistful of Dollars* and *For A Few Dollars More* had already been big box office hits; and helped to finance the better production values, and better cast for this showcase third installment. By the way, I coined the term Provolone Western as a term to replace Spaghetti Western because of all of the ham in these great flicks.

Good Will Hunting – 1997- Directed by Gus Van Sant and starring Matt Damon as a blue collar math genius from South Boston, Will Hunting, Ben Affleck as Chuckie Sullivan, his townie friend who works in construction with him, and Robin Williams as Sean Maguire, the psychiatrist that probes Will's need for academic obscurity, while engaging in self-destructive behavior. This sleeper of a film came out of nowhere to make over twenty times its cost at the box office, win two Academey Awards, and explode both Affleck and Damon into overnight stars. It could have been called *The Boston Dead End Kids with a Brain.*

Gorky Park – 1983 - Directed by Michael Apted and starring William Hurt, Lee Marvin and Brian Dennehy in the principal roles. This seemed like a sure thing when it was released, but it fell a bit short on the big screen. Still interesting to watch because of the good talent in the film.

The Gospel According to Matthew (Italy) – 1994 - Directed by Pier Paolo Pasolini and starring Enrique Irazoqui as Jesus Christ. The completion of the film by an avowed atheist caused a sensation at the time of its production. But upon closer inspection, the film turned out to be a masterpiece that was venerated by audiences and critics, alike. The relatively low-budget film, shot in black and white, captures what many felt was the true essence of Christ; his humanity and passion.

The previous films about Christ out of Hollywood were generally spectacles like *The Greatest Story Ever Told* and *King of Kings*, shot in glorious Technicolor, and portraying Christ as a long-haired, almost saintly, personality, as opposed to the *Gospel of Matthew*, which portrays Christ as a young Jewish man common to his times, who wore his hair short, and was often the same with his temper. Director Pasolini used austere sites to film at, and presented Christ in the most common way he possibly could have. This resulted in the humanization of the Christ character, and greater association by the viewing audience with the person on the screen as a person, and not a God. The music was nominated for an Academy Award. I can recommend this film highly as the best film about Christ ever made.

Go Tell the Spartans– 1978 - Directed by Ted Post and starring Burt Lancaster as the ill-fated Major Asa Barker, and Craig Wasson as Corporal Coursey, an idealistic young man who learns about war the hard way (is there any other way to learn about it?). This production actually ran out of money, but Burt Lancaster forked over the last payment to make sure the film was completed. In his opinion, it was a great script by Wendell Mayes, based on a novel written by Daniel Ford, and I would have to agree with him. The film was also well-shot by Harry Stradling Jr., with a number of eerie images. The French tried to teach us, but we did not learn from history. Highly recommended.

Gotti -1996 – Directed by Robert Harmon and starring Armand Assante as the Dapper Don. An examination of the head of the Gambino crime family in New York. Just another Italian crook who made it tougher for honest Italian-Americans to live in their communities. Nice production values.

The Graduate – 1967 - Directed by Mike Nichols and starring the love triangle members, Dustin Hoffman as Benjamin, a recent college graduate, who is now pursuing more adult pleasures, Anne Bancroft as the decadent and immortal Mrs. Robinson, and Katherine Ross as the real object of Benjamin's pure love. This coming-of-age film depicts the plight of a recent college graduate (Hoffman was 27 when he made it), who is conflicted about his career and his love life, but not in that order. He initially dates Elaine Robinson, (Katherine Ross), who is the daughter of Mrs. Robinson, who later seduces Benjamin in a famous bedroom scene.

The triangle is a bit more complicated than most, because it includes a mother and a daughter. The film is mesmerizing in part, because of the iconic sound track provided by Simon and Garfunkel; songs from which have become classics like: *Sounds of Silence, Scarborough Fair,* and *Mrs. Robinson*. Any one of these would have won an Academy Award in any given year for best song in a film, but this movie had three of them.

PLASTICS! Highly recommended for those new to cinema.

Grand Hotel – 1932 - Directed by Edmund Goulding and produced by the legendary Irving Thalberg. The cast includes such greats as Greta Garbo as Grusinskaya, a star dancer who is aging. This is the film that utilizes her famous line "I Want to Be Alone". Other major players in the film include John Barrymore as the Baron Felix von Gaigern, who has his own worries, Joan Crawford as Flaemmchen, a stenographer with loose personal morals (not much of a stretch there), Wallace Beery as the bullying General Director Preysing, Lionel Barrymore as Otto Kringelein, and Lewis Stone as Dr. Otternschlag. Other minor roles include Jean Hersholt as Senf, the Porter, Robert McWade as Meierheim, Purnell Pratt as Zinnowitz, Ferdinand Gottschalk as Pimenov, and Moran Wallace as the chauffeur. This is one of the last great films of Berlin and Germany before the onset of the Nazi era. There is not even a mention of Hitler or the Nazi Party. This film won best movie of the year at the Academy Awards. Highly recommended.

Grand Illusion – 1937 - Directed by Jean Renoir and based on the book of the same name by Norman Angell. The cast includes Jean Gabin as Lieutenant Marechal, a French officer under house arrest, Marcel Dalioas Lieutenant Rosenthal, a second French officer under house arrest, and Pierre Fresnay as the third French officer POW, Captain de Boeldieu. These three plot an escape.

Also featured is Erich von Stroheim as Captain von Rauffenstein, a German officer in charge of the POWs in a mountain fortress. The supporting cast includes Dita Parlo as Elsa, a widowed German farm woman, Julien Carette as Cartier, a showoff, Georges Peclet as an officer, Werner Florian as Sgt. Arthur, Jean Daste as a teacher, Sylvain Itkine as Lieutenant Demolder and Gaston Modot as an engineer. Recommended.

Grapes of Wrath – 1940 - Directed by John Ford and starring Henry Fonda with a strong supporting cast, this film is considered a classic of the Great Depression. The story of the Joads and their trip from Oklahoma to California is an inspiring saga for any viewer of any age. Harrowing experiences begin with roadblocks and signs saying that out of state people should turn around and go home. The camp they do manage to make it to, is nothing more than an organized exploitation farm, a method to extract the most possible work out of a man and his family for the least possible amount of money that can be paid. It was truly a blot on the history of America.

The Joads move on to the next camp and it is almost as bad as the first. Their companion, Jim Casy (John Carradine) gets involved in a fight with some bullying guards and gets himself killed, while Tom Joad gets badly bruised and becomes a fugitive after killing the guard that murdered Jim. The family hides Tom as they sneak out of camp and barely have enough gas to get to a third camp that is a legitimate government settlement for workers. But it is too late for Tom Joad; as he is now a hunted criminal. He must strike out on his own in the world and he vows to become a social activist for the rest of his life.

This film won an Academy Award for John Ford's directing, in addition to a well-deserved Best Supporting Actress award for Jane Darwell. The communist/socialist overtones of the film soon became a moot point because World War 2 began the following year. After the release of the film, communist Russia soon became our ally. It would be another ten years before socialism/communism then fell again into disfavor in American society. Highly recommended.

The Great Beauty – 2013 – Italy – Directed by Paolo Sorrentino and starring Toni Servillo in the lead role as an aging writer who is having a bit of angst over his past before he moves on to continue writing in the future. A very incisive film that examines a problem that many of us might face one day. Recommended.

The Great Buck Howard - 2009 - Directed by Sean McGinly and starring a slew of talent including John Malkovich as Buck (Amazing Kreskin?), Tom Hanks as his real life son's screen father, Colin Hanks, who does an admirable job as Buck's assistant, Ricky Jay, who is always great whenever he is on the screen in any film, and Emily Blunt as a reporter covering Buck and falling for Colin. Great stuff, and not to be missed.

The Great Dictator - 1940 - Produced, written and directed by Charlie Chaplin and co-starring a still hot (at the time) Paulette Goddard. This is a thinly veiled attack on the personality of Adolf Hitler, and is hilarious considering this was produced before WW 2 in the US. Chaplin was a master of comedy.

The Great Escape – 1963 - Directed by John Sturges and starring Steve McQueen as Captain Virgil Hilts, a motorcycle enthusiast, James Garner as Lieutenant Bob Hendley of the RAF (I did not buy Garner as a Brit), Richard Attenborough as RAF Squad Leader Roger Bartlett, James Donald as Captain Ramsey, Charles Bronson as Lieutenant Danny Velinski of the RAF (even more unbelievable as a Brit than Garner), Donald Pleasence as Lieutenant Colin Blythe, in an interesting role as a forger going blind, James Colburn as Louis of the RAF, who is a bit more believeable, but not much as a Brit, David McCallum as Eric, and a fine supporting cast of Germans playing Germans and Brits playing Brits. (CHARLES BRONSON as a Brit???? Give me a break!).

Great Expectations (England) - 1947 - Directed by David Lean, who was a master at handling spectacle and all-star casts, and starring Jean Simmons, John Mills and Valerie Hobson as well a great supporting cast. This is easily the best of all the Dickens works ever brought to the screen (with the exception of *Christmas Carol*).

The Great Imposter – 1961 - Directed by Robert Mulligan, and starring Tony Curtis as Ferdinand Waldo Demara, a man who is very similar to the character portrayed in the recent *Catch Me If You Can* with Leonardo DiCaprio. Also featured in the fim is Edmund O'Brien, Karl Malden, Gary Mierrill, Arthur O'Connell, Raymond Massey, and Frank Gorshin, which is fairly ironic, because Gorshin used to do stage imitations featuring Jimmy Cagney. He was considered to be a top notch imposter.

The imposter in this film, however, is quite different. Among Demara's impersonations were a ship's doctor, a civil engineer, a deputy sheriff, an assistant prison warden, a psychologist, a hospital orderly, a lawyer, a child-care expert, a monk, a cancer researcher and finally, the easiest job to fake in the world, because I know from experience, a teacher.

Had Demara the credentials, most of his employers would have been more than happy with his performance. Demara possessed a photographic memory and had a very high IQ. He was able to memorize textbooks easily. He was raised in a small town in Massachusetts. His family was negatively impacted by the Great Depression, and this event angered Demara. He ran away to a monastery and joined the Benedictine monks for four years. Then he enlisted in the Army after Pearl Harbor. He went AWOL, and borrowed a name from one of his army buddies. He joined two more monasteries, faked a suicide, and then borrowed another name.

He successfully scammed a college in Pennsylvania into believing he was a psychologist and he became a professor for them. The FBI caught up with him for desertion, and he did a year and a half in prison. After getting out, he studied law, and then medicine, after which he practiced being a surgeon on a Royal Canadian war ship in Korea. Having saved 16 lives, the Canadians did not press charges. He then went on to become a founder of a college, and an assistant to a warden at a state prison. The philosophy of Demara was that there was always a vacuum of power in almost every bureaucratic organization. All you had to do was fill that vacuum, and assume your personal power base within it. You never opposed anyone, or anyone's view, you merely created your own office and committee. This system worked a staggering number of times. Actually, Curtis was not the best casting for this film, as in real life, Demara was quite overweight. In retrospect, Jackie Gleason might have been a much better choice. Recommended with reservations.

The Great Man - 1956 - A-Written, directed and starring Jose Ferrer as a broadcaster who is about to take over for an Arthur Godfrey-type TV personality, except that Ferrer discovers the Great Man was not so great in real life. Also starring Dean Jagger, Keenan Wynn, Ed Wynn, Jim Backus and a great supporting cast. Must see.

The Great McGinty – 1940 - Directed by Preston Sturges in his first film effort, and starring Brian Donlevy as Dan McGinty, a bartender in a nameless South American country who recalls his past to a dancing girl at the bar. Also featured in the film are Akim Tamiroff as a local political boss, William Demarest, a future Sturges troupe mainstay, as a political hack working for the boss, Muriel Angelus as the woman McGinty marries for political convenience, and a highly professional, well-chosen supporting cast that Sturges became famous for later in his career.

Great Northfield Minnesota Raid– 1972 – Directed by Philip Kaufman and starring Cliff Robertson and Robert Duvall inthe lead roles. This depiction of the James and Younger gangs robbing the biggest bank in the West is a classic, and is really well-made. Recommended.

The Great Raid - 2005– Directed by John Dahl and starring James Franco and Benjamin Bratt in a WW2 story about the freeing of Bataan POWs at the end of the war before the Japanese could slaughter them, as they usually did with their POWs in WW2. Not bad.

The Great Santini – 1980 - Directed by Lewis John Carlino and starring Robert Duvall as Lieutenant Colonel Wilbur "Bull" Meechum, also known as the Great Santini, which is a sarcastic reference to his many accomplishments as an ace pilot, who does not have the same success at home with his wife and family. Also featured in the film is Blythe Danner as his longsuffering wife, who must always take care of the family while he is away, Micheal O'Keefe as Santini's basketball player son, Lisa Jane Persky as his daughter, and other minor roles featuring his other children.

The Great Ziegfeld - 1936 - Directed by Robert Z Leonard and starring William Powell, Myrna Loy, Luise Rainer, Frank Morgan (*The Wizard of OZ*), Fannie Brice and Ray Bolger (also *The Wizard of OZ*). A great supporting cast adds to the production values. This is a biopic of Florenz Ziegfeld, the man who put together the best live shows on Broadway.

Green For Danger (England) - 1947 - Directed by Sidney Gilliat and starring Alastair Sim, Trevor Howard, and Sally Gray as the principal actors in this murder mystery during the War in England. Sim is always great, and he is very good here as an inspector investigating a suspicious death at a hospital. A real hidden gem.

Green Hat (China)– 2004 - Directed by Liu Fendou and starring Li Congxi as a cop and Liao Fan as a criminal. But this is not a cops and robbers flick. Both men are having trouble keeping their wives faithful at home, and both are wearing what the Chinese call a Green Hat (you are a cuckold). Unfortunately, this is not just a comedy, either. It is somewhere in between. An oddity of a film; but worth seeing.

The Grey Fox - 1982 - Directed by Phillip Borsos, and starring Richard Farnsworth in a role he was nominated forby the Academy. He is amply supported by a fine cast that depicts life in Canada at the dawn of the 20th century. Richard is a bank robber, by the way, and he is inspired to rob a train from a movie he sees. Good stuff.

Greystoke: The Legend of Tarzan, Lord of the Apes - 1984 - Directed by Hugh Hudson, and starring Christopher Lambert as Tarzan, and a great supporting cast. This story of Tarzan in infinitely superior to most of the older Tarzan films, and remains the benchmark to this day. A must see.

The Grifters – 1990 - Directed by Stephen Frears and starring a miscast John Cusack (who is not meant for film noir), Anjelica Huston (who is perfect for film noir) and Annette Benning (who is also good casting for film noir). This slick production suffers from just one thing; the wrong man in the role as a young grifter. Otherwise, it is first-rate.

The Groove Tube - 1974 - Directed by Ken Shapiro and featuring Chevy Chase in a few of the skits. This collection of comedy skits is fairly average, except for one sensationally funny skit on venereal disease; be sure to catch it (the film, not the disease). Will probably not survive this list in a few years.

Groundhog Day - 1993 - Successfully directed by Harold Ramis (one of the original Ghostbusters) and starring another former Ghostbuster, Bill Murray with the funny-looking Andie MacDowell as his female sidekick. This mundane storyline of a man reliving the same day over and over is quite funny under the guidance of Ramis.

The Guide – India - 1965 - Directed by Vijay Anand and starring his brother, Dev Anand and Waheeda Rehman as illicit lovers. Anand plays a guide that falls in love with the young wife of a rich man. This soap aided by the music of S. D. Burman was a big hit when it was released.

Gun Crazy - 1950 - Directed by Joseph M Lewis and starring that two-pistol packing mama, Peggy Cummins, who is the only woman ever featured on a poster that wields two guns at the same time. A precursor to *Bonnie and Clyde*. Good noir.

Gunfight at the OK Coral - 1957 - Classic Western directed by John Sturges, who occasionally had trouble pacing his films. Despite lulls in this one, Lancaster and Douglas pull out all the stops and make it worthwhile. Douglas later recruited John Ireland for *Spartacus* a few years later. Best scene, of course, is the last one. Watched this one with my first girlfriend, Julie Bottone, over her house.

The Gunfighter – 1950 - Directed by Henry King and starring Gregory Peck and a peck of B actors with a C script. Somehow, Peck succeeds with his character, despite his ridiculous mustache. This film will not last more than a few years on this list.

Gunga Din – 1939 - Directed by George Stevens and starring Cary Grant, slightly miscast as Sergeant Cutter in the British Indian Army. His two sidekicks are Ballantine, played by the dashing Douglas Fairbanks, Jr., and a third sergeant, MacChesney, played by Victor McLaglen. Also featured in the cast is Sam Jaffe, as the loyal self-sacraficing Indian, Gunga Din, and Joan Fontaine as Emmy, the fiancée of Ballantine, who wants him to retire and go into the tea business. A fine supporting cast fills out the troupe.

Gunsmoke –1953– Directed by Nathan Juran and starring the diminutive Audie Murphy in the lead role of bad-guy killing machine. A bit more violent than most Westerns of the era; most likely due to the presence of Murphy.

Guns of Diablo – 1965– Directed by Boris Sagal and starring Charles Bronson and Kurt Russell (as a teen) in a story about a wagon train trip across the West and the perils that are encountered. Nothing new here, but watchable.

The Guns ofNavarone - 1961 - Directed by J Lee Thompson and starring Gregory Peck, David Niven and Anthony Quinn. These three disparate actors seldom appeared together, so the chemistry was interesting to watch. The great music by Dimitri Tiomkin softens the shock of seeing Irene Papas' face on the big screen. Good supporting cast and lots of action.

H

Hacksaw Ridge –2016 –Directedby MelGibson and starring Andrew Garfield as an exceptional young man who is a conscientious objector who refuses to carry weapons, but not hesitate to put his life on the line 75 times to save 75 individuallyinjured soldierson the ridge. Truly awe-inspiring, and one of the few war movies thatis truly awe-inspiring,

Hail Caesar! – 2016 – –Directed by the Coen Brothers, so you know the film will be zany and unconventional. The film stars George Clooney, who loved working with the Coens in the past, and Josh Brolin, among others. This tale of a Hollywood producer trying to keep the massive egos of his stars in line is hilarious. Very funny.

Half Nelson – 2006 – Directed by Ryan Fleck and starring Ryan Gosling (I'm sure there was great cconfusion on the set when anyone yelled out "Ryan!"). This tale of a drug-addicted teacher teaching students in a drug-ridden area has some unusual insights. Interesting.

Halls of Montezuma - 1951 - Directed by Lewis Millstone and starring more tough beef than you would find in a steakhouse in China. The line-up of tough guys included Richard Widmark, Jack Palance, Karl Malden, Richard Boone, and Jack Webb for starters. Great cast and action.

Hamlet – England – 1948 - Directed, produced and starring Laurence Olivier as Hamlet. This is obviously Olivier's baby from beginning to end, and it was as close to a compete success as you can have (the only exception was not having massive box office results). Olivier had wisely cut almost two hours from the content of the original play, knowing that movie audiences would get restive after two hours. This resulted in a production that purists found to be disappointing, but movie-goers found to be very entertaining. The rest of the sterling cast included Basil Sydney as King Claudius, the killer of Hamlet's father, and the plunderer of his mother, Eileen Herlie as Queen Gertrude, who naively marries Claudius after the death of Hamlet, Norman Wooland competently plays Horatio, Hamlet's stable friend, Felix Aylmer as Polonius, the father of Ophelia, Terence Morgan as Laertes, whose father is killed by Hamlet and his sister driven mad by him, and Jean Simmons, one of the most beautiful women in the history of cinema, as Ophelia; the casting for her role was so perfect that she was nominated for a best supporting actress award. Speaking of awards, this picture won for Best Movie of the year in 1948 as well as Olivier winning for Best Actor of the year for the only time in his career. Although nominated nine times, this would be his only triumph. Jean Simmons would go on to star in films such as *Spartacus* and Elmer Gantry and would have the most successful film career of all the women in the film. Highly recommended.

Hamsun (German) - 1996 - Directed by Jan Troell and starring Max Von Sydow and Ghita Norby as his wife. A prominent couple in Norway supports Hitler, and lose everything. Historically interesting, because it is a true story.

Hangmen Also Die – 1943 – Directed byFritzLang andstarring Walter Brennan and Brian Donlevy in a tale about theCzechResistance during WW 2 and the events after an assassination to get the killer out of the country. Not bad.

Hangover Square - 1945 - Directed by John Brahm and starring my favorite British actor, George Sanders, along with Linda Darnell. The film deals with the seedy part of town being a hangout for the rich and famous. They have everything to lose, and the lowlifes have nothing to lose. A good lesson for all.

Hannah and Her Sisters -1986 - Written and Directed by Woody Allen, who also stars in the film, but the female cast dominates the action as we follow a group of sisters and their romantic involvements. Would have liked more Woody here, and less of the sisters. Michael Caine is always good, Mia Farrow is OK, Carrie Fisher is good, Barbara Hershey is OK, Lloyd Nolan was better off on Guadacanal, Maureen O'Sullivan was better off in the Jungle with Johnny, Daniel Stern is out of his depth here, Max Van Sydow belongs in European films and is lost here, Diane Wiest is usually neurotically interesting, as is this film, if you like soap.

Hannibal - 1959 - Directed by Edgar G. Ulmer, an old dependable studio director from the B movie lots who was famous for making Detour , a low-budget film-noir classic. Some Italian hack director was also listed, but he probably got in Edgar's way more than he helped. The film was relatively interesting because of Mature and the plot of the film which was the threatening of Rome by elephants and Hannibal crossing the Alps. He would have gotten it done, too, if he hadn't mixed business with pleasure. His captured princess falls in love with him and ruins everything. So much for ruling the world. Good fun.

Hard Day's Night – 1964 — Directed by Richard Lester and starring John Lennon, Paul McCartney, Ringo Starr and George Harrison, the least popular member of all the Beatles.

Much to the credit of manager Brian Epstein and music editor George Martin, the film does not get bogged down with an artificial script or professional actors; it is sort of a free verse visual expression of the actual lives of the Beatles at the time, but with a bit of creative license.   Some critics thought the film was brilliant, and I was one, at the time, who did not understand what they meant.   But now I see what the critics of the 60s were clamoring about; the film has a sense of great authenticity; it is not overly artificial. Not only is it realistic, but it is very funny at the same time. The idea that the Beatles had become prisoners of their own fame was not farfetched in the least.

Hard Eight – 1996 –Directed by Paul Thomas Anderson and starring Philip Baker Hall, John C Reilly, Samuel L Jackson, and the only person associated with the film with just two names, Gwyneth Paltrow. The tight script and superb cast make this a real treat to watch. All the characters are sleazy and the film has no socially redeeming value whatsoever. What fun!.

The Harder They Fall —1956 - Directed by Mark Robson and starring Humphrey Bogart as the good guy trying to clean up the fight game, and Rod Steiger as the highly believable heavy. Jan Sterling is also featured. In real life, they would have just shot Bogey. But fun to watch, anyway.

Harry and Tonto – 1974 - Directed, written and produced by Paul Mazursky, and starring Art Carney of *Honeymooners* fame as Harry Coombs, an older widower who cannot stay in his NYC apartment after it is condemned, Herbert Berghof as Jacob Rivitowski, Ellen Burstyn as Shirley Mallard, Geraldine Fitzgerald as Jessie Stone, Larry Hagman as Eddie Coombes, Chief Dan George as Sam Two Feathers, and a slew of aging, over the hill actors who can still do a good job in small roles, as evidenced by this film.

Harry and Tonto has more aging actors in it than a home for the aged in Hollywood. But don't let that fool you into thinking this is a film for just the 55 and over set. The film is entertaining on many levels for all ages. The story begins with Harry leaving his condemned apartment and moving in with his child, Norman (played by Joshua Mostel), who has a comfortable house in Long Island. He is bored to tears there. So he plans a cross-country trip with his cat companion, Tonto.

His performance is so understated and riveting, that one can easily see why he won the Academy Award that year for the Best Actor in a film. It was no easy accomplishment either; he had to beat out the finest actors of a younger generation, Dustin Hoffman, Jack Nicholson and Al Pacino, who many thought was a lock to win for Godfather II. Some have speculated that these three heavyweights somehow split the vote in just a way that Carney was able to sneak in with the win. But no one ever asks the score in a championship game; they just want to know who won. Highly recommended for all ages.

Hart's War -2002 – Directed by Gregory Hoblit and starring Bruce Willis and Colin Farrell in a WW2 tale that you would expect to have lots of fireworks with all that estrogen in the lead roles, but it is wasted on a dreary investigation of possible POW misdeeds. Still interesting

Hatful of Rain – 1957 - Directed by Fred Zinneman of *A Man for All Seasons* fame. Don Murray and Eva Marie Saint struggle against the evils of drug addiction in an emotional film that just falls short, but is still interesting to watch.

Headhunters (Norway) –2011 –Directed by Morten Tyldum and starring unknown actors from Norway who do a superb job thanks do the great screenplay by Lars Gudmestad and Ulf Ryberg. This tidy little thriller about corporate recruiting will hold your attention from beginning to end.

The Heartbreak Kid – 1972 - Directed by Elaine May, who knows funny, and starring a great cast including Charles Grodin (perfectly cast), Jeannie Berlin, who is great, and a smoking hot Cybil Shepherd. Eddie Albert as a psycho dad is really not too much of a stretch for him, but he is good, nevertheless. This story of unrealistic expectations is very funny. A must see.

Heat - 1995 - Directed by Michael Mann and starring Al Pacino and Robert DeNiro, who never worked together outside of the Godfather 2 film. Both actors are subdued here and give each other plenty of room in the scenes, so the end result is pretty good. Val Kilmer adds to the cast quality.

Heaven and Earth- 1993– Directed by Oliver Stone and starring Tommy Lee Jones, Joan Chen, Thuan K Nguyen, and a solid supporting cast. This story portrays the struggle of a Vietnamese woman during the war in Vietnam, and after the war in the US. Powerful material.

Heaven and Earth (Japan) -2001- Directed by Haruki Kadokawa and starring Enoki Takaaki, Tsugawa Masahiko, Asano Asuko, Zaizen Naomi, and Nomura Hironobu as various warriors. This is a great action movie, and is photographed beautifully, as well as having great music. A must-see film.

Heaven Can Wait – 1943 – Produced and directed by Ernst Lubitsch and starring Don Ameche as Henry, a man who has to convince the devil that he belongs in Hell (that will be quite easy for me to do), Laird Cregar as the Devil, Spring Byington as Henry's mother, Louis Calhern as Henry's father, Charles Coburn as Henry's mischievious grandfather, Gene Tierney as Martha, the romantic interest, and wife of Henry, and a fine supporting cast, including the popular Marjorie Main as the mother-in-law from Hell (no relation to the devil in this film).

Heaven Can Wait – 1978 -- Directed by and starring Warren Beatty and a great supporting cast including the always hot Julie Christie, James Mason, Charles Grodin, Dyan Cannon, Buck Henry (who is always funny), Vincent Gardenia taking time off from his Death Wish duties, and Jack Warden as the usual grouch he plays. A number of these cast members would follow Beatty forShampoo later on. Very funny.

The Heiress – 1949 - Directed by William Wyler and starring Olivia DeHaviland, Montgomery Clift, Ralph Richardson, and Miriam Hopkins in a super-soap. I really loved the slam-bang ending of this film, which I will not reveal, but suffice it to say it is fitting. Picture highlights the difficulty of initiating a meaningful relationship when you are rich.

Hell in the Pacific – 1968 - Directed by John Boorman and starring Lee Marvin and Toshiro Mifune in the lead roles. Most of the money for this production went to the actors, but it was still entertaining; although I didn't care for the ending. Worth viewing. Story is about the only two men on an island fighting each other. It was supposed to be symbolic. This film will not last long on this list.

Hell is For Heroes - 1962 - Directed by Don Siegel and starring Steve McQueen and James Coburn in a can't miss war movie. However, it missed. Still worth viewing as a decent actioner, but promised so much more than it actually delivered. Another soon to be departed from this list film.

Hell's Angels – 1930 -Credited as directed by Howard Hughes (but not really), the film was actually directed by James Whale, the master director of horror films at Universal Studios. What better choice for the horrors of war than the best director of horror films? What Hughes knew about directing could probably be taught in a three day seminar, so there was no way he could have directed a professional film like this one. But money does buy a lot of credit.

Starring in the film is Jean Harlow as Helen, as the woman of easy virtue who prefers the sexy and more experienced brother, Monte over his less experienced brother, Roy, who treats Helen as if she deserves to be on a pedestal. Monte knows better, and treats her the way she deserves to be treated. At this point in time, Harlow was the marquee actress of the film, and much better known than anyone else in the cast. Monte is played by Ben Lyon, a relatively unknown actor from the thirties. James Hall, a better-known actor from that time period, plays the naïve Roy. A talented cast of supporting actors fills out the troupe for this intense tale of WW 1 fighter pilots.

Hellzapoppin – 1941 - Directed by H.C. Potter and starring Ole Olsen, Chic Johnson and Martha Raye. This was the last fun film before the outbreak of WW2, and as such, does not have that WW2 pall hanging over the plot like every other comedy of the forties. Of course there is no plot in this zany piece, but that is just fine. Lots of fun.

Henry V – England - 1946 - Directed and starring Laurence Olivier as Henry V, Leslie Banks as the Chorus, Felix Aylmer as the Archbishop of Canterbury, Robert Helpmann as the Bishop of Ely, Vernon Greeves as the English Herald, Gerald Case as the Earl of Westmoreland (no relationship to the Vietnam-Era American general), Griffith Jones as the Earl of Salisbury, Morland Graham as Sir Thomas Erpingham, Nicholas Hannen as the Duke of Exeter, Michael Warre as the Duke of Gloucester, Ralph Truman as Mountjoy, Ernest Thesiger as the Duke of Berri, Frederick Cooper as Corporal Nym, Roy Emerton as Lieutenant Bardolph, Robert Newton of Long John Silver fame, as Ancient Pistol, Freda Jackson as Mistress Quickly, George Cole as an unnamed boy, George Robey as Sir John Falstaff, Harcourt Williams as King Charles VI of France, Russell Thorndike as the Duke of Bourbon, Leo Genn as The Constable of France, Francis Lister as the Dukeof Orleans, Max Adrian as the Dauphin, Jonathan Field as the French Messenger, Esmond Knight as Fluellen, Michael Shelpy as Gower, John Laurie as Jamy, Niall MacGinnis, as MacMorris, Frank Tickle as the Governor of Harfluer, Renee Asherson as Princess Katherine, Ivy St. Helier as Alice, Janet Burnell as Court, Arthur Hambling as Bates and Ernest Hare as the final person that is credited with an appearance in this film as a priest.

Well over half the theater was sold out on opening night just from the actors in this film and their families. The film begins with an insult to Henry V from the French Dauphin; a can of tennis balls (and they are not even as good as Wilsons). So Henry raises an army and invades France. At the Battle of Harfleur, Henry rouses his troops to victory and then to an unbelievable upset at the Battle of Agincourt, where he is greatly outnumbered. After a great victory, he goes on to another by wooing Katherine of France. There sure is nothing like great sex after a great battle. Despite the unending introduction of far too numerous characters, the play is still my favorite of all the Shakespearean pieces.

Henry V (England) – 1989- Directed and starring Kevin Brannagh as Henry V, Derek Jacobi as the Chorus, Simon Shepherd as the Duke of Gloucester, James Larkin as the Duke of Bedford, Brian Blessed as the Duke of Exeter, Paul Gregory as Westmoreland, Charles Kay as the Archbishop of Canterbury, Alec Mcowen as the Bishop of Ely, Fabian Cartwright as the Earl of Cambridge, Stephen Simms as Lord Scroop, Jay Villers as Sir Thomas de Grey, Edward Jewesbury as Sir Thomas Erpingham, Ian Holm as Fluellen, Daniel Webb as Gower, Jimmy Yuill as Jamy, John Sessions as Macmorries, Shaun Prendergast as Bates, Pat Doyle as Court, Michael Williams as Williams, Richard Briers as Bardolph, Geoffrey Hutchings as Nym, Robert Stephens as Pistol, and Robbie Coltrane as Sir John Falstaff

Also featured are Christian Bale as the Boy, Dame Judi Dench as Mistress Quickly (I love that name), Paul Schofield, who was actually the best qualified actor to play the Archbishop of Canterbury, since he won an Academy Award for that role in *A Man For All Seasons*, but chose to play Charles VI of France instead, Michael Maloney as Louis, the Dauphin, Harold Innocent as the Duke of Burgundy, Richard Clifford as the Duke of Orleans, Colin Hurley as Grandpre, the French Lord, Richard Easton as the Constable, Christopher Ravenscroft as Mountjoy, Emma Thompson, the former wife of Brannagh, as

Katherine, the love interest of Henry V, David Lloyd Meredith as the Governor of Harfleur, David Parfitt as the Messenger, Nicholas Ferguson as Warwick, Tom Whitehouse as John Talbot, Nigel Greaves as the Duke of Berry, Julian Gartside as Bretagne, and Mark Inman, Chris Armstrong as soldiers. Once again, sales from the families of all these actors on opening night was quite brisk. See the previous description of the plot from the Olivier film. Brannagh is just as good; and is a bit more visceral.

Hercules - 1958 - Directed by Pietro Francisci and starring Steve Reeves as Hercules. Wikipedia has him as the titular lead in the film, but I would have to disagree, and say that honor belongs to Sylva Koscina, the princess; although it was close. Fun to watch.

Here Comes Mr. Jordan– 1941 - Directed by Alexander Hall and starring Robert Montgomery, Claude Rains and Edward Everett Horton in a screwball comedy made before the outbreak of WW2. There were very few of these made after WW2 began. Still funny.

Hero (China)– 2002 - Directed by Zhang Yimou, one of the two premier Chinese directors (Chen Kaige is the other) and starring Jet Li, Tony Leung, Zhang Ziyi (the skinny successor to Gong Li, as the queen of Chinese cinema), and a sound supporting cast for a period epic on China. Great eye candy.

Heroes For Sale – 1933 - Directed by the talented William Wellman, who would go on to make *A Star is Born, Beau Geste*, and *Public Enemy* among many other fine films, and starring Richard Barthelmess as Thomas Holmes, a luckless World War One hero who not only fails to get his proper credit in the War, but also becomes additcted to opiates as a POW, Aline MacMahon as Mary Denis, the promising Loretta Young as Ruth Loring Holmes, Gordon Wescott as his cowardly friend, Roger Winston, Robert Barrat as Max Brinker, Berton Churchill as Mr. Winston (ironic eh?), Grant Mitchell as George W. Gibson, Charles Grapewin as Pa Dennis, Robert McWade as Dr. Briggs, G. Pat Collins as a communist sympathizer, and James Murray as a blind soldier.

This little gem of a film is extremely entertaining from a number of different perspectives. First, it clearly captures the plight of the World War One veteran who came home from the war in less than perfect condition. There was no Vetrean's Administration at the time, and practically no long-term care for veterans who returned from the war with various maladies. Tom was one of those unfortunates. While on a mission to capture a German soldier for intelligence, his buddy Roger freezes with fear and hides in a foxhole. Tom manages to capture a German prisoner, and bring him back to the foxhole, but is wounded during the capture. His friend Roger offers to take the prisoner back to the lines and leaves Tom in the foxhole to be captured by the Germans. What a pal. While in German custody, Tom becomes addicted to opiates administered by the German doctors to kill his pain. Roger, on the other hand, gets a medal for his bravery for capturing the German soldier. Highly recommended for a good slice of life during the Depression, and some insight to the treatment of WW 1 vets.

He Walked By Night - 1948 - Directed by Alfred L Werker (also known as one-movie wonder Al) and starring the appropriately named lead actor, Richard Baseheart as a grusome serial killer on the loose. Interesting film-noir.

Hidden Fortress (Japan) - 1958 - Love the poster. Your typical Akira Kurosawa-direction of major star, Toshiro Mifune as a warlord hunkering down and regrouping before resuming hostilities. This film was actually a metaphor for the recovery of Japan after WW 2. One of Kurosawa's best.

High and Low– 1963 –Japan- Directed by Akira Kurosawa and starring his usual lead actor, Toshiro Mifune, in a story about a chauffeur's son being kidnapped and held for ransom.   B Kurosawa films are better than most other B movies.

The High and the Mighty - 1954 - Directed by William A Wellman and starring John Wayne as the large and in-charge guy, Clare Trevor, Jan Sterling and Lorraine Day as the helpless women, Robert Stack before he became Elliot Ness, Phil Harris, who was cracking jokes about planes, and decent production values. They never seemed to show this one on airline flights.

High Noon – 1952 - Directed by Fred Zinneman and starring Gary Cooper as Will Kane, a sheriff who is about to retire with his pacifist wife to become a storekeeper, Grace Kelly as Amy, his Quaker wife, who insists he run away from almost certain death. And Ian MacDonald as Frank Miller, the leader of a small pack of criminals, who has vowed to kill Kane after getting released from prison. He and his gang will arrive on the noon train. This is a nice, practical Western for a change. Heroes that are reluctant, rather than gung ho, are far more interesting to watch on the big screen. Kane is a true anti-hero; he really does not want to be there, and he is plenty scared.

   I can recommend this as one of the best Westerns ever made, with a message that the Old West was not as heroic as we were led to believe when we were kids. As a matter of fact, this Zinneman film is the complete antithesis of films made by Frank Capra, where a man's friends are the most important assets they have. After living a fairly long time, I would have to agree more with the Zinneman philosophy and reality, although Capra may have one or two points in his favor.

High Plains Drifter – 1973 - Directed by and starring Clint Eastwood in a run of the mill vigilante Western before Clint refined his talents as a director. A bit overstylish and lacking a bit of substance. These minor excesses were eliminated in his later works. Still worth viewing.

High Sierra – 1941 - Directed by Raoul Walsh and starring Humphrey Bogart as Roy Earle, a man just released from prison, Donald MacBride as Big Mac (no, McDonalds did not steal this from here), an aging gangster, not the burger, Cornell Wilde in one of his first major roles, as Mendoza, a worker in the resort, Arthur Kennedy as Red, and Alan Curtis as Babe. The very talented Ida Lupino plays Marie, a woman who eventually falls for Roy, Joan Leslie plays Velma, a young, innocent woman with a clubfoot, but unlike the character in the novel, this woman is a lot stronger (should have been named Elise).

   The story begins with Big Mac planning a robbery of a California resort casino. He wants an experienced con like Roy to lead the group. Roy eventually meets up with all the members of the gang, and the heist is carefully planned. Of course, there is always a complication in these types of heist films and this one is no exception. Roy drives to a remote home in the mountains where the girl with the club foot, Velma, lives. Roy pays for the surgery necessary for Velma to get back on her feet. Roy falls in love with Velma, and asks her to marry him, but she loves another. When Velma's betrothed arrives, Roy bids farewell to Velma and with his heart broken for almost twelve hours, he begins to look at Marie and shacks up with her, instead (a much better choice). I know this is supposed to be some kind of classic, but I really didn't have much sympathy for Roy. He had two clear chances to make it in society, and he blew off both of them. Recommended only for Bogart fans.

High Tide – 1947 - Directed by John Reinhardt and starring a cast of B actors utilized in flashback film-noir technique. Nice low-budget production is suspenseful from the beginning because the tide will come eventually and drown the trapped car victims. Hidden gem.

High Wall - 1947 -B- Directed by Curtis Bernhardt and starring Robert Taylor and Herbert Marshall in a noir as dark as it gets. Man is committed for killing his wife after an affair; but did he do it? Tune in and find out.

Hildago -2004 - This is one of my three favorite horse films. The others are *The Black Stallion* and *The War Horse*. If you enjoyed those, you will like this one. If you don't like horse films than maybe you prefer asses, or films viewed by them.

The Hill – 1965 - Directed by Sidney Lumet and starring Sean Connery in an attempt to cash in on his popularity in the Bond series with this mediocre screenplay and overwrought acting. Despite the holes in the film, a good supporting cast saves the day and the film is watchable.

His Girl Friday – 1940 - Directed by Howard Hawks and starring Cary Grant and Rosalind Russell in a classic screwball comedy. Also featured are Ralph Bellamy and Gene Lockhart without Lassie.

His Kind of Woman - 1951 - Thought to be a bit tawdry in the early fifties, this film is now very tame compared to modern sexual mores. Directed by John Farrow and starring the hot combo of Robert Mitchum and Jane Russell as happenstance lovers and adventurers, along with an understated (that will be the day) performance from Vincent Price.

His Majesty O'Keefe – 1954 - Directed by Byron Haskin and starring Burt Lancaster as the adventurer, David O'Keefe, a sea captain who has grand ambitions, Joan Rice as an island girl, Dali (they could never name their child Salvador), Andre Morell as Afred Tetins, Abraham Sofaer as Fatumak, the Medicine Man, and Charles Horvath as Bully Hayes. This relatively unknown film is completely carried by Burt Lancaster in a bravado performance. Burt used to smile and flash those pearly whites more than Tom Cruise, but was a much better actor

A sea captain seeks to make his fortune in the South Seas and begins to employ natives to harvest copra, but runs into complications such as jealous chieftains and German colonialists. In an interview with Burt, he mentioned to me that the Fiji Islands were not all that romantic to live in for an extended period of time. The food was horrendous, and he had a bad case of dysentery to boot. This is not a must see film, but you certainly can relax and enjoy your popcorn watching this one.

Hitchcock -2012 — Directed by Sacha Gervasi and starring the multi-talented Anthony Hopkins as the Master of Suspense. He is ably supported by a great cast including Helen Mirren, Jessica Biel, and

Scarlett Johansson. Oddly enough, Hitchcock had little respect for actors and actresses, and just considered them props for his stories and cinematography, which he considered paramount.

The Hitchhiker - 1953 - Directed by the multi-talented Ida Lupino and starring Frank Lovejoy (the most oxymoronic name in film) and Edmund O'Brien (of *DOA* fame). - There is real tension is this indie production that made it to the big screen and got thumbs up from every critic. A must-see on how to make a good low-budget film.

HM Pullham Esq. - 1941- Directed by King Vidor (doesn't a director have enough power already without being named King?) and starring Hedy Lamarr, Robert Young (lose that mustache, please) and Ruth Hussey (great stage name). Your usual triangle screwball melodrama of pre WW2. Fun to watch.

The Hoax – 2006 - Directed by Lasse Hallstrom and starring Richard Gere, who fits the bill in one of his more erudite roles. I have a great appreciation for hustler and hoax films, and this is a fine specimen. I can recommend it.

Hoffa- 1992 - Directed by Danny DeVito, who also has a major role in the film as Bobby Ciaro, the right-hand man of Hoffa. The film also stars Jack Nicholson as Hoffa, the iconic labor leader of the sixties, Armand Assante, as the sleazy Carl D'Allesandro, J.T. Walsh as Frank Fitzsimmons, the successor to Hoffa, John C. Reilly as Hoffa's betrayer, Frank Whaley as a young trucker, Kevin Anderson as Robert F. Kennedy, John P. Ryan as Red Bennett, Robert Prosky as Billy Flynn, Natalia Noguich as Jo Hoffa, Nicholas Pryor as Hoffa's lawyer, Paul Guilfoyle as Ted Harmon, Karen Young as a young female official, and Cliff Gorman as Solly Stein. There were a dozen ways this film could have been a disaster, but DeVito avoided all of them and turned out a nice finished product.

Hollywood Ending - 2002 - Directed, written and starring Woody Allen, Debra Messing, Mark Rydell, Treat Williams and the under-appreciated Tea Leoni, in a tale about director's block (like writer's block, but more expensive). A semi-autobiographical film about Allen trying to recapture his "earlier, funnier films" as generally described by his legions of fans.

Hollywoodland – 2006 - Directed by Alan Coulter and starring Adrien Brody, Diane Lane, Ben Affleck, and Bob Hoskins. A solid cast delivers the goods in this real life film noir biopic of the original Superman. Some stirring moments.

Hombre – 1967 - Directed by Martin Ritt and starring Paul Newman as Hombre, aka John Russell, a white man raised as an Apache, Paul Newman as John Russell, the hero, the veteran Fredric March as Dr. Alex Favor, Richard Boone, who steals the film as the slimy Cicero Grimes (such an appropriate last name!), Diane Cilento, a slightly miscast Italian actress as Jessie, the boss of a boarding house that Russell sells a herd of horses, Cameraon Mitchell as Frank Braden, (another veteran actor who could have played the Boone role with ease) are featured.

Also, Barbara Rush as Audra Favor, the good doctor's wife, Peter Lazer as Billy Lee Blake, a young lover who overestimates his sexual prowess, Margaret Blye as Doris Blake, who is the young lover's wife who seems a bit unsatisfied, Martin Balsam as Henry Mendez, Skip Ward as Steve Early, Frank Silvera as a Mexican bandit, (I have always wanted to play this role ever since I was a kid when I saw *The Treasure of Sierra Madre* with the misquoted line "We don't need no stinking badges!"), David Canary as Lamar Dean, Val Avery as Delgado, and Larry Ward in a very interesting small role as a cowardly soldier in the stagecoach waiting room.

The Homecoming - 2009 - Directed by Morgan J Freeman and starring newcomers Mischa Barton, MattLong and Jessica Stroup. These actresses will be around for a long time because they have got what it takes. This little gem showcases the both of them in the tradition of *Fatal Attraction*.

Honeymoon Killers - 1972- Leonard Kastle directs this wonderfully trashy exploration of lowlife crooks who will do anything, including murder, for a few thousand bucks. Tony Lo Bianco gives the performance of his career, and Shirley Stoler is letter-perfect. A bit violent, and visually disgusting.

Hoodlum Priest - 1961- Directed by Irvin Kershner, and starring Don Murray as a priest who hangs out with the people who sin the most; the poor, the disenfranchised, and the morally bankrupt. A powerhouse of a biopic, and based on a true story as well.

Hoop Dreams – 1994 - Directed by Steve James. This is a documentary that follows the fortunes of two of the best basketball players in the nation for 1994. The story begins with two Afro-American basketball players from Chicago who have dreams of becoming players in the NBA. William Gates and Arthur Agee are both recruited by Saint Joseph High School in Westchester, Illinois.

Would either of these young men have been recruited for this predominantly white high school had they been average black students without great basketball expertise? Not very likely. Saint Joseph's had a great tradition of winning basketball games, and that was the only reason these young men were recruited. The two young boys have to take an hour and a half to get to and back from this school. It is horribly inconvenient for them. They both endure long and difficult workouts, and have few social friends at the school. Gates and Agee must learn new skills to compete at the very highest level of competition in the state.

The families of Gates and Agee must support their children through this very difficult ordeal. But are they supporting them to get an education, or are they supporting them in the hopes they will eventually land an NBA contract? How likely are they to even get a scholarship at the college level without superior intellectual skills? The film shows the struggles of both young men to academically make it into a decent college, but both fail academically to keep up with their college work and eventually drop out.

The film clearly shows that the coaches and school administrators are far more concerned with the successes of the athletic teams, than the intellectual development of the players on those teams. Both young men are merely pawns in the game of coaching and jockeying for recruitment. The sad aftermath of the film is that neither Gates or Agee made it into the NBA. They just did not have the overwhelming skills that were required to make it.   There are only about 300 jobs for players in the NBA. Every year there are at least five or six veterans on every team that are guaranteed to make the roster. That allows less 60 jobs a year to open up for rookies from the NBA draft. The top thirty or so will have very little problem making some pro team roster, but after number 30, 31-60 are a crap shoot.

Anyone in the top 120 players to come out of the college ranks can make it into the 31-60 range if they have a particular set of skills that a team may be looking for. But the bottom line is that 60 of the top 120 will be out of luck. The other graduating 1200 players will not even get an invitation to an NBA tryout camp. So only 5% (or less) of the graduating college basketball players even get a shot at the NBA. Gates and Agee didn't even make it into the pool of 1200. Fortunately, both young men made better lives for themselves in the aftermath of this film. Better housing for their families, and new life choices were results of this film experience. I can highly recommend this film for all budding basketball players who think they will play in the NBA. Think again.

Hoosiers - 1986 - Directed by David Anspaugh and starring a totally in-control Gene Hackman, Barbara Hershey, and an Oscar-nominated performance by Dennis Hopper, as a basketball junkie, who is also the town drunk. This film REEKS of authenticity and believability. Every scene is just like being in the Midwest in the fifties. The clothes, mannerisms, and every other detail are meticulously handled by the expert hands of the director. Must see.

Hopalong Cassidy – 1935 –Directed Nate Watt and starring William Boyd in the lead role that would lead to a TV series in the early1950s. Gabby Hayes adds great humor as a sidekick and the film spawns a sequel for the next year.

Hope and Glory – 1987 - Directed by John Boorman and starring Sarah Miles, Ian Banne and an all-British B actor troupe. The director successfully recreates the tense period of war-torn England during the Blitz and other German incursions of WW2. We see the war through the eyes of a young boy, and it is an interesting lens.

Hors-La-Loi (Outside the Law) (Algeria) - 2009 – Directed by Rachid Bouchareb and starring Jamel Debbouze, Roschdy Zem and Sami Bouajila as three Algerian brothers who try to overcome enormous odds and almost constant mistreatment from the French before, during, and after the Algerian independence movement. This film was nominated for, and should have won, Best Foreign Film of the Year. And except for one minor flaw in the film that could have been easily corrected by Bouchareb, it would have won. I am a neutral observer of the Algerian-French conflict, so I recognize a film when it too one-sided politically.

Unlike *Z*, which was the only Algerian film ever to win the Best Foreign Film Award, *Hors-La-Loi* does not have even one sympathetic Western or French character. Every Frenchman is demonized; there are no French good guys. On the other end of the spectrum, every Algerian is portrayed as a good guy; there are no bad Algerians, except possibly a brief scene at the beginning when the Algerian landlord evicts the brothers and their parents off their farm. In real life, it is never this way. There are always good and bad people of all nationalities, and the vast majority of directors have come to realize that in their films.

Bocuhareb has not, and that is why none of his three nominated films have won in the past. And they will never win, until his films are more balanced with reality. Reality does not only occur for one side in a conflict, as so wonderfully illustrated by Clint Eastwood with *Flags of Our Fathers* and *Letters From Iwo Jima* which expertly showed two sides of the same coin. Maybe for the third installment of the trilogy, Buchereb, a terribly talented director, will remember that no pancake is so flat that it doesn't have two sides. Highly recommended.

The Hospital – 1971 - Directed by Arthur Hiller, and starring George C. Scott in his Academy-Award nominated role as Dr. Herbert Bock, a hard-nosed hospital administrator who has to make nearly impossible decisions on a daily basis. Also starring in the film is a highly competent supporting cast including: Diana Rigg as Barbara Drummand, a love interest of Dr. Bock; she is the daughter of a patient, Robert Walden as Dr. Brubaker, Barnard Hughes as Edmond Drummond, the father of Barbara, who is a patient, Richard A. Dysart as Dr. Welbeck, Stephen Elliot as Dr. John Sundstrom, Andrew Duncan as William Willie Mead, Donald Harron as Dr. Milton Mead, Nancy Marchand as Mrs. Christie, as the icy Head of Nurses (she steals every scene she is in).

Also featured is Jordan Charney as Hitchcock, part of the bureaucratic, unfeeling hospital administration that makes budget decisions, Robert Blossom as Guernsey (you wouldn't think there would be a cow in a hospital movie), Lenny Baker as Dr. Howard Schaefer, Richard Hamilton as Dr. Ronald Casey, Kate Harrington as the sympathetic Nurse Dunn, Katherine Helmond as Mrs Mead, the wife of William, Frances Sternhagen as Mrs. Sally Cushing, and an unknown Stockard Channing before she became famous, as an emergency room nurse. Good drama.

Houdini – 1953 - Directed by George Marshall and starring Tony Curtis as Houdini, the legendary escape artist and Janet Leigh as Mrs. Houdini. Make no mistake about this film; it is a one-man movie that uses its female co-star, Ms. Leigh, merely as window dressing. There is hardly a scene in the entire film that does not include Curtis as he gives a powerhouse performance of the the greatest escape artist of all time.

Hound of the Baskervilles -1939 - Directed by Sidney Lanfield and starring Basil Rathbone as Holmes and Nigel Bruce as the classic Watson. A sturdy supporting cast adds to the production values. This tale of mysterious murder and greed (with the emphasis on the greed) has been done over two dozen times. This edition is the eeriest.

Household Saints – 1993 -Directed by Nancy Sivoca and starring Tracy Ullman, Vincent D'onofrio and Lili Taylor as a tightly wound Catholic family that goes through three generations of Catholic angst, which is amply captured on screen by the director in numerous shots. Interesting.

House of Fear – 1944 - Directed by Roy William Neill and starring Basil Rathbone and Nigel Bruce in another Holmes tale. This one is not quite as good as most of the others, but it is still a notch better than most of the other mysteries of the period. Worth seeing, but will not make the list in a few years.

House of Flying Daggers (China) - 2004– Directed by Zhang Yimou and starring Takeshi Kaneshiro asJin, the new leader of the Flying Daggers, a group of gangsters in ancient China, Andy Lao as Leo, another gang member, and Zhang Ziyi, who has desperately tried to replace Gong Li as China's leading actress, but always seems to fall short in that area as Mei, a blind dancer, who is the daughter of the former gang leader. With the eternal love triangle set in place at the beginning of the film, we are now ready for the events that follow. The film was very well done technically, and the story was quite interesting, until the silly finale. Much better to have let the events naturally affect the main actors rather than have some forced, unrealistic showdown. The film is still good enough for me to recommend it to all audiences, and I enjoyed watching the plush production values that Yimou films always seem to have.

House of Games – 1987 - Directed and written by David Mamet, and starring Lindsay Crouse as Dr. Margaret Ford, a renowned psychologist who bites off more than she can chew when she gets involved with professional gamblers and scammers, Joe Mantegna as Mike, a professional scammer, who underestimates the ability of Dr. Ford to figure out the scam she is involved in, Ricky Jay as George, a grade A, slimeball scammer, who almost steals the movie, and William Macy as Sgt Moran. The rest of the cast is ably directed by Mamet in their roles as counselors and lowlifes.

The film begins with Margaret publishing her book about compulsion. One day, in her office, she is in a session with a compulsive gambler, Billy, who tells her his life is in danger. He owes 25 gees to a criminal figure and will be killed if he doesnt pay. Margaret visits the pool hall and bar called the House of Games, and confronts the man Billy owes money to, Mike. Margaret figures Mike is a tough talker, but not a violent gangster. Mike surprises her by saying Billy only owes eight hundred dollars, and will forgive the debt if Margaret comes with him to a high-stakes poker game as his girlfriend. This is one of the best small-budget films ever made. It is in my top hundred films of all time. I highly recommend it as classic film noir, even though it is made well after the golden age of that genre.

The House of Rothschild – 1934 – Directed by Alfred Werker and starring a great cast, including George Arliss, Boris Karloff, Loretta Young, and Robert Young. This loose interpretation of the famous Rothschild financial empire is mostly about the romance between the two Youngs. Isn't it great if you don't have to change your last name if you get married?

House of Sand and Fog – 2003 – Directed by Vadim Perelman and starring Jennifer Connelly and Ben Kingsley as combatants for a desired piece of real estate. A lot of interesting issues are raised, since one of the combatants is a recent immigrant from a Muslim country.

House of the Seven Gables - 1940 - There is more ham in this film than in a very large butcher shop. Don't get me wrong, however. I loved George Sanders in almost every role he was in and I have a great appreciation for Vincent Price as well. But let's be honest here. These are about the two hammiest actors of the forties and fifties and they are in the same film! (the only one that I am aware of that they starred in together).

House of Usher - 1960 - Directed by Roger Corman, so you know the film came in under budget, and starring Vincent Price as a member of a dysfunctional family (I saw worse in Jersey City). Written by Poe and the first of eight Corman/Poe partnerships. Not too bad, although there a lot of ham here.

House on 92nd Street - 1945 - Directed by Henry Hathaway and starring Gene Lockhart, Leo G Carrol of Topper fame, and a professional supporting cast in a story about rotten Nazi spies and how the FBI and J Edgar smash their ring. The film is done in semi-documentary style. Pretty decent.

How Green Was My Valley – 1941- Directed by John Ford, who divided most of his filmmaking between great Westerns featuring John Wayne, and Irish-centered films usually featuring Victor McLaghlin, makes a film about the Welsh without either of his staple actors. Starring in this one is Walter Pidgeon, who appears to be slightly miscast as a Welchman, Mr. Gruffyd, but pulls it off with the help of veteran Ford actress Maureen O'Hara as Angharad Morgan, who was featured in many of Ford's Westerns and Irish films.

    Also starring in the film are some quality supporting actors including Anna Lee as Bronwyn, the wife of Ivor, Patric Knowles as Ivor, Donald Crisp as Gwilym Morgan, and Roddy McDowell as Huw Morgan, the young brother of Angharad. The film uses a limited voiceover of the Roddy McDowell character as he relates his memories for the film. The setting is in a harsh Welch mining town which is perfectly captured in the stark filming technique of black and white which Ford excelled in in previous Irish/English films such as The Voyage Home and The Informer. This is one of the best mining films ever mad,e and without sensationalistic scenes; it is still capable of rendering tremendous emotional impact. I can recommend it highly.

Howard's End – 1992 - Directed by James Ivory,which is extremely appropriate, because this is soap at the very highest level and done very well, at that. The sterling cast includes heavyweights such as Anthony Hopkins, Vanessa Redgrave, Helena-Bonham Carter and Emma Thompson. The scenes between Thompson and Hopkins are electric.

The Hucksters – 1947 - Directed by Jack Conway and staring Clark Gable as Victor Albee Norman (why they wanted to give such a pretentious name to a character that is trying to depict honesty and simplicity is beyond me), Deborah Kerr, in her American film debut as Kay Dorrance, the predictable love interest for Gable (it even tells us so on the movie poster), Sydney Greenstreet as the wonderfully deplorable Evan Llewellyn Evans, who is perfectly cast as an adverertising mogul, Adolphe Menjou as Mr. Kimberly, a slightly dishonest advertising executive who has pangs of honesty, Ava Gardner as Jean Ogilvie, the seasoned cynical office manager, Keenan Wynn as the perfectly cast immoral, but likable ad-man who will do anything for a sale, and Edward Arnold as his usual hard-nosed businessman. This highly capable cast is also supported by an army of supporting actors that the MGM studios had been famous for. This army, unfortunately, began to break up after WW 2 because of the advent of television and the gradual breakdown of the classic studio production model. The film is fun to watch from a period piece standpoint, but there isn't a shred of reality in the entire film.

Hud – 1963 - Directed by Martin Ritt and starring Paul Newman as Hud, son of Homer and older nephew to Lonnie, and a modern-era cowboy with an irreverent attitude toward people and society in general, Melvyn Douglas as the serious Homer, who embraces all the time-honored values of hard work and ethics, Patricia Neal as the unconvincing love interest of Hud (If I'm not attracted to her in the slightest, how could a stud like Hud be attracted to her?), and Brandon De Wilde, all grown up since he was featured in *Shane*, shows us why he never got another significant role in film as an adult.

    Somehow, Neal won an Academy Award for this role as a lead actress, when she was on the screen less than DeWilde! Neal was a fine actress when cast properly, but this was not a role for her. Ann

Margaret or Diane Carroll would have been much better (even Jane Fonda). She won out of sympathy for her disfiguring car accident in real life. Douglas won for his role in the Best Supporting Actor category, and that was deserved. And of course, the great James Wong Howe certainly deserved the Best Cinematography award he received. The film is almost pure Western soap, with overtones of Tennnesse Williams imitations of characterizations and dialogue. One could have easily imagined Brando in the role of Hud, but then his romance with Neal would have really been laughable.

Hugo – 2011 –Directed by Martin Scorsese, who was fearless in doing a type of film he had never done before (fantasy), and starring Asa Butterfield, Ben Kingsley,and a virtually unrecognizable (it took me a full five minutes to realize who this character was being played by) Sasha Baron Cohen in a relatively straight role (although he will never be able to play a straight role again, because the audience will laugh as soon as they see him, as one of the world's funniest men). The plot is rather unique; a boy lives in a Paris train station and takes care of the clocks. Recommended.

Human Condition – 1959–-Japan - Directed by Masaki Kobayashi and starring a group of unknown Japanese B actors in a solid tale about a weasel in the Japanese army who tries to avoid combat, but fails. Top notch.

Human Desire -1954 - Directed by Fritz Lang and starring Glenn Ford and Gloria Grahame along with Broderick Crawford. Good film noir by a master of the art. Worth seeing.

The Human Stain - 2003 - Directed by Robert Benton and starring Anthony Hopkins and Nicole Kidman as a couple that meet at a lakeside cabin after the demise of both Hopkins' career as a professor and the death of his wife. His deep dark secret is that he is a black man posing as a Jew. (It didn't bother Sammy Davis Jr). In New York, they wouldn't give it a second thought, but in New England......

Hunchback of Notre Dame – 1939 - Directed by William Dieterle and starring Charles Laughton as The Hunchback of Notre Dame, Quasimodo, a highly sympathetic figure who protects an accused murderess, Esmeralda, played very well by Maureen O'Hara. Sir Cedric Hardwicke plays Frollo, while Edmond O'Brien is satisfactory as the protective Gringoire. The film had an absolutely stirring music sound track created by Alfred Newman which deservedly won the Academy Award that year for best music. This was no small feat considering the tremendous sound track from *Gone with the Wind* that was in competition with this one for that year.

   Also starring in the film are Thomas Mitchell as Clopin, Alan Marshal as Phoebus, Walter Hampden as the Archdeacon, Harry Davenport as King Louis XI, and a highly competent supporting cast that is well-directed by Dieterle for great dramatic effect.   Almost a completely perfect film from beginning to end and highly recommended.

Hurricane – 1937 - Directed by John Ford, who usually excelled in great Westerns, but was also at home in tales of the Seven Seas, starring Dorothy Lamour before she became famous for the Hope-Crosby films, as Marama, Jon Hall as Terangi, the sexy savage of the islands, Mary Astor, as the proper French lady, Madame De Laage, C. Aubrey Smith as Father Hall, who believes Godis stronger than any hurricane, Thomas Mitchell as the worldly Dr. Kersaint,

Raymond Massey as the self-righteous Governor De Laage, John Carradine in his creepy best, as the cruel warden, and a sound supporting cast that gives substance to lush surroundings in the film. The hurricane, which is more like a typhoon, is beautifully shot, and one can almost touch the force of nature in the film. Recommended

Hurt Locker – 2008 - Directed by Kathryn Bigelow and based on a screenplay by Mark Boal, who was a freelance writer embedded as a journalist with a US military forces bomb squad in 2004. The film is nominated for numerous awards this year and I am picking it to win Best Picture of 2009. Even though the film was made in 2008, it was not released in the US until 2009. I also think it will win Best Screenplay and Best Director. If Bigelow is successful in winning the award for best director, she will be first woman to do so.

Starring in the film are a cast of relatively unknown actors as soldiers including Jeremy Renner, Anthony Mackie, and Brian Geraghty. This film is far more complex than most of the war dramas we have come to see on the big screen over the decades. Most of the so-called war movies are about battles between countries and armies of men. This film centers on the battle some soldiers have within themselves and, unfortunately, the casualties of war are not always the ones we see on the battlefield. Highly recommended.

714

I

I Accuse – 1958 - Directed and starring Jose Ferrer with a solid B actor cast supporting the lead actor. The story about corruption and anti-Semitism in the French Army has become an historical classic - A must see.

I Am a Fugitive From a Chain Gang - 1932- Directed by Mervyn Leroy and starring Paul Muni as Robert Elliot Burns, known as James Allen in the film. The movie was produced just prior to the new film code that would have censored several of the scenes that were depicted in this film. Attacking the legal system of a state, for instance, would have been banned by the subsequent code. Some of the more graphic acts of violence would have also been omitted. But almost every scene in the film seems to ring true, and there is not an ounce of Hollywood slick that would become very common after the implementation of the code. The story is about a man who leaves the army after World War 1 and has a difficult time returning to civilian life and finding a job.

This film riled the prison system in Georgia, and a warden from that state sued the studio for damages. The end result was that chain gangs across America were all examined for excesses and the system was greatly improved. Although nominated for Best Actor for this film, Muni lost out to a tie between Fredric March and Wallace Beery. There were a slew of critics (including myself) who thought Muni's performance was much better than either of the winners. This film was produced during the pre-code era, so it was possible to show a number of dramatic situations that were not available to filmmakers after the code was implemented. This film is on the top 100 best films of all-time list from numerous critics throughout the United States and the rest of the world. It is also on my top twenty list. I can recommend this film as the greatest prison film ever made, and also as a great representative of film noir. Films rarely get any darker than the material that is portrayed in this one.

I Am Cuba (Cuba) – 1964 - Directed by Mikhail Kalatozov and completely neglected for over thirty years until rediscovered by Martin Scorsese (gee, that guy finds some great stuff). The story of the Cuban revolution as told by a Russian with great camera work.

Iceman – 1984 - Directed by Fred Schepisi and starring Timothy Hutton as Stanley Shephard, an anthropologist at an arctic base who discovers the body of a prehistoric man, played by John Lone. David Strathairn plays Dr.Singe, a rather cold-blooded scientist, who treats his find more as a scientific experiment instead of a human being. Strathairn is always convincing in any role he tackles as evidenced by his successes in *Eight Men Out* and *Good Night and Good Luck*. Also featured in the film is Lindsay Crouse as Doctor Diane Bradley in another intellectual role that she seems to excel at. She was quite brilliant in another intellectual role in the Mamet film, *House of Games*. The balance of the supporting cast is subdued and professional under the direction of Schepisi.

I Confess – 1953 - Directed by the MASTER of suspense, Alfred Hitchcock and starring Montgomery Clift and Anne Baxter. Clift was an early version of an Anthony Perkins-type actor. Good in this one.

If I Had a Million - 1932 - Directed by seven different directors (the best of which is Ernst Lubitsch) and starring an All-Star cast of anyone who was funny in the early thirties with the exception of Charlie Chaplin, the film goes on to depict lucky recipients of a million dollars from the clear blue sky. The TV show, The Millionaire would take this concept and translate it into a successful TV show in the fifties. In the deep depression, a million dollars was an enormous life-changing sum; today, you need that just to retire. Great viewing.

Ikiru (Japan) - 1952 – Directed by Akira Kurosawa, the recognized master of Japanese cinema, and starring Takashi Shimura as Kanji Watanabe, a minor Tokyo bureaucrat who seeks greater meaning in life. One of Kurosawa's best.

I Know Where I'm Going! (England) -1947 - Directed by Michael Powell, so you know the photography will be superior. This soap starring Wendy Hiller is reminiscent of films like *Brief Encounter* and even a bit of *Wuthering Heights*. Soap lovers will love it.

The Illusionist – 2006 - Directed by Neil Burger and starring the talented Edward Norton as Herr Eisenheim, a renowned illusionist accused of necromancy, Paul Giamatti as Walther Uhl, a Chief Inspector who believes Eisenheim has committed a heinous crime, and a very sexy Jessica Biel as Sophie, the Duchess von Teschen, who is trapped in an unhappy promised future marriage to the crown prince Leopold, who is known to be an abuser of women. The crown prince is competently played by Rufus Sewell. This was a great story with compelling performances and is on my top 100 films of all time. I recommend it highly.

Il Postino – Italy – 1994 - Directed by Michael Radford and starring Mossimo Troisi, Maria Grazia Cucinotta and Philippe Noiret. Noiret plays Pablo Neruda, the famous Chilean poet who acts as a modern-day Cyranno in getting a shy postman involved with a beautiful woman he admires. Great stuff and good music as well.

I'm Alright Jack – England - 1959 - Directed by John and Ray Boulting (two brothers who got along, obviously) and starring Peter Sellers, Terry-Thomas and Ian Carmichael in the principal roles. Richard Attenborough and Margaret Rutherford, two heavyweight actors, do a fine job in support. Satire of workers and owners funny from beginning to end.

The Imitation Game – 2014 - Directed by Morten Tyldum and starring Benedict Cumberbatch in an Academy-Award worthy role as Alan Turing, a scientist who develops a code-cracking machine (a forerunner of the computer), that helps the Allies break the difficult code of the Nazis during WW2. Cumberbatch is ably supported in the film by Keira Knightley as his romantic interest.

Immortal Sergeant – 1953 – Directed by John M Stahl and starring Henry Fonda, Maureen O'Hara and Thomas Mitchell. This tale of a shy Canadian soldier who is inspired by the death of his rough sergeant is a classic.

In a Lonely Place - 1950 - Directed by Nicholas Ray and starring Humphrey Bogart and Gloria Grahame in a class- A film noir treat. This is a story about trust and decadence. It is very well done and is one of Bogart's more sympathetic performances.

Informer – 1935 - Directed by John Ford, more noted for his American Westerns, but also one of the leaders of the Irish Mafia in Hollywood, and starring Victor McLaglen in his Academy-Award winning role as Gypo Nolan, a stereotypical Irish brawler and boozer, who is eventually marginalized so badly within the repressed Irish society under the English, that he must choose to sacrifice his integrity, and his loyalty to his friends and the Irish Republican Army that he is a part of.

Inherit The Wind -1960- Directed by Stanley Kramer, who was also famous for another courtroom drama a few years later, *Judgement at Nuremburg*, and starring Spencer Tracy in his Academy-Award nominated performance as Henry Drummond (Clarence Darrow in real life), the liberal lawyer defending a high school teacher who had the audacity to teach natural selection in his classroom, Fredric March in a very nice turn as the conservative Matthew Harrison Brady (William Jennings Bryan in real life), who advocates a Biblical approach to education and Dick York, as the harried high school teacher, Bertram Cates, who is actually a fictional portrayal of John Scopes, the actual teacher who was put on trial for teaching about Darwinism.

The formidable supporting cast includes: Florence Eldridge as Sara Brady, Gene Kelly as E. K. Hornbeck of the Baltimore Herald (patterned after Henry Mencken), Donna Anderson as Rachel Brown, Harry Morgan as Judge Mel Coffey, Claude Akins as Rev. Jeremiah Brown, Elliott Reid as Prosecutor Tom Davenport, Paul Hartman as Deputy Horace Meeker – Bailiff, Philip Coolidge as Mayor Jason Carter, Jimmy Boyd as Howard, Noah Beery Jr. as John Stebbins, Norman Fell as WGN Radio Technician, Hope

Summers as Mrs. Krebs - Righteous Townswoman, Ray Teal as Jessie H. Dunlap and Renee Godfrey as Mrs. Stebbins. Good stuff.

The Insider – 1999 - Directed by Michael Mann and starring Al Pacino as Lowell Bergman, Russell Crowe as Jeffrey Wigand, Renee Olstead as Deborah Wigand, Christopher Plummer as Mike Wallace, Diane Venora as Liane Wigand, Philip Baker Hall as Don Hewitt, Lindsay Crouse as Sharon Tiller, Debi Mazar as Debbie De Luca, Stephen Tobolowsky as Eric Kluster, Colm Feore as Richard Scrugs, Bruce McGill as Ron Motley, Gina Gershon as Helen Caperelli, Michael Gambon as Thomas Sandefur, Roger Bart as the Seelbach Hotel Manager and Jack Palladino as Jack Palladino playing himself. This is the story of the outrageous behavior and irresponsibility of Big Tobacco.

In The Electric Mist - 2009 - Directed by Bertand Tavernier and starring Tommy Lee Jones and John Goodman in the lead roles. Goodman always has that edgy approach to his acting, and it is perfect for this film. Jones is very good as well as a cop in the Bayou country trying to solve some difficult crimes. Good viewing and underrated.

In The Shadow of the Moon (England) – 2007 - Directed by David Sington and Christpher Riely. This is the ultimate documentary of the manned space flights of the United States to the moon. Fascinating in many respects; especially photographically and historically.

In The Valley of Elah – 2007 – Directed by Paul Haggis and starring Tommy Lee Jones, Charlize Theron (I watch every one of her films immediately because she is never in a bad one), and a solid supporting cast including Susan Sarandon. This unraveling of a mystery and the revenge that follows is done with the right mixture of directorial influence. The Valley of Elah refers to the place David beheaded Goliath.

In Time – 2011 - Directed by Andrew Niccol and starring Justin Timberlake and a solid cast of B actors who take an intelligent script and run with it. A very believable future scenario of divided economic populations using time as currency. Great production values without overbearing special effects.

The Intruder - 1962 - Directed by Roger Corman, the self-proclaimed king of B movies, and starring William Shatner before he became Kirk. Shatner plays a racist in a small Southern town who tries to induce racial tension. This was before Kirk started to woo Ohura. Interesting from both a historical and cinematic perspective.

The Invaders (49th Parallel) – 1941 – Directed by Michael Powell and starring B actors with a very unique story line. Nazi U-Boat survivors raid Canada and try and make it to the US border because the US is neutral at this point in time during WW2. Great photography (as usual) from Powell.

Invasion of the Body Snatchers – 1956 - Directed by Don Siegel, this science-fiction thriller was made for less than half a million dollars in the mid-fifties. It made ten times that or more in profits at the box office. Most science-fiction films made in the fifties were terrible. The ratio of good science-fiction films to bad ones is easily one in five and probably even lower than that. This was one of those wonderful surprises that occasionally popped up in theaters without any warning. All the bad science-fiction films, as well as the good ones, were often ballyhooed in radio and TV ads just prior to their release. You could tell just from the advertising, that another bomb was well under way to delivery in your neighborhood theater.

It was such a joy when one actually provided the thrills it promised. This film starred Kevin McCarthy as Dr. Miles Bennels, our protagonist in the film, who gradually finds out that we are being invaded, dammit. Dana Wynter, a lifelong B actress, is the love interest in the film, but love is the last thing that anyone is looking for on the screen with all of these creepy aliens taking over the earth. The film comes from a novel by Jack Finney called *The Body Snatchers*, and got his novel serialized in *Colliers Magazine* in 1954. The vast majority of science-fiction films of the fifties could not match the writing levels of this one. The agonizing suspense and terror are wonderfully translated onto the big screen through the skills of the very talented Don Siegel, who went on to make many more significant films in his future. Highly recommended and superior to all sequels in almost every way.

Invasion of the Saucer Men -1957 - Directed by Edward L. Cahn and starring Frank Gorshin (the Jimmy Cagney imitator) and several other B actors caught in this turkey (included in the Turkey Farm) with terrible production values and a script that will leave you laughing (unintentionally). Why is it here? Because it is funnier than most modern comedies.

The Invisible Man – 1933 - Directed by the legendary James Whale, who was a perfectionist of the monster genre, and starring Claude Rains as the Invisible Man, Dr. Jack Griffin, Gloria Stuart as Flora, his fiancée, and a lively supporting cast that adds great atmosphere to the entire proceedings. Monster films were a staple of Universal Studios in the thirties and this is one of the best of the genre.

In Which We Serve – England - 1942 - Directed, written, produced and starring Noel Coward, who humbly proclaims the film to be the greatest motion picture of our time. No, its not, but it is decent viewing. It is primarily a British Navy propaganda film using excellent talent.

The Ipcress File – 1965 - Directed by Sidney J Furie, who uses some unusual filming techniques to highlight the world of the spy. Micheal Caine follows up his success in *Zulu* with this adequate spy thriller.

I, Robot - 2004 - Directed by Alex Proyas and starring Will Smith as the bad robot-hunter in film that tries to reproduce the success of Harrison Ford in *The Blade Runner*. It nearly succeeds because the robot is quite fascinating, and upstages Smith in almost every scene. Worth viewing.

Iron Man - 2008 - Directed by Jon Favreau and starring Robert Downey Jr as Iron Man. Downey takes the film from cartoon to believable sci-fi on the strength of his superb acting. This is one of Marvel's best superhero films.

I Served the King of England (Czechoslovakia) - 2006 - Directed by Jiri Menzel and starring Ivan Barnev and Oldrich Kaiser as Jan Dite as a young and older man, respectively. This is a tale of poor judgment and greed, and some might say of survival. Please, no Czech please, jokes. Ethics were at a minimum during the Nazi occupation of Czechoslovakia. Interesting story line.

Ishtar – 1987 - Directed by Elaine May and starring Warren Beatty and Dustin Hoffman in an unlikely tale of two terrible lounge singers trying to make a living in Morocco. This fun movie was horribly panned by numerous critics, who, in my opinion, were unfair to the actual end result of the film. Roger Ebert was excessively critical of the film, but I thought it was mildly funny. After all, Roger, it wasn't meant to be *Lawrence of Arabia*.

Island in the Sky -1953 - Directed by William Wellman and starring John Wayne in one of his more unusual roles. A good supporting cast including Lloyd Nolan, James Arness, and Andy Divine help with the production. This is primarily a survival film and keeps the viewer engaged.

Island of Lost Souls – 1933 - Directed by Erie C Kenton and starring Charles Laughton, Bela Lugosi, Richard Arlen and Kathleen Burke. Burke plays the smoking hot Panther woman. This stuff was written by HG Wells (everything he wrote was great). This film is no exception. Scarier than a lot of other contemporary slasher films.

It Came From Beneath the Sea - 1955 - Directed by Robert Gordon and starring a plethora of B actors; all who do a decent job. The real star of the film is the giant octopus that attacks the Golden Gate Bridge in a very cool scene. Decent sci-fi.

It Came From Outer Space - 1953 - Directed by Jack Arnold and starring Richard Carlson as an amateur astronomer and film actor, Barbara Rush and a bunch of other B actors in Universal's first 3D movie, which did not add an iota to the actual impact of the film (3D is for morons; I hate when I am forced to watch modern films in 3D against my will). Still fun to watch the Ray Bradbury story.

It Happened One Night – 1934 -Directed by Frank Capra and starring Clark Gable and Claudette Colbert. This film dominated the Academy Awards for that year by winning Best Actor and Best Actress as well as other major categories. Capra won for Best Director and, of course, this film won for Best Picture of the year. The material is the film is a bit dated, which explains its low standings for the top one hundred films. Also, this Capra film does not have the same social messages that his other films of this period had like *Grapes of Wrath*.

Gable plays a reporter seeking the location of a missing heiress. The plot would be considered pretty absurd in modern times, but audiences liked to believe that such things were possible back in the days of the Depression. A romance develops, but then goes sour when the Colbert character finds out that Gable has been playing her for a fool. Gable is unable to tell her that, yes, he started to hustle her, but then fell in love with her himself, despite his best efforts to remain aloof. Of course, you will be able to figure out the ending pretty much because they did not believe in unhappy endings during the Depression. Recommended for the crisp dialogue.

It Happens Every Spring -1949 - Directed by Lloyd Bacon and starring Ray Milland and a solid supporting cast of B actors. Milland plays a professor who discovers how to throw a baseball that can't be hit (something the Yankee pitching staff could really use). The movie is great fun.

It's a Gift – 1935 - Directed by Norman Z Macleod (as if anyone could direct WC Fields) and starring WC Fields, Baby Leroy, and a solid supporting B actor troupe. The story is about a grocery store owner who is besieged from all sides in life and tries to find a little bit of comfort in the bottle. One of Field's best.

It's A Wonderful Life – 1946 - Directed by Frank Capra and starring Jimmy Stewart and Donna Reed along with a great supporting cast of B actors. It is a rather dark Christmas story about the financial struggles of a man who tries to do everything morally correct, but always seems to come out with the short end of the stick every time. Fun to watch.

Ivan the Terrible Part 1 (Russia) - 1943 - Made right smack in the middle of a life and death struggle with Germany in WW 2 by master director Sergei Eisenstein (I still don't how he got it done) and starring a cast of unknowns. It is the biopic of Ivan the Terrible and you have to see it to realize that most of these things actually happened in history. Must-see.

Ivan the Terrible Part 2 (Russia) - 1943 - Directed again by the incomparable Sergei Eisenstein and starring the same troupe of B actors that was in the original Part 1 release. The film goes on to show the descent of Ivan the Terrible from horrific despot to a completely mad animal with control over millions of people; sort of like my first wife. Some critics offered that these two films were metaphors for Hitler in Germany. Great cinema.

I, Vitelloni (Italy) - 1953 - Directed by Federico Fellini and starring a group of unknown Italian actors playing a group of spoiled post-WW2 Italian youths who are having trouble fitting into the post WW 2 world (as did most other people as well). The stark contrast of how their parents suffered in relation to the good times they are having weighs heavily on some of the young men. Great insight to post-war Italy.

Ivy – 1947 - Directed by Sam Wood and starring a very amorous Joan Fontaine, who wants three men at the same time (at the very least). This is dark soap, and has no protagonist except the third lover, Herbert Marshall, who repels Joan's advances. When rich men do this, it's too boring to be a movie. Worth seeing.

I Wake Up Screaming - 1941 - Directed by H Bruce Humberstone, who was famous for doing Charlie Chan films, and starring Betty Grable, Victor Mature, and Carole Landis as well as a solid supporting cast. Dark soap on a grand scale will be highly enjoyed by soap-lovers.

I Walk Alone – 1948 - Directed by Byron Haskin and starring Burt Lancaster, Kirk Douglas and the smoking hot Lizabeth Scott (she is actually smoking and is actually very hot in the poster). This film noir piece, although containing the sissy actor, Wendell Corey, still has a great supporting cast and story. Of course, in real life, Noll would have just had Burt killed in an hour or so. (By the way, poster art is terrible; guy looks nothing like Lancaster or Douglas.)

J

Jackie – 2016 – Directed by Pablo Larrain and starring Natalie Portman as Jackie Kennedy Onassis and her memories of John F Kennedy and her children. Portman does a very nice job. Would have liked to have seen more of the Onassis period, however.

Jason and the Argonauts -1963 - Directed by Don Chaffee with special effects by Ray Harryhausen. The cast of unknown B actors is irrelevant when stacked up against the special effects and photography. Lots of fun.

Jaws – 1975 - Directed by Steven Spielberg and starring Roy Schneider, Richard Dreyfuss, and Robert Shaw. This film kept an awful lot of people out of the water during the summer of 1975 and afterwards. The film was banned or rejected for show houses at various shore theaters because of the negatlve impact it had on bathers.

Jerimiah Johnson - 1972 - Directed by Sidney Pollack and starring Robert Redford as Jeremiah Johnson, a legendary mountain man who was left for dead after a tangle with a grizzly bear. Not the greatest movie or Western of all time, but a pleasant 90 minutes or so of good acting and a fine story.

The Jerk – 1979 - Directed by Carl Reiner and starring Steve Martin in his feature film debut, which was a smash hit and cemented his role as a leading comedian of the eighties. Plot is idiotic, just like the character, but it really doesn't matter as long as it makes us laugh, right?

Jerry Maguire - 1996 - Directed by Cameron Crowe and starring Tom Cruise as a grinning, insincere, hustler (this was a tremendous stretch for Cruise, but somehow he pulled it off). Cruise is an agent for Cuba Gooding Jr, who plays an elite athlete trying to obtain a big contract. Renee Zellweger is one of Cruise's love interests (the other is himself, of course). Where is the money! Fun to watch.

Jersey Boys- 2014- Directed by Clint Eastwood and starring Christopher Walken and a solid cast of unknowns in the story of the Four Seasons, a singing group from the badlands of New Jersey that made several hits in the 60s and 70s. Great stuff.

Jesse James – 1939 - Directed by Henry King and starring Tyrone Power, Henry Fonda and Randolph Scott as well as a great supporting cast. John Carradine is the dirty little coward that shot Mr. Howard in the back. Film accurately portrays the James Brothers as good guys fighting against greedy railroad land grabbers.

Jesus of Montreal (Canada) - 1989 - Directed by Denys Arcand and starring a great cast of unknown Canadian actors. This is an allegorical presentation of the story of Jesus set in the modern era (something that is terribly delicate and difficult to achieve). The director and actors succeed in their attempt by utilizing creative scenes, crisp dialogue and a grand sense of humor. Not sacreligious in any way. Very interesting.

Jezabel- 1938 - Directed by William Wyler and starring Bette Davis in her attempt to compete with *Gone With the Wind*, which would come out the following year. Warner Brothers thought that a better actress (everyone agreed that Davis was a better actress than Leigh) would be able to out-Southern Belle Vivian Leigh. Unfortunately, they did not have a strong enough male lead as good as Gable, or a supporting cast as good as DeHaviland and Howard. So Gone with the Wind made the public completely forget about this film one year later.

JFK – 1991 - Directed by Oliver Stone and starring Kevin Costner as the embattled New Orleans DA, Jim Garrison. Costner excelled in roles where he played someone with integrity, and the public firmly believed (and still believes) that the Kennedy Assassination was more than just a one-man show. See it for yourself and judge for yourself.

Jiao Yulu (China) – 1990 - Directed by Wang Jixing and starring Li Xuejian as an exemplary cadre in the early Chinese Communist Movement of the 1950s. Although some view the film as primarily communist propaganda (and at least some of it was), there is still a strong genuine socialist concern for the land and the masses that is evident in the film. These people were certainly a lot better off under socialism than they ever were under the landlords of capitalism. See it and judge for yourself.

Jim Thorpe, All American - 1951- Directed by Michael Curtiz, the best director on the Warner Brothers lot, with *Casablanca* under his belt. Curtiz's sense of the dramatic allows this to be more than just a rah-rah jock film. Burt Lancaster also adds great depth to the role, and Charles Bickford does his best work in this film. A truly inspiring sports film in the top ten sports films of all time.

Johnny Belinda - 1948 - Directed by Jean Negulesco and starring Lew Ayres, Jane Wyman and the competent Charles Bickford and Agnes Moorhead. This is some of the finest soap ever produced by Hollywood. It won an Academy Award for Jane Wyman as Best Actress (and was richly deserved). The story of an abused deaf mute woman who fights back is irresistible. A must see.

Johnny Eager - 1941 - Directed by Mervyn Leroy and starring Robert Taylor, a very sexy Lana Turner and Van Heflin in an Academy-award winning performance as Best Supporting Actor. This film noir classic also includes one of Edward Arnold's specialties as a heavy, adding to the production values. Although the plot is a bit convoluted and sometimes unbelievable, it certainly is never dull. Good movie-making.

Johnny Got His Gun - 1971 - Written and Directed by the talented and blacklisted Dalton Trumbo (he had the audacity to challenge knucklehead Joe McCarthy) and starring Timothy Bottoms as a WW 1 veteran who literally was blown away by a shell. All he has left are his torso, genitals and his brain. One of the most aggressively anti-war films of all time, and for good reason. Relentlessly depressing, yet inspiring at the same time. A must see.

Johnny Guitar - 1954 -Directed by Nicholas Ray and starring a very severe-looking Joan Crawford (she had the appearance of a virile Montgomery Clift). Mercedes McCambridge chews up her scenes as well, as one of the best cat fights in the history of cinema comes to a throbbing conclusion. The men and events in the film are merely props for the great final confrontation. Not to be missed. This was voted the second toughest woman poster of all time (after *Gun-Crazy*).

Johnny O'Clock – 1947 - Directed by Robert Rossen and starring Dick Powell (a lightweight noir guy) and Evelyn Keyes (a veteran B actress). The best actor in the film is Lee J Cobb who plays a great cop. Good film noir that comes in on a budget.

Journey Into Fear - 1943 - Directed by Norman Foster (as if anyone would be able to direct Welles) and starring Orson Welles, Joseph Cotton, his long-time associate at Mercury, Dolores Del Rio (who is out of her depth here), and Ruth Warrick, another veteran from Mercury. A good Nazi spy film promised so much more because of the great cast and title. Be happy the film is better than average and enjoy it.

Journey to the Center of the Earth – 1959 -Directed by Henry Levin and starring Pat Boone in a non-singing role with James Mason, who can't sing at all. Diane Baker adds to the eye candy as the female lead, but has no substantial dialogue. The real star of the film is Jules Verne's story and the special effects which are to be immensely enjoyed by anyone with an active imagination. Good fun.

Journey to the Far Side of the Sun (England) —1969 - Directed by Robert Parrish and stars a crop of British B actors and a B sci-fi script that shows the other side of the Sun. Any beginning astronomer will tell you that there are 360 X 360 sides to the sun as one degree becomes a vast distance away from the next degree in just a few light years. But for the mathematically disadvantaged, the film will still be fascinating. Recommended as an oddity. Look at that spaceship in the poster; I've seen more exciting trash receptacles.

The Joy Luck Club - 1993 - Directed by Oliver Stone, who although an excellent director, may have been the wrong choice for this film, which required a very delicate hand. The film starred Ming Na, Rosalind Chao, Lauren Tom, France Nuyen, Tamlyn Tomita, Kieu Chinh, Lisa Lu, and Tsai Chin. An outstanding musical score (one of the best of the decade) was written for the film by Rachel Portman and the script came from Amy Tan's best-selling book. Great dynamic between Chinese mothers and their daughters. How could the film miss? A must-see.

Judgment at Nuremburg – 1961 - Directed by Stanley Kramer and starring an international cast led by Maxmillan Schell as the Allied prosecutor, Marlene Dietrich, as a WW 2 survivor, Burt Lancaster, as an honorable Nazi, and Spencer Tracy, fittingly, as a judge. A bit cumbersome at times, but generally very entertaining.

Ju Dou (China) – 1990 -Directed by Zhang Yimou and starring Gong Li. This team of Zhang and Gong dominated Chinese cinema for almost fifteen years. In this film, Zhang expertly directs Gong as a purchased wife of the brutal Yang Jinshan, a silk trader, played by the steady Li Wei, a perennial favorite of Zhang. A nephew of Jinshan, Yang Tianqing, played by Li Baotian, another favorite of Zhang, falls in love with Ju Dou and they have a secret affair. Ju Dou gets pregnant with Yang's child, but attributes the pregnancy to Jinshan due to necessity. I will not reveal the ending, but it is Shakespearean in nature and not your traditional happy Hollywood ending. This is one of China's highest grossing films and is recommended as a great visual treat.

Jules and Jim – 1962 – France – Directed by Francois Truffaut and starring Jeanne Moreau, Oskar Werner (*Fahrenheit 451*), and a solid supporting cast of B actors in a story about two men who are in love with the same woman. Tragic.

Juliet of the Spirits – Italy -Directed by Federico Fellini and starring a group of B Italian actors in an ensemble piece held together by fine directing. The story of life in modern Rome is visually stunning, but emotionally less satisfying than some other Fellini works.

Jungle Book – 2016 – Yet another hit full-length cartoon produced by Disney. This one is written by Terry Gilkyson, who did a wonderful job with the script. Celebrity voiceovers of this boy in the jungle adventure include Bill Murray (when is he ever NOT funny), and a convincing straight bit by Ben Kingsley (when is he NOT convincing). I also enjoyed the bit by Christopher Walken, who is always entertaining. Great kid movie.

Jurassic Park – 1993 - Directed by Steven Spielberg, so you know no one who is nice will die. Starring Sam Neill, Laura Dern, Jeff Goldblum (the smuggest actor in film history), and a professional supporting cast. The music by John Williams is first-rate and stirring. The real stars, however, are the dinosaurs on the dinosaur farm. Top-notch sci-fi.

785

K

Kagemusha - Japan - 1980 - Directed by Akira Kurosawa and starring Tatsuya Nakadai as the lowly bandit who assumes the role of great general who is dying in order to save the army from defeat. A bit like *El Cid* with a body double. One of Kurosawa's best. Must see.

Kansas City Confidential - 1952 - Directed by Phil Carlsen and starring John Payne, a solid B actor who once had a hit in *Miracle on 34th St*. Colleen Gray provides a good female lead. This is classic film noir at the B level. Worth seeing as a case study on how to make a good B movie on a slim budget.

The Karate Kid - 1984 - Directed by John G Avildson, who was adept at making Rockytype films because he made the original Rocky and starring Ralph Macchio as the kid , Pat Morita as the closet martial-arts expert, and Elizabeth Shue as the kid's mother. This film is now an icon of American Cinema and has been copied, satirized, and immortalized. Must see.

Keeper of the Flame - 1943 - Directed by George Cukor, who was better known for light fare, and starring Spencer Tracy with Katherine Hepburn and a group of solid B actors in supporting roles. This is a story about a writer who is doing research on the husband of widow Hepburn in order to write a fluff piece. Unfortunately, Tracy finds some dirt. Interesting.

The Kennel Murder Case - 1933 - Directed by Michael Curtiz of *Casablanca* fame and starring William Powell as Philo Vance (that's right; the one Soupy Sales used to make fun of) and Mary Astor (good at playing rich dames), a niece of a murdered dog show exhibitor, and a sidekick of Vance during the case. I had wished to call this film a dog, but in good conscience I must say it was entertaining. I never knew dog exhibiting was so dangerous. I will now view *Best in Show* in a new light.

Kentucky Fried Movie - 1977 - Directed by John Landis and starring various Hollywood non-entities. The film is series of tasteless skits that are totally unrelated. Because the film was crass, tasteless, but extremely funny, it was a gigantic hit with the American public, the vast majority of which fall into the same category (crass and tasteless, such as myself).

Key Largo -1948 - Directed by the gritty John Huston and starring Humphrey Bogart, Edward G Robinson, Lauren Bacall, Lionel Barrymore and Claire Trevor. The stellar cast delivers the goods in practically one or two movie sets; quite similar to *The Petrified Forest*, to which this film obviously has similarities (Bogey was the heavy in that one, but the hero in this one). A classic and must see.

Khartoum (England) - 1966 - Directed by Basil Dearden and starring Charlton Heston as the protagonist, the immortal General Gordon of England, who had no business being there in the first place. Laurence Olivier is absolutely perfect as Mahdi, the antagonist who eventually kills Gordon and kicks the British out of the Sudan. When I was a kid, I used to root for the British in these films. Now, as an educated adult, I always root for the natives, instead. Root for Heston if you believe colonization is a good idea. Fun film.

Kid Glove Killer - 1942 - This film marked the directorial debut of the talented Fred Zinnemann, who went on to win the Academy Award for *A Man for All Seasons*. The movie stars the capable Van Heflin, Marsha Hunt and a number of other B actors who do a reasonable job. Heflin plays what is now known as a forensic crime investigator. Very interesting.

The Killer is Loose - 1956 - Directed by Budd Boetticher and starring Joseph Cotton, Wendell Corey and Rhonda Fleming. I tend to disagree with the poster. Wendell Corey is dreadful and is about as threatening as Barney Fife in Mayberry. Rhonda Fleming is hot, though. Worth it, because of the story line.

The Killers – 1946 - Directed by Robert Siodmak and starring Burt Lancaster in his film debut. Also starring in the film are Ava Gardner and Edmond O'Brien in support roles. The film is based on a short story by Ernest Hemmingway. It is a classic of film noir, and the mood is set early by the capable director. The story is about an unsolved crime and a lot of missing money. We find out that The Swede, played by Lancaster, was in the middle of the entire string of events, including the crime, itself.

Albert Dekker makes a great crook and Edmond O'Brien is a natural for a cop. So the casting was just about letter-perfect for this film. The music by the incomparable Miklos Rozsa is first-rate and the cinematography is perfect for the genre. This is a must see film if for no other reason than to marvel how quickly Lancaster made the transition from circus acrobat to capable Hollywood actor.

The Killer That Stalked New York - 1950- Directed by Earl McEvoy and starring a cast of Hollywood B actors who do an adequate job. The reason the film succeeds is because it has a decent director and an A script. Diamond smuggling and a smallpox outbreak at the same time; how can you beat that? Nice story.

The Killing -1956- Written and directed by Stanley Kubrick, who would go on to do much different material in the future and starring Sterling Hayden (a great film noir actor) and Coleen Gray, one of the top B actresses. This story of a first-class heist at a racetrack is very cool and the ending (which I will not reveal) is poetic. Great noir.

The Killing Fields (England) – 1984 - Directed by Roland Joffe and starring Sam Waterston of *Law and Order* fame as well as John Malkovich. Haing S Ngor plays a key role as the real-life Dith Pran, who worked for the NY Times in Cambodia and lived through the Khmer Rouge killings and other horrors of Cambodia at the time. Fascinating to watch.

Kill the Messenger- 2014 - Directed by Michael Cuesta and starring the usual suspects for B films with minimal production values. What saves this film is the story, which is based on fact. True stories are almost always more compelling than twenty-something fantasies. Reporter uncovers CIA drug and contra action in Nicaragua. Interesting

Kim - 1950 - Directed by Victor Saville and starring Errol Flynn, Dean Stockwell, Paul Lukas in an India adventure yarn. Unfortunately, the only women you will see in this film is the one on the poster, as women are of no importance in the story. Still worth viewing for early Dean Stockwell.

Kind Hearts and Coronets – England - 1950 - Directed by Robert Hamer and starring Alec Guinness as half the royalty in England (he plays eight roles). If my memory serves me correctly, only Tony Randall ever nearly played as many roles in one film; in the *Seven Faces of Dr. Lao*. The quality of Guinness' roles are better, though. Price great, also.

King David - 1985 - Directed by Bruce Beresford and starring Richard Gere as King David, the slayer of Goliath and the inspiration for lined diapers for adults. Watching Gere prance around in white diapers is enough for most women to see this film, but the story line is rather interesting as well. No small animals were injured in this film.

Kingdom of Heaven -2006 - Directed by Ridley Scott and starring Orlando Bloom (miscast), Liam Neeson (perfect), Jeremy Irons (also perfect), Ed Norton (always perfect), and a good supporting cast. Great music by Jerry Goldsmith added to the production values as well as wonderful cinematography. When I was a child, I rooted for the Europeans; now, as an educated adult, I find myself rooting for the natives. The moral of the story; stay home and make money. Great battle scenes (what else would you expect from Scott?)

King Kong – 1933 - Directed by Merian C Cooper and Ernest B Schoedsack and starring Fay Wry, Robert Armstrong, and Bruce Cabot. There is also a thrilling musical score by Max Steiner, who went on to do *Gone with the Wind* six years later. The real star of the film, however, is King Kong himself and all the special effects that went into the movie. This film was the first true box office success of a major special effects effort.

The story revolves around an egomaniac showman, Carl Denham, played by Armstrong, who will stop at nothing to get fame and fortune. Ann Darrow, played by Wray, is a sympathetic character, unlike Denham. She is obviously working to make ends meet and falls in love with Jack Driscoll, who is one of the few survivors of the original rumble in the jungle. This is, of course, a must see film and on just about every critic's top one hundred list.

King of California - 2007 - Directed by Mike Cahill and starring Michael Douglas. The real star of the story is the story. Cahill wrote a very inventive story line that succeeds in engaging the audience. Although far-fetched (some might say completely crazy), the story pays off in more than one way. Interesting.

King of Kings - 1961 -Produced by Sam Bronston (before there was *El Cid*) and directed by Nicholas Ray (normally a tough guy specialist) and starring a very beautiful Jeffrey Hunter (if I were to turn gay (like Cary Grant stated in one of his films), then this would be the guy I would chase). Robert Ryan is also featured in his usual cruel persona. The music by Miklos Rosza and the cinematography are better than the acting. (great eye candy).

The King of Marvin Gardens - 1972 - Directed by Bob Rafelson and starring Jack Nicholson, Bruce Dern (lightweight actor) and Ellen Burstyn (A actress). The story focuses on a missed opportunity in Atlantic City before the casinos arrived. I really didn't buy Nicholson as a simpleton, but the story was really interesting, so I forgave the characters. Worth seeing.

The King of Masks (China) – 1996 - Directed by Wu Tianming, who won the Best Director award in China for this film and starring Zhu Xu as Wang, the magician who performs bian lian, the Chinese art of changing masks in opera. The film also stars Zhou Renying, as the little orphan girl that is adopted by Wang. It is one of the best movies ever made in China according to many critics. The scenes depicting Bian Lian WITHOUT special effects are what make the film so spectacular, and stand above other Chinese films, with the possible exception of *Farewell, My Concubine*.

The story of a bian lian master with no male heir to pass on his skill is the primary plot of the film. Wang adopts what he believes to be a male heir only to find out that it is a female child later on. The child stubbornly sticks to Wang despite his disappointment, but runs away after accidentally setting his small hut on fire. Eventually, Wang is falsely jailed and rescued by the orphan later in the film. This is a must-see film, not only for Chinese films , but as a universal film.

King of the Children (China) - 1987 - Directed by the talented Chen Kaige and starring Chen Shaohua as a man sent away to the countryside near the end of the brutal Cultural Revolution. There he becomes king of the children. Interesting story drew a great deal of criticism from Chinese government, originally, but then relented. Good story.

King Rat – 1965 -Directed by Bryan Forbes and starring George Segal as King Rat, the big cheese in the POW camp. Supporting Segal is Tom Courtenay, Patrick O'Neal and John Mills. Good music by John Barry and the story written by James Clavell of *Shogun* fame. Interesting dynamic.

King Solomon's Mines – 1950 - Directed by Compton Bennett and starring Stewart Granger with Deborah Kerr. Tale of husband and treasure hunting could have been better with less emphasis on the jungle and more on the mines. But still some good acting and scenes. Worth seeing.

Kinsey- 2004- Directed by Bill Condon and starring Liam Neeson as Kinsey. Fine supporting cast includes John Lithgow, Chris O'Donnell, and Timothy Hutton. Film concentrates on the serious, academic aspects of Kinsey's research, and therefore, not that appealing to mass audiences. Watchable.

The King's Speech – 2010 - Directed by Tom Hooper with an original screenplay written by David Seidler and starring Colin Firth as King George VI and Geoffrey Rush as speech therapist, Lionel Logue. A fine supporting cast including Helena Bonham Carter as the wife of King George VI, Queen Elizabeth, whose daughter Queen Elizabeth II, currently has reigned as Queen for over 58 years.

Also in the cast are Guy Pearce, perfectly cast as the abdicating King Edward VIII, and an ironic casting of Derek Jacobi as the Archbishop of Canterbury. (Jacobi gained fame decades ago portraying the Roman Emperor, Claudius, in 1976 and winning the Best Actor award for that year in television. Claudius was a notorious stutterer and Jacobi created an unforgettable character in that production, just like Firth creates one for this film.) The director does a great job of developing the characters of both the trainer and the king at the same time.

Kiss Me Deadly - 1955-Directed by Robert Aldrich and starring Ralph Meeker, a good B actor and a supporting cast of adequate B actors. Written by Mickey Spillane, so you have an A script, at least. In glorious black and white film noir. Lots of fun.

Kiss of Death – 1947 - Directed by Henry Hathaway and starring Victor Mature, Brian Donlevy and Coleen Gray. This is one of the best B movies ever made. The cinematography is outstanding and the actors put everything they have into their roles. Film noir at its very best.

Klute – 1971 - Directed by Alan J Pakula, who is very good with serious subjects and starring Jane Fonda in her Academy-Award winning role as hooker with a heart of Charlie Chan. Fonda helps detective played by Donald Sutherland to solve a crime. A notch above the average detective film.

Knife in the Water (Poland) - 1962 - Directed by Roman Polanski and his only legitimate good movie. All downhill after this one. Cast includes Polish unknowns, but the real star of the film is the story, which is first-rate. Should you ever go on a date with one woman and two guys? Not if you're a guy. Tense thriller is in doubt until the very end of the film.

The Knot (China) - 2006 - Directed by Lin Yi and starring Chen Kun, Vivian Hsu, and Li Bing Bing in a first-rate soap that will easily make it into the House of Soap. War creates the usual triangle which then creates emotional difficulties. This plot has never been done before. (I'm being sarcastic, as you may have guessed). For soap-lovers only.

Knute Rockne, All American- 1939- Directed by Lloyd Bacon, which is quite appropriate because there is plenty of ham in this sports extravaganza. Pat O'Brien goes way over the top and Ronald Reagan as the Gipper is just too good not to see. Still fun to watch.

Koyaanisqatsi – 1983-Japan - Produced and directed by Godfrey Reggio with great music from Philip Glass and great photography by Ron Fricke. The stars of the film are the people in charge of the production; the director, writer, music composer and photographer. They create a masterpiece documentary.

K-PAX - 2001 - Directed by Lain Softley (I suspect this is not a real name) and starring one of my favorite actors in a quirky role, Kevin Spacey, as an alien (or maybe he isn't). It is mystery sci-fi. Jeff Bridges plays the psychiatrist who does not believe Spacey is an alien, and tries to cure him. Very amusing.

Kramer vs. Kramer – 1979 - Directed by Robert Benton and starring two of the best in the business; Meryl Streep and Dustin Hoffman. You really believe these two were married. The film is unusual in the sense that it is very realistic and unrealistic about divorce at the same time. Divorce does mess up kids; no contest there. But to think the father will have the same influence in the child's life as the mother is a pure fantasy. The mother will influence the child much more over 90% of all divorce cases (see New York University school of Social Research results). Nice fantasy film for divorced fathers, though.

The Krays -1990 - Directed by Peter Medak and starring Billie Whitelaw and Tom Bell as the Krays (as in CRAY-ZEE), two young British thugs who kill their way to the top of the crime lords in England. Overly-violent, but probably accurate. Interesting.

Kundun - 1997 - Directed by Martin Scorsese and starring mostly unknown Asian actors. The story is about the selection and abdication of the Fourteenth Dali Lama of Tibet, even though it was filmed in Morocco. The film portrays the Chinese Communist Party in a very poor light, even though Buddhist feudalism was responsible for very low average wage and living conditions in the region.

   The film does not mention the substantial increase of wages and living conditions since the CCP takeover of Tibet in 1959, nor does it mention the repressive nature of the Buddhist clerics who ruled the region as if all citizens of the region were assumed to be Buddhists. A complex religious/political situation to say the least, but Scorsese goes out of his way to avoid too much political claptrap and sticks to the beautiful filming and story, which are extremely well-done. Very interesting.

Kung-Fu Cyborg - China-2009- Directed by Jeffrey Lau and starring Hu Jun, Betty Sun, Alex Fong, Ronald Cheng, and Wu Jing of Hong Kong (you can usually recognize Hong Kong names because they have English first names; this is not foolproof or stereotypical, but just a good indicator of where the film was made). This transformer film (I hate most of them) is much better than the usual transformer film because it actually has a story and interesting character development. The best of the transformer films.

Kung-Fu Hustle (China) -2004 - The funniest film ever made in Chinese cinematic history. Directed, produced and starring Stephen Chow . Also starring Yuen Wah, Yuen Qiu, Danny Chan, and Bruce Leung.

I agree 100% with Roger Ebert about this film. It is hilarious, and I laughed harder at this Chinese film than any other I have ever seen (and I have seen just about all of them). A must see.

L

Lacombe Lucien (France) - 1974 – Directed by Louis Malle and starring Pierre Blaise as Lucien Lacombe, a young man who falls in love during the German occupation of France late in World War 2, Aurore Clement as France Horn, the romantic interest of Lucien, who happens to be Jewish, and a sound supporting cast that lends authenticity and depth to a very human story of human reactions to events that are overwhelming. The story is supposedly based on events that happened during the filmmaker's own youth during the German occupation. Though nominated for best Foreign Film in 1975, it did not win, but did win the Golden Globe for best Foreign Film. Recommended.

LA Confidential - 1997 - Directed by Curtis Hanson and starring Kevin Spacey, Russell Crowe, Guy Pearce, Kim Basinger, Danny DeVito and David Strathairn. Good mood music provided by Jerry Goldsmith enhances the production values. Great screenplay about LA Cops, celebs and a bit of corruption in both. Recommended.

La Dolce Vita – Italy - 1960 – Directed and written by Federico Fellini and starring Marcello Mastroianni as Marcello Rubini, a reticient reporter who covers nefarious assignments, Anita Eckberg as Sylvia, the sexy Swedish-American actress who is the object of Marcello professional and sexual curiosity, Anouk Aimee as a beautiful and wealthy heiress whom Marcello makes love to in the course of his other duties, Walter Sentesso as Paparazzo, the professional photographer sent with Marcello to photograph the rich and famous (and if this name sounds familiar, it should, because it is the origin of the term Paparazzi, or intrusive Italian professional photographer which came from this film).

Lady and the Tramp - 1955 – Produced by Disney Studios and starring Tramp, a common street dog and Lady, a pampered high-pedigree bitch. This film found enormous appeal to both young and old during the mid-fifties. The two main characters are amply supported by an amusing group of dogs and humans, all of which are subservient to the romance between the two main characters. Disney art and storytelling skills are at Golden Age levels in this film.

There is never a dull moment on the screen and there are plenty of memorable ones such as the sharing of spaghetti in an Italian restaurant. Both dogs kiss as a result of the strand of spaghetti running out of room at the end. This was truly an inspired scene and is now a film icon in Hollywood history. As usual, this Disney film has little violence and is quite suitable for children of all ages. By this time, the Disney Studios had already garnered a string of financial successes from their full-length cartoon features and this one would be one of the most popular because of its universal theme and appeal. The social translation for older viewers was that it really didn't matter where you came from as far as pedigree, as long as you had the right stuff, you could be successful in life or with the opposite sex. America had a long tradition in film of stressing that love was more important than money in relationships and this feature only reinforced that still debatable proposition. I can recommend this full-length cartoon as one of Disney's best productions of all time. There probably wasn't a kid or parent who didn't see it at one time or another in the 1950s.

Lady Eve – 1941 - Directed by Preston Sturges and starring a fast-lane Barbara Stanwyck and a slow-lane Henry Fonda who meet and fall in love on a luxury liner during a cruise. Sturges is at the top of his game in this one and Stanwyck is perfect. Recommended.

Lady From Shanghai - 1948 - Directed, produced and starring Orson Welles and Rita Hayworth (a worthy adversary for Welles) along with a very capable Everett Sloan (another veteran from Citizen Kane. The twisted plot includes a murder, a frame, a hot wife, and a fall guy. I will let you figure out who does what to whom. Very engaging. on asandlady, Louisa, who.

Lady Killers (England) - 1955 - directed by Alexander Mackendrick and starring Sir Alec Guinness as Professor Marcus, a mastermind thief, Katie Johnson as an elderly landlady, Louisa, who rents out rooms to Professor Marcus and his gang, Cecil Parker as Major Courtney, one of the more gentlemanly gang members, the talented Peter Sellers in an early role as the Cockney, Harry Robinson, and Herbert Lom, who would go on to make many future films with Sellers during the Pink Panther series as the vicious gangster Louis Harvey.

The wonderful screenplay was written by William Rose and deservedly was nominated for, but did not win, an academy award for best screenplay for that year. It did win other screenplay awards, however. The direction of Mackendrick is almost at a manic state and the action moves at breakneck speed. One must be very quick to gather all the little subplots that are proposed in the plot.

Lady on a Train - 1945 - Directed by Charles David and starring Deanna Durbin in a screwball comedy along with Ralph Bellamy as her foil. A competent supporting cast including Edward Everett Horton and others provide plenty of laughs. Recommended.

Lady Sings the Blues – 1972 - Directed by Sidney J Furie and starring Diana Ross as Billie Holliday in a film treatment loosely based on her life. The movie was nominated for a slew of awards, but did not win any. Especially disappointing was Ross losing the Best Actress award to Liza Minnelli, which many critics thought was an injustice. Film was very popular.

Lady Vanishes – England - 1938 – Directed by Alfred Hitchcock and starring Margaret Lockwood as Iris Henderson, the romantic interest of Gilbert, a young Michael Redgrave as Gilbert, a musicologist who befriends Iris, Paul Lukas as the dubious Dr. Hartz, who may or may not be a spy, May Whitty as Miss Froy, the woman who vanishes from the train who was a governess, and who is actually a major spy for England. A fine supporting cast of likely spies and counterspies that work very well together. The real star of the film, of course, is Hitchcock himself as the director. The direction of the film is impeccable, and the location of the major portion of the film taking place on a train allows the director to control almost every single aspect of the film from beginning to end. A train is almost like performing a play on stage; the space is limited and the sets are easy to change.

As a matter of fact, I cannot think of a better film to translate into a play. Hitchcock uses a wide variety of his tricks including having the audience guess the nature of each of the actors as well as how the escapade will be accomplished. Very few, if any, will be able to figure out the ending of the film which I will not reveal. The complications are at the same time predictable and unpredictable. We are familiar with the plot, but never see the solution coming. This is Hitchcock at his very best and he would repeat his successful train motif in some of his other films such as North by Northwest, and of course, his most famous train movie, *Strangers on a Train*. I can recommend this film heartily and it would a shame if you have seen other Hitchcock films and miss this one, because it is one of his best.

La Femme Nikita – France - 1991 – directed and written by Luc Besson and starring Anne Parillaud as Nikita, a teenage drug addict who murders a policeman and is sentenced to life imprisonment, Tcheky Karyo as Bob, a CIA-type wet-work operator, Jean Hugues Anglade as her male love interest, who is primarily a prop, and veteran actress Jeanne Moreau as Amande, a trainer for the secret agency, who trains Nikita to become a killing machine Recommended with reservations for the violence.

Lake of Fire – 2017 – Tony Kaye directs this gripping documentary on abortion. A very even-handed approach to both sides of the issue (because every issue has two sides). Kaye maintains his English attitude of fair play for both sides with great skill. Recommended.

Lamumba – 2000 – Directed by Raoul Peck and starring Eriq Ebouaney as the legendary Patrice Lamumba, the John F Kennedy of the Congo, as dubbed by the media by some, and as a communist agitator by others. See the film and judge for yourself. But one thing was certain. Lamumba was not assassinated by anyone from the Congo; that would leave Europe and the US as the most likely suspects. Recommended.

Land of the Pharaohs - 1955 -Directed by Howard Hawks and starring Joan Collins and Jack Hawkins (Joan was way too fast for him). The story of a king building his own pyramid is interesting, but the rest of the plot is rather commonplace.

Larceny Inc. - 1942 - Directed by Lloyd Bacon and starring Edward G. Robinson, Jane Wyman, and Broderick Crawford. This is your fantasy-world of gangster land where you can avoid getting whacked by the competition, plan idiotic heists that succeed, and still wind up with a happy ending. Totally ridiculous plot, but fun to watch.

Last Angry Man - 1959 - Directed by Daniel Mann and starring Paul Muni as a doctor who is the subject of TV show. Muni tries mightily to raise the level of mediocre script, but ultimately, it is merely very good soap. Worth watching for Muni's Academy-Award nominated performance.

Last Bandit – 1949 – If only it were true. Directed by Joseph Kane and starring Forest Tucker and Andy Devine (who lends levity to the proceedings) in a story about a man who has to make a choice between a life of crime and going straight. A bit different from your usual Western.

Last Command – 1928 (Silent)- Directed by Joseph Von Sternberg and starring Emil Jannings as the memorable General Sergius Alexander, a cousin of the deposed Czar of Russia, Evelyn Brent as his romantic interest, Natalie Dabrova, a budding film actress, and an early appearance by William Powell of *The Thin Man* series, who plays a Hollywood director with flawless precision. Von Sternberg would go on to make other films that highlighted men who fell for women of questionable character. His most famous, of course, was *The Blue Angel*, starring Jannings and Marlene Dietrich.

The Last Emperor -1987 - Directed by Bernardo Bertolucci and starring John Lone, Joan Chen, Peter O'Toole, and a number of mainland Chinese actors, most notably Chen Kaige, who is now considered to be one of China's finest directors. Columbia Pictures wisely included the mainland Chinese film industry in this production and obtained the cooperation of the CCP for shooting in the Forbidden City and other sensitive areas of China. That is the best way to make a film in China.

The movie was a big commercial and critical success and portrayed the life of Puyi, who is known to every child in China, but was pretty much a mystery to everyone in the US until this film. The cinematography is outstanding. The film won Best Picture of the year and a slew of other Academy Awards including Best Director. Bertolucci has a taste for the sumptuous in his filmmaking cinematography, and there are few venues that are more photographic than the Forbidden City and other Chinese locations.

Peter O'Toole gives a bravado performance as the personal tutor and mentor of the young emperor. Of course, like all other great O'Toole performances for one reason or another, it was always ignored in Hollywood by the Academy voters. The scope of the film is enormous. Just to cover Puyi's life in the Forbidden City would have been more than enough for a magnificent picture. This is a must see film on China, and is on numerous top 100 lists.

Last Gangster – 1937- If only it were so. Directed by Edward Ludwig and starring Edward G Robinson as your classical thirties gangster. Also starring Jimmy Stewart. A solid cast of B actors helps with the atmosphere, which MGM was noted for creating in most of its films. Worth watching for Robinson.

Last King of Scotland - 2006 - Directed by Kevin MacDonald and starring Forest Whitaker as Idi Amin, the bloodthirsty dictator of Uganda. Whitaker gives a tour-de-force performance that won the Best Actor Academy Award. A must-see film that is chilling.

Last Night – 1998 –Directed by Don McKellar and starring Sandra Oh (the only A actress in the film) and a decent supporting cast, including the director in a story about different reactions of people to their last night on earth. How would you spend your last night on earth?

The Last of Sheila - 1973 - Directed by Herbert Ross and starring some A talent such as Richard Benjamin, James Coburn, and James Mason. A solid supporting cast makes the mystery/comedy even more enjoyable. A pleasant way to spend 90 minutes.

Last of the Dogmen – 1995 – Directed by Tab Murphy and starring Tom Berenger and Barbara Hershey in the lead roles in a story about a bounty hunter (dogman in American Indian folklore because he tracks down men like a dog) in Montana who solves the killing of three wanted men. Not bad.

Last of the Mohicans - 1936 - Directed by George B Seitz and starrring Randolph Scott, Binnie Barnes and Bruce Cabot as Magua, the treacherous Indian. The film is great in every respect except for the depiction of Magua, which fails to come close to the portrait of Magua in the solid remake of the film many years later. Bruce Cabot is just not convincing as an Indian. Great fun to watch.

The Last of the Mohicans - 1992 – Directed by Micheal Mann and starring Daniel DayLewis, Madeliene Stowe, and the unforgettable portrayal of Magua by Wes Studi, who almost steals the film away from Lewis. Mann is relentless in maintaining the breakneck pace of the film and there is never a dull moment. He has a particular knack for action sequences and there are numerous thrilling encounters all throughout the film. Day-Lewis is very convincing as the Last of Mohicans and is manly enough to make any maiden's heart go pitter-patter. Madeliene Stowe gives the best performance of her career in this film and is also very sexy.

She is no little weak-kneed damsel in distress. She can handle herself in a fight and is not afraid to handle a gun of any type. The real star of the film, however, is Wes Studi, whose character Magua, is so compelling for every second he is on the screen that one cannot literally take their eyes off him for a second. This was easily the greatest role of his career. The duels on the cliffs between Magua and a few of the main characters are beautifully done and are an example of how one on one combat scenes should be photographed. This is a must-see film and consistently in the top hundred films of all time on just about every movie critic's list.

Last Picture Show - 1971 - Directed by Peter Bogdanovich, who always excelled in filming in black and white (see *Paper Moon*). The film has an extremely talented cast of A actors including Timothy Bottoms, Jeff Bridges, Ellen Burstyn, Ben Johnson, Cloris Leachman and Cybil Shepherd. Even Randy Quaid is good in this one. A must see.

La Strada – Italy - 1956 - Directed by Federico Fellini and starring Anthony Quinn as Zampano, a brutish strongman who treats women as if they are merely props for his show, Giulietta Masina as Gelsomina, a simple farming peasant who replaces her sister as a prop for the unfeeling Zampano and his show, and a very unlikely Richard Basehart, a thoroughly American actor playing an Italian clown (and quite well, for that matter) known as the fool, who falls for Gelsomina but comes to a tragic end.

There is also a highly capable supporting cast that augments the fine performances of the lead actors. Fellini, who usually excels in surrealistic endeavors, is working with neorealism here and succeeds just as well. This film shows the extraordinary talent and range of the master director. The film is considered a masterpiece of acting in Italian cinema, and it won the very first Academy Award for Best Foreign Film that was presented that year. This was my mother's favorite film of all time, and I remember seeing, but not understanding it as a child. It is recommended for these fine performances and because my mother would beat me if I didn't recommend it.

Last Tango in Paris -1973 - Directed by Bernardo Bertalucci and starring Marlon Brando and Maria Schneider in a story about two dysfunctional adults who enter into a perverse sexual arrangement. The man is grieving over the loss of his wife, and the woman is engaged and obviously not in love with her betrothed. The sex scenes were considered controversial at the time and were later toned down by censors. Interesting to see Brando win an Academy Award for one of his lesser pieces of work here.

Last Train From Gun Hill - 1959 - Directed by Hal Wallis and starring Kirk Douglas and Anthony Quinn in a story of passion and violence in the Old West. Two of the more passionate actors in the business make this soapy oater believable. Fun to watch.

Last Tycoon - 1976 - Directed by Elia Kazan and starring Robert DeNiro in his least-known role along with many other good actors wasted on this Harold Pinter catastrophe taken from an overblown F. Scott Fitzgerald unfinished novel of the same name. There was a reason he never finished it; its boring. Better to have done *The Diamond as Big as the Ritz*, which was much far more interesting than this story about the rich and powerful. Who cares? In the top 2000 just to see DeNiro.

Last Voyage - 1960 - Directed by Andrew L. Stone and starring Robert Stack, Dorothy Malone, Edmond O'Brien and the always-entertaining George Sanders in a story about a cruise liner sinking in the Pacific. Fun to watch.

Last Wave – Australia - 1977 – Directed by Peter Weir and starring Richard Chamberlain in a tale about the coming of a gigantic tidal wave that will engulf Australia. Builds up to a decent climax. Could even have been better.

L'Atalante (France) - 1934 - Directed by Jean Vigo and starring Michel Simon, Dita Parlo and Jean Daste. This is a simple story of newlyweds who have a bit of difficulty adjusting to married life. A soap-lover's treat.

La Terra Trema (Italy)- 1947 - Directed by Luchino Visconti and starring a number of unknown B Italians, some of which were complete amateurs. Despite that (or maybe because of the inexperienced cast), the film was well-received by the critics in Europe. A solid film.

Laura – 1944 — Directed by Otto Preminger and starring the dreamy Gene Tierney and Dana Andrews with an outstanding supporting cast including the talented Clifton Webb, Vincent Price and Judith Anderson. The music from this film is haunting and became a hit many years after the film was forgotten.

Lavender Hill Mob - 1951 -England- Directed by Charles Crichton and starring Alec Guinness and Stanley Holloway as an inside and outside crooks planning a bank gold heist. This film has similarities to *The Producers* which came later because the main character was a life-long honest man who is talked into a crime by a shady character. A lot of fun to watch.

Law-Abiding Citizen - 2009 - Directed by F. Gary Gray and starring Gerard Butler in a breakthrough role as a man determined to make the system pay for its excesses and Jamie Foxx as the prosecutor who tries to stop him. The audience is rooting for the convict all the way. A real rouser.

Lawman - 1971 - Directed by Michael Winner and starring heavyweights Burt Lancaster, Robert Ryan and Lee J Cobb. That's enough ham for four butcher shops. Burt is a marshal dedicated to dishing out justice with the barrel of a gun. Law and Order addicts will absolutely adore this film. Recommended.

Lawrence of Arabia – 1962 - Directed by David Lean and starring Peter O'Toole, who somehow did not manage to win the Academy Award for Best Actor that year despite easily giving the best performance of any actor, not only for that year, but most likely for the entire decade. A brilliant supporting cast included Anthony Quinn, Omar Sharif, Sir Alec Guinness, and a host of other highly accomplished actors.

The story is based in fact about a major in the British army in WW 1 who becomes the unlikely leader of the Arab armies fighting against the Ottoman Empire in Arabia. The Battle of Acaba was brilliantly photographed and the large all-star supporting cast was solid in every respect. This film is generally accepted by most critics to be the best of all the blockbuster movies ever made. The sweep and richness of the filming, the crisp dialogue and the first-rate performances make it an unforgettable film. By last count, I have seen this film at least a half dozen times and it never seems to get tired. Lean is a master of this sort of film, as evidenced by his previous success with *The Bridge On the River Kwai*, which was also a multi-award winner. Lean kept numerous actors from that ensemble for this production, including Guinness. There are more than a dozen memorable scenes in this film and there are too many to note individually. This is a must-see movie.

A League of Their Own -1992 -Directed by Penny Marshall and starring Madonna, Rosie O'Donnell, Geena Davis and Tom Hanks. This story of a touring WW 2 period all-woman's baseball team hits a home run and delivers the goods (I can't think of another cliche right now). Great fun.

Left Hand of God- 1955 - Directed by Edward Dmytryk and starring Humphrey Bogart, Lee J Cobb and Gene Tierney. Cobb, a very good actor, is miscast here as there were plenty of good Chinese actors available to play the role better. Bogart and Tierney are good, but the script is really not up to snuff. I love priests who are good with a gun, though.

Legend of Tian Yun Mountain (China) - 1980 - Directed by Xie Jin and starring Wang Fuli, Shi Jianlan, Shi Weijian, and Zhong Xinghuo. The film depicts the seldom-told story of the political in-fighting within the Chinese Communist Party during the 1950s and the Rightist movements of that period. Very interesting.

Le Jour Se Leve (France) – 1939 - Directed by Marcel Carne and starring Jean Gabin, a French legend, Jules Berry and Arletty. This seemingly simple tale of a man consumed by violence takes on more levels of understanding before the climax and makes for interesting cinema. Recommended.

Lenny – 1974 - Directed by Bob Fosse (who was generally more successful with directing musicals) and starring Dustin Hoffman as Lenny Bruce, the controversial stand-up comedian of the 1960's who was convicted for obscenity violations which are now commonly heard on cable TV cartoon shows like South Park every week. Valerie Perrine very good in supporting role. Recommended with reservations about Bruce's drug addiction.

Les Miserables - 1935 - Directed by Richard Boleslawski and starring Fredric March, Charles Laughton and Cedric Hardwicke. There were few actors who could convey the air of self-righteousness as well as Laughton, and the film production values are first rate. A must see.

The Letter - 1940 - Directed by William Wyler and starring Bette Davis and Herbert Marshall in a compelling courtroom drama about a woman who might or might not be involved with another man, and is accused of killing him for reasons other than self-defense. Compelling drama.

Letter From an Unknown Woman (China) - 2004 - Directed by Xu Jinglei and starring Dong Ping, Xu Jinglei, Zhao Yijun, and Ma Paobing. This story about about a forgotten affair revived by a communication from someone in the past is a universal theme. Extremely well done by the director, Xu.

Letters From Iwo Jima - 2006 - Directed by Clint Eastwood and released after the failed *Flags of Our Fathers*, which did poorly at the box office. It appears the very original Japanese view of the battle and the aftermath were more interesting than the cliche-ridden American view. A must see.

Letter to Three Wives - 1949 - Directed by Joseph L Mankiewicz and starring Jeanne Crain, Linda Darnell and Ann Southern as the three wives and Kirk Douglas, Paul Douglas and Jeffrey Lynn as the husbands. Thelma Ritter adds to the production. A great soap about three marriages that may or may not be on the rocks.

Leviathan – 2014 – (Russia) Directed by Andrey Zvyagintsev and starring Alexey Serebryakov as a Russian fisherman who is in danger of losing his family's house to a corrupt mayor, who is backed by the Communist Party. Interesting.

L.I.E. - 2001 - Directed by Michael Cuesta and starring Paul Franklin Dano and Bruce Altman in the leading roles of troubled son and father, respectively. This story of family tragedy among the rich and privileged of Long Island is interesting soap, but imagine how tragic it would have been in a poor family.

Life -2017 – Directed by Daniel Espinosa and starring Jake Gllenhaal and a bunch of B actors that is befitting the storyline of the film. What saves the film, however, is the A production values which keeps our attention riveted on the screen from beginning to end.

Life and Death of Colonel Blimp -1943 - Directed by the formidable pair of Michael Powell and Emeric Pressburger and starring Deborah Kerr and some British B actors. A thoroughly entertaining romp through British military manners.

Life and Death of Peter Sellers -2004 – Directed by Stephen Hopkins and starring Geoffrey Rush as Sellers and a superior supporting cast including Charlize Theron, John Lithgow, Emily Watson, and Stanley Tucci. This life doc of Sellers hits the spot.

Lifeboat - 1944 - Directed by Alfred Hitchcock and starring a great cast including Tallulah Bankhead, William Bendix, Walter Sleazak, and Hume Cronyn. The dialogue is first-rate. One of the Master's best films. A must-see.

Life of Arthur Tafero - 2018-A- Directed by Arthur Tafero and starring Andy Garcia as Arthur Tafero, Helen Mirren as Mary Tafero, Geoffrey Rush as Arthur Tafero Sr, Matthew Modine as Doulgas King, Winona Ryder as Julie Bottone, Cameron Diaz as Mary DiGioia, Anjelica Huston as Maryanne Bannon, Gong Li as Wang Lijun, and Joseph Tafero as himself. This tale of fate travels from New Jersey to New York, to Florida and then China. Finally, the tale ends in Florida, where redemption and closure finally take place. Only one print of this film. Selected by Insomniacs Anonymous as the film most likely to put you to sleep.

Life of Emile Zola - 1937 - Directed by William Dieterle and starring Paul Muni as Emile Zola, the great writer with a focus on the Dreyfuss Affair in France. One of the best biopics ever made and Academy Award winner for Best Picture that year.

Life of Pi - 2012- Directed by Ang Lee and starring Suraj Sharma, Irrfan Khan, Tabu (the successor to Sabu), Adil Hussain, Gerard Depardieu in a cameo, and Rafe Spall. Make no mistake, this is Sharma's film all the way and quite an accomplishment it is. It is a wonderful combination of Castaway and Black Stallion, all rolled up into one with a little Siddhartha thrown in for good measure. I enjoyed the film immensely as it took me away from my earthly worries for over two hours. Do not try to read too much into the film and you will enjoy it even more. One of the finest Indian films ever made in the US. Highly recommended.

Life on a String (China) -1991 - Directed by the talented Chen Kaige and starring Liu Zhongyuan, Huang Lei, and Xu Qing in this great film about a blind musician and his disciple who believes his teacher will see after breaking 1000 strings. Great movie making.

Life With Father - 1947 - Directed by Michael Curtiz of Casablanca fame and starring William Powell, Irene Dunne and Elizabeth Taylor. This amusing turn of the century comedy will keep you laughing. Recommended.

Lion Has Wings – 1940 – Directed by Michael Powell and starring Merle Oberon and Sir Ralph Richardson in a story about the struggle of the British Air Force during WW 2 in England against the onslaught of the Nazis.

Lion in Winter -1968 - Directed by Anthony Harvey and starring Peter O'Toole and Katherine Hepburn in an academy-award winning role. A great supporting cast which included Anthony Hopkins and a young Timothy Dalton helps the production values. O'Toole snubbed once again as Best Actor, deserved better.

Lion King – 1994 – Animated feature directed by Roger Allers and Rob Minkoff about a relationship between a father lion and his son. The evil uncle adds to the plot. Disney at its best in this production. I am a sucker for any father and son plot.

Lion of the Desert (England) -1981 - Directed by Moustapha Akkad and starring Anthony Quinn as Omar Muhktar, the *Lion of the Desert*, who opposes the modern fascist army of the Italians before the outbreak of World War 2, Oliver Reed as General Rodolpho Graziani, the Italian General who defeats Muhtar and eventually has him hanged, Rod Steiger as Mussolini (a very well-cast role), who appoints

Graziani to conquer Libya, and Raf Vallone as Diodiece, a disillusioned Italian officer. There are also small cameo roles by prominent actors, John Gielgud and Irene Pappas, who had co-starred with Quinn much earlier in the successful *Zorba the Greek*.

Listen to Me, Marlon – 2015 - Directed by Stephan Riley and starring Marlon Brando at various points in his long and legendary career. We hear sound bytes of Marlon espousing various thoughts throughout his many roles and challenges in life. Good documentary.

The List of Adrian Messenger - 1963 – Directed by John Huston and starring George C. Scott, Kirk Douglas, Tony Curtis, Frank Sinatra, and Burt Lancaster. Sinatra seldom appeared with any of these other actors. A solid mystery, and hard to recognize one or two of the characters. Good fun.

Little Big Man - 1970 - Directed by Arthur Penn and starring Dustin Hoffman as the little big man, Faye Dunaway, Chief Dan George, Martin Balsam and other competent B actors. This is a revisionist Western (those are Westerns where the Indians are the good guys and the soldiers are the bad guys, unlike the old days of Hollywood) that has a comedic touch, but is also filled with the ample tragedies of the American Indian. Interesting to view.

Little Caesar - 1931- Directed by Mervyn Leroy and starring Edward G Robinson in an iconic role. Douglas Fairbanks Jr. is also featured in the film, but Robinson chews up every scene he's in, and makes a name for himself in Hollywood. A must-see.

Little Dieter Needs to Fly- 1998 - Directed by the talented Werner Herzog and starring Dieter Dengler playing himself in a documentary that is both astounding and tragic. Talk about survivors. This guy makes those survivor champions on television look like sissies in comparison.

The Little Fugitive - 1953 - Directed by Ray Ashley, Morris Engel and Ruth Orkin, who all do a wonderful job on a very limited budget. Every parent's worst nightmare. Richie Andrusco plays the little boy lost in Coney Island. A prime example of how to make a low-budget film.

Little Miss Sunshine -2006 - Directed by Jonathan Dayton and Valerie Faris and starring Greg Kinnear, Steve Carill of *Office* fame, Alan Arkin (who is great here) and Abigail Breslin who steals the film when she is on camera. Could have been called how to make 100 million from an 8 million investment. Great fun.

Little Women – 1941- Directed by George Cukor and starring Katherine Hepburn, Joan Bennett, Paul Lukas, Frances Dee and Jean Parker in principal roles of Louisa May Alcott's well-known novel. Class A soap all the way.

Live in Peace (China) -1997 - Directed by Hu Bingliu and starring Pan Yu (but not in this case), Bai Xueyun, Sun Min, Wang Hong, Huang Jinchang, Kong Xianzhu and Li Tuan in a story that shows Chinese families can be just as dysfunctional as Western families. Fun to watch.

The Lives of a Bengal Lancer - 1935 - Directed by Henry Hathaway and starring Gary Cooper, Franchot Tone, Richard Cromwell and Guy Standing in a tale of colonialism that is now viewed quite differently than when it was filmed. We are more inclined to root against the colonials these days. Great action and story, though.

The Lives of Others (Germany) - 2006 - Directed and written by Florian Henckel von Donnersmarck and starring Ulriche Muhe, Martina Gedeck, Sebastian Koch and Ulrich Tukur in the principal roles in a film about East German espionage during the Cold War. Won Best Foreign Film for 2006.

Living in Oblivion – 1995 - Directed by Tom DiCillo and starring Sal Buscemi as an unfortunate independent film director. This film is hilarious, and Buscemi is absolutely letter-perfect in the role, and makes the entire film highly enjoyable. Director DiCillo is also on the top of his game. A great peek into actual independent film production.

Local Hero (Scotland) - 1983 - Directed by Bill Forsyth and starring Burt Lancaster and Peter Riegert with a great supporting Scottish cast in a comedy about a large company buying land on a remote Scottish isle. Keep an eye out for the mermaid.

The Lodger - 1944 -Directed by John Brahm and starring Merle Oberon, Laird Cregar and George Sanders. This version of Jack the Ripper is not as spectacular as others, but it gets the job done in high style (with Sanders leading the way). Fun to watch.

Logan's Run - 1976 - Directed by Michael Anderson and starring Michael York, Peter Ustinov and Farah Fawcett. This diverse crew acts out the crime of aging over 30 which has dire consequences in the future (right now its 60, but I can see the trend). Still good sci-fi.

Lola (Germany)-1982- Directed by Rainer Werner Fassbinder and starring an unknown German group of B actors who capture the decadence of post WW2 Germany, and the moral cesspool that almost everyone in the film dives into. A really interesting study of human nature.

The Loneliness of the Long Distance Runner (England) - 1962 - Directed by Tony Richardson and starring Tom Courtenay, Michael Redgrave and a very good supporting cast in a story about rebellious youth and how class distinctions push you into predictable behaviors. Good stuff.

The Lone Ranger - 1956 - Directed by Stuart Heisler and starring Clayton Moore and Jay Silverheels. How could I not include this B Western? The usual mundane plot of greedy land-grabbers does not dampen the enjoyment of watching a full-length film of an American icon.

Lonesome Jim -2006 - Directed by the talented Steve Buscemi and starring Casey Affleck, Liv Tyler and Mary Kay Place along with a very good supporting cast. The story about a failed novelist going back home to live with his parents is a perfect setting for comedy.

Lone Star - 1996 - Directed by John Sayles, who was finally given a well-deserved solid budget after great success on shoestring budget films, and starring Chris Cooper, Kris Kristofferson, and Matthew McConaughey in a police mystery that is deliciously unraveled in expert fashion by Sayles.

Long Day's Journey Into Night - 1962 - Directed by Sidney Lumet and starring Katherine Hepburn, Sir Ralph Richardson, Jason Robards Jr. and Dean Stockwell as members of a dysfunctional family with hidden addictions. Famous O'Neill play translates well to the screen.

The Longest Day - 1962 - Directed by Darryl F Zanuck and a crew of assistant directors and starring an all-star cast and a musical score by Maurice Jarre. This story about the D-Day invasion of WW2 is covered in minute detail. The paratrooper scene was the most memorable. Top of the line action.

The Long Good Friday - England -1982 – Directed by John MacKenzie and starring Bob Hoskins in a sensational performance in his first major role as Harold Shand, a common gangster who aspires to become a businessman as a developer of a future Olympics real estate project, Helen Mirren (long before she became famous for playing the Queen of England) as Harold's girlfriend, Victoria, Eddie Constantine, as a leading American mafia figure, and an amusing cameo debut by Pierce Bronson, who plays an IRA hit man. This is one of best gangster films ever to come out of England, and was made for less than a million pounds (1.6 million US dollars roughly). I can recommend it without reservation.

The Long Voyage Home - 1940 - Directed by John Ford and starring John Wayne, Thomas Mitchell and a solid supporting cast. This is a tale of merchant seamen who risked their lives carrying high explosives from the US to England before the entry of the US into the war. Covers the seedy side of shipping as well as the heroic side.

Look Back in Anger – (England)- 1959 - Directed by Tony Richardson and starring Richard Burton, Claire Bloom and Mary Ure. This is a play based on a dysfunctional family and how they deal with class differences in England in the post WW2 era. Burton always dynamic.

Loose Shoes - 1980 - Directed by Ira Miller and starring Bill Murray and Howard Hesseman featured in a number of sophomoric skits presented in coming attraction (trailers) form. Some of the skits are very funny and some miss, but Murray fans will have a ball.

Lord Jim - 1965 - Directed by Richard Brooks and starring Peter O'Toole, James Mason, Eli Wallach, Jack Hawkins, Curt Jurgens and veteran star, Paul Lukas. This Conrad adventure yarn about cowardice and redemption met with mixed reviews, but I am a big O'Toole fan and I enjoyed his performance, despite some uneven moments.

Lord of the Flies - 1963 - Directed by Peter Brook, who was meticulous in every detail, and starring pretty much an unknown cast. It is the Golding story that is the star of the picture and the tension holds for over an hour in the film. A must see.

Lord of the Rings -The Fellowship of the Ring - 2001 - Before there was Harry Potter, there was *Lord of the Rings*. Directed by Peter Jackson and starring Viggo Mortensen, Elijah Wood, Ian McKellen, and Orlando Bloom among others. We are introduced to the main heroes and learn of their quest in this Tolkien classic. Reading the book helps a lot.

Lord of the Rings II- The Two Towers -2002 - The second installment of the trilogy is primarily a massive battle that lasts for over an hour. The state-of-the-art special effects at the time were spectacular. Makes little sense unless you saw the first film, however.

Lord of the Rings III - 2003 - The Return of the King - This is the third part of the trilogy, and it won Best Picture of the year for 2003. This film ties together all the loose ends, as well as culminating in another terrific battle sequence.

Los Olvidados (Mexico) - 1950 - Directed by Luis Bunuel and starring a cast of Mexican unknowns that turn in a first-rate job. This is a story about youth living in one of the worst slums in the world inside of Mexico City. The poverty, violence and tragic results cannot be explained in print; you must see the film.

The Lost City of Z – 2017 – Directed by (no, not Costa Garvas) James Gray and starring unknown Charlie Hunnam in the lead role of an explorer in the early 20th century who finds an ancient civilization in the Amazon that had some amazing aspects. Love films like this.

The Lost Continent- 1951 - Directed by Sam Newfield and starring Cesar Romero (horribly miscast), Hillary Brooke (star of the TV *Abbott and Costello* show) (also horribly miscast), and a collection of out of work C actors in a low-budget production about a lost continent. This was a lost continent all right. It was lost on the back lot of some second-rate studio in Hollywood. Hilarious from start to finish. Really belongs in the Turkey Farm, but enjoy.

Lost Horizon -1937 -Directed by Frank Capra and starring Ronald Colman, as the immortal Robert Conway. This film often tops the list of best films of all time by numerous critics. It is a story rich in both characterization and in plot. The cinematography is magnificent, and the music is memorable. The fine supporting cast is a testimony to the efficiency of the golden age of studio central casting.

Frank Capra has often mentioned that this was the most difficult production he was ever involved with at several levels. He once stated that he did not know whether he had a bomb or a hit on his hands. History has shown that this was considered his greatest work, and that is a substantial statement considering all of the successes that Capra had experienced in his career. This is also Ronald Colman's greatest role within a great career. Several of the cast members point to this film as the zenith of their careers.

The story is innovative and engaging. A diplomat in China, Robert Conway, is assigned to evacuate civilians from China's war-torn city of Baskul. This film is as uplifting as cinema can be. Frank Capra had mentioned that this movie was the apex of his career, although the film was a financial disaster at the box office, originally.

Lost in America - 1985 - Written, directed and starring Albert Brooks and Julie Hagarty in a story about hitting the road with a Ralph Kramden idea (that would be one of the schemes that Ralph always came up with in the *Honeymooners* that always led to a financial disaster).

Lost in Translation - 2003 - Directed by Sofia Coppola and starring Bill Murray and Scarlett Johansson in a story about an actor and a college student who befriend each other in Japan because they are both lonely. Well done soap.

The Lost Patrol - 1934 - Directed by John Ford and starring Victor McLaglen and Boris Karloff in a tense WW1 adventure revolving around access to water in the desert. Good suspense and tension.

The Lost Weekend - 1945 - Directed by Billy Wilder, who was well known for much lighter fare and starring Ray Milland in his Academy-Award winning performance as an alcoholic. Jane Wyman and a supporting cast add to the production, but Milland gives us a tour-de-force performance. A must-see.
Love Affair -1939 -Directed by Thornton Freeland and starring Humphrey Bogart and someone named Dorothy Mackaill who had top billing! (she must have known a Columbia exec very well at the studio). Despite this film being pure soap, still worth watching for Bogart.

Love and Anarchy (Italy) -1973 - Directed by the talented Lina Wertmuller and starring Giancarlo Giannini as Tunin, a budding anarchist who desires to assassinate Mussolini, but would probably be more likely to shoot himself in the foot, the very sexy Mariangela Melato as a prostitute, Salome, who becomes a political activist and aides Tunin in his quest to assassinate Mussolini, and Lina Polito as another prostitute, Tripolina, who joins in the conspiracy, and becomes the love interest of Tunin.

The pace of the film is very quick, and the sure hand of Wertmuller makes the relationship between Tunin and Tripolina seem as profound as possible in such a short period of time. The characters are very believable and their incompetence is even more realistic. They are all amateurs trying to become professional killers. Wertmuller somehow takes a very serious plot, and keeps it bubbly for an hour and a half with sexual tension, comedy and pathos.

This was the film that made Wertmuller's career. It also made a major star out of Giannini, who emerged from this role as the leading Italian actor of the seventies. I always thought that Lina Polito would also become a major star, but that reality never materialized for her. There were a half dozen ways this film could have fizzled under the heavy atmosphere of a political plot to assassinate Mussolini. Wertmuller wisely went for the light side of the incident; she was able to milk the romance and comedy for well over an hour.

Giannini was absolutely riveting on screen; you could not take your eyes off of him. He seemed to be a combination of Charlie Chaplin and Rudolph Valentino (how's that for a mixed bag?). It is so unbelievably difficult to do a serious film with comedic and romantic overtones, but somehow Giannini and Wertmuller pulled it off. The film as a whole is wonderfully entertaining and should not be missed; especially for the spectacular debuts of Wertmuller and Giannini.

Love and Death -1975 - Written, directed and starring Woody Allen and his sidekick Diane Keaton in another of their farce comedies lampooning the overly-serious *War and Peace*. Nobody does it better than Allen.

Love in the Afternoon - 1957 - Directed by Billy Wilder and starring the miscast Gary Cooper (not really a great romantic lead) and the perfect Audrey Hepburn, (who carries Cooper with ease) as well as Maurice Chevalier (the human version of Pepe Lapew). This is first-rate soap for those who need a good dose.

The Lovely Bones - 2009 - Directed by Peter Jackson and starring Saoirse Ronan, Mark Wahlberg (who seems never to make a bad film), Rachel Weisz, Susan Sarandon and Stanley Tucci. This film and its performances came out of nowhere to impress even the most jaded critic in a story about the supernatural. A real accomplishment by Jackson and new actress, Saoirse Ronan.

Lovers and Other Strangers - 1970 —Directed by Cy Howard and starring Bea Arthur, who steals the film, Richard Castellano (of *Godfather* fame), who became famous for the line "so what's the story?", and Bonnie Bedelia, who is also very good. One of the best comedies ever.

Love Story-1969- Directed by Arthur Hiller and starring Ali MacGraw and Ryan O'Neal in the number one iconoclastic soap of all time. Ray Milland adds to the production values. There were about five women in the entire country who didn't read the book or see the movie, or utter the phrase "love is never having to say you're sorry".

Loving - 1970 - Directed by Irvin Kershner and starring George Segal and Eva Marie Saint in a stark film about greed, adultery and selfishness. In reality, there is very little loving going on in the film, and the title is an oxymoron.

Lumumba – Germany – 2000 - Directed by Raoul Peck and starring unknown actor Eriq Ebouaney as Patrice Lumumba. The film starkly describes the coup to remove Lumumba with the aid of the United States and its covert agencies. Then the US installed Joseph Mobutu as President of the Congo. Very disturbing to see the USA in such a bad light.

The Lunchbox – 2013 – India – Directed by Ritesh Batra and starring Irrfan Khan and Nimrat Kaur as a couple of destiny derived from a lunch being delivered to the wrong person. A wonderfully amusing and human film that is reminiscent of classics like *Brief Encounter* and *Bridges of Madison County*. A soap-lover's dream.

Lured (1947) - Directed by Douglas Sirk and starring a wonderful cast including Lucille Ball (who was a fine dramatic actress), one of my favorite actors, George Sanders, Boris Karloff, and Charles Coburn as a Scotland Yard detective. The film even playfully adds a character from Sherlock Holmes, Moriarity. However, the plot is more sophisticated than we might imagine.

Lust, Caution (China) - 2007 - Directed by Ang Lee and starring Tony Leung Chiu Wa, Tang Wei, Joan Chen, and Leehom Wang. This neatly conceived tale of espionage during WW 2 is quite similar to the the plot for the film, Mata Hari starring Greta Garbo, which was about a femme fatale during WW 1. Good stuff.

Lust for Gold – 1949 – Directed by Silvan Simon and starring Ida Lupino, Glenn Ford, and Gig Young in the lead roles. This B Western is several cuts above most others because of the talented cast, especially Lupino. Tale of greed for gold a bit mundane.

Lust For Life -1956 - Directed by Vincente Minnelli and starring Kirk Douglas and Anthony Quinn in the primary roles. This tale of Vincent Van Gogh is told with gusto and a first-rate musical score provided by Miklos Rozsa (*Ben Hur*, *El-Cid* and many others).

Luther -1973 - Directed by Guy Green and starring Stacy Keach as Luther. There have been many renditions of Luther, but this is one of the best and does not candy-coat his life. The director does a first-rate job.

941

M

M (Germany) - 1931 –A- Directed by Fritz Lang and starring Peter Lorre as one of the greatest human monsters on the big screen (second only to Hannibal Lechter). This film traces the crimes and eventual cornering of a child killer in a German city. The cinematography for this film is absolutely mesmerizing. There are few scenes without suspense and Lang is superb in crafting the web for the loathsome Lorre character. I will not reveal to you how he is caught, but it is a very creative mechanism. Lorre was a relative unknown before this film and he went on to become a major Hollywood star in supporting roles for many years afterwards.

Fritz Lang had already gained notoriety for his previous silent film work, and as it turned out this first sound film for him was to be his best effort in film. This is the best German film in the history of their cinema and ranks in the top thirty films of all time on virtually every film critics list. Instead of using sordid scenes of violence, Lang uses the power of suggestion much more effectively. The emotional impact of the crimes on the unfortunate parents are brought to the fore and the sense of community, even in a city, is really eye-opening. Lang gets more horror out of one scene of suggestion than the vast majority of directors get with several scenes of violence and gore. Highly recommended as one of the greatest German films ever made.

MacArthur – 1977 - Directed by Joseph Sargent and starring Gregory Peck and Ed Flanders. This biopic covers the military career of Douglas MacArthur and his great triumphs in the Pacific.

MacArthur's Children -Japan- 1985- Directed by Masahiro Shinoda and starring Ken Watanabe, Matsako Natsume, and Shiima Iwashita as inhabitants of a small isolated island community who grow up under the occupation of American forces in Japan.

Madadayo – Japan - 1993 -This is Akira Kurosawa's last film as a director and it is one of his best. He does a great job capturing the *Goodbye, Mr. Chips* atmosphere that was a hallmark of that great film and putting it into this one from the Japanese perspective. Highly recommended.

Madame Curie -1943 - Directed by Mervyn Leroy and starring Greer Garson and Walter Pidgeon as the the husband and wife team of world-famous scientists. This biopic was very popular as it took the world's mind off of WW2 for a few hours with stellar acting by both cast members.

Madigan - 1968 - Directed by Don Siegel and starring Richard Widmark, Henry Fonda, Inger Stevens, Harry Guardino and James Whitmore. This slice of life in the NYC law enforcement world is often brutal and violent, but as realistic as any filmed.

The Magdalene Sisters (England) -2002 - Directed and written by Peter Mullan and starring an unknown, but effective cast of Irish actors. This story of slave labor utilized by the Catholic church shocked many when it came out (but not a lot of Catholics). Extremely enlightening for those not associated with Catholicism.

The Magic Box - England - 1951 - Directed by John Boulting and starring Robert Donat with guest appearances of Laurence Olivier and Peter Ustinov. This great biopic shows the unfortunate demise of the inventor of motion pictures, who had poor marketing skills, and so lost the honor of being credited for his discovery to others. Fascinating.

The Magician (Sweden) -1958 - Directed by Ingmar Bergman and starring Max Von Sydow and Ingrid Thulin. This film about a Swedish hustler magician is engaging from beginning to end. Not the usual Bergman angst.

Magic Town - 1947 - Directed by William A Wellman and starring James Stewart and Jane Wyman in a story about public opinion polling (as in Neilson) in a small town that goes awry. Funny stuff.

The Magnificent Seven -1960 - Directed by John Sturges and starring Yul Brenner, Steve McQueen, Charles Bronson, Robert Vaughn, James Colburn, Horst Buchholz, and the most forgotten member of the seven (like Bashful in Snow White), Brad Dexter. Eli Wallach as Calvera almost steals the film from the other seven with his tour-de-force performance.

Some critics believe this is the greatest American western ever made and I am one of them. Sturges creates some of the greatest Western action sequences ever captured on film and sets them to the magnificent music created by Elmer Bernstein, one of the greatest scorers of film music in the history of film. Brenner gives a sterling performance as well as McQueen. Bronson gives a rock-solid performance as well. Vaughn is wonderfully slick and psychotic, while Colburn creates one of the most dramatic knife scenes ever made. Buchholz seems a little bit out of his depth in the film, but one hardly notices this little blip; at least they did not choose him for the romantic interest because he was a guitar player like Ricky Nelson and a host of other musicians of the times who weaseled their way into various westerns so they could deliver their big numbers (including Elvis).

Of course the least remembered member of the team was Brad Dexter, who gives a credible performance, but still remains the trivia question that most people cannot answer when asked to name the seven actors who played these roles. Wallach's performance is the best of anyone in the film. This film is better on all levels than Kurosawa's film. Better ingredients, better pizza. This is a must see film, unless you hate westerns, and is on everyone's top 100 list except for the elitist, pompous asses at the New York Times.

The Magnificent Yankee – 1950 – Directed by John Sturges and staring Louis Calhern as the prestigious Oliver Wendell Holmes, arguably the greatest Supreme Court Justice in the history of the US. Nice biopic.

Magnum Force -1969- Directed by Ted Post and starring Clint Eastwood and Hal Holbrook in a story about vigilantes and corruption within the police department. Sometimes the justice system does not work properly and vigilantes take the law into their own hands. Are they right? The viewers must decide for themselves.

Major Barbara – England - 1951 - Directed by Gabriel Pascal and starring Wendy Hiller and Rex Harrison along with Robert Morley and a fine supporting cast. Hiller plays a Salvation Army Major who tries her best to keep her followers on the side of clean living. Good clean fun.

Make Way for Tomorrow -1937 - Directed by Leo McCarey and starring Beulah Bondi and Victory Moore as an aging couple who have their house foreclosed and are forced to live with their kids (none of which has room for them). The movie is far more topical and less dated than one might suspect. Good dialogue.

Malcolm X - 1992 - Directed by Spike Lee and starring Denzel Washington as Malcolm X. Great performance by Washington and crisp direction by Lee makes for fine viewing regardless of your political persuasion. Viewed with an open mind, some actually change some opinions about him.

The Maltese Falcon – 1941 -Directed by John Huston and starring Humphrey Bogart, Mary Astor and Peter Lorre. This film is sometimes criticized for not having a clear plot and lacking a bit of logic. Who cares?. The only thing that counts is if you keep my eyes and ears glued to the screen, and I really enjoy watching you play your character.

A Man and a Woman – France - 1966 - Directed by Claude Lelouch and starring Anouk Aimee with Jean-Louis Trintignant in one of the best soaps of all time. This film was a sensation when it came out in 66.

A Man Called Horse -1970 -Directed by Elliot Silverstein and starring Richard Harris as Horse. This film came out of nowhere to become one of the best films of the year about an English aristocrat abducted by American Indians and then eventually becoming their leader. Fascinating to watch.

The Manchurian Candidate -1962 - Directed by John Frankenheimer and starring Laurence Harvey, Frank Sinatra, Janet Leigh and a devilishly good Angela Lansbury. This tale of a Korean POW who becomes brainwashed is gripping from beginning to end.

A Man Escaped - 1957 – France – Directed by Robert Bresson and starring a cast of B French actors in a story about a daring escape by a member of the French Resistance from the occupying forces of the Nazis. Not terribly original, but watchable.

A Man For All Seasons - 1966 - Directed by Fred Zinneman and starring Paul Scofield in his academy-award winning role as Thomas More. Also featured is Robert Shaw and Orson Welles. Film also won 5 other awards including Best Picture.

The Man From Colorado - 1949 - Directed by Henry Levin and starring William Holden and Glenn Ford in the lead roles. The superior cast make this Western a cut above most other B productions. Good action sequences as well.

The Man From Laramie - 1955 - Directed by Anthony Mann and starring James Stewart with Arthur Kennedy and a sound supporting cast. Succeeds despite the mundane plot of selling rifles to the Indians.

The Man From Planet X - 1951 - Directed by Edgar G. Elmer and starring a cast of C actors. What makes this film interesting is the story and the setting is in Scotland, which is a bit unusual. Fun to watch.

The Man From the Alamo -1953 - Directed by Budd Boetticher, noted Western expert, and starring Glenn Ford as the man from the Alamo. Interesting story about the only survivor of the Alamo makes good viewing.

Manhattan - 1979 - Directed and starring Woody Allen, Diane Keaton and Meryl Streep in Allen's specialty of life in New York City. One of the more low-key Allen films and a very entertaining story line.

Manhattan Murder Mystery - 1993 - Directed and starring Woody Allen and Diane Keaton along with Anjelica Huston and Alan Alda. You have to admit that Allen always gets the best talent available for his films, even if the story lines are not all that original. Fun to watch.

Man Hunt - 1941 - Directed by Fritz Lang and starring Walter Pidgeon and Joan Bennett. Lang was the equivalent of Hitchcock before Hitchcock became famous. This film is a testimony to his skill and mirrors his efforts in M. Solid suspense.

Manhunter - 1986 - Directed by Michael Mann and starring William Petersen and other competent B actors in a gripping prequel to Silence of the Lambs (almost, but not quite as good - sorry, but Entertainment Weekly is a bit too effusive).

The Man in the Grey Flannel Suit - 1956 - Directed by Nunnally Johnson and starring Gregory Peck as the man in the suit. This story about one man's quest for quality of life instead of making money is still very topical. Engaging story.

Man in the Iron Mask - 1939 -Directed by James Whale, which gives the story a horrific feel, and starring Louis Hayward, Joan Bennett and a solid supporting cast of B actors. The A story and director make the film click.

The Man in the White Suit –1952- Directed by Alexander Mackindrick and starring Alec Guinness in a little-known sci-fi gem about a man who discovers a valuable fabric for clothing and its applications in science and industry. Great script, and the only film ever made with a fabric as the centerpiece of a movie plot.

Man of a Thousand Faces- (1957) - Directed by Joseph Pevney and starring James Cagney and Dorothy Malone. The film chronicles the struggles and accomplishments of Lon Chaney, the master of disguise. Interesting.

Man of Iron – Poland – 1980- Directed by Andrzej Wajda and starring a cast of unknown Polish actors who do an excellent job chronicling the rise of the Solidarity movement in Poland, which not only got the Russians out of Poland, but caused the fall of communism in the USSR. A must see.

Man of Marble – Poland- 1977 - Directed by Andrzej Wajda and starring a cast of unknown Polish actors in a prequel to Wajda's Man of Iron classic featuring Solidarity. This earlier film depicts the beginning of unrest in the worker's milieu in Poland before the Big Bang. Engaging.

Man of the West – 1958 – Directed by Anthony Mann and starring Gary Cooper, Lee J Cobb and a miscast Jack Lord (Hawaii 5-O) in the lead roles. Cooper was getting a little long in the tooth to be playing these action roles. Mundane story picked up by good cast.

Man on the Moon – 1999 – Directed by Milos Foreman and starring Jim Carrey as the tragic Andy Kaufman along with a solid supporting cast in a story about the meteoric rise and sudden death of a talented comedian. The film is interesting, but falls short of expectations of great promise.

Man on the Roof – Sweden- 1977 - Directed by Bo Widerberg and starring a group of unknown Swedish actors who do a good job carrying the action. This story of the police besieging a killer holds your attention.

Man Who Could Work Miracles – England -1936 -Directed by Lothar Mendes and starring Roland Young and Ralph Richardson. The real star of the movie is HG Wells and his great story about a man with unusual powers. It will hold your attention every minute.

Man Who Came to Dinner - 1942 - Directed by William Keighley and starring Monty Woolley, Bette Davis and Anne Sheridan combine for a riotous comedy about a man who is injured on someone's property and decides to live with them instead of suing them. Very funny.

Man Who Fell to Earth - 1976- Directed by Nicholas Roeg and starring David Bowie as the man who fell to earth, an alien searching for water for his planet. Bowie is very good in his debut and the production values are very nice.

Man Who Lived Again – England - 1936 - Directed by Louis Stevenson and starring the incomparable Boris Karloff as a mad professor who delves into brain transplants. One of the more underrated Karloff films.

Man Who Loved Women - 1983 - Directed by Blake Edwards and starring Burt Reynolds and Julie Andrews. This remake of an earlier Truffaut classic is very well done and probably the funniest film Reynolds ever did. Edwards keeps the loose Reynolds in character.

Man Who Knew Too Much - 1934 - Directed by Alfred Hitchcock, who would remake the film twenty years later with James Stewart, and starring Peter Lorre with a great supporting cast. This story of espionage still holds up, despite being a bit dated.

Man Who Shot Liberty Valence -1962- Directed by John Ford and starring James Stewart and John Wayne (who never worked together before). Lee Marvin steals the film as Liberty Valance, a sober, cruel version of his character from *Cat Ballou*. The film is quite successful, despite the appearance of Vera Miles, one of the worst actresses in Hollywood history.

Man Who Would Be King - 1975 - Directed in robust fashion by John Huston and starring the unbeatable British combination of Sean Connery and Michael Caine. Christopher Plummer also adds to the production values. A rousing Kipling adventure in old Afghanistan. Gee, if two guys could conquer Afghanistan, how come it's so hard now for colonialists to conquer it?

Man Without a Star – 1951 – Directed by King Vidor and starring Kirk Douglas and Richard Boone (a nice combo there). Story of defrocked sheriff who must become a regular citizen up against sleaze is interesting.

The Man With the Golden Arm - 1957 - Directed by Otto Preminger and starring Frank Sinatra, Eleanor Parker and Kim Novak. This tale of drug addiction and gambling is probably the best film Sinatra ever made, but was not recognized by the Academy. Great music adds to the production values.

March or Die – 1977 - Directed by Dick Richards and starring Gene Hackman and Max Van Sydow (an unusual pairing) in a story about the French Foreign Legion and the rescue of buried treasure from the Arabs who actually are the rightful owners of it. Interesting.

Maria Candalaria (Mexico) -(1951)- Directed by Emilo Fernandez and starring Pedro Armendarez and Delores Del Rio in the role that catapulted her career as an indigenous Indian- Mexican woman.

Marjorie Prime – 2017 – Directed by Michael Almereyda and starring Geena Davis and a nice supporting cast in a story about tech bringing us closer to the ones we loved in life. A truly uplifting film that allows us to get answers that we did not get in our real lives.

The Mark – England - 1961 - Directed by Guy Green and starring Stuart Whitman in his best role and Maria Schell along with Rod Steiger. This tale of child molestation is chilling and was very well executed by the director.

The Mark of Zorro -1940 - Directed by Rouben Mamoulian and starring Tyrone Power as Zorro. A great supporting cast includes Basil Rathbone, among others. This version of Zorro is among the best ever made.

The Marksman -1953 - Directed by Lewis Collins and starring Wayne Morris in your run of the mill B Western of the fifties that would not have been included in this list of 2000 unless it had a very interesting story line. See for yourself.

Marnie - 1964 - Directed by Alfred Hitchcock and starring a miscast Sean Connery, but a perfectly cast Tippi Hedren as the psychotic Marnie. Diane Baker is also featured. The film could have been called The Romantic Adventures of Psychoanalysis. Top-notch soap.

Marriage Italian Style (Italy)- 1964 - Directed by Vittorio De Sica and starring Italian icons Sophia Loren and Marcello Mastroianni. Does the story really matter if these three are making the film? A must see.

The Marriage of Maria Braun -(Germany) – 1978 - Directed by Rainer Werner Fassbinder, who really captures the essence of Germany immediately after the war. This film about emotional survival is a classic and the best of all the New German Cinema period.

The Martian – 2015 – Directed by Ridley Scott and starring Matt Damon in a story about an astronaut that is marooned on Mars after his team leaves him behind after a mission due to a terrible storm (some team). He is forced to use his wits with few supplies to survive for an unlikely rescue. Good stuff from a top notch production crew.

Marty -1955 – Directed by Delbert Mann and starring Ernest Borgnine in the role of his career that won him the academy award for Best Actor. Betsy Blair also stars. The tale of two slow lane lovers also won best film of the year. Best line is "I dunno, whadda you wanna do?" by one of Marty's friends.

MASH -1970 - Directed by Robert Altman and starring Donald Sutherland in a careermaking role along with Eliot Gould, whose career went straight downhill after this success. Kellerman and Duvall are hilarious as Hot Lips and Burns and Gary Burghoff is great (and the only original to make the TV series) as Radar. A must see.

The Mask of Demitrios - 1944 - Directed by Jean Negulesco and starring Sydney Greenstreet, Peter Lorre and a great supporting cast in a film noir classic that you know will be gripping from beginning to end. A must see.

The Masque of the Red Death - 1964 - Directed by the king of the Bs, Roger Corman and starring the king of the B actors, Vincent Price, so you know you will be getting a pretty entertaining film. This tale of let them eat cake by a local prince is reminiscent of the financial breakdown in the US with the investment bankers in the role of the prince.

Master and Commander - 2003 - Directed by the impeccable Peter Weir (Picnic at Hanging Rock, The Last Wave) and starring Russell Crowe, who is right at home playing a sea captain. Not the most memorable of films, but certainly exciting to watch.

Master of the World -1961 - Directed by William Witney and starring the only Hollywood ego capable of playing master of the world (other than Orson Welles) at the time, Vincent Price. Charles Bronson is horribly miscast, but is overwhelmed by Price, anyway. A lot of fun to watch.

The Matador -2005 - Directed and written by Richard Shepard and starring the unusual pairing of Greg Kinnear and Pierce Bronson as two unlikely cohorts; one is a hit man and the other is a salesman. Can you guess which is which?

The Match Factory Girl (Finland) - 1990 - Directed by Aki Kaurismaki and starring Kati Outinen and a group of unknown Finnish actors. This stunning film is reminiscent of the early Italian neo-realism period after WW2. The story of a withdrawn factory girl really heats up in the middle of the movie. Be patient.

Matchstick Men -2003 -Directed by the miscast Ridley Scott and starring the perfectly cast Nicholas Cage. This tale of cons and second chances is highly entertaining and Cage is absolutely hilarious.

The Matrix - 1999 - Written and Directed by the brothers Andy and Larry Wachowski and starring Keanu Reeves and Larry Fishburne in a futuristic sci-fi actioner. The film was followed by two sequels, but the first one is best. Very stylish and iconoclastic.

The Mayor of Hell - 1933 - Directed by Archie Mayo with some help from Michael Curtiz and starring James Cagney and a competent supporting cast in a story about a hood who helps kids in reform school (sort of a rough version of Boystown). A bit dated, but still very effective.

Me and Orson Welles - 2008 - Directed by Richard Linklater and starring a cast of unknowns working with an excellent story by Robert Kaplow (wrote the novel, actually). This tale of a young man getting an opportunity to work with Orson Welles is fascinating. Highly recomeneded.

Mean Streets - 1973 - Directed by Martin Scorsese and starring Robert DeNiro and Harvey Keitel with an uncredited appearance of David Carradine as a drunk who gets beat up in a bar. The Carradine appearance seems to have been missed by some online critics who have every other detail of the film.

   The story follows the characters of Charley, a serious Catholic, and aspiring gangster and Johnny Boy, played by Dinero, who is strictly just a loose cannon. The two make an unlikely couple, but their chemistry is undeniable. After a series of loans and non-payments, Johnny Boy gets in trouble with the bookies and pays the price. This was a breakthrough film for Scorsese, Dinero and Keitel, all of whom went on to make several more great films in the future. This is a must-see film and is listed on the top 100 of most film critics.

Mechanic - 1972 - Directed by Michael Winner and starring Charles Bronson and a good supporting cast in a story about a professional killer and his various tools of the trade. Bronson perfect for the role.

Mediteranneo –Italy -1991 -Gabriele Salvatores and starring a group of unknown Italian actors who work with a great script by Enzo Monteleone under the direction of a very good director who won the Academy Award for best foreign film of the year.

Medium Cool -1969 - Directed by Haskell Wexler and starring Mayor Daley and the Chicago city police as the heavies in a semi-documentary about the Chicago riots during the Democratic National Convention. A real eye-opener for American citizens.

Meet Boston Blackie - 1941 - Directed by Robert Florey and starring Chester Morris as Boston Blackie, in a spy thriller that is top of the line B material. The entire series is just as good as the Charlie Chan series.

Meet John Doe -1941 - Directed by Frank Capra and starring Gary Cooper and Barbara Stanwyck in a socialist classic. Edward Arnold plays a great mean capitalist. If only American politics were this simple seventy years later. A must see.

Melvin and Howard -1980 - Directed by Jonathon Demme, who is miscast as a light comedy director, and starring Paul Le Mat as the buddy of Howard Hughes. Jason Robards also adds to the story of a drifter who accidentally meets Howard Hughes and then suffers a string of personal misadventures.

Memories of Underdevelopment - 1973 -Directed by Tomas Guitierez Alea and starring Sergio Corrieri in a tale of a Cuban writer who stays behind in Cuba after the Revolution while his family and friends flee to Miami. Very incisive to living in Havana during the Castro years.

The Men -1950 - Directed by Stanley Kramer and starring Marlon Brando as a disabled World War 2 veteran. This film is primarily Born on the Fourth of July without color film and lavish production values. Of course, Brando is a much better actor than Cruise, so the end result is better.

Men in War - 1957 - Directed by Anthony Mann and starring Robert Ryan and Aldo Ray in a gritty little tale about an undisciplined army unit cut off from the main contingent. This Korean War flick is still entertaining even though it does not have the authenticity of most WW 2 films.

Merry Christmans, Mr. Lawrence – 1983- Directed by Nagisa Oshima and starring David Bowie, Tom Conti, and Jack Thompson with Japanese actor Ryuchi Sakamoto. This prison camp film is a notch above most others and very interesting to watch because Bowie is a very good actor.

Metropolis -1927 - Silent - Directed by Fritz Lang and starring a group of unknown German actors. The real star is the story of a futuristic hell on earth and the tight direction of Lang brings the desperation of the inhabitants right into your psyche. A must see.

Michael Collins-1996 - Directed by Neil Jordan (The Crying Game) and starring a heavyweight cast including Julia Roberts, Liam Neeson, Aidan Quinn, and Alan Rickman (one of my favorite over-the-top actors). The lead role is performed nicely by Ian Hart as the ideological Michael Collins, who sought independence for Ireland from England. Well done.

Midnight -1939 - Directed by Mitchell Leisin and starring Claudette Colbert and Don Ameche John Barrymore, Francis Lederer and Mary Astor in supporting roles in a rather engaging love story that is much better than the average soap.

Midnight Clear - 1992 - Directed by Keith Gordon, who makes a successful transition from actor to director. This tale of a surrender that goes terribly wrong is a microcosm of how things get out of control in war. A really good film.

Midnight Cowboy – 1969 - Directed by John Schlesinger and starring Dustin Hoffman and Jon Voight as two street hustlers in New York who have a hard time making \their way through life. This was the first X-rated movie to ever win the best picture Academy Award. The rating for the film was toned down to an R after its critical success. It also marked the first major film for Jon Voight, who went on to do several more fine films and cemented Dustin Hoffman as a legendary film icon. Somehow, neither actor was able to garner the award for Best Actor that year.

The theory was that they split such a large vote for best actor that they allowed the third best performance of that year, John Wayne's *True Grit*, to win. Also, there was a great deal of sentimentality attached to the Wayne nomination, as he had never won before and Hoffman was assumed to be nominated many more years to come for future roles. The chemistry between Hoffman and Voight is undeniable and they played very well off each other. There were a lot of ways this film could have gone wrong, but they were all avoided by the able director, Schlesinger. A eclectic supporting cast added a great deal of authenticity to the film and it really captured the flavor of the streets of New York at the end of the 1960s.

Midnight Express – 1974 - Directed by Alan Parker and starring Brad Davis as Billy Hayes, Randy Quaid and John Hurt. Parker does an outstanding job of creating a great film by utilizing the energetic acting talents of Brad Davis and the entire supporting cast. The film begins with a heart-pounding sequence and never seems to slow down. John Hurt is infinitely believable as a drug-riddled inmate who helps Hayes to escape and Randy Quaid brings a bit of humor to this otherwise relentlessly brutal tale of Turkish prison and drug offenders. The supporting cast, and the Turkish prison warden, in particular, are very effective in their roles. The production values of the film vary wildly from very good to almost amateurish, but it all somehow works because of the nature of residing in a grim prison does not really call for exceptional production values.

The music is fabulous and is a driving force behind the pacing of the film. This is the story of Billy Hayes and his harrowing experiences in the Turkish legal system. I was actually rooting for the Turkish legal system in this film because Billy Hayes got what he deserved. I thought the Turks treated him very fairly despite the racist stance of the film that depicted every Turk in the picture as an ignorant pig. The guy was a drug smuggler. You do the crime, you do the time. That said, the film is excellent under the reins of director Parker. This film is on many top 100 lists.

Midnight Run - 1988 - Directed by Martin Brest and starring Robert DeNiro and Charles Grodin as a bounty hunter and the bounty, respectively. This is a very funny film and has more double crosses than a cemetary. The mob, FBI, the bail bondsman, the bounty hunter and the criminal are in constant chaos with each other.

Mighty Aphrodite -1992 - Written, directed and starring Woody Allen with F. Murray Abraham, Claire Bloom, Helena Bobham Carter, Olympia Dukakis, Mira Sorvino, Jack Warden and Peter Weller without his Robocop suit on. One of the reasons that Allen is almost always successful in his films is that he spares no expense in casting and building a great ensemble. This is a prime example.

Mighty Wind - 2003 - Directed by Christopher Guest and starring the gang from Second City Television plus Fred Willard in a mockumentary about folk singers reuniting after decades for a one night concert. Absolutely hilarious, even though lovingly done.

Mildred Pierce -1945 - Directed by Michael Curtiz and starring Joan Crawford as Mildred Pierce in the ultimate you and me kid against the world soap. An ungrateful daughter is every woman's nightmare and Joan handles it with aplomb. A must see for her Academy-Award winning role.

Milk - 2008 - Directed by Gus Van Zant, who handles the delicate material with ease and starring Sean Penn in perhaps his most challenging role as Harvey Milk, the honest and courageous gay politician in San Francisco who came to a tragic end. A must see.

Million Dollar Baby -2004- Directed by Clint Eastwood and starring Clint Eastwood, Hillary Swank and Morgan Freeman in an original story of the rise of a woman boxer. Swank did a great job and deserved all the awards she received for the role. Great action.

The Mind-Benders (England) -1963 - Directed by Basil Dearden and starring Dirk Bogarde in a British thriller about dangerous experiments with the mind. The term "that blows my mind" comes from this film. It became part of the sixties lexicon.

The Mind of Dr. Soames - England – 1970 - Directed by Alan Cooke and starring Terrance Stamp and Robert Vaughn in a tale of developmental psychology. A man who has been in a coma since birth, comes out of it as a baby. His behavior is quite similar to a number of politicians in Washington. Fascinating.

Ministry of Fear – 1944 - Directed by Fritz Lang and starring Ray Milland, Dan Duryea and Alan Napier. This noir tale of Nazi spies is wonderfully developed and craftily structured by a master director. A must see.

Minority Report -2002 - Directed by Stephen Spielberg in possibly the worst-named sci-fi film of all time which sounds more like a civil rights film than a sci-fi movie. The film stars Tom Cruise as part of the futuristic pre-crime police. These are professional profilers (I thought that wasn't PC?) who prevent crimes before they are committed (how do you prosecute that in a court of law?). Interesting though.

Minute to Pray, Second to Die -1972 – Directed by Franco Giraldi and starring Alex Cord, Arthur Kennedy, Robert Ryan, and a bunch of Italian cowboys trying to reproduce the success of A Fistful of Dollars.......They weren't able to, although it is watchable.

Miracle – 2004 - Directed by Gavin O'Conner and starring Kurt Russell as Herb Brooks, the coach of the miracle USA ice hockey team of 1980 that defeated a much more talented Russian team that was highly favored. Good stuff.

Miracle at St. Anna – 2008 - Directed by Spike Lee and starring a relatively unknown cast (with the exception of Turturro and Leguizamo) as members of 92 Infantry Division, a segregated unit that is patrollling captured Italian territory. The story is inspiring, but bogs down occasionally as this is not Lee's strength (war genre).

Miracle in Milan (Italy) -1951 --- Directed by Vittorio De Sica and starring a group of unknown Italian actors with the exception of the director, himself. This fantasy about the dispossessed in Milan has heavy religious overtones (miracles, angels, flying off to heaven), but is tastefully done by De Sica, who is a a master of fantasy.

The Miracle of Morgan's Creek —-1944 - Directed by Preston Sturges and starring Eddie Bracken and Betty Hutton in a screwball comedy about a girl who is in trouble after her soldier husband goes off to war and leaves her in a family way. By the way, she married him after one night and cant even remember his name. Very funny.

Miracle on 34th Street —1947 - Directed by George Seaton and starring John Payne, Edmund Gwenn, and Maureen O'Hara. Natalie Wood plays the little girl who believes in Santa Claus. Gwenn steals the film as Santa and proves beyond a doubt that there is a Santa Claus.

The Miracle Worker - 1962 - Directed by Arthur Penn and starring Anne Bancroft and Patty Duke in their Academy Award-winning roles. Bancroft won for Best Actress and Duke won for Best Supporting Actress. The story about Helen Keller is inspirational and a must see film. Bancroft gives the best performance of her career in this film.

Mirage – 1965 - Directed by Edward Dmytryk and starring Gregory Peck and a miscast Diane Baker in a tale of intrigue and false identities. Walter Matthau is also featured and is very effective in his role. A cost accountant who is actually a scientist is a pretty strange twist.

Misery - 1990 - Directed by Rob Reiner, who does a great job transferring his comic sesibilities to what is basically a horror movie. The film stars James Caan as a famous writer and Kathy Bates in a breakthrough role as his number one fan. Watch out for those number one fans.

Missing —-1982 - Directed by Costa Garvas, who excels at political thrillers and starring Jack Lemmon and Sissy Spacek as the father and wife of an American jounalist who was \killed in Chile by persons unknown during a military coup. Garvas accused the US of killing him and the US State Department denied it. Decide for yourself.

The Mob - 1951 – Directed by Robert Parrish and starring Broderick Crawford, Ernest Borgnine and Richard Kiley. This is a tale of an undercover cop trying to break the hold of a gang of hoods who are running the docks of the city. It reminded me of Hoboken and *On the Waterfront*.

Moby Dick - 1956 - Directed by John Huston, who excels in such films, and starring Gregory Peck and a sound supporting cast in the immortal Hermann Melville Tale about the Great White Whale. Fairly well done, but might have even been better with a different lead (Spencer Tracy, Walter Brennan, or my pick, Charles Bickford)

Modern Times – 1936 - Silent- Written, Directed and starring Charles Chaplin in one of the last silent films ever made until 2011. The tramp takes a job in the factory while hanging out with Paulette Goddard (who is ravishing). There are a number of socialist statements made in the film (all of them relatively tame by today's standards), but it was enough to get Chaplin eventually blackballed by a number of theaters. Fun film to watch.

Modigliani - 2005 - Directed by Mick Davis and starring Andy Garcia in the lead role in a story about an Italian sculptor and painter in the early 20th century within Spain who worked mainly with nudes. Interesting, but not earth-shattering.

Mommie Dearest - 1981 - Directed by Frank Perry and starring Faye Dunaway in one of her best roles as Joan Crawford. The film has the feel of a horror movie, not a biopic and is told from the perspective of Crawford's adopted daughter, Christina, played very well by Mora Hobel. A must see film.

Mona Lisa —1986 - England - Directed by Neil Jordan and starring Bob Hoskins and Michael Caine as the A actors. Cathy Tyson is also featured. This film about an ex-con who helps a call girl is average stuff, but the direction of Jordan raises the story line.

Mongol - 2007 - Directed by Sergei Bodrov and starring a relatively unknown cast. The producers were wise to put the money in the production values instead of name actors and came up with a great action hit. The story of Genghis Khan is always fascinating. I love the Mongols and Mongol films.

A Mongolian Tale (China) - 1995 - Directed by Xie Fei and starring Tengger, Naranhua, and Dalasurong in a first-rate soap about two friends who are brought up together, but go in very different directions.

Monkey Business -1931 - Directed by Norman Z. McLeod (as if anyone could direct the Marx Brothers) and starring Groucho, Harpo, Chico and Zeppo Marx. This laugh-fest takes place on an ocean liner and features a number of classic Marx Brothers skits.

Mon Oncle – France - 1958 - Directed by Jacques Tati and starring Tati and a number of other relatively unknown French actors. Mr. Hulot, the character played by Tati, has trouble adjusting to the modern world and is very conservative. Recommended.

Mon Oncle d'Americque – France- 1980 - Directed by Alain Resnais and starring Gerard Depardieu. This is classic French soap about three people who are going in different directions in life and face a number of life changes. A remake of the successful 1958 film.

Monsieur Verdoux -1947 - Directed and starring Charlie Chaplin in one of his later, not so funny films (this Chaplin, not Woody Allen, who made a much better transition to serious films) about an unemployed banker that has thirties socialistic overtones, but is out of step in the late forties. Still fascinating to watch Chaplin anytime.

Monster -2003 - Written and directed by the talented Patty Jenkins and starring Charlize Theron in her oscar-winning role as a sociopath. Christina Ricci adds significantly to the storyline and turns in a fine performance. A must see film.

Monster in a Box - 1992 - Directed by Nick Broomfield and written and starring Spaulding Gray with good music by the talented Laurie Anderson. These three make a great sequel to Swimming to Cambodia, even though this film has nothing to do with the previous one. I always wished Gray had done another one or two of these.

Monster's Ball - 2001 - Directed by Marc Forster and starring Billy Bob Thornton and smoking hot Halle Berry as the widow of an executed convict. Thornton plays a prison guard and Peter Boyle plays his father. Everyone is letter-perfect and Berry won the best actress award that year.

Monte Walsh – 1970 – Directed by William A Fraker and starring Lee Marvin, Jack Palance and Jeanne Moreau in a tale about an aging cowboy that realizes the life he led is disappearing (in more than one way).

Monty Python and the Holy Grail - (England) 1975 - Directed by Terry Gilliam and Terry Jones and starring Graham Chapman, John Cleese, Terry Gilliam, Terry Jones, Eric Idle and Michael Palin in one of the funniest films of all time. Funniest comedy ensemble of the 20th century. If you do not laugh at this film, there is something seriously wrong with you.

Monty Python Live at the Hollywood Bowl- England – 1982 - Directed by Terry Hughes and Ian MacNaughton and starring the entire Monty Python ensemble plus Marty Feldman (who would go on to make films for Mel Brooks). Lots of great skits.

Monty Python's The Meaning of Life - England – 1983 - Directed by Terry Jones and starring the Monty Python ensemble in a number of very funny skits describing the foibles of the workplace and life in general.

The Moon and Sixpence - 1942 - Directed by Albert Lewin and starring George Sanders and Herbert Marshall. This liberal interpretation of the Maugham novel was welcomed by the public in 1942 as a respite from the early poor results of WW2. Two hours of getting away. Sanders is great. The old gang at Fort Washington Library (especially Miriam Fleischer and John Badarocco) would know I love this film.

Moon – (England) 2009 – Directed by Duncan Jones and starring a relatively unknown British actor, Sam Rockwell, who does an outstanding job (the British generally concentrate on good scripts, good directors, and good actors, and what is left over is spent on special effects when they do science-fiction). Hollywood usually produces sci-fi with the opposite formula. Sam is nearing a three-year stint on the moon and events begin to occur that may make his return difficult. Recommended.

Moonlighting – (England)- 1982 - Directed by by Jerzy Skolimowski and starring Jeremy Irons as Nowak, a refugee during the Solidarity period of Poland's revolution who is working in England. Man of Iron and Man of Marble are a bit better as Solidarity films, but this film has Irons, so it is a wash.

Moonstruck - 1987 - Directed by Norman Jewison, who excelled in these types of films. The movie stars Cher and Nicholas Cage as lovers, a hilarious Olympia Dukakis as Cher's mother, Vincent Gardenia and Danny Aiello. Great cast and great movie.

The More the Merrier - 1943 - Directed by George Stevens and starring Jean Arthur, Joel McCrea and Charles Coburn in a story about an overcrowded apartment during the WW2 housing shortage. Strange bedfellows makes for a very funny movie. Coburn won Oscar for his role.

Morgan! – England -1966 - Directed by Karel Reisz and starring David Warner and Vanessa Redgrave. This film actually defies description, however, it is quite funny, so you must see it for yourself. The premise is an immature man tries to woo back his divorced wife.

Morocco - 1930 - Directed by Josef von Sternberg and starring Gary Cooper, Marlene Dietrich and Adolphe Menjou in a tale of adventure and intrigue. Cooper is not really hot enough for Dietrich, but she carries him well. She should have been on top for billing.

The Mortal Storm – 1940 - Directed by Frank Borzage and starring Margaret Sullivan, James Stewart, Robert Young and Frank Morgan. This story of Germans fleeing Germany during the Nazi era was new to the US in 1940. Interesting.

The Mosquito Coast —1986 - Directed by the highly competent Peter Weir, who is good at creating suspense. The film stars Harrison Ford, Helen Mirren, and River Phoenix with music by Maurice Jarre and a great story provided by my friend (actually, I only met him once), Paul Theroux (I believe it was his best work). I really enjoyed one chilling scene.

The Most Dangerous Game —1932 -Directed by Irving Pichel and starring Joel McCrea, Robert Armstrong and Fay Wray (she always seems to running around in the jungle). Great music by Max Steiner adds to the suspense of this great short story of humans being hunted as game.

A Most Violent Year – 2014 – Writen and directed by J.C. Chandor and starring Oscar Isaac and Jessica Chastain in the lead roles. The film highlights the rotten core of the home-heating industry and the hoops that an honest man has to jump through to survive. Recommended.

Mother India (India) - 1957 - Directed by Mehboob Khan and starring Nargis, Sunil Dutt, Rajendra Kumar and Raaj Kumar in a classic tale of a mother who kills her own son because he is a criminal. A must see.

The Motorcycle Diaries (Spain) - 2004 – Directed by Walter Salles and based on the writings of Che Guevara, the film stars Gael Garcia Bernal as Che Guevara and Rodrigo De La Serna as his second cousin, Granado. Robert Redford was one of the executive producers. I believe that this was his first trip to South America since he went to Bolivia in Butch Cassidy and the Sundance Kid (although it may have been filmed elsewhere).

The film humanizes Che Guevara and gives him a sympathetic background instead of spouting political bromides that are sometimes associated with his name. The whole film, as a matter of fact, takes on attitude of the apolitical, rather than the proactive. The director does a magnificent job of humanizing the major characters and Che Guevara, in particular. Che came from a rich family and he was supposed to follow in his father's footsteps and become a doctor. But he did what a lot of other college students in the fifties did; he dropped out and went cross country. In his case, cross-country was going across South America. It is basically a story of two boys taking a joy ride through South America on their motorcycle.

They do what young men normally do; they look for women and good food and then move on. Neither has a lot of money and they survive by their wits. If the film were not about Che Guevara, it might have passed for a very enjoyable light comedy. It reminded me of the light-hearted Italian comedies of the sixties and seventies. There is almost no indication in the film about the political beliefs of either main character. They are in the film as observers, not activists. This is what makes the film successful, instead of a political bore. We learn more about South America, Facism, Socialism and the day to day events in people's lives that drive them to become what they will one day be, than about any ideology.

The movie is crammed with Socialist Humanism, and concern for the working man. Why is it that people have to label films as communist or socialist, when films like *Bound for Glory*, which didn't have that much of a socialist message as well, got labeled as a socialist film? There is not a nickel's worth of difference between this film and *Bound for Glory* (with the exception there is less good music). They were both highly entertaining films about men who hit the road to find their countries. The film won an Oscar for best song from a film and a number of other international awards, but it is the simplicity of the film that will grab you; not the awards or because it is about Che Guevara. Have you ever noticed the more I talk about a film, the more I like it?

Moulin Rouge - 1952 - Directed by John Huston and starring Jose Ferrer as Henri de Toulouse Lautrec. Zsa Zsa Gabor is also featured as an airhead singer (a tremendous stretch for her). This liberal interpretation of Lautrec's life makes for entertaining cinema. One of Ferrer's best performances ever, and one of the most incisive films on the philosophy of love. Other than singing and acting, Zsa Zsa is quite good.

Mountains on the Moon - England –-1990 - Directed by Bob Rafelson and starring an unknown cast of actors who do a decent job with a first-rate story about the discovery of the source of the Nile River. Interesting.

The Mouse That Roared - 1959- England - Directed by Jack Arnold and starring Peter Sellers in several key roles. Jean Seberg is also featured. This is a hilarious spoof on the foreign policy of the United States during the post WW2 period and the small country that takes advantage of it. Still topical because the State Department in DC still pretty much uses the same strategy.

Mr. 880 - 1950 – Directed by Edmund Goulding and starring Burt Lancaster, Dorothy McGuire and Edmund Gwenn. This is an engaging film about a counterfeiter of one dollar bills; almost impossible to track down and quite funny to boot.

Mr. Belvedere Goes to College -1949 - Directed by Elliot Nugent and starring Clifton Webb and Shirley Temple in the lead roles. The film works well because Temple is just as talented as an adult as she was as a child. But Webb steals the film.

Mr. Deeds Goes to Town - 1936 – Directed by Frank Capra and starring Gary Cooper and Jean Arthur in the lead roles in a story about an eccentric millionaire who has socialist tendencies (a common theme in Capra films). Extremely entertaining and very funny.

Mr. Holland's Opus - 1995 - Directed by Stephen Herek and starring Richard Dreyfuss as Mr. Holland. William H Macy also turns in a great job in the film. The story centers around a music teacher at a high school who realizes that teaching is almost as important as music (maybe more).

Mr. Hulot's Holiday -1954 - Directed by Jacques Tati and starring Tati as well in the lead role of a conservative old chap who goes on vacation and suffers various misadventures. Worth seeing for fun.

Mr. Roberts -1955 - Directed by John Ford, who is a bit out of his element with comedy, but does a great job with this one. The movie stars William Powell, Jack Lemmon, Henry Fonda and James Cagney. Everyone does a top-notch job.

Mrs. Miniver —1942 - Directed by William Wyler and starring Greer Garson and Walter Pidgeon and a great turn by Teresa Wright as participants in the great saga of WW 2 in wartime England. The highlight of the film is the authentic atmosphere of the Dunkirk disaster in England itself. A must see.

Mr. Smith Goes to Washington - 1939 -Directed by Frank Capra and starring Jimmy Stewart along with Jean Arthur and Claude Rains, who plays a repentant shady politician (would never happen in real life). Edward Arnold also plays a deliciously evil politician (my dream role) Good fun despite the unbelievable plot.

Mughal E-Azam (India) - 1960 - Directed by K. Asif and starring Prithviraj Kapoor, Dilip Kumar, Madhubala, and Durga Khote. This is a tale of forbidden love by a Prince, disapproval by the king and a beautiful dancer. Movie broke all box office records at the time.

Mulan (China) -2010 - Directed by Jingle Ma and starring Zhao Wei as Mulan and a sound supporting cast. This well-known tale first shown in the US by Disney, now gets a full film treatment and the result is better than the Disney version. Good action.

Mulholland Drive - 2001 - Written and directed by David Lynch, who was born to direct film noir, and starring Justin Theroux, Naomi Watts, and Anne Miller along with a solid supporting cast. Film about broken dreams won a slew of awards.

Mulholland Falls - 1996 - Directed by Lee Tamahori and starring Nick Nolte, Melanie Griffith, Chazz Palminteri, Treat Williams, Andrew McCarthy and John Malkovich. This film noir classic is about the police of LA using less than socially accepted methods of maintaining law and order during a time when such behaviour was socially acceptable.

The Mummy- 1932 - Directed by Karl Freund and starring Boris Karloff as the Mummy. Very original horror film packed in audiences in 1932 and still holds up well. Karloff will never be surpassed as the original Mummy.

The Mummy's Hand - 1940 - Directed by Christy Cabanne and starring an unknown cast of B actors, this film seemed destined for obscurity. But a lively story that was better than the 1932 plot allows it to step above mediocrity.

Murder By Decree -1979 - Directed by Bob Clark and starring Christopher Plummer and James Mason in the principal roles of Holmes and Watson. This tale of Holmes solving the Jack the Ripper murders is a notch above the other Holmes tales. Engaging.

Murder, Inc. -1960 - Directed by Stuart Rosenberg and Burt Balaban and starring Stuart Whitman, May Britt, a miscast Henry Morgan and a perfectly cast Peter Falk. Though very violent (it would be pretty difficult to do this story without violence), the film is well done.

Murder, My Sweet - 1944 - Directed by Edward Dmytryk and starring Dick Powell, Claire Trevor and Anne Shirley. This classic noir piece is about an ex-con trying to locate his ex girlfriend and has detective Philip Marlowe arriving at many dead ends. Great stuff.

Murders at the Rue Morgue —-1932 - Directed by Robert Florey and starring Bela Lugosi as a mad scientist (what a stretch). Actually the film has a great story line from Poe, so the actors give it their best effort and the result is a bit chilling. The original title, It Was Only Monkey Love, was eventually rejected.

Murphy's War -1971 - Directed by Peter Yates and starring Peter O'Toole in the lead role as a Captain Ahab-type survivor of a German massacre of his ships and mates. The Great White whale is a German U-Boat and the conclusion is similar to the Melville novel. Anything O'Toole does is good, but this is not his best.

Mutiny on the Bounty - 1935 – Directed by Frank Lloyd and starring Charles Laughton and Clark Gable. This is the granddaddy of all sea adventure films. The trip made by Bligh, which is understated in the film, is considered to be one of the greatest nautical achievements in the history of the British, or any other, navy. Director Lloyd keeps the action going at a fast pace and there is little in the film that suggests a lull. Laughton is wonderfully over the top as Bligh and none of the sequels with Blighs have ever matched his performance.

Not only was he over the top at times in the film, but he was also deliciously understated in many other scenes with that plotting mentality just under the skin of his amiable smile. It takes a certain amount of smugness to play Bligh and Laughton had that in his personality in spades and so it was a perfect match to the character. Gable, on the other hand, was merely adequate as Christian. Gable did not really fare very well in swashbuckler films; it was not his style. He made very few successful sea movies other than *Run Silent, Run Deep* much later in his career. The rest of the cast, as was the great tradition of the MGM studios, is letter-perfect in their delivery of all the minor characters. MGM had the best supporting actor system in Hollywood for decades.

The story line is fairly famous. Captain Bligh, played by Charles Laughton, is cruel and despotic (not historically correct), and Fletcher Christian, played by Clark Gable, is high-minded and big on human rights. For movie purposes, this sets up a great confrontation between Bligh and Christian, but for anyone who has a bit of knowledge of history, it does not exactly jibe with the truth. The truth of the matter on the Bounty was that men liked women and a sense of freedom, both of which were not available under Bligh and both of which were available under Christian on his trip to Pitcairn Island.

The mutiny occurred primarily due to lust and a desire to live a better life than could ever be achieved living in England or at sea with the lovable Bligh. A good film about life after the mutiny has yet to be made by Hollywood. The cinematography of the adventure is well-done, but the dialogue is what really captures your attention. The trial is very interesting as it has little to do with the real one and the entire event is twisted out of context. Nevertheless, this is a MOVIE and should be enjoyed as a movie, not as an accurate representation of a historical event. Recommended.

My Architect – 2003 – Directed by Nathanial Kahn, the son of the biopic subject, Louis Kahn, the famous Philadelphia architect who had achieved world-wide recognition for his ancient architectural style. Extremely balanced and well-done documentary

My Beautiful Launderette (England) - 1986-Directed by the highly capable Stephen Frears and starring Daniel Day Lewis and a cast of unknowns that rise for the occasion to a great storyline. The film is a masterpiece of comedy.

My Darling Clementine - 1946 - Directed by John Ford and starring Henry Fonda, Linda Darnell and a badly miscast Victor Mature (he could never do cowboys) in a story about the gunfight at OK Coral. Done better with Lancaster and Douglas years later, but still watchable.

My Dinner With Andre -1981 - Directed by Louis Malle and starring Andre Gregory and Wallace Shawn in what is virtually a two man conversation about living in the real world of New York versus living in your own dream world. There is no clear winner here, but the conversation is fascinating.

My Favorite Season - 1993 - France - Directed by Andre Lachine and starring Catherine Deneuve and a few B actors in a story of a middle-aged brother and sister who are forced to take care of their sick and elderly mother. Incisive.

My Favorite Year - 1982 - Directed by Richard Benjamin, who always has a sure hand with comedies and starring Peter O'Toole, Joseph Bologna and Mark Baker in a riotous film about a novice TV executive who tries to work with two massive egos; a washed up film star and a current TV star. Hilarious.

My Left Foot -1989 -Directed by Jim Sheridan and starring Daniel Day-Louis as Christy Brown, a disabled man who only has use of his left foot. Instead of being a depressing tale of what you can't do, it becomes an inspiring tale of what you can do. A must see and an academy award winning role for Day-Louis.

My Life as a Dog- 1987 - Sweden - Directed by Lasse Hallstrom and starring a group of unknown B actors from Sweden. This funny slice of life film shows the coming of age of a young boy who loses his mother, his dog, and his sense of direction, until he comes to his own rescue.

My Man Godfrey - 1936 - Directed by Gregory La Cava and starring William Powell and Carole Lombard in a classic screwball comedy about a man down on his luck during the Depression who meets a Manhattanite socialite during a scavenger hunt. Absolutely one of the best comedies of all time.

My Memories of Old Beijing (China)- 1982 - Directed by Wu Yigong and starring Shen Jie as a little six year old girl sent to live in the countryside who had to make new friends. Some of them are very strange, but the film is very sweet.

My Night at Maud's -1969 - France - Directed by Eric Rohmer and starring Jean-Louis Trintignant and a fine supporting cast in a story of a conservative man, his socialist friend, and a libertine woman. Very funny and similar to *My Dinner With Andre*.

The Mysterians (Japan) —1958 Directed by Ishiro Honda who went into the car business after this effort and starring a group of C Japanese actors. The story is also pretty bizarre; the aliens want our women. This film should really be in my turkey farm selections, but it is far too much fun to put there. Enjoy the madness.

Mysterious Island -1961 - Directed by Cy Endfield and starring a hearty bunch of B actors in an A story with A special effects by Ray Harryhausen. Union troops in a POW camp escape in an air balloon to an island that is more dangerous than the prison camp. Interesting.

Mystery Man – 1944 – Directed by George Archainbaud and starring William (Hopalong Cassidy) Boyd in the lead role of double feature filler that often ran before the main, big budget film at your local theaters. Those days are now pretty much gone forever. So are one film theaters. Multiplexes ruined two great movie traditions at one time; two movies at a time and large, enjoyable moviehouses and screens. Of course, you can still wander from one movie to another in most multiplexes, and IMAX is as good as several old-time theaters, but something special was lost.

The Mystery of Edwin Drood - 1935 - Directed by Stuart Walker and starring Claude Rains and a group of B actors who do a very good job on Dicken's last unfinished book. The plot of the poor young man who rises in society despite all the evil around him is a common Dicken's vehicle. Worth viewing for Rains.

The Mystery of Mr. Wong - 1939 - Directed by William Neigh and starring Boris Karloff as a Japanese crime-solver. This is up there with John Wayne being cast as Genghis Khan, but at least Karloff could act, and carries the film to its conclusion. Worth viewing.

Mystery of the Wax Museum - 1933 - Directed by Michael Curtiz who would go on to many great films like Casablanca and starring Fay Wray of King Kong fame along with competent B actors in an interesting mystery about a wax museum. Entertaining.

Mystery Science Theatre 3000- 1996 - Written, directed and starring the talented Jim Mallon along with Joel and his two lovable robots from the TV show as they roast some of the best turkeys on the turkey farm. This Island Earth is featured on the poster among others. These guys know how to carve up bad films. Great stuff.

Mystic River –- 2003 - Directed by Clint Eastwood, who also did much of the music and starring Sean Penn, Tim Robbins, Kevin Bacon and Larry Fishbourne. This talented cast takes a first-rate murder mystery to great heights.

N

Naked and the Dead - 1958 - Directed by Raoul Walsh and starring Aldo Ray, Cliff Robertson and Raymond Massey. This overrated Norman Mailer rendition of WW2 becomes even less illuminating a dozen years after WW 2 has ended. Many WW2 films suffer the same fate during the fifties. Still Interesting.

Naked City —1948- Directed by Mark Hellinger and starring Barry Fitzgerald in the best role of his Irish priest and/or IRA career. This day in the life of a NYC detective eventually became a successful TV series as well.

The Naked Gun - 1988 – Directed by Blake Edwards and starring Leslie Neilson and many of the crew that were in *Airplane* years earlier. This turn in Leslie Neilson's career launched him to comedic stardom as an incompetent police detective.

Naked Jungle - 1954 - Directed by Byron Haskin and starring Charlton Heston and Eleanor Parker in the key roles. The story of man versus armies of ants is compelling and was even better when read as a short story.

Naked Prey - 1966 - Directed and starring Cornel Wilde and a great supporting cast in a film that was a shocker when it first came out. The beginning is very intense and the action and suspense are maintained right to the end. A must see.

Naked Spur - 1953 - Directed by Anthony Mann and starring James Stewart, Janet Leigh, Robert Ryan and Ralph Meeker. A great cast is pretty much subject to an average script and cliched Western dialogue. Good production values makes it watchable, however.

Napoleon Dynamite - 2004- Directed by Jared Hess and starring Jon Hedar in his breakthrough comedy role as a high school outcast who rises above the expectations of all around him. Quite funny in a myriad of ways; slapstick humor, dialogue, unique characters and more.

Narrow Margin -1952 - Directed by Richard Fleischer and starring a no-name B movie cast including Charles McGraw, Marie Windsor and Jacqueline White. This film is about the most underrated movie in the history of cinema. It is as good a train movie as any made by any other director, including Hitchcock, and that is saying a lot. It is perhaps the finest B movie ever made or at least in the top ten. It's B films like this that make me keep combing through B films for those little gems that are often overlooked.

Nashville - 1975 - Directed by Robert Altman and starring an all-star ensemble that highlights the foibles of performing at the Grand Opry in Nashville. It follows about a half dozen characters during the film, as is the Altman specialty. Very well done.

The Nasty Girl - Germany - 1990 - Directed by Michael Verhoeven and starring Lena Stolze as the nasty girl. The girl is nasty because she is doing research on her home town in Germany and uncovers lots of worms under the rocks. Her town was rife with Nazis, concentration camps, and other uncomfortable discoveries. A gripping, compelling film.

National Lampoon's Animal House - 1978 - Directed by John Landis and starring John Belushi, Donald Sutherland, Karen Allen and Thomas Hulce among others. This classic college frat house film has all the cliches that one can imagine, yet it is still funny. Still the king of this genre.

National Treasure - 2004 - Directed by Jon Turteltaub and starring Nicholas Cage, Jon Voight, Christopher Plummer, and Harvey Keitel in the expensive roles that anyone could have played, plus a competent supporting cast. The real star is the outlandish story that the viewer has to swallow if he or she is to enjoy the proceedings. Have fun and watch it.

The Natural —1984- Directed by Barry Levinson an starring Robert Redford as the natural, Roy Hobbs and Glenn Close as the good woman in his life. The bad woman, Barbara Hershey, puts a big obstacle in Roy's success, but good will eventually overcome evil in baseball. I am a big sucker for baseball movies. Fun to watch.

Nazarin - Mexico – 1958 - Directed by Luis Bunuel and starring Franisco Rabal and a supporting cast of unknown Mexican actors in a moving portrait of a compassionate Catholic priest in a very poor Mexican town. Great direction by Bunuel.

Nazi Agent - 1942 – Directed by Jules Dassin and starring Conrad Veidt and Anne Ayars. The title pretty much tells us what the film will be about and Dassin is one of the best in the business at doing film noir. Veidt turns in a great effort in an above- average spy thriller.

Network – 1976 - Directed by Sidney Lumet and featuring an all-star cast giving strong performances. Peter Finch won the Academy Award for best actor, but died before the presentations. Faye Dunaway won for Best Actress and Beatrice Straight won for Best Supporting Actress. In one of the worst travesties of the awards, Ned Beatty did not win for Best Supporting Actor, when many thought his performance was the best of all others in the film. Beatty lost to Jason Robards, who played the editor in *All The President's Men*; at best a solid performance, but not Oscar-worthy.

Director Lumet keeps the film going at almost a delirious pace, and there is hardly time to digest the last great scene before another one begins to unfold. The performances are, at times, electric. Finch was great, Beatty was absolutely demonic, and Dunaway was as manipulative as one could possibly be with the exception of Machiavelli. Holden, who is a great veteran actor, who can hold his own with anyone on screen, actually becomes lost in this film because of the riveting performances of the other actors.

The film is about a television station that is having ratings problems with their current programming, so they need to pump up the intensity of the programs. Unfortunately, they pump up the intensity just a wee bit too much and create havoc in the interim. William Holden as Max Schumacher, tries to harness the enthusiasm of Diana Christiansen played by Faye Dunaway, but is unsuccessful. Diana discovers Howard Beale, played by Peter Finch and all hell breaks loose. Finch goes off the deep end during what was supposed to be his final appearance and coins the phrase "I'm as mad as hell and I'm not going to take it any more", which appears to galvanize the entire city This is one of my must-see films.

The Nevadan- 1950 – Directed by Gordon Douglas and starring Randolph Scott, Dorothy Malone and Forest Tucker, a solid cast that Scott was not usually given for his other Westerns. This tale of the Nevada badlands is better than average.

Nevada Smith - 1966- Directed by Henry Hathaway and starring Steve McQueen as Nevada Smith. Karl Malden, Brian Keith and Arthur Kennedy head a great supporting cast in this story of a legendary Western hero.

Never Give a Sucker an Even Break - 1941- Directed by Edward F Kline (as if anyone could direct WC) and starring WC Fields in a skit (most Fields films are a series of skits rather than an orderly film) about an aspiring screen writer and a singer. Mundane plot, but very funny.

Never On Sunday - 1960 - Directed by Jules Dassin, a master director, and starring Jules Dassin and Melina Mecouri as the hooker with a heart of gold. Dassin is an American academic (is there a lamer animal?) who tries to reform her. Very funny and great music.

Next Stop, Greenwich Village - 1976 - Written and directed by Paul Mazursky and starring the unlikely pair of Christopher Walken and Shelley Winters. The film about finding a new life in Greenwich Village was meaningful then, but is a cliche now. The film went a few million over budget trying to feed Winters, but still turned a profit.

The Next Voice You Hear - 1950 - Directed by William Wellman (well-known for his sci-fi and horror films) and starring James Whitmore and Nancy Davis as your typical American couple waiting to hear the voice of God on a radio broadcast. This is high camp at its very best and not to be missed. Fun to see Mrs. Reagan in her best film. There is not one cliche missed in the script.

Nice Guys – 2016 – Directed by Shane Black and starring Russell Crowe and Ryan Gosling as two lowlife city dwellers trying to solve a murder case of a porn star. Absolutely no socially redeeming value whatsoever in this film; but fun to watch.

Night and the City - 1950 - Directed by Jules Dassin, master of Noir and starring Richard Widmark and Gene Tierney. The film centers on a small time hustler and his half-baked schemes and the woman who is unfortunate enough to love him. Good stuff.

Nightcrawler – 2014 - Directed by Dan Gilroy, who also wrote the film, and starring Jake Gyllenhaal, who gives a Robert DeNiro-type obsessed performance (as in *Taxi Driver*) as Lou Bloom, a professional photographer who will stop at nothing to make the most money in the field. Recommended

The Night Digger - England - 1971 - Directed by Alastair Reid and starring Patricia Neal and a cast of unknowns in a story about a woman who lives in a decaying mansion and the young man on a cycle who passes through. I think we know where this one is headed, but there are a few surprises.

Nightfall —1957 – Directed by Jacques Tourneur and starring Brian Keith, Aldo Ray, Anne Bancroft and Jocelyn Brando. This is a nice piece of Noir that features stolen money, a less than moral sexpot, and a group of greedy, morally disabled night crawlers. Some nice scenes.

The Night Has a Thousand Eyes - 1948 - Directed by John Farrow and starring Edward G. Robinson and Gail Russell. Gail is frightened of stars. Apparently, she does not live in Hollywood. John Lund comes to the rescue in this classy soap.

Nightmare - 1956- Directed by Maxwell Shane and starring Edward G Robinson as a musician who thinks he has been hypnotized into being a murderer. Was he? And who is responsible? Good noir.

Nightmare Alley -1956- Directed by Edmund Goulding, a master director of B movies, and starring Tyrone Power, chubby Joan Blondell, Queen of the film noir B's, Coleen Gray, and Helen Walker. With all these women in a sleazy movie, you know there has to be a shady lady somewhere in the film.

Night Moves -1975- Directed by Arthur Penn and starring Gene Hackman and James Woods. PI Hackman discovers the world is sleazy in the Post-Watergate era. I wonder how long it took him? Interesting noir.

Night Must Fall – 1937 - Directed by Richard Thorpe and starring Robert Montgomery and Rosalind Russell in a curious story about a drifter who weasels his way into an upper class home of an invalid. Very intriguing stuff.

Night My Number Came Up – England - 1955 - Directed by Les Norman and starring Michael Redgrave and Alexander Knox (Wilson) in a story of flashbacks of passengers on a plane that is in danger of crashing.

Night of the Hunter - 1955- Directed by Charles Laughton and starring Robert Mitchum, Shelley Winters and Lillian Gish in a wonderfully creepy story about a minister who is a serial killer. The film ran over budget because feeding Winters was very expensive.

Night of the Living Dead - 1968 - Directed by George Romero in Pittsburgh for a miniscule amount of money and starring a C cast of actors. The story, however, became the blueprint for dozens of later films as zombies take over the night. Fun to watch. Now WAY too many crappy zombie films and TV shows.

Night of the Shooting Stars -1982 - Directed by Paolo and Vittorio Taviani and starring a cast of unknown Italian actors in a story about a small town's liberation by American soldiers. Great film-making.

A Night to Remember- England - 1958 - Directed by Roy Ward Baker and starring an unknown cast of B actors in a very good rendition of the actual events of the sinking of the Titanic in 1912. Sometimes no frills is more effective than special effects.

Night On Earth - 1991- Written and directed by Jim Jarmusch and starring Gena Rowlands and Winona Ryder in one of her best roles. The stories are a series of vignettes about the trials and tribulations of common people.

Night Passage –-1957 - Directed by James Nielson and starring Jimmy Stewart and Audie Murphy in the principal roles. I have to agree with Anthony Mann; Murphy not up to snuff as A actor for roles, but Stewart worth watching.

Night People - 1954 - Directed by Nunnally Johnson and starring Gregory Peck, a miscast Buddy Epson, and Broderick Crawford in a tale of espionage in the split city of Berlin immediately following WW 2. Interesting.

Night Plane From ChungKing – 1942 – Directed by Ralph Murphy and starring Robert Preston and Ellen Drew in a sequel (or remake If you prefer) of *Shanghai Express* from 1931. Not as good as the 31 film, but not too bad. Watchable.

Night Train to Munich- England - 1940 - Directed by Carol Reed and starring Rex Harrison and Paul Henreid in a spy thriller about the early days of WW2 and everyone scrambling to get back to their native countries. Very interesting.

Night Walker - 1964 - Directed by William Castle and starring Barbara Stanwyck in her last role along with Robert Taylor in one of his last roles. B movie stuff with A actors; interesting to see.

Nine Lives –-2005 - Directed by Rodrigo Garcia in his imitation of a Robert Altman ensemble production with an all-star cast. Some of the vignettes are better than others in this soap lover's dream.

Ninotchka - 1939 - Directed by Ernst Lubitsch and starring Greta Garbo as Ninotchka, a lively, funny woman stuck in Stalin Russia before the outbreak of the war. Also starring Melvyn Douglas.

Ninth Configuration – 1980 - Directed by William Peter Blatty of *Exorcist* fame and starring Stacy Keach and Jason Miller (who was a star in *The Exorcist* as well) in a misdirection film (a film that seems like a comedy, but isn't) about the sane and insane. Good stuff.

Nixon - 1995 –-Directed by Oliver Stone and starring Anthony Hopkins in a sympathetic treatment of the Nixon years. Democrats will think Tricky Dick was worse, and Republicans will think it is a hatchet job, so the film pleases very few, but is fascinating to watch.

Nobody Lives Forever - 1946 - Directed by Jean Negulesco and starring John Garfield, Geraldine Fitzgerald, Walter Brennan and Faye Emerson as various hustlers in the netherworld following WW2. This is great noir at its peak.

No Country for Old Men –- 2007 - Directed by the very original Coen Brothers, Joel and Ethan and starring brilliant newcomer Javier Bardem, who won an Academy Award for his effort along with Tommy Lee Jones in a story about a stone cold killer and the aging cop who chases him.

No Man is an Island - 1962 - Directed by Richard Goldstone and starring Jeffrey Hunter as an American soldier who outwits the Japanese for over three years before Guam is liberated by MacArthur. Fascinating true story.

Norma Rae – 1979 - Directed by Martin Ritt and starring Sally Field, Beau Bridges and Ron Liebman. This is a story about a simple factory worker who organizes the workers to get better conditions on the job.

North By Northwest - 1959 – Directed by Alfred Hitchcock and starring Cary Grant, Eva Marie Saint and James Mason as a heavy. This classic is one of Hitchcock's best. It is a story about mistaken identity and a chase across the US. A must see.

North Star - 1943 - Directed by Lewis Milestone and starring Anne Baxter, Dana Andrews, Walter Huston, Walter Brennan and Farley Granger in a story about Russian resistance to the Germans during WW2. Good stuff, but if you watch it, YOU WILL BECOME A COMMUNIST! (this is what American film censors thought in the 1950s).

Northwest Mounted Police - 1940 - Directed by Cecil B De Mille and starring Gary Cooper, Preston Foster and a smoking hot Paulette Goddard (way too hot for Cooper). This amusing Western has a ton of action and plot twists and will satisfy any film appetite.

Northwest Passage - 1940 - Directed by King Vidor and starring Spencer Tracy, Walter Brennan, Robert Young and a great supporting cast (despite being one of the worst movie posters I have ever seen; does that look like Spencer Tracy to you?) in a story about the great Northwest and the struggles to find a trading route.

Not As a Stranger - 1955 - Directed by Stanley Kramer and starring Olivia DeHaviland, Robert Mitchum, Frank Sinatra, Gloria Grahame, Broderick Crawford and Charles Bickford. Not a weak actor in the lot. This is a soap lover's dream about doctors and their romantic adventures.

Notes From Underground - 1995 - Directed by Gary Walkow and starring Henry Czerny in a tour-de-force performance about one the world's biggest losers. This character is the ultimate outcast and we are all just so happy not to be him. A must see.

Nothing But The Best – England - 1964 - Directed by Clive Donner and starring Alan Bates and Harry Andrews in a film about a man who will stop at nothing to get the better things in life. Tragic, in a way.

Nothing But The Truth - 2008 - Written and directed by Rod Lurie and starring Matt Dillon, Alan Alda and David Schwimmer. You will never see that combination again. An interesting story about the violation of the Constitution.

No Time For Sergeants- 1958 - Directed by Mervyn Leroy and starring Andy Griffith as a bumbling hayseed who succeeds despite being the dumbest guy in the Air Force. Funny stuff.

Not One Less (China) —1999 - Directed by the legendary Zhang Yimou and starring Wei Minzhi and Zhang Huike in a story about a 13 year old substitute teacher in the countryside who tracks down a missing students hundreds of miles away.

Notorious — 1946 - Directed by Alfred Hitchcock and starring Cary Grant and Ingrid Bergman along with Claude Rains in a film about a wife who doubts her husband's motives. The film had an alternative ending, but Hitchcock chose the happy one.

No Way to Treat a Lady - 1968 - Directed by Jack Smight and starring Rod Steiger, Lee Remick and George Segal. Steiger has a field day as a creepy serial killer and the script is nice and tight.

Nowhere in Africa - Germany - 2001 - Directed by Caroline Link and starring unknown German actors playing Jewish refugees in Africa shortly after the outbreak of WW2. Interesting historically.

Now, Voyager -1942 - Directed by Irving Rapper and starring Bette Davis, Paul Henreid and Claude Rains (who frequently starred with Davis). This is a story about a woman with low self-esteem who goes on a cruise and has a fling to get her groove back. A must see soap.

Nuan (China) — 2003 - Directed by Huo Jianqi and starring Guo Xiaodong, Li Jia and Teruyuki Kagawa (who won an award for his role). The story of a country boy who goes back to his childhood farm is very engaging.

Number 17 – England- 1932 - Directed by Alfred Hitchcock and starring a group of B actors, this film is about a group of thieves who hide their stash in a house near the English Channel. Good suspense.

1182

O

Objective Burma —1945 - Directed by Raoul Walsh and starring Errol Flynn along with a solid B cast in a story about the Burma Road during WW 2. Film is action-packed.

Oblivion – 2013 - Directed by Joseph Kosinski and starring Tom Cruise and Morgan Freeman in key roles. The script is a bit uneven and unbelievable, so the end result is disappointing. However Cruise and Freeman try to keep this boat afloat. Film will fade into the title in the near future, however.

October Man – England - 1947 - Directed by Ray Ward Baker and starring John Mills and Jean Greenwood in a story about a man who may or may not be a murderer. Suspenseful to the last minute.

October Sky - 1999 - Directed by Directed by Joe Johnston and starring Jake Gyllenhaal, Chris Cooper and Laura Dern in a true story about a humble young scientist from Tennessee who impresses everyone with his brilliance in rocketry.

The Odd Couple - 1968 - Directed by Gene Saks and starring Jack Lemmon and Walter Matthau as the original Felix and Oscar forced to lived together after divorce; one is dirty and the other too clean. Very funny.

Odd Man Out - 1947 - England – Directed by Carol Reed and starring James Mason and Robert Newton. This classic noir of British cinema is tightly directed and acted by the best in Britain. The poster is a bit over the top, however.

Officer and A Gentleman - 1982 - Directed by Taylor Hackford and starring Richard Gere and Debra Winger in an upbeat story of a poor boy making his way through officer's school. Great music helps the production.

Office Space - 1999 - Directed and written by the talented Mike Judge (Beavis and Butthead, King of the Hill) and starring Jennifer Aniston and a cast of unknown, but enthusiastic B actors, in a story about working in the office in the 90s. Hilarious.

Of Gods and Men – 2011 – France – Directed by Xavier Beauvois and starring an unknown group of French B actors in a story of Trappist Monks in Algeria during a period of political unrest and terrorism. Should they stay or go? What would Jesus do?

Of Human Bondage - 1946 - Directed by John Cromwell and starring Leslie Howard and Bette Davis in a film version of the Somerset Maugham novel about a man who is a slave of love to a woman who despises him. One of the great soaps.

Of Mice and Men – 1940 - Directed by Lewis Milestone and starring Burgess Meredith, Betty Field, Lon Chaney Jr., Charles Bickford and Noah Beery Jr. in a film version of the novel by John Steinbeck about two farmhands, one of which is simple-minded. Interesting.

Oldboy- Korea 2010- Directed by Park Chan-Wook and starring unknown Korean actors (except in Korea) in a film about a man who is imprisoned for fifteen years for no apparent reason, and then is released into a world of violence. Violence is the usual status quo for most Korean films, but this one has an interesting story attached to it that makes it worth seeing.

Oliver Twist- England —1948 - Directed by the great David Lean and starring Alec Guinness, Robert Newton, and Anthony Newley along with a solid supporting cast in the Charles Dickens classic of a young boy making his way through the world of London during the 1800s.

Olympia – German- 1936- Directed by Leni Riefenstahl and starring the participants of the 1936 Olympics. This is a masterpiece of cinematography, and although it is politically controversial, it should be judged on its production values. A must see.

Once Upon a Time in America - 1984 - Directed by master director Sergio Leone of Spaghetti Western fame and starring James Woods, Robert DeNiro, Tuesday Weld, Elizabeth McGovern, Joe Pesci, and Treat Williams in an epic about the development of crime families in the US. This film was a labor of love for Leone, who had his film virtually cut in half by greedy American distributors because the original four hours was too long for them to make bigger profits. The result was a choppy masterpiece. The film is being restored with the help of Marty Scorcese and will premiere in 2012 with its original length. I. for one. will buy a ticket. Great film-making.

Once Upon a Time in China (China) - 1991 - This a six film series directed by Tsui Hark, Yuen Bun, and Sammo Hung and starring Jet Li and Vincent Zhao as Wong Fei-Hong, a Chinese folk hero, in a story about the fall of Qing Dynasty and the problems of creating a Chinese republic with Sun Yatsen. Add an hour or two of great martial arts and you have a pretty good series.

Once Upon a Time in the West —1968 - Directed by Sergio Leone for some greedy guys at Paramount who insisted on chopping the film up so that they could make more money (the same exact thing happened to Leone in his later film, Once Upon a Time in America) and starring Henry Fonda in a deliciously bad guy role, and Charles Bronson as the good guy. Great stuff.

On Dangerous Ground - 1952 - Directed by Nicholas Ray and starring Ida Lupino and Robert Ryan as a cop that is out of control. Ward Bond also stars. This B film becomes an A film because of the quality actors and great direction by Ray. Good noir.

One and Eight (China) - 1983 - Directed by Zhang Junzhao and starring Tao Zeru, Chen Daoming, and Lu Xiaoyan in a story about a deserter during the Chinese-Japanese conflict preceeding WW2. Filmed by future director icon, Zhang Yimou, the movie is a break from the politically correct films of the seventies in China.

One False Move - 1992 - Directed by Carl Franklin and starring Billy Bob Thornton, Bill Paxton, and Cynda Williams in a story about three violent criminals and a cop with a checkered past. A pretty good story, albeit a bit violent.

One Flew Over the Cuckoo's Nest - 1975 – Directed by Milos Foreman and starring Jack Nicholson and a fine supporting cast including Danny Davito, Louise Fletcher, and Christopher Lloyd (not much of a stretch for him to be a nut job). Story about a con who chooses the nut house over prison (and pays a heavy price).

One Foot in Heaven - 1941 - Directed by Irving Rapper and starring Fredric March and Martha Scott in a story about the gradual liberalization of a strict minister and his family as they move from parish to parish.

One of Our Aircraft is Missing -England- 1942 - Directed by Michael Powell and starring a solid B cast of actors under the direction of an A director in a story about British airmen trapped behind enemy lines in the Netherlands. Actually, being queen of the underground is not a very good idea. The best spies in history were always the ones that no one ever suspected or knew about. Good filmmaking.

One Potato, Two Potato - 1964 - Directed by Larry Peerce and starring Barbara Barrie and Bernie Hamilton as a mixed-marriage couple that are threatened by the ex-husband of the white woman for raising their child with a black man. Racist issues of the film are no longer prevalent, but were timely at the release of the movie. Interesting.

One That Got Away - 1957 - Directed by Roy Ward Baker and starring Hardy Kruger as an escaped German POW, who makes his way all the way from Canada to Mexico in order to return to fight in Germany for the rest of the war. A decent treatment that leaves the Nazi stuff on the backburner and concentrates on the soldier aspects of German troops.

The Onion Field - 1979 - Directed by Harold Becker and starring James Woods, Ted Danson, Franklyn Seales and Ron Cox in a horrific tale of murder and an ineffective justice system. This is the film that launched James Woods' career. A must see.

On the Beach —1959 - Directed by Stanley Kramer and starring Gregory Peck and Ava Gardner along with Anthony Perkins in a story about the end of the world as we know it. Scary to see when you were a kid and still a bit scary.

On the Mountain of Tai Hang (China) - 2005 - Directed by Chen Jian, Shen Dong, and Wei Lian and starring Wang Wufu, Li Shusheng, and Xu Guangming in a story about the newly formed Eighth Route Army and their struggle against the Japanese. Good film-making.

On the Town —1949 - Directed by Gene Kelly and Stanley Donen and starring Gene Kelly, Frank Sinatra and Ann Miller in a musical comedy about two sailors who run all over town looking for a contest winner mod

On the Town —1949 - Directed by Gene Kelly and Stanley Donen and starring Gene Kelly, Frank Sinatra and Ann Miller in a musical comedy about two sailors who run all over town looking for a contest winner model even though they only have a few days left of freedom.

On The Waterfront – 1954 – Directed by Elia Kazan and starring Marlon Brando, Eva Marie Saint and Karl Malden, as well as a powerhouse performance by Lee J Cobb. This film is often in the top ten list of most movie critics in the United States. In one of the screen's greatest performances, Brando gives his character, Terry Malloy, an unforgettable portrayal.

Hoboken, New Jersey is the perfect setting for this grim and tough tale of life on the waterfront for the average dock worker. Wisely shot in black and white to bring out the grittiness of the atmosphere of working down in the docks, the camerawork is first rate as well as the movie sound track. Karl Malden gives the best performance of his life in this film, as does Cobb. Most critics believe this is Brando's best performance ever, also. Saint was never as good again in any film she made afterward, so this production has at least four actors who may have had the best performances of their lives in one film.

Kazan manipulates his actors with the finesse of Hitchcock and achieves a masterpiece. The visceral content of the film was seldom matched by others in the last half century. I used to live just above the steps down to Hoboken in Union City and I can vouch for the authenticity of the film's location. Kazan got everything perfect, down to the pigeons on the roof.

Only Angels Have Wings - 1939 - Directed by Howard Hawks and starring Cary Grant and Jean Arthur along with Rita Hayworth in a story about an air mail service in South America before WW 2. You can guess the triangle conclusion with Rita and Jean.

Open City – Italy - 1945 - Directed by Roberto Rossolini and filmed with the immediate memory of the Nazi occupation of Italy. The film stars mostly B Italian actors along with Anna Magnani, but is very effective because of the very simple, but effective, script. Nazis were ruthless.

Open Range –A- 2003 - Directed and starring Kevin Costner and two assistants (as directors) along with Annette Benning and Robert Duval in a story about cattlemen and farmers fighting over open range (not exactly an original idea), but the action is worth the viewing.

Open Your Eyes – 1999 –Spain - Directed by Alejandro Amenabar and starring Penelope Cruz in the lead role in a story about a man in car accident who loses his grip on reality (something in the film that cannot really be relied on). Interesting.

Operation Crossbow –England - 1965 - Directed by Michael Anderson and starring Sophia Loren, George Peppard, Trevor Howard, John Mills and Tom Courtenay in a WW 2 spy thriller about stopping the German V1 and V2 operations before those deadly bombs can be used. Interesting.

The Opium War (China) – 1997 - Directed by Xie Jin and starring Bao Guo'an, Lin Liankun, Sihung Lung, Bob Peck, Simon Williams, Shao Xin, Su Min, and Gao Yuan. This is the tragic story of China's unsuccessful struggle to keep opium out of the country that was imported by the British. I learned the Chinese were the good guys in college about the same time I learned American Indians were the good guys in the West.

Ordet – Denmark —1955 - Directed by Carl Theodor Dreyer and starring unknown Danish actors who do a good job under Dryer. The story is about rural life and death and all the good soap that goes with it.

Ordinary People -1980 - Directed by Robert Redford and starring Donald Sutherland, Mary Tyler Moore and Timothy Hutton in a best picture winner about a dysfunctional family. This royal soap won four awards and struck a chord with the public. Moore's best work.

Orphan on the Streets (China) - 1949 - Directed by Gong Yan and Ming Zhao and starring Longji Wang as Three Hairs (the film is also known as The Winter of Three Hairs). This Chinese classic has been seen by over one billion Chinese; or just about everyone in the country. It is the most recognizable Chinese film of all time. Many have seen it numerous times. The story is about a feisty orphan who manages to survive the mean streets of the city.

The Oscar – 1966 —Directed by Russell Rouse and starring Stephen Boyd, Elke Sommer, Milton Berle, Eleanor Parker, Joseph Cotten, Tony Bennett, Edie Adams and Ernest Borgnine as various Hollywood hopefuls during the Academy Award nomination period. Who will win, and who go home empty-handed? Good stuff.

Othello – England - 1952 - Directed and starring the only man in Hollywood history who would put his name as written by next to Shakespeare for the credit of writing this story; that would be Orson Welles. Welles gives the second best Othello performance on film (Olivier is better in 65). Eventually, Welles' ego was soon matched by his stomach in later years. Interesting.

The Other – 1972 - Directed to Robert Mulligan and starring a cast of unknown B actors performing a novel written by Tom Tryon about some really naughty children. It is a horror film of the highest order and unless you are a fan of that genre, you will be uncomfortable watching the film.

Our Brand is Crisis –2005 - Directed by Rachel Boynton and starring a group of dedicated B actors and a few professional politicians that give authenticity to the story of the selling of the Iraq War to the American public. Sobering.

Our Man Flint -1966 - Directed by Daniel Mann and starring James Coburn in the role of Flint, a spy similar to 007 without the production values. While not as good as Bond, the series provided enough action and good music to hold most audience's attention. Not bad.

Our Town – 1940 - Directed by Sam Wood and starring William Holden and Martha Scott in the classic play written by Thornton Wilder about life in a small town and all the ups and downs of the citizens of the small town are brought to the fore. Well done.

Our Vines Have Tender Grapes - 1945 - Directed by Roy Rowland and starring Edward G Robinson, Agnes Moorehead, and Margaret O'Brien in a tale about life on a farm from the viewpoint of the young daughter of Ed and Agnes. Interesting because writer Dalton Trumbo was banned from Hollywood after this film by McCarthyites because of his political beliefs. A sad chapter in American history.

The Outcast - 1954 - Directed by William Witney and starring the ill-fated John Derek and Joan Evans in a B oater that is a cut above the average. Man cheated out of his ranch by his uncle comes back for revenge. Not bad.

Outcast of the Islands —England - 1951 - Directed by the highly respected Carol Reed and starring Robert Morley, Trevor Howard, Ralph Richardson and Wendy Hiller; all fine actors in a Joseph Conrad story about losing a second chance because of lust. Good stuff.

The Outlaw Josey Wales– 1976 - Directed and starring Clint Eastwood and a cast of B actors including Sandra Locke in a dubious story about events during the Civil War. Civil War much more interesting with Eastwood and Locke than in our history books.

Out of the Fog - 1941 - Directed by Anatole Litvak and starring the dynamic Ida Lupino teamed with the moody John Garfield for about as perfect a film noir set-up as you can get. A classic in every way. A must see.

Out of the Past-1947 - Directed by Jaques Tournier and starring Robert Mitchum, Jane Greer and Kirk Douglas in a supporting role that steals the film because he a very good leading actor and a great bad guy. Great noir.

The Outsider - 1961- by Delbert Mann and starring a miscast Tony Curtis (the Indian with a Brooklyn accent) as Ira Hayes, the ill-fated Native American who helped raise the flag on Iwo Jima and then came stateside to sell war bonds and become an alcoholic. Powerful story overcomes casting.

Outland - 1981 -England- Directed by Peter Hyams and starring Sean Connery as the only law official on a moon of Jupiter. This nice original sci-fi story captured the imagination of the public and was called High Noon in Space by unfriendly critics.

Outlaws of the Plains – 1946 – Directed by Sam Newfield and starring Buster Crabbe (an Olympic athlete turned actor) in the lead role of a common B Western about good guys and bad guys with the good guys winning in the end. Crabbe should have stuck to sports. This film will disappear from the list in the next year or two.

The Overlanders - Australia – 1946 - Directed by Harry Watt and starring a B troupe of Australian actors in a story that highlights Australia's contribution to the efforts in WW2. Commissioned by the government, but still good cinema.

Overlord – 1975 – Directed by Stuart Cooper and starring a solid B cast of British actors retelling the events in England leading up to the D-Day invasion through the eyes of a recent young recruit. Not bad considering the low budget.

The Ox-Bow Incident -1943 - Directed by William Wellman and starring Henry Fonda, Dana Andrews and a great supporting cast in a classic story of vilgilanties gone bad. A must see.

The Oxford Murders- 2010 - Directed by Alex de la Iglesia and starring Elijah Wood and John Hurt in the principal roles. Leonor Watling adds to the cast values in this overly intellectual murder mystery. However, the dialogue is crisp with some great lines like " the only pure truth in the universe is mathematics". I guess you could call this math film Pi squared.

Oxhide (China) - 2005 - Directed by Liu Jiayin and starring Liu Zaiping, Jia Huifen and Liu Jiayin. Written and photographed by Liu Jiayin as well. The story of the director's family and his personal life won a few minor awards and was a great effort for a 23 year old.

1239

P

Painted Veil - 2006 - Directed by John Curran and starring Edward Norton, Naomi Watts, and Anthony Wang Chau in a Somerset Maugham story about a Western couple experiencing marital difficulties in China. Enlightening.

Paisan - Italy - 1948 - Directed by Roberto Rossellini in his second of three films about postwar Italy told in the neo-realistic style Italy became famous for in films after WW 2. All B actors but a great script and good direction make it engrossing.

The Palm Beach Story - 1942 - Directed by Preston Sturges and starring Claudette Cobert and Joel McCrea along with a solid supporting cast in a story about an unlikely situation with identical twins and a wavering relationship. Entertaining if you can put the ridiculous plot behind you.

Palm Trees in the Snow – 2015 - Directed by Fernando Gonzalez Molina and starring Mario Casas, Adriana Ugarte, and Macarena Garcia in the lead roles of a story about boy meets girl, boy falls in love with girl. Not exactly earth-shattering, but good stuff for soaplovers.

Panic in the Streets -1950 - Directed by Elia Kazan and starring Richard Widmark, Paul Douglas and Barbara Del Geddes (of *Dallas* fame) in a story of a potential plague that might engulf all of New Orleans. First film of its type and well done.

The Paper Chase - 1973 – Directed by James Bridges and based on a novel by Harvard Law student, John Jay Osborn Jr. and stars Timothy Bottoms as Hart and Lindsay Wagner as the daughter of the eminent Professor Kingsfield. Both of these characters are very good, particularly Bottoms, but both are annihilated whenever John Houseman is on the screen as Professor Kingsfield.

The camera loves Houseman in this role, and the viewer waits with great anticipation for every scene that Houseman is in. In my opinion, Houseman was just a good an actor as Orson Welles, if not better. Houseman was Welles' old movie partner in the business at Mercury, but Houseman preferred the writing and producing elements of film to the acting area. A true loss to the profession. This was his first major role and he won the Academy Award for Best Supporting Actor. You can't do much better than that on your first try.

The director of this film, Bridges, was working with a living legend and used him just the right way. The pacing of the film is great and there is never a dull moment. The music and photography are first-rate and the storyline is absolutely riveting. The story is about a struggling law student Hart, played by Bottoms, who is from Minnesota and comes to Harvard Law school, where the standards and the competition are ferocious. It is one of the top ten education theme films of all time. This is a must-see film and easily one of the best fifty films of all time as well.

Paperhouse - England - 1988 - Directed by Bernard Rose and starring Ben Cross (of Chariots of Fire fame) along with two new promising young actors, Charlotte Burke and Elliot Spiers in the key roles. Music by Hans Zimmer adds to the production values. This is a story of the helplessness of children when they are caught up in marital discord and how they must use their imaginations in order to escape from despair. Very interesting

The Paper Lion -1968 - Directed by Alex March and starring Alan Alda in the featured role as a writer doing an undercover story about what it is like to try out for a professional football team. Alex Karras was so good in the film as an amateur actor that he obtained many additional professional roles. Great fun.

Paper Moon -1973 - Directed by Peter Bogdonavich and starring Tatum and Ryan O'Neal in the best real actor father and daughter movie ever made about a travelling con man and his lovely, but now corrupt little daughter. Very funny.

Papillion – 1973 - Directed by Franklin J Schaffner and starring Steve McQueen and Dustin Hoffman as two inmates of Devil's Island. Good dialogue makes the film memorable as well as great location shooting. Good production values.

The Paradine Case - 1947 - Directed by Alfred Hitchcock and starring Gregory Peck, Ann Todd, Charles Laughton, Ethel Barrymore, Charles Coburn and a very young Louis Jourdan in a courtroom thriller about murder and the lawyer who falls for his client, thereby sabotaging his own case. One of the Master's weakest entries.

The Parallax View —1974 - Directed by Alan J. Pakula and starring Warren Beatty, Paula Prentiss, and Hume Cronyn is the principal roles about a writer who investigates an organization known for political assassinations. This is like investigating heroin deals in LA; I would think you would be placing yourself in harm's way. Interesting, though.

Passage (China) - 2004 - Directed by Wen Tang Cheng and starring Guey Lun Mei, Leon Dai, and Yukihiko Kageyama in a tight little film noir piece about a relic and a love triangle. The director does a great job of building up the suspense.

A Passage to India - 1984 - Directed by David Lean and starring Judy Davis, Victor Banerjee, and Alec Guinness in principal roles. This tale of a British woman's flirtations with an Indian man seem to be blown all out of proportion according to modern-day mores, but during the time portrayed in the film, it was taboo. Great for soap-lovers.

Passage to Marseille - 1944 - Directed by Michael Curtiz of Casablanca fame and starring Humphrey Bogart, Sidney Greenstreet, Peter Lorre, and Claude Rains among others in a tale of early WW2 intrigue about a ship headed to Nazi-occupied France.

Passport to Pimlico - England – 1963 - Directed by Henry Cornelius and starring a group of B English actors (although Margaret Rutherford is really considered an A actress by some) in a comedy about a small village that finds it is free from British rule. A bit like the *The Mouse That Roared* and very funny.

Password is Courage —England – 1963 - Directed by Andrew L. Stone and starring Dirk Bogarde as a clever English POW under the Germans who manages to get himself the Iron Cross. Completely absurd, but funny.

Pastime —1991 - Directed by Robin B. Armstrong and starring a group of B actors and a few retired professional baseball players such as Ernie Banks, Harmon Killebrew, Duke Snider, and Don Newcombe. This little slice of life in minor league baseball is about an aging pitcher who has no realistic chance of making the majors, but plays on because baseball is........everything. Great stuff.

Paterson – 2016 – Directed by Jim Jarmusch and starring Adam Driver (appropriate for his role), and hot newcomer, Golshifteh Farahani in a sensational story about the contemplations of a bus driver in Paterson, New Jersey; land of Libby's Texas Weiners, The Falls, The Capitol Theater, and home of the Little Indians of West Paterson (from *Tales of West Paterson*). How could I not love this movie?

Pather Panchali - India - 1958 - Directed by Satyajit Ray and starring Subir Banerjee, Banerjee, Karuna Banerjee, and a fine supporting cast of amateur actors that successfully imitated the neo-realism of the Italian filmmakers a few years earlier. The final result is a masterpiece made for $3000 that made millions.

Pathfinder – Norway —1988 - Directed by Nils Gaup and starring Mikkel Gaup in a tale of the Chudes versus the Samis in the frozen wastes of Norway. Now this may not sound like much, but it is riveting piece of work.

Paths of Glory -1957 - Directed by Stanley Kubrick and starring Kirk Douglas, Ralph Meeker and Adolphe Menjou in a fine story about World War 1 and the idiots that were in charge of men's lives giving idiotic orders that railed against all common sense. A must see.

Patterns - 1956 - Directed by Fielder Cook and starring Van Heflin, Everett Sloane, Ed Begley and a fine supporting cast in a powerful corporate drama written by the the master writer, Rod Serling of *Twilight Zone* fame. Not to be missed. in the lead roles with a fine supporting cast. Scott won an academy award for his portrayal and the film is quite intent on showing the thorny side of the great general.

The Pawnbroker - 1965- Deftly directed by Sidney Lumet and starring Rod Steiger as the pawnbroker in a tour-de-force performance that netted him the Oscar for 1964 in a story about a Nazi death camp survivor trying to go on with his life in New York after the war. Emotionally powerful.

Payday - 1973 - Directed by Daryl Duke and starring Rip Torn as a mediocre Country and Western singer who has a hobby of being a thief in whatever town he is playing in that night. A pretty funny film.

Peacock (China) -2005 - Directed by Gu Changwei and starring Zhang Jingchu, Feng Li, and Lu Yulai in a story about the period immediately following the Cultural Revolution in Mainland China told from the perspective of three different children. Interesting.

The Pearl of Death —-1944 - Directed by Roy William Neill and starring Basil Rathbone and Nigel Bruce as Holmes and Watson. This Holmes mystery surrounds various busts of Napolean, which may or may not be the hiding place for a valuable stolen pearl. Always entertaining.

The Pedestrian – Germany- 1974- Directed by Maximilian Schell and starring a cast of unknown B German actors, who, under the guidance of Schell's deft direction, turn out a little gem of a film about an elderly German on trial for war crimes. Schell got his experience for this film from starring in *Judgment at Nuremberg*, which covered many of the same issues.

Peking Express – 1951 – Directed by William Dieterle (famous for monster films) and starring Joseph Cotton and Marvin Miller (*The Millionaire*), among others, in an offbeat film about Chinese commies and outlaws. So, who are you going to root for? The commies or the outlaws? Interesting.

Peking Opera Blues - China - 1986 - Directed by Tsui Hark and starring Brigitte Lin, Cherie Chung, Sally Yeh, Paul Chun, Wu Ma, and Kenneth Tsang in a tale of late Qing China, just before the Revolution. Told in three voices for varying perspectives and quite engaging. Bit about Chinese understanding democracy is quite funny.

The People vs. Larry Flynt —- 1996 - Directed by Milos Foreman, who knew a little about censorship, and starring a very talented cast, including Woody Harrelson and Ed Norton with an effective performance by Richard Paul as Jerry Falwell, the zealous Christian crusader, who tries to villify Flynt.

Pepe Le Moko (France) —-1937 - Directed by Julien Duvivier and starring Jean Gabin and Gabriel Gabrio as swarthy members of the underworld in the Casbah within Algiers. This classic noir is one of the granddaddies of noir. A must see.

Perfumed Nightmare – Philippines - 1977 - Directed by Kidlat Tahimik and starring an unknown cast of Philippine actors who do a great job under the guidance of the unheralded director. This story about a Filipino who has a dream to go to America, but becomes disillusioned on the way. Very good first effort.

Peter Pan -1953 - Produced by Walt Disney and starring Hans Conried as a delightful Captain Hook in the timeless tale of refusing to grow up and going to Never-Never Land. Disney always does it the best. Originally scheduled for release in the 1940s, but postponed because of WW2.

Petrified Forest – 1936 —- Directed by Archie Mayo and starring Bette Davis, Leslie Howard and Humphrey Bogart as Duke Mantee. You can always tell which actor steals a movie if it's the only character 's name in the movie you remember. Can anyone remember the name of any of the other characters in this film other than DUKE MANTEE? I think not. It is the breakthrough role of Bogart's career and he is fascinating to watch every second he is on screen.

Mayo gives us the feel that the film is mostly a stage production because well over 90% of the dialogue and action takes place in one room. As a matter of fact, this film is perfect for a stage production just because of that fact. Davis can never be ignored as an actress in almost every one of her films, but in this one, she is shackled by a hackneyed stereotype of a waitress in a diner that is in the middle of nowhere. How else could you play the role except as a woman who is desperate to get out of her situation? Leslie Howard gives us a philosophical performance where a man rises above the physical needs of this world in order to achieve a sort of nirvana.

I was not really a buyer for this line of thought, but Howard gives it the old college try. It is Bogart who dominates the movie in every frame he is in. The simple story has escapted con Bogart holding people hostage in a small café in the middle of nowhere until he can make his getaway. The production primarily takes place in one room and is perfect as material for a play, but is difficult to sustain unless you have meaningful dialogue, and this film had it in heaps. Delmar Daves and Steve Kenyon wrote a fabulous script for the actors based on the play by Robert E. Sherwood.

The film did not win any awards and perennial winner, Walter Brennan won for the forgettable *Come and Get it* in the Best Supporting Actor category. As much as I love Walter Brennan, his role could not hold a candle to Bogart's in this film as a supporting actor to Leslie Howard. Bogart literally overwhelms both Howard and Davis; no small task. Bogart was not even nominated for a Best Supporting Actor award. This is one of the greatest snubs in Hollywood history, and akin to Peter O'Toole being snubbed for Lawrence of Arabia. This is a must see film.

The Philadelphia Story - 1940 - Directed by George Cukor and starring Cary Grant, James Stewart, Ruth Hussey and Katherine Hepburn one of the greatest screwball comedies of all time about a society girl who gets to choose among three men. Every girl should be so lucky. By the way, James Stewart had as much of a chance against Cary Grant as I do.

Phantom Lady - 1944 - Directed by Robert Siodmak and starring Franchot Tone and a solid group of supporting B actors in a story about a falsely accused husband in the murder of his wife. There is more soap in this well-made noir than in a dead horse factory, but the direction is tight and the actors on cue.

The Phantom of the Opera - 1943 - Directed by Arthur Lubin and starring the incredibly bad Nelson Eddy with the incredibly good Claude Rains as the Phantom. Would have been better with Jeannette McDonald in Eddy's role. But Rains makes it all worthwhile.

Pi —1998 - Written, Directed and Produced by Darren Aronofsky in a spectacular directorial debut, as well as a mesmerizing screenplay debut. The group of C actors are irrelevant here as the story is everything, and the direction is impeccable. A must see to see how one should debut in the world of film.

The Pianist - 2002 - Directed by Roman Polanski (who atones for many of his past sins with this effort) and starring Adrien Brody in his academy-award winning role. This cast of relatively unknown actors carried off a great team effort to produce a first-rate film about the Warsaw ghetto and survival under the Nazis. A must see.

The Piano – A-1993 - Directed by Jane Campion and starring the unlikely duo of Holly Hunter and Harvey Keitel along with a solid performance by Sam Neill. This story of desperate love in an isolated land is one of the top soaps of all time. Great music as well.

Pickup on South Street - 1953 – Directed by Sameul Fuller and starring Richard Widmark, Jean Peters and Thelma Ritter. Classic film noir with a tight story. A pickpocket picks the wrong pocket and now has a microfilm wanted by the commies. The scene with Thelma Ritter and the commie spy is especially chilling.

Picnic at Hanging Rock- Australia – 1975 - Directed by Peter Weir and starring a relatively unknown Australian cast of B actors. The story, however, is so strong and the direction is so tight, that the film reaches very high levels of suspense, but ultimately cannot satisfy the great expectations it arouses in the viewer. Still, very good movie-making. My first ever paid movie review.

The Pink Panther -1964 – Directed by Blake Edwards and starring Peter Sellers, David Niven, Robert Wagner and Claudia Cardinale. This crew teams up to make a first-rate spy spoof that was so good, that they had to make a half dozen sequels.

Pinocchio -1940 - Produced by the Walt Disney Studios shortly before World War 2 and rereleased on several occasions since. This story of a wooden toy that wants to become a real boy at any cost is one the best Disney productions of all time. A must see.

Pixote – Brazil -1981 - Directed by Hector Babenco and starring an unknown cast of Brazilian actors armed with a dynamite script and story line. This tragic story about the survival of a young boy in a reform school that is worse than some prisons is powerful stuff. Not for the squeamish.

A Place in the Sun- 1951 - Directed by George Stevens and starring Montgomery Clift, Elizabeth Taylor and an underweight Shelley Winters, who went on a crash diet for this film so she could fit in the rowboat scene without sinking it. This film has more soap in it than a Chinese laundry. Who wouldn't kill Winters to get Taylor? Let him off with community service.

Places in the Heart -1984 - Directed by Robert Benton and starring Sally Field, John Malkovich, Ed Harris and Amy Madigan along with Danny Glover and Lindsay Crouse in a soap to end all soaps with a half dozen solid actors. Not appropriate for those on insulin or afflicted with diabetes.

The Plainsman - 1936 - A Cecil B Demille spectacular about the Old West starring Gary Cooper and Jean Arthur along with Charles Bickford and a sold supporting cast. This Western actioner suffers a bit from being dated, but the action isn't dated.

Planet of the Apes -1968 - Directed by Franklin J Schaffner and starring Charlton Heston and Roddy McDowell in classic roles. Kim Hunter and James Whitmore add to the production values. The extremely original story line came compliments of Rod Serling, one of greatest sci-fi writers of all time and the host of Twilight Zone. This is the granddaddy of all the Ape films.

Platoon- 1986 – Written and directed by Oliver Stone; this became the film that epitomized the Vietnam War along with *Apocalypse Now*. The stars of the film all give strong performances, including Tom Berenger as the brutal Barnes, Willem Dafoe as the Jesus-figure, Elias, who allows himself to suffer for the sins of others, and is the first major film for Charlie Sheen as Chris. It was quite a coincidence that Sheen's father was the star of *Apocalypse Now*, the other great film about Vietnam. Oliver Stone, a

Vietnam veteran himself, had been trying to get this story to the screen for years. Stone directs the film with absolute authenticity and fearlessness. There is not a tepid scene in the entire film. He does not just make a movie; he grabs you by the throat and says here, you want to see what it's like to be in Vietnam? Try this on for size. Stone's moviemaking style is a take-no-prisoners approach to the story; the characters remain secondary.

And yet, it is the characters we remember the most instead of the story. Berenger gives the best performance of his career in this film, and Dafoe does as well. Some might argue that Dafoe's next Christ-like role in *The Passion of the Christ* was his best role, but that would be a very close call. Charlie Sheen, who generally does a good job as Chris, eventually becomes a better actor in films like Wall Street. The story is riveting. It is about a cherry (slang name for a new Vietnam replacement) who joins a combat-hardened team.

Elias tries to maintain his ethics and dignity, while Barnes completely abandons any form of social responsibility or behavior. Chris always seems to be in the middle of these opposite ends of the moral spectrum. The supporting cast for this film is loaded with recognizable names; John C. McGinley, who went on to make many more films, did a great job in this one, as did a young Forrest Whitaker. Also making appearances in the film were Johnny Depp before he grew his scissors, and Kevin Dillon as Bunny, a mindless brute in the same vein as Barnes. The music for the film, which is the haunting classical piece, *Adagio for Strings*, only heightens the tragic elements of the screen. The photography and dialogue are first-rate and this is still, in my opinion, the best film that Stone has ever done.

The Player -1992 - Directed by Robert Altman, so you know there will be a few loose ends, and starring Tim Robbins, Fred Ward, Whoopi Goldberg and Vincent D'Onafrio in key roles in a story about a corrupt movie exec and the cutthroat competition of the movie business. Actually, for an Altman film, this one is fairly neatly tied together.

Play It Again, Sam — 1972 - Directed, written and starring Woody Allen as a putz who tries to imitate Humphrey Bogart in Casablanca in order to impress his dates. Unfortunately, he cannot even control his hairdryer, much less his love life. One of earlier, funnier Allen films.

Play Misty For Me -1971 - Directed and starring Clint Eastwood in his first film as a director and it is highly successful. Eastwood shows the pacing and touch in this film that will lead to many successes in the future. Jessica Walter plays his number one fan. You know, the kind of number one fan James Caan had in *Misery*.

Point Break – 2015 – Directed by Ericson Core and starring mostly an unknown group of B actors. The star of this film is the photography and action stunts, all of which are first-rate. A real eye-candy movie you don't have to think too hard about.

Police Academy - 1984 - Directed by Hugh Wilson and starring a group of B actors who engage in various outrageous forms of slapstick comedy and adult situations. Purely for adolescent enjoyment, and the granddaddy of seven

Police Academy - 1984 - Directed by Hugh Wilson and starring a group of B actors who engage in various outrageous forms of slapstick comedy and adult situations. Purely for adolescent enjoyment, and the granddaddy of seven sequels; all pretty much the same film. This first one, however, is the funniest.

Poltergeist - 1982 - Directed by Tobe Hooper and starring Craig Nelson and Jobeth Williams in a Spielberg production that was not quite as scary as some other films of the same era, but it still did well at the box office. The TV scene is very good, and the actors are convincing. Better than average.

Pony Soldier – 1952 – Directed by Joseph M. Newman and starring Tyrone Power in the lead role in a story about a Northwest Mountie who has to stop the Cree tribe from crossing in to Montana and hunting buffalo there. Modern audiences will now be sympathetic with the Indians.

The Posiedon Adventure – 1972 - Directed by Ronald Neame and starring Gene Hackman, Ernest Borgnine, Red Buttons, Shelley Winters, Roddy McDowell, Stella Stevens and a serious Leslie Neilson, who fortunately dies very early in the film. A little known fact about the actual cause of the ship turning upside down is when Shelley Winters got up for a midnight snack and fell down the stairs causing the ship to overturn.

Posse – 1975 – Directed by Kirk Douglas and starring Kirk as well along with Bruce Dern for support. This story of a posse chasing an outlaw is unbelievably mundane and had been done 100 times already. However, Kirk knew that not every film can be *Spartacus*. Still entertaining.

Possessed - 1931 - Directed by Clarence Brown and starring Clark Gable and Joan Crawford in perhaps the best of all the Gable and Crawford films about a poor factory girl who runs away to New York City to have a better life. This film was greatly influenced by the Depression and the audiences of the US immediately identified with Crawford (especially the women).

The Postman Always Rings Twice- 1946 - Directed by Tay Garnett and starring John Garfield and a smoking hot Lana Turner in one of the great icons of noir. This story of lust, ambition, murder and final reckoning is a classic in just about every way. A must see.

Prairie Home Companion - 2006 - Directed by Robert Altman, who sometimes gets out of control with his ensemble pieces, and starring an all-star cast (which is typical for Altman). This loving piece is about the old days of radio shows and the various forms of entertainment they provided. Altman does a solid job with this one and the end result is very satisfying.

Predator - 1987 - Directed by John McTierman and starring Governor Arnold in the lead role of a special forces operative intent on rescuing hostages, but runs into a space-age hunter of humans who are capable of fighting back. Decent sci-fi and good action sequences make this movie well worth watching.

The President's Analyst - 1967 - Directed by Theodore J. Flicker and starring James Coburn as the psychiatrist of the US President. An interesting, but silly, premise, is still entertaining because of the good screenplay supplied by the director himself. Coburn does a good job with the highly unlikely situations.

Pretty Baby - 1978 - Directed by Louis Malle and starring Brooke Shields, Keith Carradine and Susan Sarandon in the most expensive sexploitation film made since *Candy* in the late sixties. The hype for this film was much more than the actual content, but the casual viewer will still be fascinated by the proceedings.

Pretty Poison - 1968 - Directed by Noel Black and starring the attractive duo of Anthony Perkins and Tuesday Weld. The film is a bit of a shocker and in the mold of *Fatal Attraction*, although Weld could never be as crazy as Glen Close. Certainly worth watching.

Pride of the Marines- 1946 - Directed by Delmer Daves and starring John Garfield and Eleanor Parker in the lead roles in a story of one marine's life before, during and after WW 2 and the Battle of Guadalcanal. Poster gives the impression of a musical, but the film is far from that.

The Pride of the Yankees - 1942 - Directed by Sam Wood and starring Gary Cooper as Lou Gehrig. Best baseball movie of all time (with the possible exception of *Field of Dreams*).

The Prisoner of Second Avenue - 1975 - Directed by Melvin Frank and starring Jack Lemmon and Anne Bancroft as two typical New Yorkers who have to deal with the myriad of problems of living in New York City (before the Giuliani improvements). Very funny and true to life in many situations. Proves New York is a great place to visit ,but......

The Prisoner of Shark Island –1936 - Directed by Western expert John Ford, and starring Warner Baxter and Gloria Stuart in a tale about the doctor who treated John Wilkes Booth's broken leg. Dr. Mudd was arrested and sent to the American version of Devils Island. The term "your name is Mudd" comes from that incident. Eventually pardoned. Good stuff.

Prisoners of the Sun – 1990 – Directed by Steven Wallace and starring Russell Crowe and George Takei (TV Star Trek) in a story about a Japanese POW camp for Australians featuring one of the earliest appearances of Crowe. Not bad.

Prisoner of War – 1954 – Directed by Andrew Marton and starring none other Ronald Reagan and other B actors in a rather lame rendition of POWS during WW2. Not quite up to Stalag 17 or other good POW films, but fun to watch Ron.

The Prisoner of Zenda - 1937 - Directed by John Cromwell and starring Ronald Colman and a fine supporting cast including David Niven without his moustache. This story about subbing for a King by being his double is always a great treat, either as a book or a film. Anthony Hope wrote the novel.

Private Benjamin – 1980 - Directed by Howard Zieff and starring a positively hilarious Goldie Hawn as Private Benjamin, a spoiled American princess who joins the Army for all the wrong reasons and winds up learning how to become a responsible woman. A must see.

Private Hell 36 - 1954 - Directed by Don Siegel and starring Ida Lupino, Howard Duff (a frequent costar), Dean Jagger, and Dorothy Malone in a tale about good cops going bad and a greedy night club singer who makes things even worse. Great noir.

The Private Life of Henry VIII - 1933 - Directed by Sir Alexander Korda and starring Charles Laughton in the lead role of Henry VIII. This was the first British production to win the Best Picture award at the Academy Awards. The British would go on to win more Best Picture awards specializing in Shakespeare and other classical material. The Private Life of Sherlock Holmes –B- 1970 - Directed by Billy Wilder and starring mostly B actors such as Christopher Lee working with an A script and director. The result is admirable and highly enjoyable for the viewer. There are two separated vignettes about Holmes and both are quite entertaining.

Private's Progress – England - 1956 - Directed by John Boulting, of the cinematic British family of Boulting, known for high quality on various efforts. The film is not your usual physical slapstick farce about military life, but a pretty funny scam carried off by one of the more enterprising members of His Majesty's troops.

Prizzi's Honor – 1985 -Directed by John Huston and starring Jack Nicholson and Kathleen Turner in a comedy about a mafia figure and his romantic interest. I am sure Richard Condon found the Mafia to be hilarious in his book and this film is pretty funny, but none of it is too realistic. Good fantasy.

The Producers – 1968 - Directed by Mel Brooks and Starring Zero Mostel as Max Bialystock, the producer and Gene Wilder as Leo Bloom, the accountant. This film was written by Mel Brooks and most critics consider it to be the best comedy in the history of film. It was the only time my brother was right about a film being the best of its genre. It has been reproduced as a film and as a Broadway play, both of which were very successful. Brooks keeps the action rolling at a frantic pace and the jokes come so quickly that we do not get all of them upon the first viewing.

But that is not a problem, because most people I know have seen this film at least twice. It seems to get better with each viewing. Mostel is perfectly cast as an unscrupulous producer and seducer of old women for their investment money. Wilder is absolutely perfect with both his character and his timing. The two make a formidable team, although they never made another movie together and were alleged not to like each other personally. Mel Brooks considers this film script the best he has ever written (although some would say *Young Frankenstein* was his best). The music and lyrics are unforgettable for such numbers as *Springtime for Hitler in Germany*. This movie was not even remotely PC by today's standards, but almost no one complained because the finished product was hilarious.

The supporting cast includes Kenneth Mars as a former nazi who is a playwright, Christopher Hewett, as Roger DeBris, a well-out-of-the-closet queen, who also happens to be a director in his spare time, and Dick Shawn as the very funny Lorenzo St. Dubois, the lead actor of the play. The plot is so outrageous, you begin to laugh just talking about it. A failing producer needs a sure-fire flop in order to keep the money from his investors.

Bialystock generally fleeces old ladies looking for a little companionship. He gives each one 50% until he has sold about 25,000% of the ownership of the play. This is, of course, illegal and a plan concocted by the naïve Leo Bloom, the creative accountant, who becomes an accomplice of Bialystock in order to make a quick profit. Bloom was only being theoretical, but Bialystock goes for the gold. In the process, they select what may have been the worst musical play ever submitted for use, *Springtime for Hitler in*

Germany, a musical depicting the last days of Hitler and Eva Braun, his mistress. How could a play like that last for more than one night? Well, it does, and now the boys are in hot water. This is a must see film.

The Professional -1994 - Directed by Luc Besson and starring Jean Reno in an electric, breakthrough performance as Leon (the name the film is known as in the rest of the world. The story about a hit man who adopts a young girl and then protects her is irresistible.

The Professionals - 1966 - Directed by Richard Brooks and starring Burt Lancaster, Lee Marvin, Woody Strode and Robert Ryan. Jack Palance, Ralph Bellamy and Claudia Cardinale add to the substantial production values, which are first-rate. Great actioner.

Prometheus – 2012 - Directed by Ridley Scott and starring B actors with an unusual script and top production values (including the director). This formula has worked several times in the past; most notably with Alfred Hitchcock, for whom actors were merely props for his stories and good production values. Promises much more than it delivers on the origin of mankind.

The Proud Ones - Mexico - 1953 - Directed by Robert G. Webb and starring Robert Ryan, Virginia Mayo and Jeffrey Hunter. Fun Western made on a cheap budget gets the nod because of the great cast and good script.

Psycho – 1960 - Directed by Alfred Hitchcock and starring Janet Leigh and Anthony Perkins with a great supporting job by Martin Balsam. This ground-breaking film was shot in black and white during a time when most films were being done in color. Hitchcock instinctively knew that shooting in black and white could often be much scarier than scenes that were filmed in color. The atmosphere of the film is often even creepier than Perkins.

There are very few, if any, directors who can hold the suspense in a film as well as Hitchcock. It is true he uses actors as props that are secondary to the story, but the actors here do a great job of moving the story along. Janet Leigh does a nicely understated job of a woman thief who steals money from an insurance company in Phoenix and runs away on the road. Her character is almost sympathetic; we want her to get away with her crime, but it is not to be. Martin Balsam is always very convincing in any role he tackles as a second banana, and this role as an investigator is no different. He gets tantalizingly close to solving the mystery before he meets his untimely end.

Of course, this is the role that made Anthony Perkins' career and you will see why when you see the film. The story is very offbeat. It is about a woman who steals money from a company in Phoenix and then rides off into the middle of nowhere is interesting in and of itself. Finding a motel in the middle of nowhere, she stops for a breather and a shower (one you will never forget). Perkins, character, Norman Bates, seems about as harmless as one could be; but we find out he has gone completely around the bend. In the interim, one has to marvel at how the detective, Martin Balsam, is able to track down the thief to the Motel.

The other major character in the film is Norman Bates' mother, who I am sure you will remember for a long time after the film. The sets for this film were eerie and disturbing and the quicksand location is letter-perfect, as is the set for Norman Bates' mother's house. It is truly amazing to see a master of film take an interesting story line and turn it into a masterpiece through skillful direction. Perkins, of course, runs away with the film, and it seemed at the time it was released that Perkins would be a major actor with many other great roles to be added to his future, but that, sadly, was not to be. This film was the zenith of Perkins' career and he never made another film anywhere nearly as good. This film was made for less than one million dollars and made well over a hundred times its cost.

PT 109- 1963 – Directed by Leslie H. Martinson and starring Cliff Robertson as John F. Kennedy as a young man in the US Navy during World War 2. Robertson, as always, does a convincing job as JFK and the story of his adventure in Japanese waters is pretty engaging. However, if it were not JFK, the film would not be here.

The Public Enemy - 1931 - Directed by William Wellman and starring James Cagney and Jean Harlow as a red-hot couple on the wrong side of the law. This film was a sensation when it first hit the screen. A little dated now, but still a powerful story.

Pulp Fiction - 1994 - Directed by Quintin Tarantino and starring John Travolta, Samuel L Jackson, Uma Thurman, Harvey Keitel, and a slew of other stars anxious to be in a cool Tarantino film. Tarantino, who does great satire on a genre that is quite deserving of satire, makes his masterpiece with this film. It will be the one he is remembered for.

Punchline —1988 - Directed by David Seltzer and starring Sally Field (who is actually not very funny in her performance) and Tom Hanks (who is hilarious in his performance) as two struggling stand-up comedians in NYC. The film shows that stand-up is definitely not a parttime job, as is writing, acting or any other creative process. Very funny.

The Purple Plain – England - 1954 - Directed by Robert Parish and starring Gregory Peck in a tale of World War 2 and a chain of unfortunate events surrounding a Canadian pilot in Burma near the end of the war who has lost his wife in the Blitz in England.

The Purple Rose of Cairo - 1985 - Written and directed by Woody Allen in a rare film that does not include him in the cast. The screenplay is very creative and the actors, including Mia Farrow, Jeff Daniels and Danny Aiello, give nice performances. Ultimately, the film is a tragedy.

Pursued - 1947 - Directed by Raoul Walsh and starring Robert Mitchum and Teresa Wright in one of her last starring roles. This story of mass murder and revenge is a bit on the violent side, but entertaining because of the superior black and white photography by one of the best, James Wong Howe.

Pyaasa – 1953 – India – Directed by Guru Dutt and starring Guru Dutt in the lead role as an unfortunate man stuck in an insane asylum who is apparently sane and cannot prove his identity. A fascinating look at old methods of institutionalization.

Pygmalion - 1938 - Directed by Anthony Asquith and starring Leslie Howard and Wendy Hiller in the original film version of George Bernard Shaw's play. The musical play and film made many years later were even more successful. The story of a poor, unrefined girl turned into a society woman by a professor is very entertaining.

1331

Q

Queen Christina - 1933 - Directed by Rouben Mamoulian and starring Greta Garbo and John Gilbert along with a solid supporting cast. This story of a royal romance that must be made a secret from the public is a sure crowd-pleaser. Garbo at her best here.

Quest For Fire – 1981 - Directed by Jean-Jacques Annaud and starring a relatively unknown group of actors that depict the discovery and preservation of fire. Quite impressive and realistic and handled very well by the director.

The Quiet Man - 1952 - Directed by Directed by John Ford and starring John Wayne, Maureen O'Hara, Barry Fitzgerald, Ward Bond and Victor McLaglen (the usual suspects in most Ford productions). This story about a an Irish romance and brawling would be considered sterotypical now, but still entertaining.

Quiz Show - 1994 - Directed by Robert Redford (and quite deftly so) and starring Ralph Fiennes, John Turturro and Paul Schofield in the sensational story about the fixing of a major quiz show in the 1950s. Schofield is letter-perfect as the Columbia professor father and Turturro does the best work of his career in this film.

Quo Vadis - 1951 - Directed by Mervyn LeRoy and starring Robert Taylor, Deborah Kerr, and Peter Ustinov in a story about the excesses of Rome under Nero and how the Christians suffered so mightily for their faith. All very inspiring, along with good production values and great music. (at least the lions in this film looked more realistic than the Pookie lion in *Demetrius and the Gladiators*).

R

Racing With the Moon -1984 - Directed by the talented Richard Benjamin and starring Sean Penn and Nicolas Cage in a poignant story about friends who signed up for military duty and the using the time they have left before they have to go. Millions of Americans have experienced these emotions.

The Rack - 1956 - Directed by Arnold Laven and starring a decent cast of Paul Newman, Walter Pidgeon, Edmond O'Brien, Anne Francis (miscast here) and Lee Marvin (perfect). Wendell Corey is also featured, but is totally unconvincing. The story of how responsible a POW should be under harsh treatment has evolved over time. The conclusions reached in this film that POWs should suffer in silence is fairly ridiculous.

The Racket - 1951 - Directed by John Cromwell and starring Robert Mitchum as a police captain and Lizabeth Scott as a hot night club singer (not much of a stretch there). Robert Ryan is also featured as the heavy who is an underworld figure. Your usual good guys/bad guys cop movie. Might have been better if roles were reversed.

Radio Days - 1987- Directed and narrated by Woody Allen and one of his few films that he does not appear in. The film stars his former wife, Mia Farrow, Diane Weist, Danny Aiello, Jeff Daniels and Tony Roberts. The film is a faithful reenactment of radio in the late forties after the war; just before the explosion of TV.

Raging Bull – 1980 - Directed by Martin Scorsese and starring Robert DeNiro in a tour de force performance as Jake Lamotta. Many consider this film to be the best work that Scorsese ever accomplished.

Raiders of the Lost Ark – 1981 - Directed by Steven Spielberg and starring Harrison Ford as Indiana Jones. Karen Allen is the love interest prop for this film. This is the first of many successful Indiana Jones adventures; all of which made a load of money at the box office. The first of almost any series of films is usually the best and this is the case with this series. The actors play their roles straight; I really loved the Gestapo Major Toht character played to the hilt by Ronald Lacey, who replaced Klaus Kinski. Kinski had a very low opinion of the script and turned it down. That was always a problem with Kinski; he was a cinematic snob, who is now not really known for any particular role (with the possible exception of *Aguirre: The Wrath of God*). Even Karen Allen is passable in this movie.

Ford, of course, will always be known for this role and his Star Wars character, Hans Solo. How odd that he went virtually unnoticed in his first big role in *Apocalypse Now* a few years earlier. The story overwhelms the characters in its richness and breakneck pace, ably handled by Spielberg without missing a beat. Although all the Nazis are bad and every philosophical situation in the film is clearly black and white, we dismiss the realities of real war and just get comfortable rooting for the good guys to beat the bad guys. The music and cinematography are of the highest levels and the action sequences are classics. The story begins at a leisurely pace and then grinds up to an incredible speed. The main character might have been aptly named Indy 500 instead of Jones.

Railroaded! - 1947- Directed by Anthony Mann, an A director, but with a B cast and script. The film stars John Ireland and Hugh Beaumont of *Leave It to Beaver* fame. The plot is rather mundane, but the direction is very good, so it is entertaining.

Railway Man – 2014 - Directed by Jonathon Teplitsky and starring Colin Firth and Nicole Kidman in the lead roles. A man tormented in a Japanese prisoner of war camp finds his tormentor after the war. An interesting premise, and good insight into the insensitivity of Japan and Japanese soldiers in World War Two.

Rain - 1932- Directed by Lewis Milestone and starring a very hot Joan Crawford as the hooker Sadie Thompson and Walter Huston the religious zealot who torments her. But Somerset Maugham, the writer of the piece, has a few surprises for the viewer. Good stuff.

Rain Man – 1988 - Directed by Barry Levinson and starring Dustin Hoffman and Tom Cruise. This film won best picture for 1988 as well as the best actor award for Hoffman, best screenplay and best director for Levinson. The movie is about a savant, Raymond, played by Hoffman, who is an unusual mix of a genius and a person with mental disabilities. His brother, Charlie, a selfish yuppie, comes to know of his existence only after he finds out his father left Raymond all his money.

   The bonding of the two is the essence of the film and the various sequences of Raymond's powers are real eye-openers. Hoffman gives us a tour-de-force acting demonstration "Judge Wapner, five o'clock", "I'm a good driver", and various other lines from his character have entered into the lexicon of the American language. Tom Cruise, for whom I have very little respect for as an actor, tries his very best to keep up with Hoffman, but it is a losing battle. I would say this was still the best effort of his entire acting career, despite being overwhelmed by the Hoffman character. The director does a wonderful job of slowly molding the bonding process between the two dissimilar brothers and the pacing of the film is excellent. The casino sequence is hilarious. . This is truly a fascinating film. This is a must see movie and is on practically every top 100 films of all-time list of most critics.

Raise the Red Lantern (China) - 1991 – Directed by Zhang Yimou and starring Gong Li as Songlian, third concubine to a wealthy businessman. Gong Li is sensational in this film and Zhang Yimou is at the top of his game in directing her in this role. This film is among the best films ever made in China and is always ranked in the top ten best Chinese films of all time. Somehow, it did not win the best foreign film award for 1992, losing to the good, but not great, *Indochine*, due in part by sympathy for Catherine Denueve, who was far better known to audiences than was Gong Li at this time. The snub did not change the popularity of the Zhang film, however, which has outsold *Indochine* over the years by a wide margin as a DVD. This is a must see film and is listed on several critics' top 100 films of all time lists.

Raising Arizona – 1987- Directed by the maniacal Coen Brothers and starring a perfectly cast Nicholas Cage and Holly Hunter as a redneck couple trying to make ends meet by any means necessary. Very funny stuff.

Ran – Japan – 1985- Directed by Akira Kurosawa and starring a cast of thousands as they would say in the good old days. There are literally thousands of extras in this visually sumptuous extravaganza filmed by one of the best in the business. The power struggle of Shoguns is a must-see film.

Rancho Notorious- 1952 - Directed by Fritz Lang and starring Marlene Dietrich, Arthur Kennedy, and Mel Ferrer in a story about Western sleazeballs and a man who seeks revenge against them. Interesting to see how Lang handles the Western genre.

Random Harvest- 1939 - Directed by Mervyn LeRoy and starring two heavyweights, Ronald Colman and Greer Garson. This is a two hanky primo soap. Not to be missed, even by those who are not big fans of soap. The film will grab you from beginning to end.

The Rapture – 1991 - Directed by Michael Tolkin and starring Mimi Rogers and David Duchovny of *X-Files* fame. This a religious cult film with all the bells and whistles. For those of you curious about the hereafter, this film may have extra value. Interesting. .

Rashomon (Japan) – 1950 - One of best foreign films of all time and the best Japanese film of all time was directed by Akira Kurosawa and starring Toshiro Mifune. It was the first film in history to have three alternate endings within the same film. The mystery is to be able to tell which one of the three versions is correct. An American version of the film, *The Outrage*, with Paul Newman, was shot many years later, but did not have much box office success.

This is the defining role of Mifune's acting career. Kurosawa is primarily known in the West for this film and the *Seven Samurai* (which was the basis for the greatest American Western film ever made, *The Magnificent Seven*). Each primary actor in the film had to play three versions of the same character. One version was the character as they saw themselves in the incident, the second version was how the other primary actors saw them in the incident and the third version, which was the most complex of all, was the truth and what the characters really did. Kurosawa had to direct all three versions of the same sequence quite differently since each of the major players had different versions of their personality in each sequence.

It took a sure-handed director to pull off such a tricky stunt and Kurosawa was up to the challenge. This is a film you could watch without subtitles or knowing a word of Japanese and you would still be mesmerized by the film. This movie won a special honorary Academy Award in 1952.

Rasputin and the Empress - 1932 - Directed by Richard Boleslavsky and starring the Barrymores, Ethel, John and Lionel, along with a fine supporting cast in a story about the effect of a bizarre holy man and his relations with the Royal Family of the Russias. Takes liberties with some historical facts, but is still very entertaining.

The Rat Race- 1960 - Directed by Robert Mulligan and starring Tony Curtis, Debbie Reynolds and Don Rickles. The story has Curtis coming to New York to be a musician, but finds the going tougher than he imagined. He finds Reynolds in his life and complications for a good soap begin.

Raw Deal - 1948- Directed by the highly competent Anthony Mann and starring John Ireland and a solid supporting cast including Raymond Burr. This classic noir story is about a double-crossed con who escapes prison to run away to another country with his girlfriend. There is just one catch; he is in love with a social worker taken prisoner by his framer, a sadistic mob boss, wonderfully played by Burr.

Rawhide -1951- Directed by Henry Hathaway, a competent director, and starring Susan Hayward and Tyrone Power, who really did not do Westerns very well. This story of a stagecoach adventure and romance is good with Power, who is better in the saddle than he is in the saddle.

Ray - 2004- Directed by Taylor Hackford and starring Jamie Foxx as Ray Charles along with a competent supporting cast. This authorized biopic of Charles is not all sugar-coated and captures the essence of the man and his life. Highly recommended.

The Razor's Edge - 1946 - No, this is not a slasher film for you knuckleheads out there; this a serious Somerset Maugham novel adapted to the big screen with all the bells and whistles. The film stars Tyrone Power in the best role of his lifetime (unfortunately, he did not win an Academy Award for his performance) as Larry, a WW1 veteran, who rejects all the attractions of life in the upper classes and seeks the meaning of life. Also starring in the film are Gene Tierney, Clifton Webb, Anne Baxter (in another great role), and John Payne. This is a three-hanky special and has more soap in it than most better-known soaps. It is also a coffee-house film with a big budget; something you seldom see in today's big film market. One of my favorites.

The Reader - 2008- Directed by Stephen Daldry and starring Kate Winslet, Ralph Fiennes, and a solid supporting cast. David Kross also gives a promising performance in a key role. This tale of a Nazi camp worker who is later put on trial is fascinating and gives the black and white moral issues of nazis a bit of grey area. Engrossing.

The Real Glory – 1939 – Directed by Henry Hathaway and starring Gary Cooper and David Niven. This is a tale of American colonialism in the Philippines. At the time of its release, audiences were inclined to root for the Americans, but modern political developments have made this type of film unpopular with audiences, as more educated viewers now consider foreign interventions to be a thing of the past. Also, this film came out in 1939, which, if not the greatest Hollywood year for good films, is very close to the top year and this film was lost in that landslide of superior films. Still interesting to view from a historical perspective, however.

Rear Window – 1954 - Directed by Alfred Hitchcock and starring James Stewart, Grace Kelly, Thelma Ritter, and Raymond Burr. This was the first and last time Hitchcock used Wendell Corey; for good reason. Corey was a problematic actor from the period who was not strong enough for lead roles and not very noticeable in supporting ones. Burr, on the other hand, was terrific. This story of a peeping tom who gets more than he bargains for is a classic.

Rebecca – 1940 - Directed by Alfred Hitchcock and starring Laurence Olivier and Joan Fontaine in one of the few condensed soaps created by the master of suspense. The effort to make this simple story into a spectacular blockbuster really does not work very well, but audiences of the 30's had no TV and there were no soaps on during the daytime, so this film was very popular at the box. These days, it would be considered to be a bit heavy-handed and over the top. Still, a very interesting work.

Rebel Without a Cause - 1955 – Directed by Nicholas Ray and starring James Dean and Natalie Wood. This is the film that made James Dean an icon in American film. He died in a car accident only one month before the film was released. That aside, this is easily one of the most overrated films in American history. In addition, James Dean is easily one of the most overrated actors in the history of American film.

He was believable at times, but most of the time, he came across as a whiny, spoiled little brat who had very little to do with the mainstream of the American public. In most of the families I observed growing up in the poorer section of town, you didn't buy your kid a car (you made them work for it). You also made sure your kids worked from an early age to understand the importance of a dollar. This film shows none of those family values. You will see much more realistic teenage rebel stuff about adult passage in *The 400 Blows*.

The film is about two teenagers who have trouble accepting their roles in society. They want more excitement and want to free. Free to love, run wild and do what they want. In other words, the film is about the typical teenager's yearning to break free from the control of their parents. Sometimes parents exert a gentle touch with teens growing up and, as in this case, sometimes they spoil them so much, that they begin to think they are self-sufficient adults. Who paid for the car this young teen was driving? Who paid for his clothes, food and housing? His parents paid, of course. But some teens think they are entitled to all of these things and more, so they contradict the wishes of their parents for simple things like going to school or getting a job.

This film does not explore those possibilities, it merely shows the black and white, the good and bad of the mean old parents and the poor, unfortunate teens, who have to drive around and go anywhere they want. They truly are rebels without a clue. Working for a living would have wised them up a lot faster. As a film, the character of Jim is interesting, but dated. and so is the character of Sal Mineo, who does a nice turn in the film. Judy, played by Natalie Wood, could have been played by any airhead teen from the fifties, but she at least adds some substance to the typical female mannequin of the late fifties. This is a liberal's coming-out party. Some of the scenes are overbearing and hammy, but it is fascinating to watch the development of Dean as an actor and it was tragic that he died at such an early age. This film is often included in many critics' top 100 films of all time, but for me, it barely makes the top 2000 and is more of a visual oddity.

The Red Badge of Courage -1951 - directed by John Huston and starring Audie Murphy and a solid supporting cast in the classic story by Stephen Crane about the necessity of all young men to prove themselves in battle in order to gain social acceptance. The film shows the hypocritical attitudes of those who judge courage according to the ability to wage war. A good lesson why all wars are a complete waste of time

Red Beard – 1965 –Japan - Directed by Akira Kurosawa and starring his number one tool, Toshiro Mifune in the lead role in one of the better Kurosawa films about a doctor in a rural village who teaches a younger doctor some tips on reality.

Red Cliff (China) - 2008 - Directed by John Woo, Takeshi Kaneshiro, Zhang Fengyi, Chang Chen, Lin Chi-Ling, Zhao Wei, and Hu Jun in a modern treatment of the classic tale of The Romance of Three Kingdoms. Not exactly historically correct, but great cinema because of the production values and great cast.

Red Dust - 1932 - Directed by Victor Fleming and starring Clark Gable and Jean Harlow as two people thrown together in an exotic location far from their original homes. In real life, Gable and Harlow were an item and you can see the chemistry up there on the big screen. Triangle with Mary Astor, a high class broad, makes things a bit interesting. Great soap.

The Red House - 1947 - Directed by Delmer Davies and starring Edward G Robinson in one of his creepier roles as a disabled farmer trying to hold on to his adopted daughter who has a new boyfriend. Intentionally atmospheric, and achieves more than it sets out to do. Good to see Robinson in a different role.

Red River – 1948 - Directed by Howard Hawks and starring John Wayne, Montgomery Clift, Walter Brennan and Joanne Dru in tale of adventure and romance in the old West. This film had a problem with Clift, who supposedly had a fight with John Wayne. You would have to have several drinks to believe that Clift would last thirty seconds in a fight with Wayne. Aside from that unbelievable scene, the film is done very well, just like *From Here to Eternity*, when Clift again was forced to do romantic and fight scenes that were totally unbelievable. Hawks wisely cut all of the romantic scenes with Clift very short. Still, a great Western.

The Red Shoes – 1948-Directed by Michael Powell, so you know the film will be visually stunning. and starring Moira Shearer, miscast as a ballet dancer (take a look at that poster and tell me you think that this full-bodied woman is a top ballerina), Anton Walbrook and Marius Goring also star in this sumptuously-filmed masterpiece. As good as The Turning Point, another well-made ballet film.

Reds – 1981 - Directed by Warren Beatty and starring Diane Keaton and Jack Nicholson along with Beatty and a superb supporting cast. This film about the most prominent American communist in Russian history makes for interesting viewing. Engaging, despite its left-wing tilted philosophy. ten lists as well.

The Red Violin – 1999 - Canadian classic directed by Francois Gerard is perhaps the best film ever made in the history of Canada. It stars Carlo Cecchi and Jean-Luc Bideau as owners and players of the famous "Red" violin. Samuel L. Jackson also does a very neat turn in the film as a purchaser for a major auction house that is buying a large collection of violins that had been kept safe by a dedicated Chinese musician during the *Cultural Revolution*, when groups of ignorant students in China were going around the countryside destroying anything older than themselves. The mystery of the plot is how the violin got its red color and the plot is ingenious.

The movement of the violin from country to country and continent to continent is breathtaking. The film moves as quickly as the violin and the passion of the filmmaker is almost as great as the creator of the violin, itself. The real star of the movie is not any of the actors, but the Red Violin. The violin survives a shot from a gun, terrible sea voyages, the Cultural Revolution in China, and a host of other adventures that are so unbelievable that they must be true.

The pace of the film is as quick as some of the authentic gypsy music that is in it and the photography is so lush, one wonders how many days each shot must have taken. There is truly not one dull second in this entire movie. It is an awe-inspiring film. It is on my top ten list of all time and on many other critic's top ten lists as well. . This film is a classic and highly recommended.

Reign of Terror – 1949- Directed by the capable Anthony Mann and starring the miscast Robert Cummings and Arlene Dahl in the lead roles. The story of the French Revolution and Reign of Terror is compelling, but not enough to overcome the miscasting of its two leading stars. The film is more for soap-lovers, but is still interesting to watch because of Mann's direction.

The Remains of the Day – 1993 - Directed by James Ivory and starring a restrained pair of excellent actors, Anthony Hopkins and Emma Thompson, both of whom can go over the top on occasion, but certainly not in this super-soap. A soap-lover's dream film about a restrained British relationship between two long-time house servants

Rembrandt -1936- Directed by Alexander Korda and starring Charles Laughton in the lead role. Laughton gives it his best shot, but the directing style of Korda is so classical, that the character becomes more sainted than realistic. Still interesting to watch.

Rendezvous 24 – 1946 - Directed by James Tinling and starring an unknown cast of B actors depicting the events of an East German underground movement against the Russians, who are now controlling the area. Because it was made in 1946, it has a great deal of authenticity.

Rendition- 2007 – Diurected by Gavin Hood and starring Reese Witherspoon and Jake Gyllenhaal in a tale about America's Islamophobia gone to extremes. The story is about an Aryan wife trying to track down her Egyptian husband (who must be terrorist, right?). The truth of the matter is,even if you are completely innocent of a crime or a terrorist plot; if you know someone who is a terrorist, you will be severely tested and questioned. A real ethics puzzle. Recommended.

Requiem for a Heavyweight – 1956- Directed by Ralph Nelson and starring Jackie Gleason, Mickey Rooney, and Julie Harris in supporting roles to Anthony Quinn, who plays Mountain Rivera, an over the hill heavyweight contender with a bit of talent. This film is the antithesis of Rocky, and nowhere nearly as exhilarating. However, it certainly hits the mark from the dramatic standpoint and is highly entertaining. First directed by Rod Serling of *Twilight Zone* fame on *Playhouse 90* years before.

Rescue Dawn - 2007 – Directed by Werner Herzog and starring Christian Bale as a pilot shot down in Laos (not in a war with the US at the time), and his struggles to get back to friendly lines back in Vietnam. Not the most sympathetic of characters, but interesting.

Resurrection – 1980 - Directed by Daniel Petrie and starring Ellen Burstyn as a crash survivor who develops an unusual capability as a result of her close call. Also starring Sam Shepard and a fine supporting cast. This piece of sci-fi certainly has its moments, but never seems to deliver all that it promises. Certainly worth viewing for Burstyn's performance.

The Return of Frank James- 1940 – Directed by Fritz Lang and starring Henry Fonda in the lead role assisted by Gene Tierney as the love interest. This Hollywood version of the surviving member of the James gang is fairly entertaining.

Return of the Jedi - 1983- Directed by Richard Marquand, who is not nearly as good a director as George Lucas, and starring the original stars of the first two films of the trilogy (that eventually became a lackluster double-trilogy later). Hamill proved to be a lightweight actor, as was Fisher, but Harrison Ford went on to have a sterling career. The third entry neatly ties up the first two (a bit too neatly) and everyone lives happily after. Still good viewing and a number of interesting scenes (not to mention better than all later three sequels).

The Return of The Man Called Horse – 1976 – Directed by Irvin Kershner and starring Richard Harris reprising his role as Horse, a white man adopted by an Indian tribe. In this sequel, Horse is bored being rich and successful and, oh so civilized. He longs to go back to the savagery of the West. Not too believable, but watchable.

Reuben, Reuben – 1983 - Directed by Robert Ellis Miller and starring Tim Conti in the lead role supported by the smoking hot Kelly McGillis, in a convoluted story about an alcoholic, deadbeat, overrated poet and the lives he unfortunately enters. Fortunately, the ending is extremely satisfying and worth viewing, as the majority of the audience gets its wish.

The Revenant – 2016 – Directed by Alejandro G Innarito and starring Leonardo DeCaprio in a rare convincing role as a hardy survivor. I've always wondered why he doesn't like bears, and now I know why. This tale of survival will grab you from beginning to end. Excellent filmmaking.

Reversal of Fortune – 1990- Directed by Barbet Schroeder and starring the perfectly cast duo of Jeremy Irons and Glen Close as the Von Bulows. There is also a nice turn by Ron \Silver as the defense attorney. Did Doc murder Sunny? Most likely. But the film certainly keeps you guessing right up the last minute. Recommended.

Rhapsody in Blue - 1945 - Directed by Irving Rapper and starring Robert Alda, Joan Leslie and Alexis Smith. The real star of the film, however, is the Gershwin score, which among the best ever in film. The Hollywood soap treatment of the script bears little resemblance to real life, however.

Richard III – 1956 - Directed and starring Laurence Olivier in the classic Shakespearean tale of diabolical connivance by a brother of the king who manages to wrest the throne away from not only his brother, but his other adversaries as well. Great direction and acting. A classic at all levels.

Rich Hill -2014 – Directed by the brother and sister team of Andrew Droz and Tracy Droz Tragos and starring the Jewell family of Missouri in the story of three boys growing up in poverty in rural Missouri. A subject seldom covered in film.

Rickshaw Boy (China) – 1982 - Directed by Ling Zifeng and starring Siqin Gaowa and Zhang Fengyi in a tragic story about a struggling rickshaw boy and the women who fall in love with him. This award-winning book by Lao She (sometimes confused with the ancient poet Laozi) fully captures the hopelessness of the underclass in China. Great viewing.

Ride Lonesome – 1959 - Directed by Budd Boetticher and starring Randolph Scott in a rather mundane story of transporting a criminal to justice. However, the introduction of three emerging stars of the sixties, Pernell Roberts of Bonanza, Lee Van Cleef of the Clint Eastwood Pepperoni Westerns, and James Coburn, soon to be a star in the Magnificent Seven, spice up the film.

Rider on the Rain – France - 1970 - Directed by Rene Clement and starring Charles Bronson in an offbeat role as a drifter who first picks up a lonely woman and terrorizes her. The supporting cast is relatively unknown, but does an effective job of bringing good tension to the screen.

Riding Shotgun – 1954 – Directed by Andre De Toth and starring Randolph Scott in the lead with an early appearance of Charles Bronson (*Magnificent Seven*). This Scott effort not as good as most of his others as a guard for stagecoach, but still entertaining.

Ride the High Country – 1962 - Directed by Sam Peckinpah and starring Randolph Scott and Joel McCrea as old friends on the opposite side of the law. The final confrontation will decide whether old friendships hold fast or whether money is more important. Good action.

Ride the Pink Horse – 1947 - Directed and starring Robert Montgomery along with a relatively unknown supporting cast in a story about a returning GI who is bent on avenging the death of his wartime buddy in a small town. Great atmosphere and a film noir classic.

Riding Alone For Thousands of Miles – China - 1985 - One of the lesser-known films directed by Zhang Yimou and starring Ken Takakura, a Japanese actor, in the lead role. This is one those family reunion films where the displaced missing father tries to reconnect with a son he has hardly known. Even though the plot is not very original, the cast pulls off the story with the help of Yimou.

Rififi – France - 1956 - Directed by Jules Dassin and starring Jean Servais, Carl Mohner and Robert Manuel along with a decent supporting cast. This is classic film noir with a great touch by the director in an extended sequence without dialogue or music. One feels like one of the thieves committing the jewel heist. Highly recommended.

The Right Stuff – 1983 - Directed by Philip Kaufman and starring an all-star cast including: Dennis Quaid, Fred Ward, Sam Shepherd, Ed Harris, Scott Glenn, Barbara Hershey, Lance Henriksen, Veronica Cartwright and Kim Stanley. This tale of the early American astronauts and their families is an iconic piece of American History. The music by Bill Conti is one of the best soundtracks for a film ever created. A must see.

Rio Bravo – 1959 - Directed by Howard Hawks and starring John Wayne, Angie Dickinson, Walter Brennan and Ward Bond. Also featured are two singers, Dean Martin and Ricky Nelson; neither of which are very convincing actors. There is plenty of action, though, to make up for the singing cowboys and Wayne always delivers. Worth watching.

Rio Grande – 1950- Directed by John Ford and starring many members of the usual troupe that acted for Ford, including John Wayne, Maureen O'Hara, Ben Johnson, Harry Carey Jr, Chill Wills, J Carrol Naish and, of course, Victor McLagen. This tale of reckless battles on the frontier of the American West has always been a crowd pleaser. Plenty of action.

Rise of the Planet of the Apes - 2011 – Directed by Rupert Wyatt and starring James Franco, Andy Serkis, David Olelowo and John Lithgow. Franco plays Will Rodman, a pharmaceutical engineer who is doing genetic research for a cutting edge drug company. He is desperately searching for a cure for Alzheimer's Disease which has afflicted his father, Charles, played wonderfully by John Lithgow. Franco does not go over the top and gives a very nice understated performance that fits in very nicely with the dramatic ape revolution which is the centerpiece of the film.

   Andy Serkis does a masterful job of playing the wunderkind ape, Caesar, who possesses not only superior skills to all other apes on the planet, but superior skills to most humans as well. I cannot remember a prequel that was as well-planned and executed as well as this film was. It is easily one of the best prequels ever. Making prequels is a tricky business. *Godfather 2* comes to mind as the best of all time in that category, but this one is almost as well done.

   A great supporting cast includes David Olelowo as the greedy, heartless manager of the genetics lab and Tom Felton as the cruel animal handler of the incarcerated apes. The action is almost non-stop once it gets rolling and the script is very tight. The dialogue treats its audience with intelligence rather than just trite throwaway lines. This is one of the biggest assets of the film. I can recommend this film as highly as any science-fiction film I have seen in recent memory and I have just about all of them.

Risky Business -1983 - Directed by Paul Brickman and starring Tom Cruise in a career-defining role as a spoiled young man who makes the most of his parents' wealth. An absolutely smoking hot Rebecca Demornay completely steals the film from Cruise (not easy to do) as a temptress supreme who complicates Tom's life.

The River's Edge - 1957 - Directed by someone named Allan Dwan (never to be heard of again) and starring a miscast Ray Milland, Anthony Quinn, and Debra Paget in your usual action triangle action film. The script and film would have worked much better with Quinn as the heavy and Milland as the good-guy rancher instead of the other way around. Still interesting.

River's Edge – 1987 - Directed by Tim Hunter and starring Crispin Glover, Keanu Reeves and Dennis Hopper along with a solid supporting cast. A group of teens finds out that one of their party is a murderer and the dynamic of how they handle that fact is fascinating.

The Road Home (China) – 1999- Directed by Zhang Yimou and starring Zhang Ziyi in her first major role, Sun Honglei,Zheng Hao and Zhao Yulian in a story about a country teacher and his effect on an entire community who honors him later in life. A good look at Chinese rural ethics and customs.

Road to Bali – 1952 - Directed by Hal Walker and starring the highly successful trio of Bing Crosby, Bob Hope and Dorothy Lamour in one of the most popular comedy troupes ever assembled. The stories were not really all that important, but the dialogue was hilarious and the interaction of Hope and Crosby is first-rate comedy.

Road to Hong Kong – 1962 - Lamely directed by Norman Panama and starring Bob Hope and Bing Crosby trying to make the sexy Joan Collins funny (they didn't succeed). This is the worst of all the road films because of the stereotypes shown in the film and a lame story line. But Hope and Crosby make it watchable.

Road to Morocco – 1942 - Directed by David Butler (as if the director of any of these road films matters; no one directed Hope and Crosby) and starring Bob Hope, Bing Crosby and Dorothy Lamour along with a nice piece of comedy by Anthony Quinn. Of course the plot is irrelevant; just enjoy the fun.

Road to Rio – 1947 - Directed by Norman Mcleod and starring Bob Hope, Bing Crosby and Dorothy Lamour in the fifth installment of this highly successful series of comedies. This one takes place in Brazil and the boys get to do a bit of dancing. Lots of fun as audiences never tired of this formula until the very last film in 1962.

Road to Singapore – 1940- Directed by Victor Schertzinger and starring Bing Crosby,Bob Hope, and Dorothy Lamour in the principal roles of the first road movie ever made. There would be many successful sequels to this successful debut. Lots of fun. Look for an early, tongue-in-cheek performance by Anthony Quinn.

Road to Utopia – 1946 - Directed by Hal Walker and starring Bob Hope, Bing Crosby and Dorothy Lamour in the fourth installment of the popular comedy series. Two Vaudeville performers go on a hunt for a gold mine. This plot actually won a Best Screenplay nomination at the Academy Awards for 1946! It was obviously a very weak year for writers.

Road to Zanzibar - 1941 - Directed by Victor Schertzinger and starring Bing Crosby, Bob Hope and Dorothy Lamour in the sequel to Road to Singapore, which had been very successful at the box office a few years earlier. This film was just as well-made and ensured a long line of future sequels.

Road to Perdition - 2002 - Directed by Sam Mendes and starring actor icons Tom Hanks and Paul Newman along with a nice turn by Jude Law in a story about the downfall of an Irish crime family during the early days of the Great Depression. Gorgeous cinematography that thoroughly deserved the Academy Award it won makes the production values top notch.

The Road Warrior (Austrailia) – 1982 - Directed by George Miller and starring Mel Gibson in a sequel that was far superior to the original Mad Max (this is usually not the case for the vast majority of sequels). George Miller would go on to become famous for his action sequences, many examples of which he demonstrates in arguably his best film ever. His sure hand in action sequences made him a director in high demand for hundreds of films whose primary attraction were action sequences Good action scenes equal money at the box office.

One only has to look at the inferior action films of Hong Kong that repeat the same action sequences over and over and yet still make millions of dollars. Miller was superior to those filmmakers by a mile. Gibson, on the other hand, though still pretty raw in the second Mad Max film, shows flashes of the future Mel Gibson with various mood swings within this movie. Gibson would go on to make dozens more action films in the future, but this was his baptism. The action sequences are spectacular and the music is pulsating. This is a must see film and listed on numerous top 100 lists throughout the film industry.

Roaring Across the Horizon (China) – 1999 - Directed by Chen Gaoxing and starring Lu Guangda, Li Youbin, General Feng Shi, and Li Xuejian in a documentary/propaganda film about the first nuclear weapon detonated by China in response to the US/Russia arms race. A really fascinating view into the mindset of the Chinese Communist Party at the time.

The Roaring Twenties - 1939 - Directed by Raoul Walsh and starring heavyweights James Cagney and Humphrey Bogart. Priscilla Lane is cast as the love interest. This gritty Warner Brothers release was a smash hit when it came out and made Bogart a big-time star. A classic.

RoboCop – 1987 - Directed by Paul Verhoven and starring Peter Weller (although you really don't get to see much of him) and a great turn by Ronny Cox as a sleazy corporate suit. This film was a big hit with audiences who literally cheered and applauded when Robocop laid into the crooks of Detroit. Law and order is alive and well in this flick.

Rocco and His Brothers – 1960 –Italy - Directed by Luchino Visconti and starring the smash debut of Alain Delon as Rocco, the youngest and most naive member of an Italian family trying to make it in the big city (Milan). Never a good thing when brothers love the same woman. Great directing and a classic piece of Italian neo-realism.

Rocketeer - 1991 - Directed by Joe Johnston and starring unknown Billy Campbell and an able supporting cast including Jennifer Connelly, Alan Arkin, Timothy Dalton and Paul Sorvino in a sci-fi tale about a young man who gets his hands on state of the art technology and turns himself into a superhero. Great stuff and sadly not made into a sequel because it only made 20 million at the box office in profits. This poster was voted best of the decade by collectors.

Rocky – 1976 - This is the granddaddy of all boxing films and easily the best one in the history of film. Directed by John Avildson and starring Sylvester Stallone and a rock-solid supporting cast. The film received mixed reviews, but most of them were favorable. The pompous critic at the New York Times, Vincent Canby, thought the movie and direction were second-rate; what was second-rate was Canby's ability not to get off his high horse and be able to keep an open mind. The music for the first Rocky was first-rate, as well as the sometimes gruesome photography.

Avildson had a sense for the raw, as shown with his previous work in Joe and Save the Tiger. In contrast to those films, he added some very slick editing in this one that made at least three of the sequences highly memorable. The steps scene, the eye-cutting scene and the finale are all classics. The supporting cast included Talia Shire as Adrian, Rocky's mousy love interest, and Burgess Meredith as his manager, who believes Rocky could have been much better earlier in his career had he been more serious about training.

Burt Young does a nice turn as Adrian's overbearing brother, and Carl Weathers rounds out the cast with great in-ring authenticity to the role of Apollo Creed. This film is often rated in the top ten films of all time on numerous lists of critics, but I believe it belongs in the second ten or even the third. That said, this is still a pretty high position for a film to occupy. I wonder where Canby would put it?

Rocky II - 1978 - Directed by Sylvester Stallone and starring the same crew that was in the first Rocky film, except this one was directed by Stallone and not John Avildsen. Stallone does a great job of directing the action and the soundtrack by Bill Conti is even better the first film. A great sequel.

Rocky Mountain - 1950- Directed by William Keighley and starring Errol Flynn and a B actress named Patrice Wymore (why indeed). This convoluted story about the Civil War and its memories does not translate very well with a B cast and an A actor in great decline. However, it is fascinating to watch Flynn struggle to keep his dignity.

Roger and Me – 1989 - Directed by Roger Ebert and starring the idiots at GM who drove the city of Detroit into a lengthy depression. A great documentary on how American car executives are among the least competitive and savvy businessmen on the planet. Very funny. .

Romancing the Stone- 1984 - Directed by Robert Zemeckis and starring Michael Douglas and Kathleen Turner in the lead roles of a romantic comedy that makes the grade as both a soap and a decent action film. Good dialogue.

Roman Holiday – 1953 - Directed by William Wyler and starring Gregory Peck and Audrey Hepburn in a soap about a love affair between Peck and Hepburn while on holiday in Rome. Eddie Albert adds to the supporting cast. Soap lovers will love this one.

The Rookie - 2002 - Directed by John Lee Hancock and starring Randy Quaid as the over the hill baseball coach of a high school team that decides to make one last try for the major leagues as a relief pitcher. Based on a true story and fascinating to watch.

Room at the Top – 1959 - Directed by Jack Clayton and starring Laurence Harvey and Simone Signoret in the lead roles of a soap triangle. Signoret won the academy award for best actress for this soap lover's dream film.

Rope - 1948 - Directed by Alfred Hitchcock and starring James Stewart and Farley Granger in the lead roles of one the master's lesser works about a murder and the solving of same that takes place practically in one room for the whole film. Better off as a play, and not as suspenseful as most other Hitchcock works.

Rope of Sand - 1949 - Directed by William Dieterle, who was more comfortable doing monster films. This one starred Burt Lancaster, who carries the film as adventurer in South Africa who tries to connive his way into getting some free diamonds. Paul Henreid, Claude Rains and Peter Lorre add to the cast values, but C actress Corinne Calvet almost sinks the film. Still good viewing.

The Rose Tattoo – 1955 - Directed by Daniel Mann and starring Burt Lancaster as a roving husband and Anna Magnani as his suffering wife. Magnani won the academy award for best actress for her suffering. Lancaster, one of my favorite actors, is miscast in this one. This film begged to be done by Italian directors and actors.

Rosemary's Baby - 1968 - Directed by Roman Polanski and starring Mia Farrow in the lead role of a woman who is used by a satanic cult to bear the child of Satan. Great supporting cast and good atmosphere adds to the intensity of the film. We always knew the devil lived in New York City.

The Rounders – 1965 – Directed by Burt Kennedy and starring the formidable duo of Henry Fonda and Glenn Ford. This cattle opera has a few twists and turns that make it superior to most other Westerns in the B category.

Round Midnight – 1986 - Directed by Bertrand Tavernier and starring Dexter Gordon, an amateur actor, as a jazz saxophonist in Paris during the 1950s. A subject rarely done in film; it studies the jazz scene of Paris and the difficulties of staying sober to enjoy one's success.

Royal Hunt of the Sun – England - 1969- Directed by Irving Lerner and starring Christopher Plummer and Robert Shaw in the story of the tragedy of the Incas and their invasion by the Spanish. Shaw is perfect as Pizzaro, but Plummer is a bit miscast as an Inca king. Interesting to watch.

Rudy - 1993 - Directed by David Anspaugh and starring Sean Astin in the role of a very small college football player who tries to make the team at Notre Dame, the cathedral of college football. Based on a true story, the film is inspirational and helped by a solid supporting cast and good direction.

Ruggles of Red Gap – 1935 - Directed by comedy master Leo McCarey and starring Charles Laughton and Zazu Pitts along with a solid supporting cast in the tale of a British butler who is forced to work in a Western boom town among the savages in America (I am referring to the townspeople and not the Indians). Hilarious comedy classic that is not to be missed.

The Rules of the Game – 1939 - France - Directed by Jean Renoir and starring Nora Gregor, Paulette Dubost, Marcel Dalio, Jean Renoir and Roger Desormiere in a tale of romance and soap triangles during the pre-WW2 days of France. Soap lovers will love it, but it is a bit dated.

The Ruling Class – 1972 - Directed by Peter Medak and starring Peter O'Toole as a raving madman (not much of a stretch there). A good supporting cast including the perfect Alastair Sim adds to the production values. O'Toole plays a member of the House of Lords who becomes homicidal after finding out he is not God. The lesson here is that a raving lunatic and a raving politician can seldom be identified as to which is which.

Runaway Train – 1986 - Directed by Andrei Konchalovsky and starring Jon Voight and Eric Roberts as an odd couple who hijack a train and then lose control of it. Wasted in the film is the smoking hot Rebecca DeMornay. Still a great actioner.

The Running Man – 1963 – Directed by Carol Reed and starring Laurence Harvey, Lee Remick and Alan Bates in a story about an insurance scam where Harvey fakes his death in order to collect his insurance, but runs into Alan Bates, a careful insurance investigator. This film is compared to, but not as good as Double Indemnity, a story with a similar plot. Still worth watching.

Running on Empty - 1988 - Directed by Sidney Lumet and starring Judd Hirsch, in his career-defining role (although he is now better known for *Numbers* and *Taxi*, two TV shows). Also starring in the dated anti-Vietnam war film was River Phoenix and Christine Lahti. Interesting from a historical perspective.

Russian Ark – 2002 –Russia - Directed by Aleksandr Sokurov and starring a cast of unknown B Russian actors who do a wonderful job with a brilliant script and screenplay (not to mention outstanding cinematography) about a man fantasizing interaction with 200 years of Russian History. One of the best Russian films of all time.

Rushmore – 1998 - Directed by Wes Anderson and starring Jason Schwartzman (who never did another major film), Bill Murray (perfectly cast) and Olivia Williams. The story is about a talented? high school student who tries to make his mark on society and on a female primary school teacher. Hilarious in spots. See it for yourself.

Ruthless – 1948- Directed by Edgar G. Ulmer and starring Zachary Scott, Louis Hayward and Sydney Greenstreet. This is a poor man's version of Citizen Kane and comes off as a knockoff of that classic. Interesting to see the rise and fall of a ruthless man, however.

Ruthless People – 1986 - Directed by Jim Abraham and the Zucker brothers, David and Jerry (this was the wackiest brother team of directors until the Coen Brothers). The film stars Danny Da Vito and Bette Midler in an acting match made in heaven. The film is hilarious, even though the plot is ridiculous. A classic comedy from beginning to end with great dialogue.

1449

S

Sabotage – England - 1936 - Directed by Alfred Hitchcock and starring Sylvia Sydney, John Loder and Oscar Homolka in a story about spies, sabotage, and a heroine in Pre-WW2 London. The film is a bit dated and not as good as his later spy films, but still is a clear notch above other spy movies. Good viewing.

Saboteur - 1942 - Directed by Alfred Hitchcock and starring Robert Cummings as the innocent bystander caught up in sabotage and intrigue. Some critics feel that this film is dated, but I disagree. Good suspense is never dated. Completely different from other Hitchcock sabotage film.

Saddle the Wind – 1958 - Directed by Robert Parish and starring Robert Taylor, who is fine, but Julie London and especially John Cassavettes are miscast in this film written by Rod Serling, who is also out of his element writing Westerns. Serling, a great sci-fi writer and very good with East Coast settings, is not authentic here. Cliche plot with retired gunslinger done many times before and much better. Good to view everyone trying, however.

Safe Conduct – France - 2002 - Directed by Bertram Tavernier and starring a group of unknown French actors (even in France). The real star of the film is the storyline, which is fascinating. The French film industry during the Nazi occupation makes a great setting for suspense and intrigue. Worth viewing.

Sahara – 1943 - Directed by Zoltan Korda and starring Humphrey Bogart, J. Carrol Naish (the future TV Charlie Chan), and Lloyd Bridges (the future TV Sea Hunt star). This film looks at the trials and tribulations of a tank unit deployed in North Africa. With Bogart in the middle of the action, you know you will be entertained.

Sailor Beware - 1952 - Directed by Hal Walker and starring Dean Martin and Jerry Lewis in one of their better films. Even though the plot is rather mundane (recruitment and serving together in the Navy, falling for some girls etc.), the earlier Martin and Lewis films had an energy that the later ones did not have. This is a good example.

Saints and Soldiers – 2010 - Competently directed by Ryan Little and starring newcomers Corbin Allred, Alexander Niver, Kirby Hayborne, and Lawrence Bagby as American soldiers caught behind German lines. An interesting variation on a mostly cliched plot.

Salaam Bombay! – India - 1988 - Directed by Mira Nair and starring Shafiq Syed, Tara Iasrado, Hansa Vithal, Chandra Sharma, Anita Kanwar, Nana Pataker and Raghuvir Yadav in a tale about a jealous brother who leaves the family and goes through various unfortunate adventures that do not get him any closer to returning home. Interesting.

Salesman – 1969 - Directed by the threesome of the Maysles brothers and Charlotte Zwerin and starring four real-life salesmen as they scurry around New England and Florida selling Bibles door to door. At times depressing and at other times, pretty funny.

Salvador – 1986 - Directed by Oliver Stone, so you know it will be an intense film that needs an intense actor. That intense actor would be James Woods (you can't get much more intense than Woods). This is an intense story about a journalist covering the civil war in Salvador. Very Intense.

Salvatore Giuliano – Italy - 1962 - Directed by Francesco Rosi and starring unknowns Salvo Randone and Frank Wolff in one of most underrated Sicilian crime family films ever made. A real insight to the mindset of the Mafioso who ran Sicily after World War 2. A must see neo-realistic classic.

Samson and Delilah - Directed by Cecil B DeMille (so you know the film will be BIG) and starring Victor Mature, Hedy Lamarr, George Sanders and a sexy Angela Lansbury. This classic Biblical tale with a great deal of creative film license makes for interesting viewing.

San Antonio – 1945 - Directed by David Butler, who needed two assistant directors to help him (Robert Florey and Raoul Walsh) and starring Errol Flynn and Alexis Smith in a cliched story about rustlers in Texas. Worth watching for Flynn.

Sanders of the River- England - 1935 - Directed by Zoltan Korda and starring some B actors in a story of slave traders and colonials in Nigeria in the 1930s. Despite all of these drawbacks, Nigeria was better off then than it is now; a lawless state in constant civil war.

The Sand Pebbles - 1966 - Directed by Robert Wise (who was more comfortable with musicals) and starring Steve McQueen and a miscast Richard Attenborough, Richard Crenna, and Candice Bergen. The casting director must have been drunk while making these selections. This film promises so much, but delivers very little. See it for yourself and see why. Film could have been made in New Jersey instead of China for all the authenticity of its Chinese setting. Interesting.

Sands of Iwo Jima - 1949 - Directed by Allan Dwan and starring John Wayne, Forrest Tucker, John Agar, and Adele Mara in an earthy tale of Marines during the invasions of Tarawa and Iwo Jima. Some very good scenes and an Oscar nomination for Wayne in his best film ever.

San Francisco - 1936 - Directed by Woody Van Dyke and D W Griffith and starring Clark Gable, Spencer Tracy and Jeannette McDonald in a rollicking tale of San Francisco at the turn of the century just before its great earthquake. Very entertaining. Sansho the Bailiff – Japan - 1969 - A - Directed by Kenji Mizoguchi and starring Kinuyo Tanaka, Yoshiaki Hanayagi, Kyoko Kagawa, and Eitaro Shindo in a tale of ancient Japan where a good governor is unjustly accused of abusing his office and is forced to be exiled with his family. An interesting plot.

The Satan Bug - 1965 - Directed by John Sturges and starring Dana Andrews, Richard Basehart, Anne Francis and George Maharis. This film was absolutely frightening when it first came out because it was one of the first to deal with bacterial terrorism. It really hasn't dated very much since its release and will still grip your attention.

Saturday Night and Sunday Morning – 1961 - Directed by Karek Reisz and starring Albert Finney and Rachel Roberts in a study of the mating habits of some British professionals in the early sixties. A very incisive film that concerns much more than sex. Very well written.

Saturday Night Fever – 1977 - Directed by John Badham and starring John Travolta in his career-defining role. Retailers sold over a million of these disco suits worn by Travolta after the film was released. More ham in this film than in a German deli. A must see.

Savages - 2007 - Directed by Tamara Jenkins and starring Philip Seymour Hoffman and Laura Linney. Philip Bosco plays the aging father the uneasy older children must find a way of assisting his final few months on earth. A perceptive script examines some issues that almost all of us will have to endure at one time or another.

Saving Private Ryan – 1998 - Directed by Steven Spielberg and starring Tom Hanks, Edward Burns, Matt Damon and Tom Sizemore in a first-rate tale of the Normandy invasion and the attempted preservation of the last remaining brother in a family decimated by World War Two. Done previously with the *Fighting Sullivans*, but not with the great production values or emotional impact that this film has. The scene with the mother is an unbelievable emotional wallop. A must see.

Scandal in Paris – 1946 - Directed by Douglas Sirk and starring George Sanders and Carole Landis along with Akim Tamiroff and Gene Lockhart in a romantic adventure in Paris. No one can do stuff like this as well as George Sanders. This is what separates A soap from B soaps.

Scaramouche - 1952 -Directed by George Sidney and starring Stewart Granger, Eleanor Parker, Janet Leigh and Mel Ferrer in a romantic adventure tale about the French aristocracy in old France. A stellar cast makes this production first-rate.

Scarface – 1932 -Directed by Howard Hawks and Richard Rosson and starring Paul Muni in the lead role as Scarface. Many critics feel this version is more textured than the later one with Pacino. George Raft and Boris Karloff add considerably to the production values.

The Scarlet Claw – 1944 - Directed by Roy William Neill and starring Basil Rathbone and Nigel Bruce in the Holmes tale about murder and mystery in a small village. One of the better Holmes films.

The Scarlet Pimpernel – England - 1935 - Directed by Harold Young and starring Leslie Howard in the principal role. Merle Oberon and Raymond Massey add to the production values. This is a rousing romantic adventure set in the Revolution of France amid a nest of spies. How could you ask for more?

Scarlet Street – 1945 - Directed by Fritz Lang, a master craftsman, and starring Edward G Robinson, Dan Duryea and Joan Bennet. This is a sad tale reminiscent of Of Human Bondage, a role created by Leslie Howard years earlier. It is a good try by Robinson, who departs from his usual stereotypical roles.

Schindler's List – 1993 - Directed by Steven Spielberg and starring Liam Neeson, Ralph Fiennes and Ben Kingsley. This film is often ranked in the top ten movies of all-time list of many film critics. Spielberg had never done any serious films about World War 2 or the Holocaust before this film. He seemed to be right at home with the entire genre. His brilliant use of black and white photography was essential to establish the feel of the period.

Some directors try to shoot World War 2 films in color, and they generally fail to create anything that resembles an authentic period film. Liam Neeson does a great job in the lead as Schindler and captures the tenseness of having a small amount of access to the outside world from the inside of a Jewish ghetto. There were very few venues, if any, for Jews to escape the death sentence of various concentration camps after the campaign to "cleanse the Ayran race" was established by the Nazis. Schindler provided one for them, provided they had some type of technical skill. Ralph Fiennes has a delightful time playing the evil Amon Goth, who kills Jews for sport. Rounding out the fine cast is the highly proficient Ben Kingsley, who plays one of the saved Jews and aids Schindler is saving hundreds of others through various schemes. This is a must see film on several levels.

Scott of the Antarctic – England - 1948 -Directed by Charles Frend and starring John Mills as the legendary Scott of the Antarctic, one of the most daring explorers of all time. This is a fascinating film that might have been even better in black and white.

The Sea Hawk - 1940 - Directed by Michael Curtiz, which almost ensures an A film, and starring Errol Flynn and Claude Rains in a tale of high adventure during the period of conflict between Spain and England. A good rousing show.

The Searchers – 1956 - Directed by master John Ford and starring his favorite vehicle, John Wayne and a miscast Jeffrey Hunter (he could never do Westerns well). This is a story of a man who hunts down the kidnappers of a young woman played by Natalie Wood. One of Wayne's best.

Searching for Bobby Fischer – 1993 - Directed by Stephen Zaillian and starring child actor, Max Pomeranc along with veteran actors, Ben Kingsley, Larry Fishburne and Joe Mantegna. Joan Allan plays his mother. The story is not about Bobby Fischer, but a child prodigy like Fischer, who must learn to survive in a world of adult competition on his own terms. Good stuff.

The Sea Wolf – 1941 - Directed by master Michael Curtiz and starring Edward G Robinson,John Garfield and the brilliant Ida Lupino as a great cast carries off a good Jack London story to perfection. Mystery on the high seas done the right way.

Seconds - 1966 - Directed by John Frankenheimer and starring a surprisingly good Rock Hudson along with a solid supporting cast in a great sci-fi story about replicants taking our places in society. An interesting concept and well done.

Secret Honor – 1985 - Directed by Robert Altman, who is not noted for very tight direction of a single character (he usually does montage pieces with an ensemble) and starring Philip Baker Hall in a tour de force performance as Richard Nixon contemplating his career. Fascinating to watch to try and pick the truth from fiction.

Secrets and Lies – England - 1996 -Directed by Mike Leigh and starring a cast of unknowns who do a pretty good job of playing out this first class soap about a woman who seeks out her true birth parents. It's been done before, but this one is done rather well, so I can recommend it.

Secret Garden - 1949 - Directed by Fred M Wilcox and starring Margaret O'Brien in her final film at MGM along with a very young Dean Stockwell and the dependable British actor, Herbert Marshall. This story of children escaping from the miserable world of adults is a classic and has been made three times on film. A must see.

The Secret of Santa Vittoria – 1969 - Directed by Stanley Kramer and starring Anthony Quinn and Anna Magnani in a story about a small Italian village that tries to hide its wine from the Nazis during World War 2. An amusing tale done well with veteran actors.

The Secret in Their Eyes – Argentina – 2009 - Directed by Juan Jose Campanella and starring a relatively unknown (except in Argentina) cast in a story about an unsolved murder case and the clues that are tracked down by an investigator into the crime. Interesting cinema.

Seduced and Abandoned – Italy – 1963 – Directed by Pietro Germi and starring Aldo Puglisi, Stefania Sandrelli, Paola Biggio, and Saro Urzi in a film that could only have been made in Italy. One the most underrated comedies from any country. Edgy too.

The Seduction of Mimi – Italy – 1972 - Directed by Lina Wertmuller and starring the great duo of Giancarlo Gianini and the absolutely smoking hot Mariangela Melato as two lovers thrown together in the political hotbed of Italian politics. One of the funniest films ever made.

Seize the Day – 1986 - Directed by Fielder Cook and starring Robin Williams doing his version of Death of a Salesman. Williams was wise to choose this vehicle instead of the Arthur Miller tale because this one better utilizes his scope as an actor. A man who starts over in New York City and tries to communicate with his father is a solid plot for the film.

Selma – 2014 - Directed by Ava DuVernay and staring David Oyelowo as Martin Luther King, this film about the 1960s Civil Rights movement captures the atmosphere of the time. The march from Selma to Montgomery helped get the attention needed to get the Voting Rights Act of 1965 passed and sounded the death knell for any state's segregation policies. Recommended.

Seminole – 1953 – Directed by Budd Boetticher and starring the formidable cast of Rock Hudson, Anthony Quinn, and Lee Marvin. Hugh O'Brien (*Wyatt Earp*) is also featured. This Western about the Seminole Indians in more interesting than most other Indian films because they were never defeated by US forces.

Separate Tables - 1958 - Directed by Delbert Mann and starring Burt Lancaster, Deborah Kerr, David Niven, and Rita Hayworth in a power-packed cast that delivers the super soap plot without missing a beat. Great performances.

Seraphim Falls – 2007 - Directed by David Von Ancken and starring the unlikely pairing of Liam Neeson and Pierce Brosnan as veterans of the Civil War. One is a bounty hunter (Neeson) and the other is a fugitive (Brosnan). A more complex plot than you would imagine, but the film has difficulty with its conclusion. Worth viewing.

Serenity – 2005 - Directed by Joss Whedon and starring a cast of unknown or B actors in a tight sci-fi tale of a struggle of a crew ship in space to evade an assassin who is trying to eliminate the member of the crew who is telepathic. Interesting.

Sergeant York – 1941 - Directed by Howard Hawks and starring Gary Cooper in an academy award winning role as Alvin York, the most decorated soldier in American History. Walter Brennan adds to the cast production values and once again teams up with Cooper to add a bit of humor to the proceedings. A classic and must see.

Serpico – 1973 - Directed by Sidney Lumet and starring Al Pacino early in his career as an undercover cop in the narcotics unit. This was one of the first films to explore police corruption and undercover police work and it is a powerhouse of a story.

The Servant – 1963 - Directed by Joseph Losey and starring Dirk Bogarde and Sarah Miles in a tale of class distinctions and love relationships among those classes. The film explores the shifting role of servant for a rich employer. Interesting.

The Set-Up – 1949 -Directed by Robert Wise of *Sound of Music* fame and starring the dependable Robert Ryan as a boxer caught up in a fight-fixing scheme. He is caught between the criminals and his own pride. Also starring a solid supporting cast that holds up the film noir tradition.

Seven - 1995 - Directed by David Fincher and starring Brad Pitt and Morgan Freeman in a story about a serial killer who uses the seven deadly sins as his guide for murder. A very interesting crime story.

Seven Beauties – 1976 – Italy- Directed by Lina Wertmueller and starring Giancarlo Gianinni and Fernando Rey in the story of one man's survival through World War Two including several romantic adventures, life as a criminal and a stretch of time in the death camps. Visually stunning.

Seven Days in May - 1964 - Directed by John Frankenheimer and starring Burt Lancaster, Kirk Douglas, Fredric March, Ava Gardner, Edmond O'Brien and Martin Balsam in a story conceived by Rod Serling that doesn't quite deliver what it promises, but it is still very entertaining. It is a story about the takeover of the US by the Pentagon. This was only the second time in the career of Burt Lancaster that he played the heavy in over one hundred films; the other film was *Vera Cruz* with Gary Cooper.

Seven Days to Noon – 1950 - England- Directed by John and Roy Boulting and starring Barry Jones in a tightly directed and acted thriller about a nuclear bomb threat from a nuclear scientist who wants England to end all nuclear weapon stockpiling. Great plot that almost delivers what it promises.

Seven Faces of Dr. Lao - 1964 - Directed by George Pal, the man who gave us The Time Machine and starring Tony Randall in a demanding seven-character role. The film also stars Arthur O'Connell and Barbara Eden of TV fame. Fun to see Randall play many different characters.

Seven Men From Now - 1956 -Directed by Budd Boetticher and starring his perpetual leading man, Randolph Scott, who always delivered. Also starring an early version of Lee Marvin. Always fun to watch Scott in action.

The Seven Samurai - Japan – 1956 - Directed by Akira Kurosawa and starring Tishiro Mifune and Takashi Shimura. The Japanese copied this film from *The Magnificent Seven* ....only kidding; *The Magnificent*

Seven, made a few years later, copied this film in many scenes and both films were great successes. The story of seven warriors defending a village is irresistible.

The Seven-Ups - 1973 - Directed by Philip D'antoni and starring Roy Schneider in a star-making role (before Jaws). Also starring the capable Tony Lo Bianco in a story about kidnappers and counterfeiters, but the real star of the film is the great chase scene that is in the middle of the movie. It rivals or surpasses *The French Connection* and *Bullit*.

The Seventh Cross - 1944 - Directed by master Fred Zinnemann (of *Man For All Seasons* fame) and starring Spencer Tracy in his greatest role (according to the poster, but not really) in a story about seven escapees from a Nazi death camp. One of the few American films where the hero is a communist. Film clarifies that not all Germans were Nazis.

The Seventh Veil – 1945 - Directed by Comton Bennett and starring James Mason, Ann Todd and Herbert Lom in a story about a psychologically troubled woman who is in therapy. Lom is in a straight role here and I expected Peter Sellers to pop out any moment. Good soap.

The Seventh Voyage of Sinbad – 1958 - Directed by Nathan H Juran and starring a relatively unknown cast of B actors. The real star of the film is the stop animation of Ray Harryhausen. Sinbad gets the girl in the end and gives up his new cabin boy.

Seven Years in Tibet - 1997 - Directed by Jean-Jacques Annaud and starring Brad Pitt in one of his first successful dramatic roles as an Austrian escaping to Tibet during World War Two during the transition of Tibet to Chinese possession. The depiction of events is rather one-sided and does not highlight the vast improvement of basic human needs of the majority of the population under the Chinese. Other than that omission, and overt sympathy for the Dali Llama, the film is beautifully shot and quite engaging. The final result was that food, shelter and clothing with more economic opportunity and social equality was far more attractive than religion for the vast majority of Tibetans.

Sex, Lies and Videotape – 1989 - Directed by Stephen Soderbergh and starring Andie McDowell, Peter Gallagher, James Spader, Laura San Giacomo, and Ron Vawter in a frank exploration of couples and their problems with sexual difficulties. An interesting subject for mature audiences.

Sexy Beast – England - 2001 - Directed by Jonathan Glazer and starring an amazingly transformed Ben Kingsley along with a fine supporting cast. Kingsley positively steals the film with his physical presence. He is Gandhi on steroids. His transformation from sensitive small-bodied actor to absolutely buff crime action-figure is truly remarkable and a must-see.

Sgt. Bilko - 1996 - Directed by Jonathan Lynn, who does not do a very good job at controlling the action. The film stars the talented Steve Martin, who tries his best, but cannot match the original humor of Nat Hiken's TV *Bilko* starring Phil Silvers. Mostly sight gags and physical comedy in this remake. Add one star if you have never seen the original TV show.

Shadowlands – England - 1993 - Directed by Richard Attenborough and starring Anthony Hopkins and a miscast Debra Winger. This film succeeds to a degree because of the great acting skills of Hopkins, who can carry any film and cast strictly with his own persona. Very loosely based on the life of CS Lewis. Primarily for soap-lovers.

Shadow Magic – China - 2001 - Directed by Ann Hu and starring a relatively unknown cast of Western and Chinese actors who do an excellent job under the master supervision of the director. Based on a true story of the introduction of cinema to turn of the century China. The *Cinema Paradiso* of China. Absolutely fascinating and a must-see for all movie buffs.

Shadow of a Doubt – 1943 - Directed by Alfred Hitchcock and starring Joseph Cotten and Teresa Wright along with supporting actors MacDonald Carey and Hume Cronyn. This courtroom thriller has a wonderful twist ending which I will not reveal, but suffice it to say that you will be well-entertained.

Shadows and Fog - 1992 - Directed by Woody Allen, who tries to do his imitation of Bergman, but falls quite a bit short. Starring a serious Woody Allen, Mia Farrow, Jody Foster, Madonna and John Malkovitch as wasted talented actors and actresses in this irrrelevant story about 20's Europe. Only for very strong Allen addicts, as I peg this film to be the worst film he ever made.

Shakespeare in Love- 1998 - Directed by John Madden and starring Gwyneth Paltrow, Joseph Fiennes, Geoffrey Rush, Colin Firth, Ben Affleck (what's he doing here with these great actors?), and Judi Dench. An almost all-star cast delivers a great performance in one of the best love stories ever captured on film. A must-see. This was my pick for Best Film of the year and it deservedly won.

Shallow Grave – 1994 - Directed by the talented Danny Boyle and starring a relatively unknown cast including Ewan McGregor in a quirky little film about three roommates who find a fourth roommate dead, but lots of cash. They agree to split the money and bury the body in a desolate spot. Of course, there are complications. Entertaining.

Shampoo - 1975 - Ably directed by Hal Ashby and starring Warren Beatty, Goldie Hawn, Julie Christie, Carrie Fisher (she is in over her head here), and a great performance by Jack Warden in a story about the relationships of customers of a hairdresser. Positively hilarious and entertaining. Perfect casting (except for Fisher).

Shane – 1953 - Directed by George Stevens and starring Alan Ladd in the lead role, Jean Arthur, Van Heflin, Brandon De Wilde (in his only good role ever), Jack Palance, who is always great, and Ben Johnson in a simple classic western about bullies and heroes. Great stuff.

Shanghai Dreams (China) -2005 - Directed by Wang Xiaoshuai and starring Gao Yuanyuan, Li Bin, Tang Yang, Wang Xiaoyang, and Yao Anlian in a story about displaced city folk in a rural setting shortly after the Mao period ended in 1983. Haunting in spots and complete with an authentic disco scene. Visually and emotionally fascinating.

Shanghai Express – 1932 - Directed by Josef von Sternberg and starring Marlene Dietrich and Anna May Wong. This is the original and much better than the campy version done in the modern era by Madonna. Anna May Wong is head and shoulders above most modern Chinese actresses (with a few exceptions) and Dietrich as a femme fatale is rarely matched. A classic.

Shanghai Story (China) - 2004 - Directed by Peng Xiaoliang and starring Joey Wang and Josephine Koo along with Feng Yuanzheng and Zheng Zhenyao in a story about victims of the Cultural Revolution, a re-occurring motif of Chinese cinema. This story concerns a prominent family made destitute by the mindless hordes that roved during the *Cultural Revolution*. Bittersweet.

Shanghai Triad (China) - 1995 - Directed by Zhang Yimou and starring Gong Li in the lead role. The story of gangsters in 1930's Shanghai has a *Godfather* feel to the film, but while visually stunning, the characters are not fully developed except for the amusing house boy, whose experiences are shown through his eyes in the film. Still gorgeous to view.

The Shawshank Redemption - 1994 - Directed by Frank Darabont and starring Tim Robbins and Morgan Freeman along with a superlative supporting cast in a story about a man who tries to retain his and his inmate friends' dignity while in prison. An above-average prison film that stresses the psychological aspect of prison rather than the mere brutality of incarceration.

She -1935 - Directed by Lansing C. Holden and starring Randolph Scott, Nigel Bruce (of Sherlock Holmes fame) and a relative cast of unknowns including someone named Helen Gahagan in the lead female role. Evocative music is provided by Max Steiner and the story is very engrossing. The Queen in this film and her costume influenced Disney in his making of *Snow White*. The story revolves around a lost civilization ruled by a queen who believes she is immortal. Follow up to King Kong was both disappointing at the box office and on the big screen, but still better than the average fare available at the time.

She Done Him Wrong - 1932 - Directed by Lowell Sherman and starring Mae West, Cary Grant and Gilbert Roland. Grant and West made a great pair on the screen, although Grant was a bit younger and West was at the height of her fame and ability. This soap about a bar girl as a moll for a gangster that falls for a Salvation Army type is fairly hackneyed as a plot, but we are not watching the film for the plot; it is for the great chemistry between West and Grant. Grant had been in this type of role before in Blonde Venus with Marlene Dietrich, but the chemistry wasn't there. It is here.

The Sheriff of Medicine Bow – 1948 – Directed by Lambert Hillyer and starring Johnny Mack Brown in his third effort under this director as a sheriff trying to clean up a corrupt town. Such an unusual plot for a Western. Hackneyed, but fun to watch.

Sherlock Holmes - 1932 - Directed by William K Howard and starring Clive Brook as Sherlock and Reginald Owen as Watson. A nice turn by Ernest Torrence as Professor Moriarty adds to the production values. Owen, however, is far too serious in the role as Watson, and both Basil Rathbone and Nigel Bruce would go on to have much greater chemistry in the title roles in later years. Interesting as a curiosity.

Sherlock Holmes and the Secret Weapon – 1942 - Directed by Lionel Atwill and starring the dynamic duo of Basil Rathbone and Nigel Bruce as Sherlock Holmes and Dr. Watson, respectively, in a story about a fictional secret weapon that the Nazis are about to develop to win the war. Interesting at the time, but quite dated now. However, the banter of Rathbone and Bruce is worth the price of admission.

Sherlock Holmes Faces Death – 1943 - Directed by Roy William Neill and starring Basil Rathbone and Nigel Bruce. By this time, the story lines were relatively hackneyed or convoluted like this one; a family member grabs for the inheritance; how original. Only the banter between Rathbone and Bruce saves this turkey. Hillary Brooke, the female lead of the film, would go on to much more success on TV with *Abbot and Costello*.

Sherlock Holmes in Washington - 1943 - Directed by Roy William Neill and starring Basil Rathbone and Nigel Bruce in the lead roles. This fifth installment of the series goes through the motions of a nazi spy ring trying to steal a microfilm from a British spy in Washington. Holmes, of course, saves the day, and the hackneyed script with his wonderful banter with Watson.

Sherlock Holmes The Sign of Four – 1939- Directed by Graham Cutts and starring the relatively unknown acting pair of Arthur Wontner and Ian Hunter as the principal leads. Holmes becomes involved in a relatively convoluted plot of prison escape, stolen treasure and revenge. If you can suspend disbelief long enough, the film is entertaining.

She Wore a Yellow Ribbon – 1949- Directed by John Ford and starring John Wayne, Ward Bond, Ben Johnson and Victor Mclaglen, the usual crew of Ford's cast of choice for many of his films. This crew always delivered the goods when it came to action westerns and this film is no exception. Watch the Duke spank those Indians.

Sherman's March – 1986 - Directed and completely created by Ross McElwee, the Southern version of a young Woody Allen, who is obsessed with his romantic relationships instead of producing his documentary on *Sherman's March to the Sea*. The film shows all his distractions and why he cannot make any progress toward his original goal. I agree with the Times. This guy and film are goofy, but funny.

She's Gotta Have It – 1986 - Directed by Spike Lee and starring Tracy Camilla Johns, Spike Lee, John Canada Terrell, and Tommy Redmond Hicks in a love rectangle (as opposed to the usual triangle). Why these guys want this woman is beyond me; she is chubby and homely, and not very sexually attractive. However, this is Brooklyn, where men are sometimes desperate for female companionship. The three suitors are quite funny, actually. They all have great deficiencies of their own, and Nola's personality overwhelms all three of them. This is primarily a male fantasy because Nola does not match the other 99% of the desires of the women in the world. Those women generally want one good man and a family. Of course, there are a few women like Nola, but I have never met a happy one. Interesting to watch.

Shine - 1996 - Directed by Scott Hicks and starring a perfectly cast Geoffrey Rush as a psychotic pianist along with Lynn Redgrave (*Georgy Girl*) and Sir John Gielgud in a story about a complete nervous breakdown and recovery through great patience and care. An inspiring story and a must see. A career-maker for Rush as he won the Academy Award that year for this film.

Ship of Fools – 1965 - Directed by Stanley Kramer and starring an all-star cast including Vivien Leigh, Simone Signoret, Jose Ferrer, Lee Marvin, Oscar Werner, Elizabeth Ashley, George Segal, Michael Dunn and a fine supporting cast. Music by Ernest Gold adds to the production values. Would you believe that some of these people heading for Nazi Germany were anti-Semitic? Shocking! This story of a diverse group of people headed for Nazi Germany in 1933 is missing just one thing; no one cares about any of the characters. The dialogue, however, is interesting in parts.

The Shipping News – 2001 - Directed by Lasse Halstrom and starring Kevin Spacey, miscast as Quoyle (Quoyle was a big oaf with an oversized chin; Spacey is a smallish man with a good-looking chin). This type of challenge has never stopped Spacey in the past (see his Bobby Darin role) and, of course, he succeeds despite his miscasting. The film also stars Julianne Moore, perfectly cast as Wavey, Judith Dench, perfectly cast as Agnis Hamm, and Kate Blanchett, appropriately cast as the psycho, Petal. Actually, the novel by E Anne Proulx probably had more homely people in mind than these four leading actors, but everyone in Hollywood wanted a piece of the action in this classic film, so we get some of the best-looking people in the history of Newfoundland instead. The movie features one daughter instead of two (believe me, there is a world of difference in trying to bring up two kids instead of one) and is a major change in the script. It does, however, allow for greater development of the redemptive romance of Quoyle and Wavey. This film is very good on several levels, just as the book was great on several levels. The theme of second chances and redemption run through both the book and the film. A must see and a must read.

Shock Corridor – 1963 - Written and Directed by Samuel Fuller and starring a B cast of actors that are allowed to get really hammy as nut cases. The saving grace of this film is the story, which is interesting because a writer is willing to have himself committed to the nut house in order to win a Pulitzer. I could see this happening in real life. Be careful what you wish for.

Shockproof - 1949 - Directed by Douglas Sirk and written by Samuel Fuller, so you know you will at least have a dose of reality in the film. Cornel Wilde and Patricia Knight have the lead roles in this story about a parole officer who falls for one of his assigned cases. The ensuing triangle becomes the basis for the film. Not bad for a B film.

Shoeshine (Italy) – 1947 - Directed by Vittorio De Sica and starring a group of unknown B Italian actors who do a great job with a very good script that describes post-WW2 Italy through the eyes of a young shoeshine boy who is forced to live in poverty with hundreds of other orphans of the storm from that conflict. Compelling film-making at every level.

Shoot the Moon - 1982 - Deftly directed by Alan Parker (*Midnight Express*) and starring Albert Finney and Diane Keaton (in a rare dramatic role) in a well-scripted story about the devastating effects of divorce. This is probably the best film of all time about the subject of divorce. The final scene is unforgettable.

Shoot the Piano Player – 1962 - Directed by Francois Truffaut (*400 Blows*) and starring Charles Aznavour and a group of B French actors in a story about a piano player who tries to recover his life after the suicide of his wife. Not the best of Truffaut, but better than most other directors. Soap lovers will like it.

The Shop on Main Street – 1965 - Directed by Jan Kadar and Elmar Klos and starring an unknown cast of B Czechoslovakian actors who do a good job with a decent script. This story of anti-Semitism in WW2

Czechoslovakia is not really earth-shattering in its revelations and has been done a hundred times, but the acting is very good and we sympathize with the victims. Winner of the Best Foreign film for 1965.

A Shot in the Dark – 1964 - Directed by Blake Edwards and starring Peter Sellers and Elke Sommer. The real star of the film, of course, is Sellers as Inspector Clouseau and Herbert Lom as his suffering boss. Every scene with Sellers is hilarious. A must-see comedy classic.

Shrek – 2001 - Directed by Andrew Adamson and Vicky Jenson and starring the voices of Mike Myers, Eddie Murphy, Cameron Diaz and John Lithgow. I was stuck in a violent rainstorm in New York City one day and just to get out of the rain, I went to this film (which I would not normally have chosen to review). I wish I could say I spent two hours in an enchanted world of make-believe and wonder, but that would be a lie. It was dry in the theater and I needed a rest from a busy day. The production was ok, but does not really stack up that well against Disney classics from the past (which all animated films must sooner or later be compared to). At least the main character, Shrek was entertaining, and the story was watchable, but not earth-shattering. Good for the kiddies.

Sholay (India) - 1975 - Directed by Salim Javed and starring Dharmendra, Sanjeev Kumar, and other Indian B actors who do a very good job with a genre that Indian films are really not known for; action/adventure. I have nothing but the highest regard for Indian films as long as they do not contain a Bollywood dance number. This film is one of those serious Indian films without a Bollywood dance number. This is considered a Hindi classic and I agree with that assessment.

Shower (China) - 1999 - Directed by Zhang Yang and starring Zhu Yu, Pu Cunxin and Jiang Wu in a simple story about a Beijing bathhouse that is run by two partners who are consumed by life's continuous challenges and problems; relationships, money, and friendship. A great little film from China that is not about old dynasties, the Communist Party, or a corny relationship in Beijing.

Sid and Nancy- 1986- Directed by Alex Cox and starring an over-the-top Gary Oldman (one of my favorite actors) and Chole Webb in the sensitive love story of Sid Vicious and his beloved Nancy Spungen as they wade through the cesspool of alcohol, drugs and sex in the Lower East Side of New York. Often presented in the same classes in school that show car wrecks and mayhem as a result of drunk driving.

Siddhartha - 1973 - Directed by Conrad Rooks and starring Shashi Kapoor, Simi Garewal and Romesh Sharma in the classic tale of Hermann Hesse's masterpiece, *Siddhartha*. The film is relatively faithful to the book and the photography by Sven Nykvist is outstanding. A highly underrated film that did not get the attention that it deserved at the time (this was a period of American obsession with sex and violence; which was the complete opposite of the content of this film). Highly recommended.

Side Street - 1950 - Directed by Anthony Mann and starring Farley Granger (*Strangers on a Train*) and Cathy O'Donnell along with a convincing supporting cast in a story about a unsuccessful gas station owner who falls into thirty thousand dollars. Of course the money is illegal, so he is in trouble from the start. A good film noir piece by a talented director.

Sideways - 2004 - Directed by Alexander Payne and starring Paul Giamatti, Thomas Haden Church, Virginia Madsen, and Sandra Oh in a wonderfully acted romantic comedy about two elitists who go on a wine-tasting trip and become romantically involved with two women while on the trip. Giamatti and Oh stand out in particular. This film was Best Screenplay for the year 2004.

Siege At Red River – 1954 – Directed by Rudolph Mate and starring Van Johnson and Richard Boone in the lead roles. Watch for Jeff Morrow (TV *Combat*) as one of the bad guys. Film saved by Johnson and Boone.

The Signal- 2014 —Directed by William Eubank and starring Laurence Fishburne and several B actors in a story of three MIT hackers (if they are MIT grads, why do they need to hack anything?) who come to Area 54 or a place like it in the desert and try to solve a communication from outer space. Not exactly an earth-shattering plot, but interesting enough to keep our attention.

Silence of the Lambs – 1991- Directed by Jonathon Demme and starring Anthony Hopkins as Hannibal Lechter, an individual with carnivore sensibilities and Jody Foster as a young FBI agent who is assigned to enlist the aid of Lechter to catch a serial killer. This is the greatest cop movie of all time and the cop happens to be a woman, Clarice Starling. There is a pretty good case for Hopkins' character, Hannibal Lechter, to be the greatest human monster of all time, but some would say Anthony Perkins in Psycho would rank higher. This film occasionally appears on some top ten lists. Demme seems to have a solid grip on the slimy underworld of sexual deviates and killers. His direction is wonderfully paced and there is never a dull second in the entire film.

Anthony Hopkins steals this film from the less experienced Foster, who, despite being overwhelmed by the Hannibal Lechter character, still gives an excellent performance. Any actress in her role would have met the same fate. Demme captures the creepy world of the serial killer and the psychotic becomes normal in the course of the film. There are elements of horror, the crime genre, and a study of abnormal psychology, which blend for an extremely riveting screen experience. This film is not recommended for the squeamish or young impressionable minds. This film swept the Oscars in 91 with Demme, Hopkins, Foster and the film itself winning every major award. This is the top-rated movie of the horror genre ever to win the Academy Award for best picture.

Silent Running -1973- Directed by Douglas Trumbull and starring Bruce Dern and a decent supporting cast of B actors in a tale of environmental fantasy that is technically very good because Trumbull had expertise in that area. The story is a bit far-fetched, but if we suspend disbelief, it proves to be an engrossing film.

The Silent World – (Le Monde Du Silence) - France- 1956 - Directed by Jacques-Yves Cousteau and professional director, Louis Malle. The real stars of the movie are the undersea creatures and plant life that make the film a huge success. This documentary won best documentary of the year for 1956. The underwater photography became a trademark of Cousteau.

Silkwood – 1983 - Directed by Mike Nichols, who is more famous for his cutting edge comedies, and starring Meryl Streep, Cher, Kurt Russell, Craig T Nelson and Fred Ward along with a solid supporting cast in a story of wrongdoing at a nuclear plant that was being investigated by Karen Silkwood, a union rep at the plant. Before she can uncover the truth, she dies from a mysterious car crash. The audience is then faced with the task of believing the accident was coincidence, or part of a conspiracy to silence Silkwood. Worth viewing.

Silverado – 1985 - Directed by Lawrence Kasden and starring one his favorite actors, Kevin Costner along with Scott Glenn, Danny Glover and Kevin Kline. The cast also includes Rosanna Arquette, John Cleese, Brian Denehy, Jeff Goldblum (badly miscast), and Linda Hunt. Needless to say, there was enough ham in this film to supply Ockoberfest in six cities in Germany. Everyone tried to steal every scene and only Costner was strong enough to emerge unscathed. The film is certainly a lot of fun to watch, though. The hackneyed story doesn't really matter. Just enjoy it.

Silver Lode – 1954 – Directed by Allan Dwan and starring Dan Duryea and John Payne (Miracle on34th St) in a tale about a silver mine and the greed that eventually comes in to play in most partnerships.

Silver Streak – 1976 - Directed by Arthur Hiller and starring Gene Wilder, Richard Pryor and Jill Clayburgh in a rather uneven, but funny comedy about a runaway train. There are some hilarious scenes in this film, but at other times, it bogs down in silliness or poor plot development. Worthwhile just to see Wilder and Pryor in three or four great scenes.

A Simple Noodle Story (China) – 2009 - Directed by Zhang Yimou and one of his rare misfires and starring Sun Honglei, Ni Dahong, xiaoshenyang, and Yan Ni in a comedy/horror attempt with a Chinese setting at copying Blood Simple by the Coen Brothers made years earlier. This is one of those joyous failures that really doesn't matter, so just relax and enjoy the fun.

Simple Plan - 1988 - Directed by the competent Sam Raimi and starring the talented trio of Bill Paxton, Billy Bob Thornton and Bridget Fonda in a story about amateurs trying to outfox professional criminals. The plot is fascinating, as we see a simple plan go spiraling way out of control. The moral of the story is not to try and take easy money. Nice directing job.

Sinbad the Sailor -1947 - Directed by Richard Wallace and starring Douglas Fairbanks Jr in one his last starring roles along with Maureen O'Hara, Walter Slezak, Anthony Quinn and George Tobias. This pure fantasy is shot in beautiful technicolor and is a lot of fun to watch even though we can all guess the unraveling plot and final conclusion. Fun to view.

Sister Kenny - 1946 - Directed by Dudley Nichols and starring Rosalind Russell as Sister Kenny, a role for which she was nominated for Best Actress. Also starring Alexander Knox (*Wilson*), and Dean Jagger. This story of a nurse who ignores doctors when trying to care for polio victims is a bit syrupy, but for the most part, entertaining. Good cast.

Sitting Pretty – 1948 - Directed by Walter Lang and starring Clifton Webb in his first of three Mr. Belvedere films. Also starring Robert Young and Maureen O'Hara, but Webb steals the film from beginning to end. Two sequels were made because of the success of this comedy. Fun to watch and great dialogue.

The Sixth Sense – 1999 - Directed by M Night Shyamalan and starring Bruce Willis and Haley Joel Osment in a horror film that concentrates on the mind rather than on gore and scary images. The interaction between Willis and Osment is fascinating. Recommended.

Slap Shot – 1977 - Directed by George Roy Hill and starring Paul Newman as the coach of a hockey team that is losing money. This is one of the funniest sports films ever made. Every scene with the Hanson Brothers is absolutely hilarious. A must see.

Slaughterhouse Five - 1972 - Directed by George Roy Hill and starring Michael Sacks in the lead role of Billy Pilgrim, an individual with unusual psychic ability. The scenes from war-torn Dresden are impressive as is the scene with the American POWs there. Recommended.

Slaughter on Tenth Avenue - 1957 - Directed by Arnold Laven and starring Richard Egan, Jan Sterling, Dan Duryea and Walter Matthau. This story of a dedicated DA who fights corruption and crime on the docks of New York City is both brutal and sobering. A bit dated, but still holds the viewer well.

Sleeper – 1973 - Directed by and starring Woody Allen and Diane Keaton in a story about a nincompoop who travels in the future and comes up against a number of social challenges. The scenes with the ORB are very funny, but there are a few misses along the way as well. One of the earlier, funnier Woody Allen films.

Sleepless in Seattle - 1993 - Directed and written by Nora Ephron and starring Tom Hanks and Meg Ryan in an intelligent romantic comedy that is a pleasure to watch from beginning to end. A great film to watch with your significant other. This cross-country romance has a nice touch. The characters are not wooden, but realistic.

Sleuth - 1972 - Directed by Joseph L. Mankiewitz and starring the formidable pair of Laurence Olivier and Michael Caine as the lead actors. The story revolves between two men who love playing mind games. One is a rich, spoiled aristocrat who thinks his money will protect him from everything in life and the other is an overly ambitious working-class hustler. The chemistry between Olivier and Caine is fascinating to watch. Recommended.

A Slight Case of Murder – 1938 - Directed by Lloyd Bacon and starring Edward G Robinson and a solid supporting cast in a story about a former bootlegger who tries to go straight, but is confronted by numerous problems from his past. Because of the great character actors of the period, the film is successful at creating a good melodrama. Recommended.

Sling Blade - 1996 - Written, directed and starring Billy Bob Thornton in a film about a simple man living in rural Arkansas who has to come to grips with his violent past. A fascinating portrayal of a sympathetic character who must make a decision of going back to his world of violence or shunning it completely.

Slumdog Millionaire – (India) - 2008 - Directed by Danny Boyle and starring a relatively unknown cast of Indian actors including Dev Patel, among others, in a story of a young man's escape from his past and the slums from where he was born. A Rocky-type film that has you rooting for the underdog from beginning to end. Some of the scenes are heart-rending and harrowing. Winner of the Best Film of the year in 2008.

Smile – 1975 - Directed by Michael Ritchie and starring Bruce Dern and Barbara Feldon (Agent 99) in a very funny comedy about the young Miss America beauty pageant that was held at Santa Rosa, California. This is a prime example of how truth can be so much funnier than fiction. Feldon is perfectly cast and Dern is a dyed-in-the-wool Californian, so he is perfect for this role as well. Hilarious in spots and a debut for Melanie Griffith.

The Snake Pit – 1948 - Expertly directed by Anatole Litvak and starring Olivia DeHaviland in her academy-award nominated role as a patient in an insane asylum. Often harrowing scenes and a stellar performance by DeHaviland. The fine supporting cast adds authenticity to the film (because of the research efforts of the director). Temporarily banned in England.

Snowpiercer -2014 – Directed by Joon-Ho Bong and starring Ed Harris and Tilda Swinton picking up nice checks for a B movie. The sci-fi tale of a train travelling through an icy world is fairly unbelievable fantasy, but it is at least entertaining to view because of the quality actors.

Snow White and the Seven Dwarves - 1938 - This Walt Disney production was one of the first and most successful box office full-length cartoons ever made. Some of the scenes were too scary for young children at the time, but parents ignored that problem and took the kids anyway. The evil queen steals the film. A must see.

So Dark the Night – 1946 - Directed by Joseph H Lewis and starring Steven Garay as a Jeykll and Hyde-type police inspector, who becomes a totally different person at night. An interesting study in human nature. Worth viewing.

Solaris – 1972 - (Russia) - Directed by Andrei Tarkovsky and starring an unknown collection of Russian B actors in an A-scripted film written by Polish science-fiction writer, Stanislaw Lem. The mysteries of the mind can often be more intriguing than the usual science-fiction of action and aliens. This is a prime example. The story of a small group of members on a space station who go into emotional stress is fascinating and was made into a major Hollywood production years later starring George Clooney.

Soldier Blue – 1970 – Directed by Ralph Nelson and starring Candice Bergen and Peter Strauss (Rich Man Poor Man) in the lead roles. This is one of your soapier Westerns, but retains some good action sequences as well. Good chemistry between two miscast actors.

Soldier in the Rain – 1963 - Directed by Ralph Nelson and starring Jackie Gleason and Steve McQueen is a story about two military men who have an unusual relationship as master sergeant and buck sergeant. Chemistry between Gleason and McQueen not as good as chemistry between Gleason and Newman in Hustler, but good enough despite some dated situations. Gleason always entertaining.

Soldier of Orange – Netherlands - 1979 - Directed by Paul Verheoven and starring Rutger Hauer and a B cast of Dutch unknowns in a very entertaining film about the life of Dutch college students at the time of

WW2. Told with a sense of humor and compassion that makes one feel sorry both sides of the conflict. A seldom-explored topic of WW2.

Soldier's Story – 1983- Directed by Norman Jewison and starring Denzel Washington and a solid supporting cast in a story about an investigation into a murder of a Louisiana sergeant on a military base. We see the characters of the film reveal the reasons that the sergeant was deposed and finally come to the conclusion that the sergeant had it coming and that there will be no apprehension of the murderer. An interesting film.

Solomon and Sheba – 1959 - Directed by King Vidor (don't you love names that make people instant royalty, like Duke Wayne or King Vidor?) and starring Yul Brynner and Gina Lollobrgita as Solomon and Sheba. George Sanders, who could act rings around both leads in the film, was also featured. There is enough ham in this movie to supply the army for a winter, but it certainly is a lot of fun to watch. Hard to buy Brynner as a Jew after seeing the Ten Commandments and his role as an Egyptian. I kept thinking when did the Pharoah become the king of Israel?

Somebody Up There Likes Me - 1956 - Directed by Robert Wise (*Sound of Music*), who was better noted for his musicals and starring Paul Newman and B actress Pier Angeli. A solid supporting cast helps with the production, which, at times, suffers from the syrupy direction of Wise. However, the acting of Newman and the fine photography (it won the academy award that year), make up for Wise's shortcomings in the drama area.

Some Like it Hot – 1959 - Directed by Billy Wilder and starring Jack Lemmon, Tony Curtis and Marilyn Monroe and a fine supporting cast in a screwball comedy about gangsters and cross-dressers. Condemned by the Catholic Church on its release and viewed with pleasure by millions of Catholics who realized the Legion of Decency often had no sense of humor when categorizing films.

Somewhere in the Night -1946 - Directed by Joseph L Mankiewitz and starring John Hodiak, Lloyd Nolan and Richard Conte. There are no A actors in this film, but somehow it adds up to an A film. The female lead, played by Nancy Guild is adequate, but not memorable. What is memorable, however, is the script of this cutting-edge film noir. The story pins around a WW2 Veteran with amnesia. Who is he? Is he a bad man or a good man? We are left guessing (some will get it) for most of the film. Very entertaining. Recommended.

Song of the Fisherman (China) – 1934 - Directed by Cai Chusheng and starring Wang Renmei, Luo Peng, Yuan Congmei, and Lan Hangen in a story about the simple lives of Chinese fishermen. This film is a bit dated now because most of these jobs are gone. But the message is not dated and the emotions are genuine. Recommended.

Sons and Lovers – England - 1960 - Directed by Jack Cardiff and starring Trevor Howard, Dean Stockwell and Wendy Hiller in a soap deluxe treatment of the potboiler written by D.H. Lawrence. Not as good as other Lawrence soaps, but better than most other writers.

Sons of the Desert - 1933 - Directed by William A. Seiter and starring the legendary comedy team of Stan Laurel and Oliver Hardy. This story about two nincompoops going to a convention without the knowledge of their wives is a classic. Arguably the best of all Laurel and Hardy films. A must see.

Sorcerer - 1977 - Directed by William Friedkin and starring Roy Scheider and a fine supporting cast in a great remake of the classic Wages of Fear. This story of desperate men performing desperate deeds to try and change their lives is powerful stuff. The photography is outstanding and the suspense, at times, almost unbearable. Great film-making.

Sorry, Wrong Number – 1948 - Directed by Anatole Litvak and starring Barbara Stanwyck and Burt Lancaster in a rare bad-guy role. This story captivated readers of a national magazine for weeks. The story of a kept man by a rich woman who is the object of an attempted murder. Suspenseful from beginning to end. Hitchcock wanted this film, but lost out to Litvak.

Source Code – 2011 - Directed by Duncan Jones and starring Jake Gyllenhaal and a decent supporting cast in a story about a soldier who continuously goes back in time to stop a bomber of a train. This is a serious sci-fi version of *Groundhog Day*. Interesting to watch.

The Southerner – 1945 - Directed by Jean Renoir and starring Betty Field and Zachary Scott in the lead roles as two poor cotten farmers in Texas. This simple story with B actors is skillfully delivered by master director Renoir, who got an Oscar nomination for this film. A soap-lover's delight. Watch for J Carroll Naish (the TV Charlie Chan), as the heavy, Devers.

South Park - 1999 - Directed by Trey Parker and starring the usual gang of miscreants in a three-episode length version of the TV show. You either love or hate South Park; there really is no middle ground. I happen to be a fan. The film includes a war against Canada and a sub-plot between Satan and Sadaam. Recommended only for those who like the show.

The Spanish Prisoner - 1997 - Directed by David Mamet and starring a serious Steve Martin, who is very good, Ben Gazzara, Felicity Huffman, Mamet regular Ricky Jay (*House of Games*), and a sound supporting cast in an elaborate con that is similar to, but not quite as satisfying as *House of Games*, the finest con movie ever made. Still better than *The Sting*.

Spartacus – 1960 - Directed by Stanley Kubrick, who is remembered far more for *2001: A Space Odyssey*, and starring Kirk Douglas, in the greatest role of his career. Make no mistake; this is Kubrick's finest film, and he has made many of them. The same holds true for Douglas who had over a dozen fine performances in his career, but none that matched this one. It was ironic that one of his best friends, Burt Lancaster, won for Best Actor that year for *Elmer Gantry*. Although nominated three times in his career, Douglas never did win the award. This film was his best shot, in addition to the critically acclaimed, but mediocre box office film, *Lust For Life*.

Spartacus was a novel written by Howard Fast and adapted to the screen by Dalton Trumbo, a blackballed Hollywood writer from the Commie Scare period. Peter Ustinov won a Best Supporting Actor award for his highly amusing stint in the film. The cinematography was outstanding for this movie because most of it was done by Kubrick himself, who was a master with the camera. The musical score by Alex North was first-rate. The supporting cast was resonant, and included wonderful portrayals by the very sexy Jean Simmons as Virinia. It was also fun to see Charles Laughton, as a Roman Senator, verbally dueling with Laurence Olivier, a Roman General. Woody Strode was very effective in his role, also, as a gladiator who befriends no one because you might have to kill them some day in the arena.

Despite his amusing Brooklyn accent, Tony Curtis was moving in his role as a Greek slave to a Roman General. *Spartacus*, of course, is based on true historical events along with some literary and cinematic license. In this case, the end result was extremely satisfying. Highly recommended.

Speed -1995 - Directed by Jan De Bont and starring Keanu Reeves and Sandra Bullock in the lead roles. Dennis Hopper, of course, overwhelms both of these actors with his role of the heavy, and great lines like "Don't try to grow a brain". The plot of a disgruntled employee terrorizing a bus by remote control is very original, and engages the viewer from beginning to end. Recommended.

Spellbound – 1945 - Directed by Alfred Hitchcock and starring Ingrid Bergman and Gregory Peck in the lead roles in a story about the world of psychoanalysis, an innocent man with amnesia, and a dubious home for rich, troubled patients. Bergman plays one of the doctors and Peck one of the patients; it might have been more realistic the other way around. Good Hitchcock, though.

Spiderman - 2002 - Directed by Sam Raimi and starring Tobey Maguire in his career-defining role. Willem Dafoe, Kirsten Dunst, James Franco, and Cliff Robertson also star. Do I really need to tell you the story about Spiderman's origin? A nice film treatment with all the bells and whistles shows the proper respect for this comic book icon.

The Spider Woman – 1944 - Directed by Roy William Neill and starring Basil Rathbone, Nigel Bruce and Gale Sondergaard as the Spiderwoman. This creepy little tale of a series of suicides has Holmes faking his own death in order to catch a female version of Moriarity. One of the better Holmes films.

The Spiral Staircase – 1946 - Directed by Robert Siodmak and starring Dorothy MaGuire, the singer, George Brent the actor, and Ethel Barrymore, a member of Hollywood royalty. This tale of a series of murders of handicapped women in a New England town is a bit different from most other murder mysteries. It will keep you in suspense for a while.

Spirited Away - Japan– 2001 - Directed by Hayao Miyazaki, and starring the voices of B Japanese actors and actresses. This children's world of spirits and monsters is right in line with ancient Japanese Shitois, which is a derivative of ancient Chinese religious Taoism (which differs from philosophical Taoism). The full length cartoon won the Academy Award for best animation film.

The Spirit of Saint Louis - 1957 - Directed by Billy Wilder and starring a perfectly cast James Stewart (who in real life had been a pilot). The film becomes very intense in the second half and has an exhilarating climax. Great photography and direction by Wilder.

Spotlight – 2015 – Directed by Tom McCarthy and starring Marc Ruffalo and Michael Keaton in the leading roles. This hard-bitten look at a Catholic Archdiocese cover-up of sex crimes committed by various parish priests gives us a good insight to the inconsistency of the Catholic Church in maintaining its internal discipline in this area. A chilling portrait.

Spray of Plum Blossoms - China- Silent -1933 - Directed by Bu Wancang and starring icon Ruan Lingyu and Jin Yan as well as a solid supporting cast in a soap-lover's delight. For romance addicts, it doesn't get any better than this. Follow the exploits of two military academy grads and their amorous adventures.

Spring Fever (China) – 2009 - Directed by Lou Ye and starring Qin Hao, Chen Sicheng, Zhuo Tan, Songwen Zhang, Jiang Jiaqi,Jintao Li, Yue Wang, and Wu We in the leading roles. This story of rash behavior during the Spring Festival holidays in China is a recurring motif in many Chinese films. This is a holiday designed for new beginnings.

Springfield Rifle – 1952 - Directed by Andre De Toth and starring Gary Cooper and a group of B actors in a tale of civil war espionage and horse rustling. The title of the film is a bit misleading. The story, however, is fairly unique and interesting to watch.

Spring in a Small Town (China) -1948 - Directed by Fei Mu and starring Wei Wei, Zhang Hongmei, Cui Chaoming, Wei Li, and Shi Yu in a story about romance and life in a small town during Spring Festival, the most important Chinese holidays of the year. This is considered one of the best Chinese films ever made. A must see.

Spy – 2015 – Directed by Paul Feig and starring a feisty Melissa McCarthy (who does really make the perfect spy) and Jude Law in a nice piece of work as a supporting actor (I don't know how he was able to keep a straight face) in this farce comedy about a fat housewife spy. Great characterizations and very funny.

Squaw Man – 1931 – Directed by Cecil B DeMile and starring Warner Baxter in the lead role in a story about a cowboy who becomes involved with an Indian squaw and the complications that arise from that relationship. Interesting to watch.

Stage Door – 1937 - Directed by Gregory La Cava and starring Ginger Rogers, Lucille Ball, Katherine Hepburn, Ann Miller and Adolphe Menjou in a great ensemble film that shows the problems of breaking into show business. A classic and a must see film. Stagecoach – 1939 – A - Directed by John Ford and starring John Wayne, Claire Trevor, Thomas Mitchell, John Carradine and Andy Divine (*Andy's Gang* with Froggy) in the icon stagecoach film of Westerns. The story examines the lives of the passengers as they go through various perils including an Indian attack. A must see.

Stage Fright - 1950 - Directed by Alfred Hitchcock and starring Jane Wyman, Marlene Dietrich, Michael Wilding and Richard Todd in a story about the unsavory side of life on the stage. Hitchcock takes a mundane story lathered in soap and turns it into a pretty good suspense thriller.

Stairway to Heaven – 1946 - Directed by master director Michael Powell and assistant Emeric Pressburger and starring David Niven, Kim Hunter and Raymond Massey along with a superb supporting cast in a great fantasy romance (perhaps the best ever made) about a WW 2 pilot and his adventures in the afterlife. Reminiscent of *The Devil and Daniel Webster*, but a bit better.

Stalag 17 – 1953 - Directed by Billy Wilder and starring William Holden and a great supporting cast including Peter Graves (*Fury*) in a story about POWs in WW2 and life in the prison camp. Holden gives a great performance and try to guess the traitor.

Stalker – 1979- Netherlands - Directed by Andrei Tarkovsky and starring a group of unknown B actors who do a decent job of enacting the interesting fantasy of a place where wishes can be granted on another planet. Original script idea. Not bad; although the title could have been better.

Stalking Moon - 1968 - A - Directed by Robert Mulligan and starring Gregory Peck and Eva Marie Saint in a suspense-filled Western about an Indian that is stalking the home of a settler and his wife. Instead of waiting for the Indian, the settler goes out hunting for him. A real nail-biter all the way. A must see.

Stampede – 1949 – Directed by Lesley Selander, a B Western regular, and starring Gale Storm, who was now getting top billing over Johnny Mack Brown (and for good reasons). This mundane tale of the West is saved by Storm's presence.

Stand By Me - 1986 - Directed by Rob Reiner and starring a group of coming of age actors including River Phoenix, Keifer Sutherland, Will Wheaton, and Corey Feldman in a story by Stephen King about pre-teens exploring the landscape for a rumored dead body that is supposed to be scary, but is actually a bit of fun. Great music to boot. Similar to *Tales of West Paterson*.

Stanley and Livingstone – 1939 - Directed by Henry King and starring Spencer Tracy, Nancy Kelly and Walter Brennan. This is the true story of a newspaperman (Tracy) setting out on a safari to find humanitarian, Dr. David Livingstone, who is lost in the wilds of Africa and presumed dead. Pretty good stuff.

The Star – 1952 - B - Directed by Stuart Heisler and starring Bette Davis and Sterling Hayden in a story about a washed-up leading (age gets almost all of them) actress, who eventually comes to face her new status. Davis could have been drawing on her own career at this point in time, but she went on to make a number of more fine films. Intriguing.

Stardust Memories - 1980 - Directed by Woody Allen and starring Charlotte Rampling, Woody Allen and Jessica Harper in a story (most likely autobiographical) about a director who frets over the fact that his fans like his earlier funnier films rather than the serious artistic films he is now making. If this isn't about Woody Allen, then I don' know anything about movies.

Stargate - 1994 - Directed by Roland Emmerich and starring James Spader, Kurt Russell and the lovely Jaye Davidson in a flawed sci-fi epic that has thrilling moments alongside some hackneyed situations, but is ultimately quite entertaining. The concept is outstanding.

Star is Born – 1937 - Directed by William A Wellman and starring Janet Gaynor and Fredric March along with a great supporting cast that is well-directed. This story about the rise of a young actress from the masses to the top of the heap has been done dozens of times in Hollywood; but never better than this version.

Starman – 1984 - Directed by John Carpenter, who was generally known for directing broad scary films, takes a very nice detour from that reputation with this light sci-fi romance that requires a very light touch. Jeff Bridges and Karen Allen are perfectly teamed here.

The Stars Look Down – 1941 - Directed by the talented Carol Reed and starring Michael Redgrave, Margaret Lockwood and Emlyn Williams in a story about the hardships faced by a British coal-mining community. Similar to *How Green Was My Valley*, but not Welsh.

Starship Troopers - 1997 - Directed by Paul Verhoeven, who is very good at this genre, and starring a smoking hot Denise Richards (where were these women when I was in the Army?) and a B cast of actors who battle aliens in defense of the earth. Totally ridiculous, but lots of fun to watch.

Star Trek Generations - 1994 - Directed by David Carson and starring the basic casts of the first two Star Trek TV shows. Somehow, Carson makes this dubious plan work with humor and the result is a lot of fun for all.

Star Trek – The Origin - 2009 - Directed by JJ Abrams and starring a group of B actors along with the original Spock, Leonard Nimoy, in an amusing telling of how the original crew got together. Nice script and tight direction make it a solid entry.

Star Trek II – The Wrath of Khan – 1982 - Directed by Nicholas Meyer and starring William Shatner, Leonard Nimoy and the original cast as well as Ricardo Montalban in a much-improved version of the first revival film. Worth viewing to see the evil Khan performance of Montalban (which is way over the top, as usual).

Star Wars – 1977 - Directed by George Lucas and starring Mark Hamill as Luke, the only significant role of his career, Carrie Fisher as Princess Leia in the only significant role in her career, Harrison Ford as Han Solo, who went on to star in many films, Alec Guinness, who had many successful starring roles, as Obi-Wan and the master of the Force (ancient Taoism) and the voice of James Earl Jones. Of all these, the voice of James Earl Jones steals the film, as does the onscreen character of Darth Vader.

Audiences fell in LOVE with Darth Vader. The Force was also another very popular topic within the film, and it became an Icon of American entertainment spawning another five financially successful films that have grossed over six billion dollars as of the end of 2010. A seventh and final film, *War of the Clones*, was not successful. The movie won seven non-acting Academy Awards, which means it was the Best Movie of the year in every single aspect except acting. The sound track is legendary. The special effects were breathtaking. Audiences were enthralled. I cannot convey the excitement of the crowd of moviegoers who saw the first week's release on the 44th Street theater in New York; it was an electric experience. Nothing like it had ever been seen before. It seemed as if one amazing special effect appeared for every minute of the film. This is an American classic and is a must-see film for all buffs.

State of Siege (France) - 1972 - Directed by Costa Garvas an starring Yves Montand as a smug CIA agent who is captured by revolutionary forces. Garvas always does a top-notch job in this genre and this film is no exception. The pounding music by Mikis Theodorakis adds to the production values.

The Steel Helmet - 1951 - Directed by Samuel Fuller, master of grit, and starring B actors who do a great job under his direction. This film has the look and feel of real combat, therefore most of the situations are highly believable. It's a relief to get out of the theater and back to civilization.

The Stepfather - 1987 - Directed by Joseph Ruben and starring Terry O'Quinn in his best performance ever. This film shocked both audiences and critics alike upon its release because Quinn gave the performance of a lifetime. His role lifts an average horror film to a higher level. This movie spawned three sequels, but none as good as this.

Steve Jobs – 2015 – Directed by the talented Danny Boyle, and starring Michael Fassbender as Jobs and a solid supporting cast including Kate Winslet and Seth Logan. This biopic promises more than it can deliver, but what it does deliver is well done, thanks to Boyle.

Still Life (China) – 2006 - - Directed by Jia Zhangke and starring Zhao Tao, Sanming Han, Wang Hongwei, Zhou Lan, Lizhen Ma,Bing and Li Zhu. The film chronicles the gradual destruction of a town by the construction of the Three Gorges Dam. Good direction.

Stir – Australia – 1980 - Directed by Stephen Wallace and starring Bryan Brown and Max Phipps in a story based on an actual prison riot in New South Wales, Australia. Gritty tale has the feel of authenticity and is fascinating to view

Stone Reader - 2003 - Directed by Mark Moskowitz and starring a great storyline that is the true star of the film, a documentary. The movie tries to retrace the life of a lost genius, Dow Mossman, who suffered a nervous breakdown after writing his one and only successful novel. A fascinating look into the creative process.

Stop Loss – 2008 – Directed by Kimberly Peirce and starring Ryan Phillippe as a Sergeant who has done more than their duty for their country coming back home to reenter civilian life....except that some lowlife in the swamp of Washington DC (who never spent one day in combat) decides to invoke a seldom-used clause in the military contract that the character, Brandon, has signed. Pathetic behavior for a country that has consistently abused its veterans from Korea to the present day.

The Story of Alexander Graham Bell - 1939 - Directed by Irving Cummings and starring a young Don Ameche, Henry Fonda and Loretta Young as Bell's wife. This class A biopic was overwhelmed by ten other blockbusters that came out in the most productive year in Hollywood history. Too bad the company spawned by the inventor (AT&T) lost 90% of its value for investors in the late 1990s.

The Story of G.I. Joe – 1945 - Directed by William A Wellman and starring Burgess Meredith in one of his finest roles (he became Rocky's manager in the 1970s). This story of a dedicated US journalist, Ernie Pyle, during the heat of battle in WW2 is a classic and a must-see.

The Story of Louis Pasteur – 1936 - Directed by William Dieterle and starring Paul Muni as Louis Pasteur, a scientist who is searching for a way to make milk less harmful for millions of children in the world by giving it a much longer shelf life. Great biopic is a must-see performance by a top-notch actor. Film deservedly won best screenplay and best actor for Muni.

The Story of Qiu Ju – China – 1992 - Directed by Zhang Yimou and starring the incomparable Gong Li as a peasant woman who does battle with the Chinese city bureaucracies to get compensation for her husband. A classic in every way.

Strait-Jacket - 1964 - Directed by William Castle, who could never rise above the B genre of horror, and starring an aging Joan Crawford (who was scary just to look at) as a reformed axe murderer (I am not kidding; that is really the plot) and Diane Baker as her suspicious daughter who might be picking up some of mom's bad habits (like hammy acting). Great over the top kitsch.

The Straight Story – 1999 - Directed by David (I will take to you the weirdest places you have ever been) Lynch and starring Richard Farnsworth in a great performance as an aging veteran who has lost his license, but uses a tractor to visit his estranged brother. Film takes you places where you have never been, but not in the usual bizarre Lynch way. Good filmmaking.

Straight Time – 1978 - Directed by Ulu Grosbard and starring Dustin Hoffman as a smalltime hood who can't catch a break when he tries to go straight. Also starring Harry Dean Stanton, Gary Busey, and Theresa Russel. Keep an eye peeked by an early appearance of Kathy Bates. A bit depressing, but watchable.

Strange Cargo - 1940 - Directed by Frank Borzage and starring real-life lovers, Clark Gable and Joan Crawford in their prime. Gable is a plantation owner and Crawford is a woman of questionable character (what a stretch) who invades his world. Peter Lorre and Paul Lukas are also featured. Great dialogue.

The Strange Case of the End of Civilization as We Know It - 1977 - Directed by Joseph McGrath and starring the talented John Cleese in a very silly parody of Sherlock Holmes. The only thing wrong with this film was that it was not made into a number of sequels. Very silly and a lot of fun.

Strange Impersonation – 1946 - A - Directed by Anthony Mann and starring Brenda Marshall and a host of B actors who do a wonderful job with an A script. Post-WW2 psychosis begins with this noir tale of revenge. Great story line and direction. Would have been admired by Hitchcock.

The Strange Love of Martha Ivers – 1946 - Directed by Lewis Milestone and starring a wonderfully sick Barbara Stanwyck, a hot Lizabeth Scott and A actor, Van Heflin. This bizarre triangle is a soap lover's dream and is recommended for Stanwyck's great performance.

The Stranger – 1946 - Directed by Orson Welles and starring Joseph Cotton, Edward G Robinson and Loretta Young in a tale of a nazi hiding in open sight in New England. Welles, of course, plays the nazi with relish and ease. I refuse to capitalize nazi. This was the only money-maker for Welles in his career.

Stranger on the Third Floor - 1940 - Directed by Boris Ingster and starring Peter Lorre along with a competent group of B actors. This very early noir (one of the first three) is about a mysterious murder and a highly suspect boarder at a rooming house. Great noir.

Strangers on a Train – 1951 - Directed by Alfred Hitchcock and starring Farley Granger and Robert Walker. Neither of these actors became big stars in their own right, but Hitchcock was oblivious to big actors, anyway, since he considered all actors as merely props in his films. The real star of the movie is the script, which is dripping with suspense and will keep you engaged from beginning to end. The story revolves around a tennis star, Guy (Granger) who is travelling by train and casually mentions to a passenger, Bruno (Walker) that he is not really in love with his current wife and would love to get rid of her. Bruno concocts a scheme about how one can commit the perfect murder if the suspect has no motive. I will not reveal the ending of the movie, but I can highly recommend it as one of Hitchcock's best films. This film is in both my and many other top 100 film lists.

Stranger Than Paradise – 1984- Directed by Jim Jarmusch and starring a B cast of actors in a C level of production values. The script is pretty bad, too. Somehow, just like *Clerks*, a film that looks like it has no chance to succeed, it does. Very funny.

Strange Woman – 1946 - Directed by Edgar G Ulmer and starring one of my favorite actors of all time, George Sanders along with a B cast. A woman will stop at nothing to control the men in her life. If this had been about a man, no one would have noticed. Says volumes about our double standards.

The Stratton Story - 1949 - Directed by Sam Wood and starring James Stewart and June Allyson. Frank Morgan is also featured with Agnes Morehead. This is a baseball story about a player who loses his leg, but continues to play ball.

Straw Dogs – 1971 - Directed by Rod Lurie and starring Dustin Hoffman and Susan George in a psychological thriller about a couple who get a lot more than they bargained for on vacation.

Streamers – 1983 – Directed by Robert Altman and starring Matthew Modine and other B actors who try to rescue a weak script about US troops in the US barracks waiting to get shipped out to Vietnam. Not as good as *Sticks and Bones*, but watchable. Altman wrong choice for stagey production.

A Streetcar Named Desire – 1951 - Directed by Elia Kazan, who also directed the successful stage production and starring Marlon Brando, Karl Malden, Vivian Leigh, and Kim Hunter in the major roles. The Pulitzer Prize winning play was written by Tennessee Williams, who also wrote the screenplay with the help of veteran screenwriter, Oscar Saul. The film copped three major acting awards; Leigh nudging out Hepburn for best actress, Hunter, for best supporting actress and Malden for best supporting actor.

The role of Blanche Dubois has become an icon of both stage and film lore. Every actress in the world over the age of forty has wanted to play this role; even in modern times, and there is no shortage of actresses who want to play this part on stage. Leigh's portrayal in *Streetcar Named Desire* as Blanche is even better than her effort in *Gone with the Wind*, for which she was much-better remembered for.

Brando, on the other hand, gives a supremely visceral performance as Stanley Kowalski, an animalistic, brute of a man who is not as stupid as he looks.

Karl Malden turns in a very neat performance as the hoodwinked suitor of Blanche, and Kim Hunter, who is surrounded by a powerhouse cast, gives it her best shot as the passionate Stella. Kazan does not miss a beat in his mesmerizing manipulation of each of the characters on the screen. You can literally feel the various levels of heat on the screen. The film was nominated for, and won a bevy of Academy Awards for 1951. This is easily one of Brando's top three performances of all time on the silver screen. I loved the job Malden did in this film; and he almost steals the movie. It is still a must-see film.

Street Scene - 1931 - Directed by King Vidor and starring Sylvia Sydney and a solid B cast in a dated New York City soap that still holds up (especially for soap lovers). Early 30s misadventure.

Street of Shame - Japan – 1956 - Directed by Kenji Mizoguchi and starring an unknown B cast of actors in a story that could have been tacky, but winds up being quite humane. Prostitutes do not choose their line of work; it chooses them.

The Street With No Name - 1948 - Directed by William Keighley and starring Mark Stevens, Richard Widmark, Lloyd Nolan and a solid supporting cast. One of the earlier undercover cop stories from Hollywood that packs a wallop. Great noir.

Stripes - 1981 - Directed by Ivan Reitman and starring Bill Murray and Harold Ramis. Second City star John Candy and veteran actor, Warren Oates add to the production values. This film about two losers who join the army is generally hilarious; especially the ESL scenes with Ramis. Murray, of course, steals the film.

A Study in Terror – England -1965 - Directed by James Hill and starring John Neville, Anthony Quayle, Robert Morley and Judi Dench in some of the lead roles. Doyle was spinning in his grave over this version. It goes against the original Holmes version with a solution to the Jack the Ripper mystery and is nowhere nearly as satisfying. The poster is positively tacky (one of the worst ever). Saved only by cast, which gives it the old college try and the fact that it was a British production, which was almost always better than Hollywood versions of Holmes.

The Stunt Man – 1980 - Directed by Richard Rush and starring Peter O'Toole and Steve Railsback. Barbara Hershey is the romantic interest prop for the film. The real chemistry is between Railsback as Cameron and O'Toole as the evil Eli Cross, a director who will do anything for a good shot. The film begins with Cameron accidentally causing the death of an actor in a film that Cross is filming. Cross blackmails Cameron into taking the dead man's place for free and uses him for dangerous stunts. I can recommend it.

Suddenly – 1954 - Directed by Lewis Allen and starring Frank Sinatra and Sterling Hayden. The story is about an assassination attempt of the President of the United States. Nicely done, but the suspense does not hold up well because we know it didn't happen.

Suez – 1938 - Directed by Allan Dwan and starring Tyrone Power, Loretta Young and Annabella. This tale about the building of the Suez Canal is a lot more exciting than the real events, but then again, we are going to the movies, not a history class.

Sugarfoot – 1951 – Directed by Edwin L Martin and starring Randolph Scott and the venerable Raymond Massey in key roles. Scott saves yet another B Western from oblivion with his skills. The fish out of water formula was getting a bit stale by now in film.

Sullivan's Travels – 1941 - Directed by Preston Sturges and starring Joel McCrea and Veronica Lake. This is one of the best depression films ever made. It views the depression with a sense of humor and a hope for the future. It is of the type of optimism usually associated with Frank Capra films from the same era. Joel McCrea plays John L. Sullivan a financially successful Hollywood director, who longs to make a "meaningful" film. He sets out with his support system, which includes his vivacious girlfriend, Veronica Lake, to become a pretend hobo for a few weeks and learn about the downtrodden.

He is impressed and thankful for what he learns and hands out five dollar bills to all the hobos. But one hobo wants more than just five dollars and ambushes Sullivan at night to get the rest of his cash. He is quickly run over by a train in the train yard and is wearing Sullivan's stolen shoes. The shoes contain emergency numbers to be contacted and the studio is horrified to find out Sullivan has been run over by a train. The real Sullivan wakes up without his shoes and no money and can't even remember who he is.

Then he really finds out what it means to part of the great unwashed. I will not reveal the later part of the film, which is really the meat and potatoes of the movie. This is a must see film and one of the best films ever made about the Depression. It is on my top 100 films of all time and on many other critics' lists as well.

Summer of '42 - 1971 - Directed by Robert Mulligan and starring an absolutely smokin' Jennifer O'Neill, Gary Grimes and B cast. This film was major fantasy fodder for thousands of young male teens across the US and made O'Neill a star. Story of woman losing young husband very touching and music by Legrand music first-rate.

Sunday, Bloody Sunday - 1971 - Directed by John Schlesinger and starring Glenda Jackson and Peter Finch as partners in a swinging three-way relationship. These things never work out, of course. The film shows us why.

Sunset Boulevard – 1950 - Directed and co-written by Billy Wilder, whose primary claim to fame previous to this film were frothier and light-hearted films. The movie stars William Holden in his prime as Joe Gillis and Gloria Swanson well past hers as Norma Desmond, a legendary actress who was a star in the silent film era, but now languishes in her mansion dreaming about the good old days.. Topping out the fine supporting cast is Erich Von Stroheim as Max, Norma's loyal butler, who may or may not have had a romantic link with her in the past, and Nancy Olsen as Joe's younger girlfriend, Betty.

The music and cinematography are highly stylized and atmospheric. Franz Waxman did the score and John Seitz did the film noir-style cinematography. Although nominated for numerous awards, it did not win in any of the major categories. Despite that, the film is listed within the top ten of all time by numerous film critics. It is not the technical aspects that make this film memorable, but the human drama of a faded actress who, despite being well past her prime in both acting and romance, allows herself to enter into an imaginary love affair with a much younger man which is destined to end in tragedy for both of them. It is the trip to the destination that is the most fun, not the arrival.

Sunshine – 2007 - Directed by the talented Danny Boyle and starring a relatively unknown cast armed with a solid script and good director. This sci-fi story about re-igniting the sun is interesting and the formula of using a great director with a good story over expensive actors worked well in the past with directors like Hitchcock, for whom actors were merely props.

Superman - 1978 - Directed by Richard Donner and starring Christopher Reeve as the Man of Steel. The film also stars Marlon Brando, Gene Hackman, and Margot Kidder in key roles. They pulled out all the stops for this one and the production values are literally sky high. This is the best of all the Supermans because it was the first and EVERYONE connected with the film put out 100% effort

Superman 2 - 1980 - Directed by Richard Lester and Richard Donner and staring the same crew as the original. The one great line in this film is "Kneel before Zod!" uttered by Terrance Stamp. This was the infamous film that Donner started, but was finished by Lester. In 2006, the real Donner film was released in a special edition.

The Suspect – 1944 - Directed by Robert Siodmak and starring Charles Laughton, Ella Raines and Molly Lamont. This Hitchcockian tale directed by Siodmak is deliciously accomplished with a great performance by Laughton.

Suspicion – 1941 - Directed by Alfred Hitchcock and starring Cary Grant and Olivia DeHaviland as his doubting wife. The tale centers on whether or not Cary Grant is an evil murderer or just a victim of circumstantial evidence. The film had two endings; one which had Grant as the evil guy, and one as the misunderstood good guy. Audiences overwhelmingly preferred Grant as a good guy since he built his screen persona over the years with screwball comedies and light-hearted characters. The stretch to an evil persona was far too much for the average moviegoer in the early forties. This film is recommended despite a plot that, at times, seems a bit too far-fetched. After all, a mediocre Hitchcock film is still twice as good as most other director's good films.

Swades – 2004 – (India) - Directed by Ashutosh Gowariker and starring a relatively unknown Hindi cast of B actors in a story about an Indian scientist who returns to his home village and fights for the rights of the poor in his community and helps them to be self-sufficient. A top Hindi film.

Swamp Water – 1941 - Directed by Jean Renoir and starring Dana Andrews, Walter Brennan and Walter Huston. This eerie story about a friendship between an ex-con and a country boy has great atmosphere and good acting. Nice film.

Sweet Bird of Youth - 1962 - Directed by Richard Brooks and starring Paul Newman and Geraldine Page along with Shirley Knight. This coming of age film for youthful, rich Southerners is entertaining in spots, but should be mainly to see Newman.

The Sweet Hereafter – 1997 - (Canada) -Directed by Atom Egoyan and starring an unknown B cast of actors who do a good job. This is a relatively depressing story of a horrific school bus accident and the toll it takes on a small town. Interesting.

Sweet Smell of Success – 1957 - Directed by Alexander Mackendrick and starring Burt Lancaster and Tony Curtis in perfectly cast roles and with equally great performances. A great inside look at the entertainment business in NYC theater, and the power that some writers (use to have). A classic and a must-see.

Swept Away - Italy – 1974 - Directed by Lina Wertmueller and starring the hilarious Giancarlo Gianinni and the smoking hot Mariangelo Melato as the rich, spoiled tourist. For some reason, Italians do these types of films better than anyone else. Very funny.

The Swimmer – 1968 - Directed by Frank Perry and starring Burt Lancaster in one of his lesser efforts. This angst-ridden film fails to float most of the time and we want some resolution, but none is forthcoming. Here only to see Burt fight the leaden script.

Swimming to Cambodia - 1987 - Directed by Jonathan Demme, who is more noted for his shock directing. The film stars a very funny Spaulding Gray doing primarily a monologue for an hour and a half. So good, you never want it to end.

Swimming With Sharks – 1994 – Directed by George Huang and starring Kevin Spacey as the boss from hell (an easy role for him lol), and Frank Whaley as his human sacrifice to the ego of a Hollywood producer. There were flashes of *The Sweet Smell of Success* in this film, with Kevin doing the Lancaster bit, and Whaley doing the Curtis bit, but that is a good thing. There needs to be more films that copy classics like that, rather than mindless and endless sequels to blockbuster films and trite superhero movies. Highly recommended.

Syriana- 2005 - Directed by Stephan Gaghan and starring George Clooney, Matt Damon and Jeffrey Wright in a political thriller that is sometimes convoluted and difficult to follow, but hits the mark most of the time. Great cast makes all the difference.

T

Take the High Ground – 1953 – Directed by Richard Brooks and starring Richard WIdmark and Karl Malden in the lead roles. This is a war tale about drill instructors getting recruits ready for the realities of the Korean War. Interesting.

Take the Money and Run - 1974 - Directed and starring Woody Allen. This tale of an inept bank robber is highly unlikely, but still very funny. One of the earlier, funnier Woody Allen movies. Mostly slapstick and not as sophisticated as his later works, but great to just relax and laugh at.

Taking Chances - 2009 – Directed by Ross Katz and starring Kevin Bacon as Colonel who is escorting the coffin of a deceased soldier who has fallen in battle back to the soldier's home town in Wyoming. If you don't well up over this one, then you must be dead inside.

The Taking of Pelham, One, Two, Three – 1974 - Directed by Joseph Sargent and starring Walter Matthau, Robert Shaw and Martin Balsam. This unlikely scenario of a hijacked subway is exciting from start to finish, thanks to the great tight direction of Sargent and the solid acting of this veteran crew.

Taking Sides – 2003 – Germany - Directed by Istvan Szabo and starring Harvey Keitel and one of my favorite B actors, R. Lee Ermey (*Full Metal Jacket*) in a tale about the real interviews of Nazi sympathizers and those who were not sympathetic. Difficult to ascertain which was which.

A Tale of Two Cities – 1935- Directed by Jack Conway (a name borrowed later by Colman in Lost Horizon) and starring Ronald Colman in this action tale of the French Revolution and two men who have completely different personalities, but have an identical appearance and love the same woman. This unlikely tale by Charles Dickens somehow was bought, hook line and sinker by the public and was very popular. Good direction as well.

Tales of Manhattan – 1942- Directed by Julien Duvivier and starring an all-star cast of practically every actor and actress at 20th Century Fox. This interesting anthology of short stories follows the trail of a piece of evening wear that have different results for all those who wear it. The Robinson sequence was the most appealing story in my opinion and the ending is a bit far-fetched, but all in all, it is a very entertaining film.

Talk of the Town - 1942- Directed by George Stevens and starring superstars Cary Grant, Jean Arthur and Ronald Colman in a tale of adventure and romance within a classic triangle; the respectable man versus the guy in trouble. You can pretty much figure which way this one will go, but still a lot of fun.

Talk to Her – 2002 – Spain – Directed by Pedro Almodovar and starring Geraldine Chaplin and a cast of Spanish B actors who try to make a hopelessly depressing film hopeful. A difficult task even for an A group of actors. Good try.

The Tall T - 1957- Directed by Budd Boetticher and starring Randolph Scott, Richard Boone and Maureen O'Sullivan in a story about a kidnapping of a ranch foreman and an heiress (a fairly original idea for a screenplay in a Western). Randolph and Boone are always outstanding

Tampico – 1944 - Directed by Lothar Mendes and starring Edward G Robinson and Victor McLaglen in a story about oil tankers getting sunk by the Nazis. I really didnt buy McLaglen in this role, but watching Robinson in action is worth the price of admission.

Tampopo – Japan - 1986-- Directed by Juzo Itami and starring a crew of unknown Japanese actors who do a great job with an A script and excellent direction. This story of food, opening a restaurant and human relationships works on all levels.

Tap Roots – 1948 – Directed by George Marshall and starring Van Heflin, Susan Hayward, Boris Karloff and Ward Bond (TV Wagon Train) in a film about a farmer during the Civil War who uses dynamite before it was invented. Very strange.

Taras Bulba - 1962 - Directed by J Lee Thompson and starring Tony Curtis and Yul Brenner in the lead roles. Christine Kaufmann provides the female eye candy. This film is lush from beginning to end; the photography is outstanding. The music action sequences are impressive as well. Highly recommended despite the sugary romance scenes.

Targets - 1968 - Directed by Peter Bogdonovich (*Paper Moon*) and starring the dependable Boris Karloff in the lead role in a tale about a mass murderer who shoots people at random. This film is far scarier than most horror movies because it is based on real life characters who commit these types of crimes. Fascinating.

Tarzan and his Mate - 1934 - Directed by Cedric Gibbons and starring Johnny Weissmuller and Maureen O'Sullivan in the classic tale by Edgar Rice Burroughs about Tarzan of the Jungle. Great stuff from beginning to end and the chemistry between the two is authentic. One of the rare instances where an athlete succeeds as an actor in a major film.

Taxi Driver – 1976 - Directed by Martin Scorsese and starring Robert DeNiro and Jodie Foster in the lead roles. This role solidified DeNiro as a superstar and also began the highly successful career of Jodie Foster (although she had made some other minor features). The story of a taxi driver in New York who falls off the cliff of sanity for a while is riveting. The scenes with Harvey Keitel are great. Cybil Shepherd also provides some very good scenes as well.

Tell Them Willie Boy is Here – 1969 - Directed by Abraham Polonsky and starring Robert Redford, Robert Blake and Katharine Ross (The Graduate) in the lead roles. This story of a native American Indian who refuses to adhere to the law of the white man is a sobering look at what really implies justice. An interesting film.

Temptress Moon (China) - 1996 - Directed by Chen Kaige and starring Gong Li and Leslie Cheung in the lead roles. This is a beautifully photographed story of crime, crime families and individual survival among the triads of Shanghai. Kaige demonstrates his mastery of the screen and directing in this masterpiece.

The Tenant – France - 1976 - Directed by Roman Polanski and starring Melvyn Douglas and Shelley Winters before she lost her savings from overeating. This tale of paranoia and supposed terror fails to deliver the goods it promises, but is at least original in its concept. Interesting to watch unfold.

The Ten Commandments – 1956 - Directed by Cecil B DeMille and starring Charton Heston as Moses. Yul Brenner almost steals the film away from Heston, as the evil Ramses, Pharaoh of Egypt. The special effects in this film rank among the best of all time, as does the film itself, which appears on many critics' top ten lists. The parting of the Red Sea still stands as one of the most spectacular special effects in film history. It is certainly one of the top ten epics ever made. DeMille was generally known to be an old-fashioned director, who was quite formal and a despot on the set. He had a good knack with conducting large crowd scenes which were essential in blockbusters like this one.

The cinematography and music in the film were first-rate and both won well-deserved academy awards. The film won almost all the technical awards in 1956. The film score by Alfred Newman (the conductor, not the Mad magazine newt), was memorable in every respect. The costume design was right on the money and very little expense was spared for the production of the film which eventually would go on to make ten times or more the money it was produced for. Recommended. Billy Crystal and I still remember the voice of Edward G Robinson in this film as he uttered the immortal words "Where's Your Messiah, Now?" Nyah.

Tender Mercies – 1983 - Directed by Bruce Beresford and starring the talented Robert Duvall in a tale of redemption of an alcoholic country and western singer by a widow and her young son. This film went on to win best screenplay in 1983 and Duvall won the best acting award which was well-deserved.

Ten From Your Show of Shows - 1973 - Directed by Max Liebman (who was more of an editor than a director on this project) and starring the greatest male-female TV comedy team of all time, Sid Caesar and Imogene Coca. Each one of these show sections is an absolute classic and hilarious. There hasn't been a funnier pair in almost seventy years on TV. A must-see.

The Terminator - 1984 - Directed by James Cameron and starring Arnold Scwartzenegger as the Terminator. Also starring Linda Hamilton in her career-making role. This futuristic horror story is compelling from beginning to end and the action is almost constant as well. There are numerous iconic scenes and lines from the film. A classic.

Terms of Endearment – 1983 - Directed by James L Brooks and starring the perfectly cast couple of Debra Winger and Shirley MacLaine as well as a nicely cast Jack Nicholson. There are dozens of great zingers in this film and all three actors get a chance to land a number of good scenes. MacLaine and Nicholson won academy awards for their roles and the film was given the best picture of the year award for 1983. The story about a mother-daughter relationship that is rocky in parts struck a chord with millions of women everywhere.

Terror in a Texas Town – 1958 – Directed by Joseph H Lewis, who specialized in B Westerns, and starring the unusual pairing (never to be seen again) of Sterling Hayden and Sebastian Cabot (miscast). This offbeat Western is noted just for being different from the usual good guy, bad guy formula.

The Testament of Dr. Mabuse (Germany) - 1933 - Directed by Fritz Lang and starring Rudolf Kein-Rogge as the good doctor. He is ably assisted by a good supporting cast, but it is the tight direction by Lang and the good story that keeps you pinned to your seat. A classic crime thriller.

The Texas Kid – 1943 – Directed by Lambert Hillyer and starring Johnny Mack Brown and a group of B actors. This Western would have been lost in the shuffle of hundreds of others were it not for the performance of Brown, who brings it a cut above.

The Texas Rangers – 1951 – Directed by Phil Karlsen and starring B actors Robert Montgomery and Gail Storm (*Annie Oakley* on TV). This low-budget production of the Texas Rangers is as good as any other that ever came to the screen……and you have Gail Storm as well (always had a crush on her).

Thank You For Not Smoking -2005 - Directed by Jason Reitman and starring relative unknown Aaron Eckhart, who does a great job along with veteran actors Sam Elliot, Robert Duvall and William H Macy. This fictional, but highly likely scenario is both hilarious and scary at the same time; a difficult trick for a director to pull off, but Reitman gets it right. The film implies that all smokers are idiots and suicidal.

That's Life! – 1986 - Directed by Blake Edwards and starring Jack Lemmon and Julie Andrews (who had a hit under Edwards with Victor/Victoria). The film is not Edwards' best, but the veteran actors help pull the lame plot through. For soap lovers.

The Theory of Everything – 2014 - Directed by James Marsh and starring Eddie Redmayne in the lead role. I was rooting for Redmayne to get the award for Best Actor after this performance. His portrayal of Stephen Hawking was unforgettable. Shows Hawking as a young man full of life and potential, who perseveres over ALS. Highly Recommended.

There's Something About Mary - 1998 - Directed by Robert and Peter Farrelly and starring Cameron Diaz, Ben Stiller and Matt Dillon in a screwball comedy about a ditzy blonde and two suitors who ignore some very funny situations. Diaz is great. A classic comedy.

There Was a Crooked Man - 1970 - Directed by Joseph L Mankiewitz and starring Kirk Douglas and Henry Fonda along with a superb supporting cast including Hume Cronyn and Burgess Meredith. This black comedy about a heist and hidden loot holds up for a while, but then strains at the end. The veteran actors, Douglas and Fonda, make it worthwhile, though.

There Will Be Blood - 2006 - Written and directed by Paul Thomas Anderson and starring multiple-Academy Award winner, Daniel Day-Lewis, as a driven oil wildcatter and the very talented Paul Dano (*Madmen*) as an overbearing religious zealot. The film is a classic, and the acting is first-rate all the way. Dano unbelievably holds his own with Lewis (almost an impossible feat).

These Three – 1936 - Directed by William Wyler and starring Merle Oberon and Joel McCrea in a soap-lover's dream about gossip and its ill effects. The story centers around a boarding school, a stolen bracelet, and a vicious student. For soap lovers only.

They Drive by Night – 1938 - Directed by Raoul Walsh and starring George Raft, Ann Sheridan, Ida Lupino, and Humphrey Bogart in a riveting Warner Brothers crime film that becomes an instant classic because of the great cast (especially Lupino) and the great direction of Walsh.

They Gave Him a Gun - 1937 - Directed by W.S. Can Dyke and starring Spencer Tracy, Gladys George and Franchot Tone in a tale that could be about any war and any veteran that returns from it, but this story is about WW 1. The film contends that some vets use their war experience to become criminals. An early form of film noir that hits the target.

They Live By Night – 1949 - Directed by Nicholas Ray and starring Farley Granger, Cathy O'Donnell and Howard DaSilva as a heavy. This film noir deluxe is a great first effort by Ray and a preview of even better efforts in the future. Good stuff.

They Made Me a Fugitive – England - 1947 - Directed by Alberto Cavalcanti and starring Trevor Howard and Sally Gray as a star-crossed couple who are drawn into a life of crime in another great film noir from across the pond. A tale of betrayal and revenge.

They Might Be Giants - 1971 - Directed by Anthony Harvey and starring George C Scott as an eccentric millionaire (not much of a stretch there) and Joanne Woodward as his sidekick, Dr. Watson. Yes, this is yet another copy of Sherlock Holmes with an A cast, but the results are mixed. Scott and Woodward are impeccable, but the screenplay by Goldman is flawed. Good fun.

They Shoot Horses, Don't They – 1969 - Directed by Sydney Pollack and starring Jane Fonda and Michael Sarazin in the lead roles as dance contestants during the Depression. There are numerous powerful images in this film and Gig Young almost steals the film as the MC. Oscar-worthy in almost every category.

They Were Expendable – 1945 - Directed by John Ford in a curiously low-key manner (he usually used big scale in his films) and starring John Wayne, Robert Montgomery and Donna Reed in the lead roles. This small film about the exploits of the small boats of the Navy in the early part of the Pacific War is as good as most of the bigger films of WW2.

They Who Dare – 1954 – Directed by Lewis Milestone and starring Dirk Bogarde and a solid supporting cast in a story British forces attacking the Luftwaffe in the Dodecanese Islands. Better than your average B war film.

They Won't Believe Me - 1947 - Directed by Irving Pichel and starring a gun-toting (see poster) Robert Young (*Father Knows Best*) and a worldly Susan Hayward (far more believable). This story of a rich slimeball using women like tissues will have you rooting for Young to get the death penalty. George Sanders would have been perfect in this role.

They Won't Forget – 1937 - Directed by Mervyn LeRoy and starring Claude Rains as an evil DA and Ed Norris as the wrongly accused murderer of a small town girl from the South (played by Lana Turner in her first role). An underrated film.

The Thief of Bagdad – England - 1940 - Directed by Michael Powell and starring Sabu and June Duprez. The underwhelming cast is more than compensated for by the lush photography of Powell, a master of the camera. Didn't anyone notice that they misspelled Baghdad?

Thieves Highway- 1949 - Directed by Jules Dassin and starring Richard Conte, Lee J. Cobb, Valentina Cortessa, and Barbara Lawrence in a gritty film noir about a returning veteran who gets revenge for his father. One of the best raw underbelly of society films ever made. A must-see.

Thieves Like Us - 1974 - Directed by Robert Altman and starring Keith Carradine and Shelly Duval. Louise Fletcher (One Flew Over the Cuckoo's Nest) is also featured. This is a lower case version of Bonnie and Clyde without the sense of humor and thrills. For Depression film addicts only.

The Thin Blue Line – 1998 - Directed by Errol Morris and starring the actual criminals involved in the murder of a Dallas police officer, Robert W. Wood, Randall Adams and David Harris. The documentary follows a series of interviews that provide more questions than answers. Similar to the infamous Tafero murder case in Florida years earlier. Chilling.

The Thing From Another World - 1951 - Directed by Christian Nyby with Howard Hawks looking over his shoulder as an uncredited co-director, The film stars a solid B cast including an unrecognizable James Arness (Matt Dillon from *Gunsmoke*) and is a story of alien life in the Arctic Circle. My favorite scene is when the liberal professor tries to befriend the alien. A must see.

Thin Ice – 2011-- Directed by Jill Sprecher and starring Greg Kinnear, Alan Arkin and Billy Crudup in a Coen Brothers-type comedy that combines elements of *Fargo*, *The Red Violin*, and *House of Games*, three diverse, but very entertaining films in their own right, into a very funny movie.

Think Fast, Mr. Moto – 1937 - Directed by Norman Foster and starring Peter Lorre as Mr. Moto, the clever Japanese detective. Nice atmosphere and good script make this series better the Charlie Chan films (no goofy comedy), and would have overtaken that seriess, had not WW2 interfered a few years later.

The Thin Man - 1934 - Directed by W.S. Van Dyke and starring William Powell and Myrna Loy as Nick and Nora Charles, the most famous husband-wife detective team in the history of cinema. Maureen O'Sullivan is also featured. The initial entry is not as good as many of the sequels it spawned, but it interesting to see the origin (especially of the name, *Thin Man*).

The Thin Red Line – 1998 - Directed by Terrence Malick and starring Sean Penn and Nick Nolte in a harrowing retelling of a fictional invasion of a Japanese Island during the Pacific campaign. The rock-solid script written by James Jones is what makes the film so believable. Jones was the master of this genre. Haunting music.

The Third Man – 1949 - Directed by Carol Reed and starring Joseph Cotton, Orson Welles and Trevor Howard and a fine supporting cast in a tale about post-war Germany and the black market for valuable medicine. Great music, great script and tight acting make this a classic of Post-War Germany.

Thirteen Princess Trees (China) – 2006- A - Directed by Lu Yue and starring Liu Xin, Duan Bowen and Zhao Mengqiao in a story about a coming-of-age film in Chinese high school. Several controversial themes are broached in this unique Chinese production. The theme of teenage mating rituals in modern China is one of them. Originally, I had thought this was a film about a princess who smoked marijuana.

Thirty Seconds Over Tokyo - 1944 - Directed by Mervyn Leroy and starring Spencer Tracy as Jimmy Doolittle, the man who bombed Tokyo only two months after Pearl Harbor. The film is based on historical fact. Robert Mitchum and Van Johnson are also featured. This raid was mostly a psychological lift for the folks back home, after the early dark days of the war.

This Gun For Hire – 1950 - Directed by Frank Tuttle and starring Alan Ladd and a rare appearance of Veronica Lake with two eyes (she usually wore her hair over one eye in almost all of her films). This classic film noir features Ladd in one of his rare bad guy roles as a hit man. Good stuff from start to finish

This Island Earth – 1955 - Directed by Joseph M Newman and starring a shaky B cast of actors. The film is advertised as two and a half years in the making; it was more likely that it took two of those years just to convince Universal to film this turkey. Often featured on *Mystery Science Theater 3000* for justifiable lampooning, but has some harrowing moments. Fun to watch.

This is Spinal Tap – 1984 - Directed by Rob Reiner in mockumentary form and is a classic spoof of rock bands. The B cast does a great job keeping a straight face and staying in character throughout the film, so that some in the audience actually think it is a real band (of course, these are the dumb people in the audience). Fun to see.

This Land is Mine – 1943 - Directed by Jean Renoir and starring a stellar cast including Charles Laughton, Maureen O'Hara and George Sanders in a tale of the French Resistance during World War 2. Although probably fictional, still interesting.

This Man Must Die – France - 1970 - Directed by Claude Chabrol and starring a B cast of French actors in a tale of revenge for the killing of a young boy. Directed with pinpoint precision by Chabrol, who, like Hitchcock, keeps us in suspense til the very end and shows that actors are secondary to a good director (like Hitchcock as well)

This Sporting Life – England -1963 - Directed by Lindsay Anderson and starring Richard Harris and Rachel Roberts in a scathing examination of the life of a soccer star in England. Great script and explosive dialogue make this a must-see.

The Thomas Crown Affair – 1968 - A - Directed by Norman Jewison and starring Steve McQueen as the original Thomas Crown along with the smoking hot Faye Dunaway as his romantic interest. Remade successfully in 1999, but not as good as the original. Great music as well.

Three Came Home - 1950 - Directed by Jean Nugelesco and starring Claudette Colbert in a sugar-coated treatment of a WW2 Japanese prison camp. The camps were far more brutal than the one portrayed in this film, but Hollywood was in the process of getting cushy with anti-communist post-war Japan at the time. One of Colbert's last films and interesting to see.

Three Comrades – 1938 - Directed by Frank Borzage and starring a stellar cast including Robert Taylor, Robert Young and Franchot Tone along with Margaret Sullivan in a tale about three young German soldiers returning to life after WW1. Very good depiction of the effects of war on normal young men.

Three Days of the Condor – 1975 - Directed by Sidney Pollack and starring Robert Redford and the sexy Faye Dunaway. Cliff Robertson also adds to the production values. This tale of a NYC reference librarian outwitting the CIA and getting to the NY Times with a sensational story is quite amusing and entertaining. Don't mess with those NYC reference librarians.

Three on the Trail - 1936 – Directed by Howard Bretherton and starring William Boyd (Hopalong Cassidy) in the lead role. Hoppy would soon leave these dreary B Westerns to begin his own brand of action in just one year. Fun to watch Boyd.

Three Strangers - 1946 - Directed by Jean Negulesco and starring Peter Lorre, Sydney Greenstreet and Geraldine Fizgerald in a highly unlikely, but highly entertaining scenario about three strangers who make a pact to buy a winning Irish Sweepstakes ticket. Performances are top-notch and Fitzgerald's best until *A Trip to Bountiful*.

Throne of Blood – Japan – 1957 - Directed by Akira Kurosawa and starring Toshiro Mifune and a solid B cast of Japanese actors in a story about guilt and ill-gotten gains. This Shakespearean-type tale is expertly directed by Kurosawa, who really kno

Through a Glass Darkly – 1962 – Sweden – Directed by Ingmar Bergman and starring Max von Syndow and a small, competent supporting cast of B actors who tell a story about four people and their psychological problems. Strictly for soap-lovers.

Throw Mama From the Train - 1987 - Directed and starring Danny DaVito and Billy Crystal in a far-fetched fantasy that mirrors the plot of Hitchcock's Strangers on a Train. Danny needs to kill his mother and everyone wants to be a best-selling writer. The dialogue is hilarious, however, and Davito's direction is perfect.

Thunder Over the Plains – 1953 - Directed by Andre Detoth (the least talented of all Randolph's directors) and starring Randolph Scott and a group of B actors. Scott is not able to rescure this mediocre script and plot, but there is no such thing as a bad Randolph Scott Western.

THX 1138 – 1971 - Directed by George Lucas and starring Robert Duvall and Donald Pleasence in a futuristic tale that is similar to 1984, but with more artistic filming. A good first effort from Lucas, but the weak female lead prevents the story from evolving too intensely. A good preview of things to come from Lucas, however.

Ticket to Heaven – Canada - 1981 - Directed by Ralph L. Thomas, and starring Nick Mancuso with a solid group of B Canadian actors in a courageous tale of exposing the horror of religious cults. Film shows how these cults break down human resistance to their ideas. A real eye-opener.

Tight Little Island – England - 1949 - Directed by Alexander Mackendrick and starring a very funny cast of talented B actors from England. In a film reminiscent of Local Hero, the local Scottish population of the island is suffering from a shortage of wartime spirits until a freighter runs aground near their shores loaded with whiskey. Based on true facts.

Timbuktu – 2015 - Directed by Abderrahmane Sissako and starring Abel Jafri as Abdelkrim, Fatoumata Diawara as La chanteuse, and Hichem Yacoubi as Djihadiste in the most difficult listing of director and leading actors playing characters in recent memory. This cautionary tale of a Muslim family trying to avoid radicals in their own country is a perfect example of how a large majority can be manipulated by a small minority fringe group. Recommended.

Time After Time - 1979 - Directed by Nicholas Meyer and starring Malcolm MacDowell and Mary Steenburgen in a wonderful science fiction tale about H G Wells pursuing Jack the Ripper through modern time. This creative coupling of two famous tales works very well on the big screen and is a real treat. Recommended.

Time Changer- 2002 – Appropriately directed by Rich Christiano and starring a forgotten cast of C actors, this unintentional comedy of a Bible professor travelling 100 years into the future is quite funny when viewed with a different perspective. Enjoy the craziness.

The Time Machine- 1960- Directed by George Pal and starring a miscast Rod Taylor as George, a tinkering inventor at the turn of the century in 1900 and the alluring Yvette Mimieux, as the futuristic love interest he discovers among a colony of harvested farm animals set for eventual slaughter and consumption. The real star of the film, however, is the time machine itself. Seeing this film in 1960 at a young age, one could not help but be inspired by the Time Machine. It set in motion my desire to be an astronaut. It was on my top ten list at one time, when, of course, I had hardly seen more than twenty or so major films.

It is still on my top 100 list of all-time great films, although I am sure most of the other critics have pretty much eliminated it by now. The special effects of the film were spectacular at the time in 1960, but would be considered pretty lame now fifty years later. The scientific and human drama of the film, however, retains its interesting premise. Man has always wondered about travelling through time and if you could, where and when would you go to? The setting for this film is far into the future (well over 100,000 years). The premise of a future divided between underground cannibals and helpless surface humans is no more farfetched than most other futuristic premises. Pal does a great job of translating the great Wells novel to the screen. Let's hope Wells is wrong for once about his predictions. This is a must see film for me, but I can recommend it to anyone.

Time Travelers Wife – 2009- Directed by Robert Schwentke and starring a cast of B actors in a nice B script about a librarian who travels in time (As a former NYC Reference Librarian, I am a sucker for librarian movies). Solid B entertainment.

The Tin Star – 1957 – Directed by Anthony Mann and starring Henry Fonda, Anthony Perkins, and Neville Brand (TV-*The Untouchables*) as a top cast in an average tale about a sheriff who has to measure the value of his life versus the money he gets paid as sheriff.

T-Men - 1947 - Directed by the competent Anthony Mann and starring a B cast including Dennis O'Keefe in a story about undercover Treasury agents trying to bust a counterfeiting ring. Told in semi-documentary style similar to Dragnet. Not exceptional, but fun to watch.

To Be or Not to Be – 1942 - Directed by Ernest Lubitsch and starring Carole Lombard and Jack Benny in a light-hearted romp through Nazi Germany. The predecessor to The Producers succeeds despite long odds and a formidable setting (Nazi Germany is not exactly the best setting for a comedy). Fun to see Benny in action.

To Catch a Thief – 1955 - Directed by Alfred Hitchcock and starring Cary Grant and Grace Kelly in a classy treatment of a hackneyed plot (woman falls in love with jewel thief). Hitchcock is able to take this run of the mill plot and turn it out as a filming gem.

To End All Wars- 2002 – Directed by David L Cunningham and starring Kiefer Sutherland in a tale about war in the Pacific and an encounters with the Japanese. Nothing terribly original here, but still effective.

To Have and Have Not – 1944 - Directed by Howard Hawks and starring Humphrey Bogart and Lauren Bacall along with the talented Walter Brennan. Based on the overrated book by overated writer Ernest Hemingway (which was substantially rewritten for the screen). This film is more famous for the smoking hot pairing of Bogey and Bacall.

To Hell and Back -1955 - Directed by Jesse Hibbs and starring Audie Murphy portraying himself during WW2. The film depicts the Battle of the Bulge as happening in sunny weather. It was, in fact, fought in wintry, icy conditions with snow and low visibility (my father was there). The film is still quite engrossing since it is based mostly on fact.

To Kill a Mockingbird – 1962 - Directed by Robert Mulligan and starring Gregory Peck and a solid supporting cast including Robert Duvall. This story of prejudice in a small town hits the mark as does the character of Boo Radley, played by Duvall. Peck won the Academy award for his portrayal.

Tokyo Olympiad - 1965 - Directed by Kon Ichikawa and starring the participants of the 1964 Olympics. The film is a superb documentary of the 1964 Olympics done with magnificent photography and editing. One of the best documentaries ever made. Up there with *Olympia* by Leni Rifenstahl as a classic.

Tokyo Story – Japan - 1953 - Directed by Yasujiro Ozu and starring a B cast of Japanese actors who do a great job of acting out a classic script about an elderly couple visiting their grown grandchildren in Tokyo, who are generally too busy to pay much attention to them. A great lesson for most of us who will face the same situation some day.

To Live – China – 1994 - Directed by Zhang Yimou and starring Gong Li and Ge You in a story about the difficulties of living and bringing up a family in China during The Great Leap Forward (which was actually a great leap backward) and The Cultural Revolution (which contained no culture at all and destroyed everything old including lives of millions of educated Chinese). Great filmmaking.

Tombstone -1993 - Directed by George P. Cosmatos and starring Kurt Russell, Val Kilmer, Bill Paxton, Sam Elliot, Powers Boothe, and Charlton Heston in a story about Wyatt Earp and his brothers that may have contained some actual history. Plenty of action.

Too Late the Hero - 1970 - Directed by Robert Aldrich and starring Michael Caine, Cliff Robertson and Henry Fonda in the principal roles. This gritty little WW2 film is fairly unknown, but delivers a pretty good wallop for early WW2 efforts in the Pacific. Worth viewing.

Tootsie – 1982 - Directed by Sydney Pollack and starring Dustin Hoffman as Tootsie and Jessica Lange, Teri Garr and Charles Durning in supporting roles. This classic comedy of a struggling actor who remakes himself into an energetic, not-too-looking woman who makes it big on TV, is a comedy classic. A must-see.

Topaz – 1969 - Directed by Alfred Hitchcock and starring a large group of B actors used as props by the Master to try and make a convoluted script into a cogent film. Not really as good as most of the other spy films done by Hitchcock, but still better than films done by other directors.

Topkapi – 1964 - Directed by Jules Dassin and starring Melina Mercouri, Peter Ustinov and Maximillian Schell in a heist caper that contains both comedy and suspense. The A director and competent acting trio makes this film work, as well as the excellent script.

Topper - 1937 - Directed by Norman Z McLeod and starring Cary Grant and Constance Bennett and a fine supporting cast in a story about a rich young couple who come back as ghosts and appear only to a stodgy middle-aged man. One of the classic Hollywood comedies and also made into a long-running TV show.

Tora! Tora! Tora! - 1970 - Directed by Richard Fleischer and starring Martin Balsam and Joseph Cotton. Most of the budget of this film was spent on the special effects and not the actors. The film shows the event from the Japanese side as well as the American side. Pearl Harbor was a disaster for the US Navy, who made a big mistake in keeping most of their ships in one place.

Torn Curtain - 1966 - Directed by Alfred Hitchcock and starring Paul Newman and Julie Andrews (miscast) in one of the rare Hitchcock films that spent money on A actors and got a B result. This convoluted tale of espionage just doesn't work with these actors, thus confirming Hitchcock's principle that a good script and good director are far more important than than A actors.

Tomorrowland 2015 -Directed by Brad Bird and starring George Clooney and a solid B cast with a decent script about an older man and a young boy who are geniuses and travel to a place called Tomorrowland (not the Disney version, but a much more serious place). Clooney seems to have a proclivity for sci-fi (Solaris). He is good in this genre.

Touch of Evil – 1958 - Directed by Orson Welles and starring a miscast Charlton Heston, Janet Leigh and Orson Welles. Heston as a Mexican? Please. The rest of the film works pretty well, but Welles gets a bit too artsy for most viewers with his unusual shooting angles. Welles is not very well cast for that matter, but the story is interesting.

Town Without Pity – 1957 - Directed by Gottfried Reinhardt with a script developed by Dalton Trumbo (at the behest of Kirk Douglas, the leading role). The story concerns a rape of a German woman by four US military personnel. The defense attorney turns out to be more vicious than any of the rapists. This was a film better known for its music to sell Gene Pitney's recording of the title song. But interesting to watch Douglas in action.

Toy Story – 1995 - Produced by Disney Studios and starring the voices of various well-known actors to tell a story of what toys do when no one is watching them. A great romp for kids of all ages to infinity and beyond. Pixel Entertainment made their mark with this film and has been a force in animation ever since.

Traffic – 2000 - Directed by Steven Soderbergh and starring an all-star cast featuring the major debut of Benicio DelToro. This gritty tale of the drug trade and its tragic effects on the population is a real eye-opener with its authenticity. Recommneded highly.

Trail of the Vigilantes - 1940 - Directed by Allan Dwan and starring the unusual pairing of Franchet Tone (better known for romance films) and Broderick Crawford (*Highway Patrol*). This tale of vigilantes was a bit off the beaten path of most Westerns produced during this period. Not bad.

The Train – 1965 - Directed by John Frankenheimer and starring Burt Lancaster in the lead role with Paul Schofield in a key role as well. This story of the rescue of precious French artwork by a train engineer is riveting from start to finish. Highly recommended.

The Transsiberian – England - 2008 - Directed by Brad Anderson and starring Woody Harrelson (miscast) and Ben Kingsley (well cast). A B actress plays the romantic prop for Harrelson. The British always do a good job with these tales of intrigue and suspense on the rails. This one is also well done.

Trapeze – 1956 - Directed by Carol Reed and starring Burt Lancaster and Tony Curtis. Gina Lollobrigida adds to the eye candy of the film. This minor tale of the circus is well-directed by Reed and well-acted by Lancaster and Curtis, so the mundane story is far more interesting than usual.

Treasure Island – 1950 - Directed by Byron Haskin and starring Bobby Driscoll (a child actor who never made the A list) as Jim Hawkins, a boy who has the adventure of a lifetime, and Robert Newton, a B actor, who has his greatest role ever as Long John Silver. The hammy Newton is perfect here, as are the production values. A must-see classic for every boy.

Treasure of Ruby Hills – 1955 – Directed by Frank McDonald and starring Zachary Scott and Lee Van Cleef (*Good, Bad and Ugly*) in the leading roles as good guy and bad guy. Can you guess which was which? Standard treasure tale.

Treasure of the Sierra Madre – 1948 - Directed by John Huston and starring Humphrey Bogart, Walter Huston, and Tim Holt in the lead roles in a tale about greed and redemption. This classic film about gold is famous for one line: "Badges? We don't need no stinking badges."

Tree of the Wooden Clogs – Italy - 1979 - Directed by Ermanno Olmi and starring amateur actors in a story about rural life in Italy in the late 1800s. This film shows what a great script and good direction can do for a production. Recommended.

Trigger Fingers – 1946 – Directed by Lambert Hillyer, who specialized in B Westerns, and starring Johnny Mack Brown in this fun rendition of dealing with bandits who are doomed to failure against the mighty Brown. This film not long for the list.

Trio – 1950 – Directed by Ken Annakin (no relation to the *Star Wars* character) and Harold French (who also directed another Maugham film, Encore) and starring a young Micheal Rennie and Jean Simmons in collection of short story episodes by Somerset Maugham (one of my favorite writers). Recommended.

The Trip to Bountiful – 1985 -Directed by Peter Masterson and starring Geraldine Page in her Academy-Award winning performance that caps her career. This sensitive story about a woman visiting her home town that has virtually vanished struck a chord with many older Americans. Film also noted for DeMornay keeping her clothes on.

Troubled Laughter (China) - 1979 - Directed by Deng Yimin and Yang Yanjin and starring Pan Hong as a troubled wife in a small rural town in China. This soap's title refers to the different types of laughs employed by the Chinese. They often chuckle when confronted with problems. Interesting.

Trouble in Paradise – 1932 - Directed by Ernst Lubitsch and starring Miriam Hopkins, Kay Francis and Herbert Marshall (all solid B actors) in a screwball comedy about a romantic triangle in the upper classes. One of the triangle is a thief, though. Very engaging, even if a bit dated.

The Trouble With Harry – 1955 - Directed by Alfred Hitchcock and starring Shirley MacLaine and Ed Gwenn (*Munsters*) in one of the Master's lesser works. Too cute for its own good and the film does not work as a comedy or a suspense thriller. But bad Hitchcock is still better than most other efforts at suspense.

Troy - 2004 - Directed by Wolfgang Petersen (who is better at small films rather than epics) and starring Brad Pitt and Orlando Bloom in the lead roles. Peter O'Toole picks up a paycheck as well. This tale about the siege of Troy has all the bells and whistles, but not the heart of the book (*The Illiad*).

True Crime - 1999 - Directed by Clint Eastwood and starring Clint Eastwood, Denis Leary, and James Woods among the more notable actors in the film. Supposedly based on Klaven's novel of the same name, but extremely reminiscent of In Cold Blood, which was better done.

True Grit – 1969 - Directed by Henry Hathaway and starring John Wayne in his Academy -Award winning role. Kim Darby and Glen Campbell do nice turns as well in a supporting effort. The film was successfully remade forty years later by the Coen Brothers. Strother Martin, Robert Duvall and Dennis Hopper make great heavies as well.

True Love – 1989 - Directed by Nancy Savoka and starring Annabella Sciorra and Ron Eldard in the lead roles as a happily married couple who have quite a few bumps on the road and don't live happily ever after. A nice, realistic look at romantic love that turns sour. Great soap.

Trumbo – 2015 – Directed by Jay Roach and starring Bryan Cranston in his best role (even better than his hit TV show) as Dalton Trumbo, the great screenwriter who refused to buckle under the witch hunt for pinkos and reds during the McCarthy era. A man's political beliefs should have nothing to do with the quality of work he produces; but in the late 1940s and early 1950s in the US, these constitutional rights were trampled upon. Highly Recommended.

Trust – 1991 - Directed by Hal Hartley and starring B actors Adrienne Shelly and Martin Donavon in a superior tale of love from strangers that is tightly directed by Hartley. You will hiss the original family and boyfriend in this one and root for the new lovers.

Tucker - 1988 - Directed by Francis Ford Coppola and starring Jeff Bridges as Tucker, a man who was not afraid to challenge the big car companies with a new car company in the late 1940s. This is a bittersweet tale told with great style by Coppola. A glorious misfire that lost money, but was a critical success, has Coppola mirroring Tucker.

Tunes of Glory – 1960 - Directed by Robert Neame and starring Alec Guinness and John Mills in a very parochial story about post-WW2 Scots on a military installation. Unless you are very familiar with Scottish culture (and very few audiences are), very little of the film will make much sense to you. Recommended for Brits and Anglophiles.

Tuya's Marriage (China) – 2007 - Directed by Wang Quan'an and starring Yu Nan as Tuya, a woman from Inner Mongolia who must divorce the man she loves, so she can marry into money to support him and her children. An absolutely fascinating film that takes us to places we have never been; both physically and emotionally.

Twelve O'Clock High – 1949 - Directed by Henry King and starring Gregory Peck and Dean Jagger, who won an Academy Award for his efforts in the best supporting actor category. This taut tale of daylight bombing raids over occupied France and Nazi Germany captures the enormous stress that these men were under. Good action and fine acting.

Twister - 1996 - Directed by Jan deBont and starring Helen Hunt and Bill Paxton. Philip Seymour upstages both of them when he is on the screen in this story of the people who actually chase these storms for research purposes. Visually stunning, but emotionally flat. Still, many fine moments on the screen.

Two English Girls – 1971 - Directed by Francois Truffaut and starring Truffaut regular, Jean-Pierre Leaud, in a soap triangle centering around a young man in Paris and two sisters who have the misfortune to fall in love with him.

Two Women – Italy - 1961 - Directed by Carlo Ponti and starring Sophia Loren in her Academy-Award winning role as a refugee mother trying to protect her teenage daughter. She is not successful, but life goes on, as the film shows. Powerful stuff. Keep an eye out for Jean-Paul Belmondo.

U

Ugetsu – Japan - 1954 - Directed by Kenji Mizoguchi and starring a cast of B Japanese actors in a story told during the feudal period of Japan's history. It concerns samurai, scheming concubines, and lots of soapy complications. Considered a classic in Japan.

The Ugly American - 1963-- Directed by George Englund and starring Marlon Brando in the lead role as an American ambassador to a fictional Southeast Asian country (Vietnam?). The film highlights William J Lederer's fine book on Western colonial practices in the 20th Century and their unfortunate results. The lesson was ignored, however, and history had to be repeated in Vietnam (we should have learned from the French as well). Interesting,although a bit dated.

Ulee's Gold - 1997 - Directed by Victor Nunez and starring Peter Fonda in the lead role as a peace-loving raiser of bees. The title refers to honey, not money. When threatened by sinister outside forces, Ulee finds a unique way to protect them. Recommended.

Ulysses - 1955 - Directed by Mario Camerini and starring Kirk Douglas as Ulysses in a very loose portrayal of Homer's Odyssey. I really enjoyed watching this film as a kid and it is even entertaining for adults. This movie began the steady stream of Italian "epics" that flooded the US for the next ten years such as Hercules and the like.

Ulzana's Raid – 1972 - Directed by Robert Aldrich and starring A actor, Burt Lancaster in the lead role. Plenty of action in this allegory of the Vietnam War told as a tale of US repression of the American Indian. The truth was probably somewhere in the middle of the lies told to us as children about the settling of the West and modern revisionism of the evils of Western Expansion.

Umberto D – Italy – 1952 - Directed by Vittorio DeSica and starring Carlo Battisti (an amateur actor, as was the entire cast) as an aging man in Post-WW2 Italy. Aging in any country can be a frightful experience, but the difficulties are amplified in this neo-realistic portrayal of a man with only one dependable friend; his dog. An Italian and international classic.

Unbroken 2014 – Directed by Angelina Jolie and starring Jack O'Connell in a story about an Olympic athlete that survives getting his ship sunk during the war, and then survives a POW camp afterwards. Pretty lucky guy.

Under Fire -1983 – Directed by Roger Spottiswoode and starring Gene Hackman, Nick Nolte and Ed Harris in a war tale about war from the point of war correspondents covering the war, and the dangers they face every day.

Under Two Flags – 1936 - Directed by Frank Lloyd and starring Ronald Colman, Claudette Colbert, Rosalind Russell, and Victor McLaglen in the lead roles. This action-packed film has a Biblical reference; as when David sent the husband of his romantic interest on a suicide mission. The outcome is different in the French Foreign Legion, though.

The Unforgiven – 1960 - Directed by John Huston and starring Burt Lancaster and a badly miscast Audrey Hepburn as a half-Indian. Also starring Charles Bickford and Audie Murphy, sho seems lost without a gun scene to play. Despite these minor flaws, the film packs an emotional wallop and has some great scenes.

The Unforgiven – 1992 - Directed and starring Clint Eastwood, this tale of revenge for the scarring of a Western prostitute is quite interesting because these women seldom, if ever, fought back against any attrocities committed against them. Also starring Gene Hackman, Morgan Freeman and Richard Harris (who is wonderfully over the top).

Union Pacific - 1939 - Directed by Cecil B DeMille, who always made "BIG" films. DeMille never spared much expense on his productions, so consequently, most of them were pretty good. This film, starring Barbara Stanwyck, Joel McCrea, Robert Preston and Brian Donlevy is no exception. Lots of action about the building of America's greatest railroad.

Unknown Pleasures (China) – 2002 - Directed by Jia Zhangke and starring Zhao Tao, Wang Hongwei, Qiong Wu, Wei Wei Zhao, and Qing Feng Zhao in an eye-opening film about the spoiled generation of only-children living together in a modern Chinese city. Sort of like Friends on Crack.

An Unmarried Woman – 1978 - Directed by Paul Mazursky and starring Jill Claburgh in her Academy-Award nominated performance as a divorcee who seeks meaning in her life. Also starring Alan Bates and Michael Murphy. A film almost every divorced woman in the US can identify with.

Unstoppable – 2010 - Directed by Tony Scott and starring Denzel Washington and Chris Pine in the leading roles. This tale of an out-of-control train is similar to Speed and Runaway Train, two great action flicks. This one is right up there with them.

The Untouchables – 1987- Directed by Brian De Palma and starring Kevin Costner as Eliot Ness, the Federal Agent responsible for bringing down Al Capone in Chicago , Robert DeNiro as a wonderfully evil

Al Capone, Sean Connery as a chief aid to Ness, Andy Garcia as another of Ness's helpers, and Charles Martin Smith as the comic relief accountant for Ness, who actually helps land Capone for tax evasion. Connery won a well-deserved Best Supporting Actor for his role in the film. What didn't win and deserved to, was the music score for the film, which was nominated, but lost to *The Last Emperor* for some obscure reason.

I like to think of myself as fairly knowledgeable on film music and there is no way the score from *The Last Emperor* (although good) was anywhere nearly as dramatic as *The Untouchables*. But, the Academy often makes oversights like this in all categories. The music was written by Ennio Morricone, the master film scorer responsible for unforgettable themes from his spaghetti Westerns, *A Fistful of Dollars*, *For a Few Dollars More*, and *The Good, The Bad, and the Ugly*. He also wrote what many consider to be his best music for *Cinema Paradiso*, years later. Look for a homage to Serge Eisenstein during the Chicago Train Station scene where there is a baby carriage going down the steps. Eisenstein used this sequence for his Russian epic, *Potemkin*. The film is about the formulation of the G-men that eventually bring down Al Capone. This is a must-see film and is listed in the top 100 of numerous film critics (including mine).

Up In The Air – 2009 – Directed by Jason Reitman and starring George Clooney and Vera Farmiga as casual lovers, but serious business people, more concerned about getting ahead than creating a more meaningful relationship. Interesting concept.

Used Cars - 1980 - Directed by Robert Zemeckis and starring Kurt Russell in a first-rate comedy about used-car salesmen. Jack Warden (perfectly cast) also adds to the production values. Film has attained great cult status and is a primer for avoiding used car salesmen.

The Usual Suspects – 1995 - Directed by Bryan Singer and starring a powerhouse cast including Gabriel Byrne, Steven Baldwin, Benecio Del Toro, Chazz Palmenteri, and, of course, the man who steals the film from everyone else, Kevin Spacey. O My God! Keyser Soze is coming to get me!

Utah Blaine – 1957 – Directed by Fred F Sears and starring Rory Calhoun in the lead role (he is not a Mormon from Utah) . The film features some exceptional shootouts that were a cut above the usual gunplay in most of the oaters of the time.

V

Vanya on 42nd Street – 1994 - Directed by Louis Malle and starring Julianne Moore and Wallace Shawn in the lead roles for Uncle Vanya, the Cherkov play which was rehearsed and finally taped at an abandoned 42nd Street movie house. The movie house was eventually restored by the Walt Disney Company. Shawn is always fascinating (*My Dinner with Andre*) and worth seeing.

Vera Cruz - 1954 - Directed by Robert Aldrich and starring a fading Gary Cooper and Burt Lancaster in the lead roles of an action Western. Lancaster was seldom, if ever, cast in a bad guy role, so this was interesting to see him enjoying himself as a heavy. Cooper shows his age in this one and it is his last action film. Worth seeing for Burt.

The Verdict – 1982 - Directed by Sidney Lumet and starring Paul Newman in the lead role. Newman is supported by a great cast including James Mason (who was nominated for an Academy Award), Lindsay Crouse (*House of Games*), Charlotte Rampling (*Zardoz*), Jack Warden (*Used Cars*) and a screenplay writtren by David Mamet (*House of Games*). Story of washed-up lawyer getting a chance at one last case great vehicle for Newman.

Vertigo – 1959- Directed by Alfred Hitchcock and starring James Stewart and Kim Novak in the lead roles. This is one of the Master's best and should not be missed. The story of a cop with fear of heights, who blames himself for the death of a strange woman is a classic.

V for Vendetta – 2005 – Directed by James McTeigue and starring a cast of unknown B actors who do a decent job. The problem is that the film promises a lot more than it can deliver. It raises our expectations, and then disappoints us in the end. Became the poster child for Anonymous. Still enjoyable.

Vicky Christina Barcelona – 2008 - Directed by Woody Allen and starring Javier Bardem, Penelope Cruz and Scarlett Johanson in the lead roles of a story concerning rich people and promiscuity. Not all that funny, like Allen's earlier films. Patricia Clarkson, Kevin Dunn, and Rebecca Hall add to the cast, but film lacks soul and sense of humor. For die-hard Allen fans. If you are tired of being a clown, you should retire; not try to become a lion-tamer.

Victim – England – 1961 - Directed by Basil Dearden and starring Dirk Bogarde and Syms in the lead roles. Closet gay is outed and blackmailed. Famous for being first English-speaking film to mention the word homosexual. Interesting to see.

The Victors – 1963 - Directed by Carl Foreman and starring an all-star cast that depicts the events of occupied Germany immediately after the war ends. The moral of the story is that there are no victors in war. A hard-hitting film that shows the true effects of war on both the participants and the civilians involved. A must-see.

Victor/Victoria – 1982 - Directed by Blake Edwards and starring Julie Andrews and James Garner in a hilarious screwball comedy about a woman pretending to be a man on stage. Julie Andrews makes a clean breast of it as well. For adults only.

Videodrome – 1983- Directed by David Cronenberg and starring the talented James Woods, and the not-so-talented actress, Deborah Harry in the lead roles. A TV programmer comes up with a futuristic format for his new line of programming. Good story, but falls short on the delivery.

Vikings – 1959-Directed by Richard Fleischer (no relation to Miriam Fleisher, the famous librarian from Upper Manhattan), and starring Kirk Douglas, Tony Curtis, Ernest Borgnine and Janet Leigh in the lead roles. There was more ham in this film than in a German deli, but despite the numerous over the top performances, the film was very popular with audiences and didn't cost an arm and a leg to produce (except for Curtis).

Village of the Damned – England – 1960 - Directed by Wolf Rilla and starring one of my favorite actors, George Sanders, who tries his level best to keep a straight face in this ridiculous story that made lots of money, and was produced by John Carpenter over thirty years later for 100 times the cost of the original (really). An object lesson on how to make a hit movie on a shoestring budget. ($200,000).

The Virginian – 1946 – Directed by Stuart Gilmore and starring Joel McCrea (a much better choice as a romantic lead the Gary Cooper version. This fourth and final remake of the title is one of the better productions of this Western soap.

The Virgin Soldiers – England - 1969 - Directed by John Dexter and starring Hywel Bennett, Lynn Redgrave and Nigel Patrick in the lead roles. This is a funny soap triangle among a new recruit, an old sarge and the daughter of an officer. Success caused a sequel. Funny.

Viridiana - Spain – 1962 - Directed by Luis Bunuel and starring Fernando Rey, Sylvia Pinal and Francisco Rabal in the lead roles. This tale of Spanish perversion among the rich is the target of Bunuel's wrath. Classcism and religious allegory (a must for all Bunuel films) is rampant. Probably his best work.

Visions of Light – 1993 - Directed by Arnold Glassman, Todd McCarthy, and Stuart Sameuls and starring the great cinematographers in the history of Hollywood. This documentary examines each of the era's men behind the camera and the secrets to their success. Fascinating.

The Visitor - 2008 - Directed by Thomas McCarthy and starring Richard Jenkins in the lead role as an academic who accidentally expands his limited world when it is invaded by a few illegal immigrants. They bring a whole new meaning to his life. A very original screenplay.

Viva Villa! – 1934 – Directed by Jack Conway (not the Jack Conway from Lost Horizon) and starring the miscast Wallace Beery (who was good at almost everything he did) and Faye Wray (King Kong) as Mexicans (I am more Mexicans than these actors) who are revolting. Despite the revolting portrayals, the film is quite entertaining. Not exactly your PC Western.

Viva Zapata! – 1952 - Directed by Elia Kazan (On The Waterfront) and starring Marlon Brando as Zapata. Brando had worked with Kazan before in Waterfront and teamed up with him again for this production that did not quite hit the mark. Story of revolutionary Zapata turning into the despot that he overthrew is interesting, though.

The Voice of the Turtle – 1947 - Directed by Irving Rapper and starring Ronald Reagan and Eleanor Parker in the lead roles. This comedy of errors was probably the best that Reagan ever accomplished, but he would have much more success as President.

Voltaire – 1933 - Directed by John G. Adolfi and starring George Arliss as Voltaire. Arliss is supported by a solid cast of B actors in this story of the famous French writer who put on plays to communicate to the king the dismal conditions of the poor of France. Nice story line.

W

Wages of Fear – France – 1953 - Directed by Henri-Georges Clouzot and starring Yves Montand in his breakthrough role as a desperate man taking enormous risks for some quick money. A classic suspense-thriller that keeps you on the edge of your seat. Remade several years later as *Sorcerer*.

Wag the Dog - 1997 - Directed by Barry Levinson and starring Robert DeNiro and Dustin Hoffman in the lead roles as Washington insiders who are able to manipulate the media for their own purposes. A disturbing, but funny illustration of how easily the American people can be fooled. The origin of Fake News?

Wagon Master – 1950 - Directed by John Ford and starring Ward Bond in the role that made him famous (and also led to a long-running TV series on NBC) as Wagon Master. Supporting Bond is Ben Johnson and Harry Carey Jr. along with Joanne Dru. This is your classic Western fare for the trip across the American Frontier.

Wait Until Dark - 1967 - Directed by Terence Young and starring a perfectly cast Audrey Hepburn as a blind woman as well as a nicely cast Alan Arkin as a heavy, in a tale about stolen heroin hidden in a doll and the lengths that some crooks go through to obtain it. The final sequence is classic suspense and almost unbearable to watch.

Wake Island – 1942 - Directed by John Farrow and starring Brian Donlevy, Macdonald Carey and Robert Preston in the lead roles. William Bendix provides some comic relief in this tale about the doomed defense of Wake Island at the beginning of WW2.

Wake of the Red Witch - 1949 - Directed by Edward Ludwig and starring the real-life romantic couple of John Wayne and Gail Russell with Gig Young in a supporting role. The problem with this soap is that there is no clear protagonist. Everyone in the film is fairly morally reprehensible and the ending is predictable. Still fun to watch.

Walkabout – Australia - 1971 - Directed by Nicolas Roeg and starring Jenny Agutter, Luc Roeg and David Gulpilil as three young people who meet in the wild outback of Australia. Sort of an Australian version of Secret Garden with a lot more nature. Fascinating to watch.

A Walk in the Sun - 1945 - Directed by Lewis Milestone and starring Dana Andrews, Richard Conte, John Ireland and Lloyd Bridges as a group of American GIs fighting the Italians and Germans in Salerno, Italy. The film highlights the ambivalence of the Italians during the war.

Walk the Line - 2005 - Directed by James Mangold and starring Joaquin Phoenix and Reese Witherspoon in the lead roles as Johnny Cash and his wife. The film is a fine biopic that outlines the highlights and lowlights of Cash's life.

WALL-E – 2008 -Produced by Pixar for Walt Disney Studios and starring Wall-e, a mobile computer that has a lot more heart and common sense than the vast majority of mankind. Top of the line animation, storytelling and total package of entertainment. One of the best ever animated films.

Wall Street – 1987 - Directed by Oliver Stone and starring Michael Douglas and Charlie Sheen in the lead roles. Also starring Martin Sheen in a key supporting role. This tale of unmitigated greed was a harbinger of things to come in the financial crisis. Great performances all the way around.

The Wannsee Conference – Germany - 1984 - Directed by Heinz Schirk and starring the real-life monsters of the nazi party discussing the Final Solution for the elimination of Jews. A chilling documentary that is totally believable in every facet. A real eye-opener.

The War Game – England - 1967 - Directed by Peter Watkins in documentary style and featuring interviews with survivors of a fictional nuclear war. The amateur actors do a superb job of communicating the potential horror of such an event. It is a film you will never forget.

War Games- 1983 - Directed by John Badham and starring Matthew Broderick in his breakthrough leading role as a young computer whiz, who accidentally? hacks into the US nuclear programming system. It is ironic that this film follows *The War Game* in the reviews, but this one has a sense of humor (if such an event could be humorous). In any event, Broderick somehow pulls it off.

War Horse – 2009-Directed by Steven Spielberg and starring Jeremy Irvine and Emily Watson in the lead roles. But the real star, of course, is the War Horse. The film traces the trials of the horse during World War 1. It is highly reminiscent of The Black Stallion in its telling of the story through the eyes of a horse. Good film making.

The Warlord - 1965 - Directed by Franklin J Schaffner and starring Charlton Heston, Rosemary Forsyth and Richard Boone (miscast). Contrary to the title, the film is mostly about a romantic triangle among the War Lord, a peasant woman and her betrothed partner. This is first-class costume soap.

The Warlords (China) – 2007 - Directed by Peter Chan of Hong Kong and starring Jet Li, Andy Lau, Takeshi Kaneshiro, and Xu Jinglei in the lead roles. This epic war drama from China was better than any epic made anywhere else in the world during this year. This is a tale of the seldom-explored war of the Taiping Rebellion. Great cinematography.

War Lover 1962 – Directed by Philip Leacock and starring Steve McQueen as a psychologically damaged man who loves the thrill of war, as many others who had become addicted to it as well in various wars. Relentlessly depressing, but some excellent action sequences.

Warm Spring (China) - 2002 - Directed by Wulan Tana and starring Chengren Tian, Ruyi Qi, Zhang Yan, Hao Yang, and Weijie Yu in key roles. This is a tale of a very young orphan who finds a new family in a village far away from her original home. A heart-wrenching story that becomes inspirational by the end of the film.

The Warning Shot - 1967 - Directed by Buzz Kulic and starring David Janssen (*The Fugitive*), Steve Allen, Joan Collins, Carroll O'Conner (*All in the Family*), Eleanor Parker, Walter Pidgeon, Stefanie Powers, Keenan Wynn, and one of my favorite actors, George Sanders. This is a story of a cop who is framed for a shooting. Sounds like a pretty dull plot, eh? Well, it was. The direction by a TV director and the script by a TV writer pretty much doomed the production to B status, despite the A cast. This bomb helped doom Janssen's film career.

War of the Planet of the Apes – 2017 – Directed by Matt Reeves and starring a bunch of people wearing monkey suits (and I don't mean ill-fitting suits off the rack from Walmart). . The only recognizable face in the film is an aging Woody Harrelson, who seems to be miscast here, but what the hell; its only a movie. Great production values (as usual in this series). Interesting.

War of the Satellites- 1958- Master B director Roger Corman gives it all he has in this sci-fi attempt at filmmaking. This complex plot has two civilizations battling it out for supremacy. This one is here for your comedic enjoyment; not serious science fiction. It's like watching an Ed Wood production

War of The Worlds – 1953 - Directed by Byron Haskin and starring Gene Barry and Ann Robinson, B television actors, who give fine performances in this classic science-fiction tale by H G Wells. In my opinion, this version is superior to the bells and whistles version with Tom Cruise made many years later.

War of the Worlds - 2005 - Directed by Steven Spielberg and starring Tom Cruise in a very loose remake of the 1953 classic of the same name. This films is able to stand on its own merits, but is still not as good as the original, despite having all the bells and whistles of a Spielberg production and making half a billion dollars. Still great viewing.

The War Wagon – 1967 – Directed by Burt Kennedy and starring John Wayne and Kirk Douglas (one of the few times they were teamed up- the other being In Harms's Way. This mundane story of stolen gold and revenge is a notch higher because of the acting talent.

Watch on the Rhine – 1943 - Directed by Herman Shumlin and starring Bette Davis and Paul Lukas in the lead roles. This WW 2 story was filmed at the beginning of the conflict and has that feel of authenticity that many films afterwards just cannot match. Good music by Max Steiner to boot makes this an A production.

The Water Diviner - 2015 – Directed by Russell Crowe and starring Russell Crowe as a father searching for his three sons who were involved in a fierce battle of World War One, *Gallipoli*. Heart-wrenching stuff.

Waterloo Bridge – 1940- Directed by Mervyn Leroy and starring Vivian Leigh and Robert Taylor in one of the top half dozen love stories of all time on film. Much better than *Gone with the Wind* and the chemistry in the love scenes is much better as well. It is a soap-lover's dream, but it also a great film for anyone. The best role of Taylor's career as well.

Way Ahead – England - 1944 - Directed by Carol Reed and starring David Niven in a rah-rah WW2 film depicting recent recruits in England after the debacle at Dunkirk. It follows the new soldiers from their training to deployment in North Africa against the vaunted Desert Fox, Rommel. Well-written by Peter Ustinov.

Wayne's World - 1992 - Directed by Penelope Spheeris and starring Mike Myers and Dana Carvey as two lovable nincompoops who have their own radio show that eventually draws the attention of bigger sponsors. This leads to a series of adventures for the two boys that include a romantic involvement and other complications. Enjoyable viewing.

Way Out West - 1937 - Directed by James W Horne and starring the funniest comedy team in history, Stan Laurel and Oliver Hardy. The boys venture out to the Far West for some predictable and some unpredictable fun in cowboy land. A classic from many angles.

The Wedding Singer - 1998 - Directed by Directed by Frank Coraci and starring Adam Sandler and Drew Barrymore in the lead roles. This is one of Sandler's better efforts and the chemistry between him and Barrymore is very good. Some very funny stuff. Recommended.

We Need To Talk About Kevin - 2011 - Directed by Lynne Ramsey, who did the screenplay as well and starring Tilda Swinton in the best performance of her admirable career as the mother of a bad seed child, played marvelously by Ezra Miller. The Academy missed this obvious nomination for Best Actress and shame on them. Not to mention they should have nominated Ramsey for at least one Award as well. A must see.

Went the Day Well? 1944 - England - Directed by Alberto Cavalcanti and starring a relatively unknown group of B actors who do a good job of depicting British soldiers performing well under extremely adverse conditions.

The Westerner - 1940 - Directed by William Wyler and starring Gary Cooper and Walter Brennan in the key roles. This tale of an interloper who invades the world of Judge Roy Bean, brilliantly played by Brennan, who won the Academy Award for Best Supporting Actor that year, is absolutely great as Bean. These two made six films together, but this is the best of them.

Western Union - 1941 - Directed by Fritz Lang and starring Robert Young (miscast), Randolph Scott, Dean Jagger, John Carradine and Virginia Gilmore is a tale of the establishment of the USA's first complete continental communication system. Action-packed as you would expect from writer Zane Grey.

Westworld - 1973 - Directed by Michael Crichton, who does an exceptional job, and starring Yul Brenner, Richard Benjamin and James Brolin in the feature roles. This Frankensteinian futuristic tale came out of left field in 1973 and wowed moviegoers for months. Brenner is unforgettable.

What Doesn't Kill You – 2008 - Directed by Brian Goodman and starring Mark Ruffalo and Ethan Hawke in the key roles. This is the poor man's version of The Town, a tale of two young men growing up as minor hoods in Boston. Different focus, though, which is on family versus friend quandry rather than on a major hood as in The Town.

When Comedy Was King - 1960 - Directed, written and produced by Robert Youngson and starring the comedy greats of all time in some of their best works. Youngson does a wonderful job highlighting some of the best comedy ever put on film by the greatest comedians in history. How could this film miss?

When Harry Met Sally – 1989 - Directed by Rob Reiner and starring Billy Crystal and Meg Ryan in the lead romantic roles. This classic love story made a big hit with American audiences. The story of a platonic friendship that blooms into love and marriage has grown in stature over the years to become an icon of this genre.

When Worlds Collide - 1951 - Directed by Rudolph Mate and produced by sci-fi expert, George Pal (War of the Worlds). The cast of B actors is fairly irrelevant compared to the story (which obviously did not happen). What is fun is to see how the end of the world was avoided. Fun to watch.

Where Danger Lives - 1950 - Directed by John Farrow and starring Robert Mitchum, Claude Rains and Faith Domergue (a B actress) in key roles. A man dumps his decent girlfriend to pursue a mentally unstable sexpot. Many of us have done the same stupid thing, so this is not really an eye-opening concept. Entertaining to watch.

Where Eagles Dare - 1969 - Directed by Bryan G Hutton and starring Clint Eastwood and Richard Burton in the lead roles as commandos posing as Germans in the Alps, so they can destroy an important German installation. This is the granddaddy of all commando films (with the possible exception of *The Guns of Navarone*). Good action.

Where the Sidewalk Ends – 1950 - Directed by Otto Preminger and starring Dana Andrews and Gene Tierney. This is some great noir done by top-notch actors armed with a good script. Although I didn't care for the unrealistic ending, which I will not reveal, the film as a whole is outstanding and will keep you in suspense for its entire length. Highly recommended.

While the City Sleeps - 1956 - Directed by Fritz Lang and starring an all-star cast with an excellent script. How could this noir tale miss? It didn't. The film stars Dana Andrews, Rhonda Fleming, George Sanders,

Howard Duff, Thomas Mitchell, Vincent Price, John Barrymore Jr., James Craig and Ida Lupino (a cast better than The Ten Commandments or Ben-Hur) for one tenth of the price. Good stuff.

Whirlpool - 1948 - Directed by Otto Premminger and starring Gene Tierney, Richard Conte, Jose Ferrer and Charles Bickford in addition to a fine script that produces a wonderful end product of a film. Not as good as some of the other noir features of the period, but worth viewing.

The Whistler – 1944 - Directed by William Castle, a master of B films during this era, and starring Richard Dix and J Carroll Naish (a future Charlie Chan) in the first installment of a highly successful film series derived from radio. Worth seeing the original, as future sequels tended to have fewer good production values.

White Dawn - 1974 - Directed by Philip Kaufman and starring Timothy Bottoms, Lou Gosset Jr, and Warren Oates in the lead roles. The actors do a great job with the creative script and the end result in a fine adventure film. The film depicts the Eskimo Indians trying to hold on to their traditions against outsiders. Good viewing.

White Heat – 1949 - Directed by Raoul Walsh and starring James Cagney, Virginia Mayo, and Edmund O'Brien in the classic gangster tale of a momma's boy who goes out with a bang. The line "Top of the World, Ma!" is an immortal American line of film dialogue. A must see.

Who's Afraid of Virginia Woolf? - 1966 - Directed by Mike Nichols, who has a wonderfully perverse sense of humor, and starring Elizabeth Taylor in her Academy-Award winning role as well as Richard Burton (who should have won instead of the limited-range actor, Lee Marvin, that year). The two stars are ably assisted by George Segal and Sandy Dennis (although she has a few too many mannerisms for me). The Albee play is brought off to perfection by pro Nichols.

The Wild One - 1954 - Directed by Laszlo Benedek and starring Marlon Brando in his iconoclastic role as a motor cycle maven. Also starring is a very convincing Lee Marvin and a very naive Mary Murphy in this highly dated film about bikers terrorizing a small Southwestern town. Great for its time, but a more than a bit dated now. Still worth watching for the outfit still worn by the Village people of New York's gay community.

Wilson – 1944 - Directed by Henry King and starring Alexander Knox in his Academy-Award winning role as President Woodrow Wilson, the man who led us through WW 1 and other crises. A fine supporting cast aids the production. Knox does an outstanding job and deserved his award. His passion for the United Nations (previously The League of Nations) is why we have one today.

Will Penny – 1968 - Directed by Tom Gries and starring Charlton Heston, Joan Hackett (one of the less attractive leading ladies of the time), and Donald Pleasence (miscast) in the lead roles. Lee Majors (Six Million Dollar Man) is also featured. Grisly Western sometimes misfires with questionable supporting acting, but Heston holds up the film well enough for it to be entertaining.

Will Success Spoil Rock Hunter? - 1967 - Directed by Frank Tashlin and starring Tony Randall and Jayne Mansfield in a comedy that mirrors its own opening credits; a series of commercials that do not deliver what they promise. Randall does his level best, but cannot get any chemistry from eye candy no-talent Mansfield. This fell under the good try, but no cigar category of comedies.

Winchester '73 - 1950 - Directed by veteran Anthony Mann and starring other veteran actors James Stewart and Dan Duryea. Unfortunately, the cast was augmented by Shelley Winters who sent the film over budget because of her excessive eating habits. Fortunately, she is not on the screen too much, so the film is still very good, as we follow the various owners of a superior rifle.

The Wind and the Lion – 1975 - Directed by John Milius and starring Sean Connery, Candice Bergen (perfectly cast), Brian Keith and John Huston in the story about Teddy Roosevelt (wonderfully played by Keith) giving Morocco a spanking for kidnapping some American nationals. Great fictional romantic adventure (it never happened).

The Window - 1949 - Directed by Ted Tetzlaff and starring a stellar B cast of actors armed with a great noir script about a boy who witnesses a murder in his apartment house, but no one believes him because he is a chronic liar. Moral of the story is don't cry wolf. Good viewing.

The Windtalkers – 2002 - Directed by John Woo and starring Nicolas Cage, Christian Slater and Mark Ruffalo in primary roles. This story about Indian code communicators during WW 2 is fascinating, and seldom presented in any other war films. Good production values as well.

The Winslow Boy – England - 1948 - Directed by Anthony Asquith and starring the talented Robert Donat (*Goodbye, Mr. Chips*) and a sterling B cast of British actors who do a fine job of bringing this drama to the screen. The story of a family willing to give up their substantial wealth and standing in the community to save the honor of their youngest son is quite touching.

Winter Light – 1963 – Sweden - Directed by Ingmar Bergman and starring Ingrid Thulin and dependable standby professional actor, Max von Sydow in a story about a pastor who begins to question his faith and how it affects the small community. Bergman's best film in my opinion.

Wise Blood – 1979 - Directed by John Huston and starring John Huston and Harry Dean Stanton in the lead roles in a story about a returning WW2 veteran in the South. He is an agnostic and he vows to spread the word of his lack of faith to as many people as he can. An interesting concept and execution by Huston.

With Byrd at the South Pole – 1930 - This a wonderful documentary produced by Jesse L Lasky and Adolph Zukor about the harrowing experiences of Admiral Byrd and his men at the South Pole. Great cinematography and unique subject matter. Great viewing.

With Friends Like These - 1999 - Directed by Philip Frank Messina with a B cast and a few cameos by famous people in a story about small-time B actors competing for a small B role in a future Martin Scorsese (who makes a cameo himself). Very funny stuff under the tight direction of Messina.

Without Limits -1998 – Directed by Robert Towne and starring Billy Crudup, Donald Sutherland, and a fine supporting cast in the bio of an average track star who aspires to make the US Olympic team. Interesting.

Witness - 1985 - Directed by Peter Weir and starring Harrison Ford as a detective posing as Quaker; quite an amusing premise. Also starring Kelly McGillis as a real Quaker. Nice tight drama is expertly directed by one of the best in the business. Will hold you in suspense for the entire film.

Witness for the Prosecution - 1957 - Directed by Billy Wilder and starring Marlene Dietrich, Tyrone Power and Charles Laughton, all perfectly cast in this courtroom thriller. This is a classic tale of misdirection (not by the director, but in the plot), which will keep you guessing right up until the final scene. A very good film.

The Wolfman – 1941 - Directed by George Waggner and starring Claude Rains, Lon Chaney, Ralph Bellamy, Bela Lugosi, and a very creepily effective Maria Ouspenskaya, who completely steals her scenes as she reveals the curse of the Wolfman. A classic in every way.

Woman in the Window – 1944 - Directed by the talented Fritz Lang and starring Edward G Robinson, Constance Bennett, and Raymond Massey. This is one of the first of the genre to become known as film noir, and the tone is rather dark. Psychologist Robinson is seduced by an evil woman, and drawn into her questionable moral world. I would have preferred the originally intended realistic ending, but the censors turned it into a different ending. Still very good.

Women on the Verge of a Nervous Breakdown – 1988- Spain – Directed by Pedro Almodovar and starring Antonio Banderas and a solid supporting cast of B actors in a classic Spanish screwball comedy. One of the best.

Wonder Woman - 2017 – Ably directed by Patty Jenkins and starring Gal Gadot and Chris Pine of *Star Trek* fame along with several other competent B actors. Several outstanding scenes for this superhero movie from DC which is a clear cut above most other superhero movies in this genre. I particularly liked the charge from the trench scene ending in the taking of a town. Deserved a Best Actress nomination. Recommended.

The World of Apu –India- 1959 - Directed by Satyajit Ray and starring Soumitra Chatterjee, Sharmila Tagore, Alok Chakravarty and Swapan Mukherjee in the lead roles. This is the third installment of the Apu trilogy. It follows Apu as a grown adult and his struggle to find his place in the world as a responsible father. The plot mirrors Siddhartha to a degree and that is not a bad model.

The World of Henry Orient – 1964 - Directed by George Roy Hill and starring Peter Sellers in the lead role. He is ably assisted by Angela Lansbury and Paula Prentiss. Tom Bosley (Happy Days) is also featured. The philandering Sellers is really not much of a stretch for him and the film is very amusing, although it is rather immoral in its content. Interesting.

The World's Fastest Indian--2005 – Directed by Roger Donaldson and starring the gifted Anthony Hopkins in the lead role of a New Zealander who rebuilds an old 1920 Indian motorcycle into a record-breaking vehicle at the Utah Salt Flats competition. I want this guy for my mechanic.

The Wrong Man - 1957 - Directed by Alfred Hitchcock and starring Henry Fonda in the lead role and assisted? by Vera Miles, a C actress, who was always a favorite target of my mother, Mary, as an actress who couldn't convince a coroner she was alive. Despite Miles, Fonda shows us how bureaucracies (like the IRS and Embassies) can make the lives of innocent people miserable.

Wuthering Heights – 1939 - Directed by William Wyler and starring the dynamic duo of Merle Oberon and Laurence Olivier. David Niven is also featured, but not involved in the steamy scenes. This is the queen of all romance films. It makes *Gone with the Wind* look like a cartoon. Very intense and a soap-lover's dream.

X

X-Men –2000-Directed by Bryan Singer and starring an all-star cast including Hugh Jackman (unknown at the time, Ian McClellan, who is always stellar, Halle Berry, who is always smoking hot, Bruce Davison and Anna Paquin of *Piano* fame. The story is derived from Marvel Comics long-running success, *X-Men*. We are introduced to the main characters and then the plot moves forward from that point onward. It is a nice treatment of the comic and the characters are well-honed. There have been a number of sequels to this film already, and the likelihood is that it will continue to spawn both more sequels and some spinoffs of primary characters. This comic film is generally better done than most of the others, because it takes its primary characters seriously, and the character of Doctor X is particularly well done by the very good actor, Patrick Stewart, of *Star Trek* fame. I can recommend the film to anyone.

Y

The Year of Living Dangerously - 1982 – Directed by Peter Weir, a master of the craft, and starring Mel Gibson and Sigourney Weaver in a tale of high adventure in Indonesia during an attempted communist coup against President Sukarno. Linda Hunt, playing a man, steals every scene she is in, and won the Academy Award for Best Supporting Actress in this film. Good stuff.

Yellow Earth (China) – 1984 - Directed by Chen Kaige and starring Xue Bai, Wang Xueqi, and Tan Tuo in the lead roles. The story revolves around a poor family in a poor village that is visited by a CCP soldier during the Chinese war of resistance against the Japanese. Many of the scenes are heartbreaking and unforgettable. Recommended.

Yellow Sky - 1948 - Directed by William A Wellman, who was more of a horror genre specialist, and starring Gregory Peck, Anne Baxter, Richard Widmark, Henry Morgan (MASH), and a sound supporting cast trying to do an imitation of Shakespeare's *The Tempest*, but fail miserably in this cacophony of senseless violence and convenient lust. That said, it is fairly entertaining.

Yesterday, Today and Tomorrow (Italy) -1962 - Directed by Vittorio De Sica and starring a smokin Sophia Loren and Marcello Mastroianni in the lead roles. Loren and Mastroianni were the masters of romantic comedies and this film is a testament to that claim. A classic.

Yi Yi: A One and a Two (China) - 2000 - Directed by Edward Yang and starring Nein-Jen Wu, Elaine Jin, Issei Igata, Kelly Lee, Jonathan Chang, Hsi-Sheng Chen, and Su-Yun Ko in the primary roles. The story traces the domestic challenges of a father with a teenage daughter and a young son in addition to caring for his aging mother. A nice trip through three generations.

Yojimbo (Japan) – 1961 - Directed by Akira Kurosawa and starring his staple lead star, Toshiro Mifune. This is the role that pretty much defined Mifune's career, while the action film pushed Kurosawa more toward mainstream audiences. Good work all the way around.

You Can't Cheat an Honest Man - 1939 - Directed by Lester Cowan (good luck trying to direct WC Fields) and starring WC Fields, Edgar Bergen and Charlie McCarthy (who is actually a dummy controlled by Edgar Bergen) in some silly story we don't care about. It is the ongoing feud between Fields and McCarthy that is hilarious.

You Can't Take It With You – 1938 - Directed by Frank Capra and starring Jean Arthur, Lionel Barrymore, James Stewart, Edward Arnold and dancer Ann Miller in a tale about a member of a rich family (Stewart) who falls in love with a working class girl from an eccentric family. Like most Capra films, a movie that appears to be a simple story, but is far more complex on several levels.

Depending on your political leanings, Capra was viewed as one of the following: a visionary, (there is a passage in the film that mentions solar energy for the first time in movies; and in 1938!), a socialist humanist, (without friends, you have nothing), a socialist, (give up your boring job and tune in; very 60s), a communist, (everyone is in the same boat and making money is meaningless), or just a hippie who wanted to live in a commune (this is also the first hippie commune film ever made, and in 1938!). It is interesting to note that the two lovers had jobs, though. Well, it appears as if Capra was ahead of his time, but that time has passed; the 60s are long gone and the philosophies that were associated with them. However, there are still some believers out there, so why not go with the flow, Joe?

There are several dated scenes and characterizations, and then there are several essential scenes that are as timely as can be. It is up to the viewer to discern which is which. How this film won the Academy

Award for Best Film of the Year is beyond my understanding; it is a good film, but Oscar-Worthy? Maybe it was just a lean year for films. I thought *Mr. Deeds Goes to Town* was better.

You Must Be Joking (England) - 1965 - Directed by Michael Winner and starring Terri Thomas and many of Carry On actors of many other British films. This collection of silly plots and twists of a scavenger hunt are carried off to perfection by these experienced comedians, unlike the similar Mad Mad World film that spent tens of millions of dollars and was a dud.

Young Adult - 2011 - Directed by Ivan Reitman and starring the very talented Charlize Theron, who is one of the few actors and actresses in Hollywood who can do comedy as easily as her dramatic roles (Meryl Streep is the only other one that comes to mind for women, and Jack Nicholson and Kevin Spacey are the only two that come to mind for male actors). This hilarious story of an arrogant former high school homecoming queen coming back to her home town for a bit of recaptured glory is a real eye-opener. Very funny.

Young Frankenstein – 1974 - Directed by Mel Brooks and starring the usual suspects of his troupe. They include Gene Wilder as Dr. Fronkensteeeeeen, Teri Garr as his lab assistant with a licentious sense of humor, Cloris Leachman as Frau Blucher, a horse trainer, Madeline Khan as herself, Marty Feldman as Igor, who has trouble getting over the hump, Kenneth Mars, the nazi playwright from *The Producers*, has a bit role as a villager, and Peter Boyle makes a wonderful monster.

There are very few comedies that make the top 100 films of all time on just about every critic's list. This and The Producers are the two that are consistently there. The dance by Boyle and Wilder is a classic and one of the funniest moments ever captured on film. There are a number of unforgettable funny scenes; far too many to recount here, and the dialogue is rich with double meanings. This is a must-see film and you have had a deprived life if you have not seen this film.

The Young Lions – 1958 – Directed by Edward Dmytryk and starring Montgomery Clift, Dean Martin and Marlon Brando. Martin is a singer and Clift cannot carry a macho military role (as he had shown in *From Here to Eternity*). However, the miscast Brando is worth watching, even though he appears to be stumbling around trying to learn how to use a German accent.

Young Mr. Lincoln – 1939 - Directed by John Ford and starring Henry Fonda as Young Abe Lincoln. The film also stars a strong supporting cast. The story follows the title of the film and traces the beginnings of Lincoln's life in Kentucky before moving to Illinois. It goes on to show his unsuccessful Senate bid against the great Douglas in a series of debates that became famous even though Lincoln lost the election. His relationship with Mary Todd is explored, and the film shows how deeply in love the two of them were from the first days of their courtship. This is a great film to show for classroom activities because it deals with so much more than just the better-known issues of Lincoln like the Civil War, slavery and his assassination. Stacks up well against the 21st century version with Daniel Day Lewis. I would recommend it highly.

The Young Savages - 1961 – Directed by John Frankenheimer and starring Burt Lancaster as a dedicated DA that is out to nail some vicious young criminals for a senseless murder. Sort of like *West Side Story* without the singing and a bit more realism.

Young Sherlock Holmes - 1985 – Directed by Barry Levinson and starring Nicholas Rowe in perhaps the best Holmes film ever brought to the screen. The script is first-rate, the story is engaging and the characters are decidedly believable, unlike the vast majority of other Holmes entries done with lesser production values and less talented directors. Highly recommended and a pity no sequels were made.

Young Thomas Edison – 1939- Directed by Norman Tourag and starring Mickey Rooney as young Tom Edison. The film also stars Fay Bainter as Nacny Edison. The story of young Edison centers on the discovery of the light bulb and not his later inventions such as modern motion picture processes and other great inventions. We learn of the struggles and failures of Edison and how success does not come easily or without a great deal of fortitude. It is a great object lesson for younger people to learn and a great film to show classrooms as a biopic. MGM was noted for having great character actors and extras in their films. It was something that they took pride in. I can recommend the movie highly.

 You Only Live Twice – 1967 – Directed by Lewis Gilbert and starring Sean Connery as 007, James Bond. This is one of the lesser entries in the series as it started to rely more on special effects and new machines and tech for Bond rather than concentrate on the Fleming story. Still worth viewing for Connery.

Z

Z – 1969 -Directed by Costa Garvas and starring Yves Montand as a political candidate that is struggling against a military dictatorship. This film is gripping from beginning to end and some of the scenes are very intense. Montand gives the best performance of his life in this film. Great music as well. The outcome of the election is in serious doubt and even the survival of the candidate is in question throughout the movie as the battle of good versus evil takes place on the screen. One of the best political thrillers ever made in film history will keep you on the edge of your seat for an hour and a half. It was such relief to go outside of the theater after the film and be living in a democracy, unlike the country portrayed in the film. Highly recommended.

Zentropa - 1992 - (Denmark) - Directed by Lars Van Trier and starring Jean Marc-Barr in the lead role as an American who comes to post-war Germany and takes a job as a train conductor. He meets a mysterious woman on the train and his downfall begins. The surrealistic scenes are intentional and the film has a dream-like quality.

Zero For Conduct (France) -1933 - Directed by Jean Vigo and starring an unknown group of young French actors who portray students at a French boarding school. Despite it's short length of 45 minutes (about the same time as a class period), the film is able to convey the frustrations of young boys sent far away from home. Very incisive.

Zodiac - 2007 - Directed by David Fincher and starring Robert Downey Jr, Jake Gyllenhaa, Mark Ruffalo and Chole Sevegny (*Boys Don't Cry*) in a story about the San Francisco serial killer who was never caught. The film grips you from the beginning and does not let you go until you leave, when you will be exhausted.

Zootopia – 2016 – This Disney production was even better than the more-ballyhooed *Jungle Book* which came out earlier in the year. The character of the Fox was so perfectly crafted, that you felt like it was a character you had known all your life. The tale of an innocent rabbit who is guided through the dangers of an inner city are pretty funny. A good tale for the whole family.

Zorba the Greek - 1964 - Directed by Nikos Kazantzakis and starring Anthony Quinn and Alan Bates in the lead roles. This melodrama highlights a devil-may-care Greek who tries to aid a clueless English businessman, who happens to be half-Greek, but all geek. Although doomed to failure, the two celebrate life. The film won the Academy Award for best cinematography that year.

Zulu – 1964 - Directed by Cy Enfield and starring Stanley Baker and Michael Caine in his first major role. It is a story of the Anglo-Zulu War of 1879 and a famous battle that was fought primarily by engineers rather than regular army troops. James Booth, Jack Hawkins and Nigel Green add their considerable talent to the entire production. The amateurs playing the Zulu warriors do an outstanding job portraying the actual warriors of 1879.

There is no mugging for the camera or halfhearted action scenes; they are completely wrapped into character and it shows in the battle sequences. It is one of the finest battle sequences in the history of film. The fighting is so intense, that you feel as if you are right in the middle of the action. This is one of the top ten war movies of all time. The soundtrack by John Barry of *Goldfinger* fame adds to the intensity of the battlefield. This is a must-see film and consistently ranks in the top 100 of many movie critics.

Zulu Dawn – 1979 -Directed by Douglas Hickox and starring pros Bob Hoskins, Burt Lancaster, and Peter O'Toole in the lead roles. Unfortunately, although I seldom pan a Lancaster or O'Toole film, this is one of the worst for the both of them. The film fails because it has no hero. There is no one to root for. Mindless violence, whether true or not, is not very entertaining, if you have no one to root for. Watchable only because Lancaster and O'Toole are in the film, and nowhere nearly as good as *Zulu*. Destined to be dropped from list.

1987

Made in the USA
Middletown, DE
20 May 2022